PRAISE FOR GARETH MURPHY'S *COWBOYS AND INDIES*

Cowboys and Indies places you at the heart of the record industry's ⌐ning moments. Far more than history, it's an artful and long-overdue look at the fantastic characters, companies and shifting cultures that have given birth to the soundtack of modern life. Essential reading.
Craig Kallman, CEO of Atlantic Records

Just when you thought the record label beast was dead and buried, along comes Gareth Murphy with a tour de force that makes you almost want to dance with that devil again.
Andrew Loog Oldham, manager and producer for the Rolling Stones

Thought I knew everything about the music business ... I learned a lot.
Seymour Stein, co-founder of Sire Records

Record labels at their best are driven by the taste, personality and ambition of one man or woman – this book fascinatingly charts their course, their perversity, their bloody-mindedness.
Martin Mills, founder of Beggars Banquet

Inside cover photos

Front: *Top* – Motown founder Berry Gordy (at the piano) with a group including Smokey Robinson (back) and Stevie Wonder (right) © Steve Kagan/Time Life Pictures/Getty Images.

Front: *Bottom* – Sun Records chief Sam Phillips (right) with Elvis Presley and his group. *GAB Archive/Redferns/Getty Images*

Back: *Top* – Rough Trade founder Geoff Travis © Geoff Travis.

Back: *Bottom* – Producer and Def Jam founder Rick Rubin © Annabel Mehran.

First published in Great Britain in 2015 by
SERPENT'S TAIL:
3 Holford Yard, Bevin Way
London WC1X 9HD
www.serpentstail.com

Copyright © 2015 Gareth Murphy.

This B-format paperback edition (Dec 2015) includes an updated final chapter.

1 3 5 7 9 10 8 6 4 2

Typeset in Garamond and Veneer to a design by Steven Seighman.

Printed and bound by CPI Group
(UK) Ltd, Croydon, CR0 4YY

The moral right of the authors has been asserted.

A CIP catalogue record for this book is available from the British Library.

ISBN 9781781254356
eISBN 978 178283 1693

THE EPIC HISTORY OF
THE RECORD INDUSTRY

GARETH MURPHY

CONTENTS

ACKNOWLEDGMENTS

This is the story of the record industry told to me by its insiders. Profound thanks to the following "record men" for all their tales, confessions and insights:

Martin Mills (Beggars Banquet, Founder)
Jac Holzman (Elektra, Founder)
Jerry Moss (A&M, Founder)
Seymour Stein (Sire, Founder)
Andrew Loog Oldham (Rolling Stones / Immediate, Founder)
Daniel Miller (Mute, Founder)
Geoff Travis (Rough Trade, Founder)
Chris Wright (Chrysalis, Cofounder)
Terry Ellis (Chrysalis, Cofounder)
Simon Draper (Virgin Records, A&R / Cofounder)
Dave Robinson (Stiff, Founder)
Ivo Watts-Russell (4AD, Founder)
Derek Green (A&M, London MD)
Laurence Bell (Domino, Founder)
Stan Cornyn (Warner Bros Records, Creative Services)
Larry Harris (Casablanca, VP)
David Enthoven (EG Management)
Tim Clark (Island, MD)

David Betteridge (Island / CBS, MD)
Andrew Lauder (United Artists / Radar / Island, A&R)
Bruce Pavitt (Sub Pop, Founder)
Craig Kallman (Atlantic Records, CEO)
Tom Silverman (Tommy Boy, Founder)
Rick Rubin (Def Jam, Founder)

Other sources:
John P. Hammond, Charly Prevost, Tom Hayes, Danny Krivit, Trevor Wyatt, Derek Birkett, Patrick Zelnik, Bob Garcia, Harold Childs, Lionel Conway, Art Jaeger, Ray Cooper, John Heyman, Tony Pye, Thomas H. White, Patrick Feaster, Rick Bleiweiss, Steve Knopper, David Ritz, Nigel House, Kathy Kenyon, Howard Thompson, Steve Lispon, Martin Kirkup, Bill Halverson and Tom Vickers.

Special thanks:
Jeff Capshew, Mark Ellingham, Rob Kirkpatrick, India Cooper, Kevin Pocklington, Drew Jerrison, Jennifer Letwack, Nicole Sohl, Andre Azoulay, Françoise Cruz, Rosita Sarnoff, Peter Pace, Sara Clarson, Lora-Jean Oliver, Pat Rowley, Paul Babin, Cassie Williams, Alison Wenham, Peter Simon, Antoine Giacomoni, Denis Stass, Kristan Krossley, Bob Kaus, Grayson Dantzic, Thomas Tierney, Gudrun Shea, Heidi Robinson-Fitzgerald, Simon Duke, Robert Hogan, Mark Doyle, Tara Murphy, Judith Azoulay and James Azoulay-Murphy.

Extra special thanks to my rock 'n' roll parents, Pat and Marie, without whom this book could never have been written.

PREFACE

Love, they say, is like the wind – you don't know where it'll come from next. The same is true of music.

To begin at the beginning, the craft of discovering and selling music isn't really an industry. It's a game. It's a way of life. It's solitary hunters chasing their muse through the wilderness. It's a marketplace of sellers. It's preachers and fanatics. It's collectors, browsers and Saturday strollers. There's plenty in this book about gambling and hustling, but the focus is on the musically literate prospectors – the indies, the midwives, the wave catchers – who source the raw material and ride it into town.

The writing of this book took some twists and turns as three years of digging threw up some surprises – in particular, a stock phrase veterans kept repeating as they described the legends in the trade. "He was a real record man," they'd say. The respectful tone in which *record man* was always evoked pointed the way to subtle distinctions inside the music business. Although deceptively simple, record man is an old term, somewhat ambiguous but nonetheless an honour reserved for a certain calibre of entrepreneur who *knows* his music.

In a game largely populated by bullshitters, being a *real* record man means getting lucky more than just once or twice. It means picking the winning ticket lots of times, often in different eras. This book maps out the life and times of the fifty or so pioneers who form the branches of the record industry's genealogical tree.

When you consider how all the major musical discoveries of the last 130 years inspired the genres that enabled clusters of record companies to finance thousands of other records, it's easy to understand the importance of *record men* in the greater scheme of things. All it takes is one big find – sometimes even just a three-minute song – to spark a cultural explosion that in turn opens up a billion-dollar gold mine.

Drawing from dead men's letters, trade journals, archives, correspondence and a hundred hours of exclusive interviews, this book has dug up thousands of things you probably don't know about music. I set out on a mission to write what I hoped would be the record business bible, the type of book I wish somebody had given me when I was seventeen years old. I imagined a living, wide-screen history book – written in the form of a road map through the decades, visiting all the important happenings and characters of the record industry's life.

The itinerary starts in Paris in 1860 and follows a timeline through Washington, D.C., New York, London, Berlin, Memphis, Detroit, Los Angeles, Jamaica, South Africa and various other locations where each record man's destiny was forged. Along that winding storyboard, musical genres come and go in a never-ending process of cross-fertilisation – vaudeville, opera, blues, jazz, hillbilly, R&B, rock 'n' roll, folk, psychedelia, progressive rock, reggae, disco, New Wave, postpunk, synth-pop, hip-hop, electronica…

Needless to say, this book was written at a time when the majority of media observers were confidently predicting the imminent death of the record-buying trade – the conventional wisdom being that nothing like the digital revolution has been experienced before. Imagine my shock to look up one day as I sifted through archives of early music-business history and find a proverbial elephant standing in the library: The record business of the twenties and thirties experienced a crash even more devastating than the recent one. Curiously, in my various interviews with today's record moguls, nobody really knew.

That forgotten crash, which began with the arrival of radio, culminated in a near-death experience in which the forty-year-old phonograph industry shrank to just *5 percent* of its former size. Left for dead by banks, a number of die-hard record men in the Great Depression tilled the desert with swing, blues and folk records. With a little help from jukeboxes, things began to pick up in the late thirties and forties. After a twenty-year dark age, a supposedly obsolete format rose from its coma and charged out of the hospital all guns blazing.

It's arguable that much of today's doom and gloom about the Internet supposedly driving the record industry into extinction is little more than a consequence of our limited knowledge of the musical world before Elvis. In this new century of rebuilding, isn't it time we take a step back, see the bigger picture? Fact is, rock 'n' roll inherited everything from that forgotten infancy: the majors, the contracts, music publishing, the collection societies, radio stations, distribution networks, equipment, jargon. As a musical experiment, it mixed up all the records of the twenties and thirties – rather like a bohemian rummaging in a secondhand clothes shop. Most of the great star spotters of the fifties, sixties, seventies and eighties learned the game in the Jazz Age. Their heightened sense of judgment was firmly rooted in musical culture. Neither futurists nor fashion victims, they possessed an innate sense of history and timelessness.

As the bigger picture illustrates beyond any doubt, the record business is inherently cyclical. Fallow periods tend to follow bumper harvests. Today's predicament, in which an ever-dwindling generation of rock 'n' roll impresarios finds itself tiptoeing into the terrifying cross-currents of the digital age, can only make sense when viewed within a complete time frame. Difficult as market conditions are today, our struggling record business has not become extinct; a tribe of indie diehards is currently trudging through the desert – surviving on weeds, puddles and their undying belief in music. In fact, today's open field is probably a place of immense opportunity. When the rivers flow again, the elected will build viaducts, hanging gardens, new temples and new marketplaces.

In a domain being constantly inherited by youngsters craving exciting new sounds and ideas, the one thing that will never change is the need for these record men. They keep the campfires burning brighter.

One thing I noticed while studying many of these characters, especially the independents, was their deep-rooted *belief.* Unlike the foot soldiers of the music business, who are notorious for their name-dropping and embellished anecdotes, the indie founders are serious, secretive, sober, immune to stargazing, wary of money and motivated by something higher. Behind every emblematic record label lies a hidden story – usually deep within the boy (and it is – nearly always – a boy). These patrons of contemporary music are the A-students of the music business, who view their role as judge and guardian.

The community is diverse and the typical cliché of "majors versus indies" is overly simplistic. Plenty of important record men worked for majors. There are two sides, however, and all record men instinctively choose one: the music or the money. Hence the book's title, Cowboys and Indies. Rather like tribal chieftains, the enlightened braves of the musical world are on a life mission – not simply to defend the village but to save a culture from extinction. In contrast, generally among the larger companies but some indies also, the cowboys run wild. Gamblers, double-dealers, or bounty hunters, they are the game players who seek money as reward. Some characters, the complex ones, are half-bloods, torn between the faith and the game.

In the movie business, it is often said that directors make better interviewees than film stars. The same, I believe, applies to the record business: Record men make more entertaining dinner guests than the stars they helped create. Being the key witnesses and catalysts, they know the real stories – who these stars really are, how the breakthroughs really happened. They saw the potential in its rawest form, negotiated the contracts, signed the royalty cheques and created the hype. Seen through their eyes, the game takes on a whole new perspective.

The strange thing is, pop stars don't always see the bigger picture. The vocation of writing and performing requires total self-absorption. Most of the time, they're under such pressure to stay on top, their best years are spent battling against themselves. In many ways, the label boss is the one concerned party actually enjoying the roller-coaster ride as it's happening. Standing in the shadows, pulling strings, counting the shekels – he's watching from the best vantage point possible.

There is a dangerous thrill to the vocation. It's like holding a monster on a leash. There are tales of manipulation and megalomania in this book, yet at the same time, with each big new musical discovery the world does keep singing and dancing. One thing is for sure, financing records is a high-risk business that doesn't make sense in purely financial terms. As any ringmaster will tell you, there have got to be easier ways of making a living.

As an intentionally panoramic voyage through the twentieth century, this book is also about migrations. The tradition of musical cross-pollination across the Atlantic and the North American plains has kept the record business constantly evolving since its very inception. Appropriately, many of the greatest record men in both America and England were themselves adventurers who crossed seas and continents in search of a new life in a big city. As the chapters unfold, various common denominators begin to emerge. This book's final destination, *"Revelations,"* reaches the deeper truths about this tribal theatre we call pop music.

Using all the great pioneers in an epic story about the record business, I set out to discover the secrets behind the curtain. To get to a high place where we can see the four horizons more clearly, let us now embark on an odyssey through all the musical crazes that drove successive generations wild with joy. In a pattern that would repeat itself several times over, it all began with a technological revolution.

1. TALKING MACHINES

THE STORY BEGINS IN PARIS. THE TANGLED BRANCHES – PRODUCERS, LABELS and recording artists – that form the record industry's genealogical tree can be traced back to one precise point. The year was 1853. In a little bookshop on rue Vivienne, a man was sitting in a chair, reading.

The man, a thirty-six-year-old typesetter named Édouard-Léon Scott de Martinville, was proofreading a physics manuscript. He turned a page and was struck by a diagram of sound waves. Fascinated by these curling lines, he began dreaming of a machine.

After chewing over the question for years, he came to a simple but ingenious conclusion – just copy nature. His sound-writing machine would have to be a type of mechanical ear attached to a pen. A barrel-shaped receptor would capture incoming sounds, the way the outer ear directs sound into the eardrum. Two elastic membranes would reproduce the work of the eardrum; a system of levers would replicate the three minute bones in the middle ear that transmit vibrations from the air to the liquid interior. A boar's hair attached to the end of this mechanical ear would engrave the vibrations on a glass surface blackened with soot.

On March 25, 1857, Scott de Martinville deposited a design with the French Academy of Sciences. Later that year he was granted a patent for his *phonautograph*, or sound-writer, the earliest known sound-recording device.

Scott de Martinville lacked the skills to build a working prototype, so he found a craftsman, Rudolph Koenig. His atelier was located on Île Saint-Louis, the little island in the heart of Paris, within walking distance of Scott de Martinville's bookshop. The two men met sporadically to assess progress, until on April 9, 1860, the earliest known recording of a human voice was engraved in soot on a glass surface. Prophetically, its inventor didn't speak but sang "Au clair de la lune," a traditional lullaby. "Under the moonlight, my dear friend, Pierrot, / Lend me your plume to write a word down. / My candle has died, I haven't got a light. / Open your door, for the love of God."

This was the golden age of science journals and exhibitions; ideas were circulating faster and over greater distances than ever before. In 1866, a telegraph cable was laid across the floor of the Atlantic Ocean, bringing Europe and America into a new era of instantaneous communication. For young, inquisitive minds with the genius to tap into the hidden wonders of science, the Victorian period was a time of immense opportunity.

In 1860, one such genius was a teenager in Scotland by the name of Alexander Graham Bell, Aleck to his family. He is remembered as the inventor of the telephone, but he also carried the work of the Paris pioneers across the Atlantic to the communications revolution about to explode in America. As a philanthropist and committed believer in sound innovation, he indirectly played midwife to Columbia Records, the industry's oldest company and one of its most prolific. The sonic unit known as a bel, as in decibel, was named after him.

What makes Bell unusual is the role of deafness in motivating his tireless research. His grandfather was a respected speech therapist for deaf children. His father, Melville Bell, invented a system of phonetic notation called Visible Speech, which showed the position of lips, teeth and tongue for each sound and was used in teaching the deaf to speak. His mother herself was deaf. From a young age, Aleck understood that deaf people suffered less from silence than from the crippling frustration of not being able to communicate. The disability landed many of them in prisons or mental asylums.

Aleck worked from the age of sixteen as an elocution teacher in London and Edinburgh. Meanwhile, Melville Bell began receiving invitations to demonstrate his Visible Speech in American universities. Increasingly intolerant of the cynicism in English scientific circles, Bell senior began to admire the spirit of curiosity and opportunity in the New World.

Then the hand of destiny struck the Bell family cruelly. In quick succession, both of Aleck's brothers died of tuberculosis, a common illness in the Victorian era of coal furnaces and damp cities. When Aleck started to look ill from the exhausting demands of teaching and researching, his heartbroken mother and father made a fateful decision to take their last son out of Britain. In 1870, when Aleck was twenty-three, they sold their properties and sailed for the New World.

Choked with bereavement, the depleted Bell family bought a farm by the banks of the Grand River in Ontario. Aleck spent his first Canadian summer in a numbed state, lying on a pillow in the middle of a field, reading vacantly, for days at a time. His slow return began with curiosity about a nearby Mohawk reservation. He approached their chief, requested permission to study the Mohawk language and was allowed to observe their school. The children's playful company lightened his heavy heart.

Seeing that his son was in need of a fresh start, in 1874 Melville Bell used his university connections to get Aleck a job in Boston as an elocution specialist. Arriving at Boston's train station, Aleck instantly fell in love with the city and returned to his routine of teaching and researching. It was during a school vacation back in Ontario that Bell built his own copy of Scott de Martinville's phonautograph and began to contemplate sound machines.

Curiosity opens eyes, but there is nothing like chance encounters to open doors. As an inspirational therapist, Bell quickly made a name for himself among Boston's deaf community. One day after a lecture, he was approached by a wealthy businessman, Gardiner Hubbard, who asked him to give private tutoring to his deaf daughter, Mabel.

While teaching Mabel Hubbard to speak, Bell began to make a lasting impression on the educated Hubbard family. A natural gentleman with impeccable manners, Bell measured six foot four, had greased-back jet-black hair and always dressed in a striking manner. He was also an excellent self-taught pianist who entertained his hosts with Highland ballads, Victorian waltzes and even some Chopin sonatas he had learned by ear.

Very quickly the Hubbards adopted Bell as a member of the family. It just so happened that Gardiner Hubbard's commercial and political energies at the time were focused on the telegraph industry. The telegraph had been the biggest communications revolution since the railway in the 1840s but had become an abusive monopoly thanks to one of America's largest companies, Western Union. In America's business and political lobbies, Gardiner Hubbard was a vocal campaigner for opening up the sector to competition.

While listening to Gardiner Hubbard's views on the telegraph, Bell confessed he was developing theories about sound transmission. He felt he was close to an important breakthrough but was concerned he didn't have a patent, or even the right to obtain an American patent, being a British citizen. Hubbard, who was an intellectual property lawyer, listened attentively and offered Bell his legal and financial support.

Hubbard wasn't the only supporter. Thanks to his father's connections, Bell befriended a professor in the Massachusetts Institute of Technology, who kept him up to date on innovations being debated in the scientific community. Bell's new landlady, Mrs Sanders, treated him as an adopted son and secretly redecorated an entire room in the house. For his twenty-seventh birthday, she organised a surprise party; surrounded by his deaf pupils and weeping with happiness, Bell was given his very own laboratory.

Working eighteen-hour days, seven days a week, the pale, exhausted Bell often suffered acute migraines. He grasped the general principle for a telephone but dared not even share his ideas, rightly sensing that other inventors were on the same trail. One night while playing piano in the Hubbard drawing room, Bell stopped dead and stood up. He had realised the significance of a game he often played on his old piano in Scotland: singing any note into the piano's sound box made its corresponding piano string vibrate harmonically. Two voices singing two different notes would vibrate the two corresponding strings. Therefore, if multiple harmonic signals could be transmitted and received through the air, they could also pass through a single wire.

Gardiner Hubbard convinced Bell to focus his efforts on a "harmonic telegraph" and used his connections to get Bell a demonstration with Western Union boss William Orton.

Two years previously, Orton had bought the patents for a system invented by a young telegraph operator, Thomas Edison, who had devised a method for four-way telegraph traffic by means of differences in current strength and polarity. Unfortunately, he had just bought the patent for a harmonic telegraph invented by a certain Elisha Gray. Smiling knowingly, the powerful telegraph mogul showed no enthusiasm for Bell's prototype.

Although the demonstration was a disappointment, it at least showed Bell and Hubbard what the competition was doing. Bell turned his attentions to the telephone. Hubbard began combing through the Patent Office to see if Bell's revolutionary idea had already been claimed. Seemingly it hadn't, but Hubbard – also sensing other inventors heading the same way – began compiling all of Bell's letters and notes in which he had mentioned a telephone.

It was a time of intense stress for Bell, who was being tugged in different directions by everyone around him. His father was pressuring him to concentrate on his day jobs tutoring deaf children and teaching Visible Speech at Boston University. As a financial investor, Gardiner Hubbard had lost patience with the little time Bell was spending in his laboratory. To complicate matters, Bell had fallen in love with Mabel Hubbard.

Ironically, Bell's lectures about deafness gave him vital clues. Using the phonautograph as a tool to illustrate the malfunctions that cause deafness, he became obsessed with its mechanical membrane. Realising that his weakness was electricity, he recruited a talented electrician, Thomas Watson, and together they stumbled on the sound-transmission possibilities of electromagnetics.

Bell's first important breakthrough was the transmitter, a sort of proto-microphone transforming audio sounds into an electrical signal. Eventually, by 1876, Bell's telephone was officially patented, in large part thanks to Gardiner Hubbard's legal prowess. Bell's crowning moment, however, was winning a gold medal at the U.S. Centennial Exposition in Philadelphia in 1876. Soon everyone in the scientific and industrial community was talking about the telephone.

Destiny or coincidence? At the Philadelphia exhibition that launched the telephone, one passing visitor viewing Bell's contraption was Emile Berliner, the man who would later invent the disc record. Although just another face in the crowd, Berliner immediately saw the Achilles' heel in Bell's contraption. The mouthpiece lacked transmission power, meaning the speaker had to shout to be heard at the other end.

Emile Berliner was the least likely candidate to even attempt improving Bell's technology. He was a poor German immigrant of Jewish origin who six years previously had arrived in America to escape enlistment in the Franco-Prussian War. Working as a janitor in a chemistry laboratory, he had no scientific education whatsoever; he had worked at various odd jobs and as a shopkeeper and travelling salesman. Since the day his ship docked in America, however, Berliner had been determined to improve his station. Not only was he attending night school, he had been carefully observing how the scientists conducted their research as he cleaned up around them.

In his rented room, Berliner began his own clumsy experiments. He eventually constructed a loose-contact transmitter, which increased the volume coming through the mouthpiece. Bell bought the patent and hired Berliner into his research unit.

There was a third man watching – Thomas Edison. Now that Bell's telephone was poised to bring upheaval to the telegraph industry, Edison reasoned that there might be a new market for vocal telegrams, replacing the old system of textual telegrams. He tried to build a keyboard telephone, a sort of typewriter capable of playing recordings.

Like Berliner, Edison had no academic discipline. He had been home-schooled by his mother in a small town in Ohio, then started working at the age of twelve selling sweets and newspapers on the railway lines. His entry into the world of science happened by accident when one day he saved a stationmaster's son from being killed by a runaway train. As a sign of gratitude, he was given a job as a telegraph operator for Western Union. Working the night shifts, Edison conducted his own experiments until he got fired for spilling acid that leaked through the floor onto his boss's desk. Thanks to the sale of his *Quadruplex* system to Western Union in 1874, he made $10,000 before the age of thirty. With this windfall he set up a laboratory in Menlo Park, New Jersey, where he conducted experiments into sound, light and wireless telegraphy simultaneously.

In the frantic months after Bell's telephone went public, Edison stumbled on a novel idea for recording sound. Because he was partly deaf, he fixed a needle to the telephone diaphragm. As it vibrated, he could feel volume levels as pinpricks. As he tinkered with this method, he realised that if modulating sound could vibrate a needle, it could indent paper and perhaps record messages the way the telegraph punched holes in a tape. His design used a needle on a revolving cylinder to engrave the sound waves.

His stroke of genius was to realise that if you could write sound, by reversing the action the sound would be reproduced. Nobody, including the brilliant Bell, had yet realised that the giant ear on a phonautograph could be reversed into a sound horn.

In late 1877, Edison shouted a nursery rhyme into his phonograph prototype. To his utter amazement, it played back the first time. Coincidentally, on April 30 a French poet by the name of Charles Cros, deposited a design for a sound reproduction device with the Science Academy in Paris, six months before Edison applied for his patent in America. It's reasonable to assume that the idea of sound reproduction was in the air. The two designs were, however, fundamentally different. The Frenchman's idea was for a revolving disc containing a spiral of laterally cut sound engravings.

The Cros design, also called a *phonograph*, remained unopened in an archive in Paris while Edison was developing his own machine. In December, Cros demanded that his sealed letter be opened and publicly read, suggesting that news of Edison's invention had reached Paris very quickly.

In that winter of 1877, American newspapers were reporting Edison's discovery of a *talking machine*, the popular moniker for all future record players. When he was invited to the White House to show his invention to President Rutherford B. Hayes, speculation began that the gadget might be a hoax. One day Edison got a surprise visit from the influential Bishop John Heyl Vincent, who shouted a flood of obscure biblical references into the trumpet. When the phonograph played back the crazy recording, the bishop declared, "I am satisfied, now. There isn't a man in the United States who could recite those names with the same rapidity."

Despite the curiosity it aroused, Edison's talking machine did not attract any investors. Fortunately for Edison, his electric light bulb flicked on a few months later. Backed by J. P. Morgan and members of the Vanderbilt family, he formed the Edison Electric Light Company and predicted, "We will make electricity so cheap that only the rich will burn candles."

Seeing that Edison had turned his attention to electric lighting, Alexander Graham Bell stepped back into the race, financing secret research to radically improve Edison's promising invention. Bell's life had changed profoundly since the telephone had become the great industrial success story of the day. In 1880, the French government awarded Bell the $10,000 Volta Prize. Not needing the money, Bell decided to set up the Volta Laboratory for his cousin Chichester Bell and another talented scientist, Charles Sumner Tainter, as his associates.

After four years of research, Bell's team completed a vastly improved variation of Edison's talking machine: the *Graphophone,* complete with waxy cylinders, a floating stylus and stethoscope tubes for clearer listening. Shopping their patents around town, their first port of call was Thomas Edison, who, feeling distracted by problems in his flourishing light bulb industry, declined. The young man who bought the Graphophone patents, Edward Easton, would prove to be the record industry's first record producer. It was with the sale of the Graphophone patent that, symbolically at least, the record business was born.

Easton was the founding father of Columbia, the record company that would produce hits for over a hundred years. Sharp-eyed and ambitious, he was a former courtroom stenographer who sold his story of the trial of President James A. Garfield's assassin for $25,000. Having gone back to college to study law, Easton, at the age of twenty-nine, was wealthy and seeking opportunity.

His short-lived partner in the venture was the older Colonel James Payne, a Civil War veteran. In 1887, the Volta Laboratory transferred its patents to Easton and Payne's new company, the American Graphophone Company. Easton and Payne's idea was to sell the Graphophone as a dictating machine to all the government offices in the Washington, D.C., area. To manufacture the machines, they rented a wing of a struggling sewing-machine plant in Bridgeport, Connecticut.

It was at this crossroads that a tycoon finally stepped in – Jesse Lippincott, the record business's first casualty. Lippincott, another Civil

War veteran, had made his fortune in the glassware trade. Following his wife's death in 1884, he moved into the Waldorf Astoria and became a familiar face in Manhattan high society. The New York press called him "*the Pittsburgh Millionaire*." Inspired by Bell's telephone, Lippincott was convinced the talking machine would be the next big thing.

He sold his glassware stock for a million dollars and convinced Edison to sell him both his phonograph patent and a majority of the stock in the Edison Phonograph Company for $500,000. Lippincott then turned his attention to Easton and Payne. With great prescience, Easton refused to sell his patent but instead suggested that Lippincott license the exclusive national sales rights for $200,000. In addition, Easton also negotiated an exemption for one sales territory: his home market of Washington, D.C., in which he set up Columbia Phonograph to sell talking machines directly to the federal administration.

Lippincott signed the various cheques and created the first and only record industry monopoly. Copying Bell's business model, he divided America into distribution zones, leasing the machines at $40 per year to licensed dealers, who in turn would lease the machines to users.

Despite a moderately promising start, Lippincott's company and all of its affiliated distributors began haemorrhaging money. Wisely, Edward Easton went out to investigate what was happening on the ground. Throughout March 1890, in what would be the first nationwide study of the nascent record industry, Easton travelled coast to coast, visiting thirty-one of Lippincott's regional branches.

To his amazement, Easton observed something nobody saw coming. A San Francisco distributor had transformed the phonograph into "pay to play" jukeboxes. Custom-built, in beautifully decorated wooden cases and fitted with coin slots, they were placed in arcades, saloons, drugstores and various strategic places of passage. The fashion spread from California to other cities. Although the average take for most of these nickel phonographs was about $50 a week, the most popular jukebox was believed to be in a drugstore in New Orleans. It averaged $500 a month.

Within a year, Lippincott's monopoly began to collapse. Cash-strapped local distributors began reneging on their rental bills; Edison and Easton were locked in disputes over their respective manufacturing quotas; a hundred creditors were knocking on Lippincott's door. By autumn 1890, Lippincott was reported to have fallen into a state of "despondent paralysis." Although he probably suffered a stroke, newspapers reported Edison's claim that Lippincott had "become insane when he lost all his money."

Edward Easton was the quickest to adapt. Jukebox operators found local entertainers to record two-minute routines, generally funny caricatures: yokel-alee, minstrelsy, operetta, fiddlers, unbelievable whistlers, exaggerated accents. Marching bands were popular in the Victorian age and being very loud they were well suited to the limitations of phonographs. By hooking up ten machines to the same trumpet, a marching band could record ten cylinders simultaneously. Singers with powerful lungs could at best record three cylinders at a time.

Columbia signed an exclusive contract with the iconic U.S. Marine Band and began wholesaling their recordings to dealers. In a taste of things to come, Columbia's ten-page music catalogue was divided into genre categories: Sentimental, Topical, Comic, Negro, Irish, Shakespearean recitals. Soon Columbia was producing 300 to 500 cylinders a day, sold mainly by mail order.

The first nationwide smash hit of the 1890s came from a black vaudeville performer by the name of George Johnson. Born a slave, Johnson made a living whistling and singing for coins in the ferry terminals on the Hudson, until in early 1890 he was spotted by local talking-machine dealers. Repeating the same routine over and over was a typical day's work for the ferryboat singer and between 1890 and 1895 he churned out 50,000 copies of his two hits, "The Whistling Coon" and "The Laughing Song."

Another popular genre on jukeboxes was Irish satire, in particular a caricature called Casey played by a Bostonian actor, Russell Hunting. For example, "Casey as a Judge" consisted of rapid back-and-forth legal banter between a judge and an accused Irishman speaking in a thick Irish brogue. Another actor, Dan Kelly, invented Pat Brady, who also made hilarious pleas in courtrooms, canvassed for election and described visiting the World's Fair.

With Columbia racing ahead, Edison had to concede that the talking machine's future lay in entertainment, not utility. He forced the crippled remains of Lippincott's company into receivership and initiated a legal battle to regain his patents. With Edison locked in a long dispute, Edward Easton reorganised and refinanced his group as its sole president, then overhauled the Graphophone with a steady-playing clockwork motor.

Intentionally making the better-known phonograph obsolete while Edison was stuck in two years of court procedures, Columbia released its new-generation Graphophone Type G Baby Grand in 1894 at a retail price of $75. Armed with his impressive catalogue of music and comedy, the wily Edward Easton sensed that the time had come to market talking machines to domestic audiences.

2. JUDGMENTS

IN A WASHINGTON, D.C., MUSEUM ONE AFTERNOON, EMILE BERLINER STOOD looking at a copy of Scott de Martinville's phonautograph. He realised that its laterally cut grooves were fundamentally different from Edison's vertically cut cylinders and further research led him to the designs of Charles Cros. Sensing that there was real potential for a patent, Berliner developed the Gramophone, which played a flat disc. Berliner still had many improvements to figure out, but he was a violinist, pianist and composer who accurately foretold the destiny of this curious science even before the first jukeboxes appeared in San Francisco.

Presenting his prototype to the Franklin Institute on May 16, 1888, with a speech entitled "The Gramophone: Etching the Human Voice," he predicted that in the coming musical explosion "future generations will be able to condense within the space of twenty minutes a tone picture of a single lifetime." Dropping lofty names such as Italian soprano Adelina Patti, he asserted that "prominent singers, speakers, or performers may derive an income from royalties on the sale of their phonautograms and valuable plates may be printed and registered to protect against unauthorised publication. Collections of phonautograms may become very valuable and whole evenings will be spent going through a long list of interesting performances."

As clairvoyant as he was, nobody was listening. By 1893, however, Berliner had better 7-inch prototypes and began publicising the killer advantage of his invention over the phonograph: the possibility of mass duplication from a single master. His other smart move was to recruit a recording engineer of immense musical culture, Fred Gaisberg – arguably the first great A&R man in the record industry's infant years. A&R stands for Artists and Repertoire, that part of a recording company that scouts talent and oversees its development.

Alas, Berliner's efforts to attract capital investment were not helped by surrounding circumstances. The aftershocks of a huge economic crash, the Panic of 1893, were reverberating through the business world. An oversupply of silver had led to huge public demand to exchange silver money for gold. When America's gold reserves reached their legal minimum and banks were forced to issue high-interest bonds, the markets eventually collapsed. In total over 15,000 companies and 500 banks went bust. The depression provoked a spate of anti-Semitism; in populist cartoons the Rothschilds were blamed for the crash.

Lacking the requisite skills of persuasion, Berliner employed a Methodist preacher to pitch his new invention to his former employers at the Bell Telephone Company. Listening incredulously to a woozy hand-driven recording of Berliner singing "Twinkle Twinkle Little Star" in a thick German accent, his former colleagues winced. "Has poor Berliner come down to this? How sad! Now if he would only give us a talking doll, perhaps we could raise some money for him."

In stark contrast, Edward Easton was aggressively advertising Columbia's arsenal of products in all of America's household magazines: *McClure's, Cosmopolitan, Munsey's, Harper's,* et cetera. Despite the recession crippling the entire consumer economy, Columbia enjoyed such a spurt of growth that Easton moved his head office from Washington to Manhattan and opened regional offices in Chicago, Philadelphia, St. Louis, Baltimore and Buffalo.

Then Edison, having succeeded in clawing back his patents, re-entered the market in 1896. Competing with Columbia on every front, Edison began his own music catalogue, slashing prices further with his own

clockwork phonograph, retailing at just $40; within a year, he was offer-
ing a $20 instrument. By Christmas 1897, Columbia hit back with a $10
clockwork Graphophone. Prices hit rock bottom with an Edison model
called the Gem at just $7.50. In the space of five years, the talking-
machine market had undergone a revolution in accessibility.

Realising they needed a spring-driven motor of their own, in February
1896 Berliner's technicians called in a handyman by the name of Eldridge
Reeves Johnson, a lanky machine artisan from Delaware who owned a
small sewing-machine repair store in Camden, New Jersey. It was to be a
lucky encounter that would change Johnson's destiny and, in time, make
him one of the richest men in America.

Although Johnson would later joke that Berliner's prototype sounded
like "a partially educated parrot with a sore throat and a cold in the head,"
he was fascinated. He was also fed up with the sewing-machine business,
having endured backbreaking years barely eking out a profit. In his spare
time, Johnson began tinkering with the Gramophone and came to understand its many subtleties. By doing away with some parts, Johnson found
a cheap solution and became Berliner's chief manufacturer.

Berliner and his partners then stumbled upon a promoter and advertising man, Frank Seaman. Confident, optimistic and above all convincing, Seaman talked Berliner into a deal: no upfront fees, just sign away
fifteen-year exclusive agency rights. Setting up a third company in the
network, Seaman moved into the music district on Broadway and began
advertising the Gramophone in magazines.

Crucially, Berliner's musical director, Fred Gaisberg, realised that
despite his company's small output, he was able to record respected singers
who would never have subjected themselves to the mind-numbing repetition involved with cylinder recording. His first big fish was an Italian
tenor, Ferruccio Giannini, who sang edited versions of arias from *Rigoletto,
Traviata, Trovatore* and *Cavalleria Rusticana*. Berliner and Gaisberg also
brought in speakers, evangelists, freethinkers, actors and orators. Even
the very popular John Philip Sousa and his U.S. Marine Band abandoned
Columbia and agreed to record exclusively for the Gramophone disc.

With demand booming, by 1898, Frank Seaman had exceeded the
$1 million mark. Nevertheless, Berliner's international expansion,

setting up Deutsche Grammophon in Germany and the Gramophone Company in England, caused consternation – both in his own camp and over at Columbia. Seaman began brooding; his sales contract with Berliner covered America only, but he had harboured hopes of commanding a global empire. Concerned by Berliner's growth, Edward Easton called in a noted patent lawyer from Washington. Although nobody could have guessed it, the following period would be a legal disaster with consequences that would shape the record business for the entire century ahead.

The fearsome attorney, Philip Mauro, placed a Berliner Gramophone on a table and began carefully studying its characteristics. He then began researching his adversary's business structures. In October 1898, Mauro filed a lawsuit against Seaman's company for copyright infringement against Bell and Tainter's principle of a floating stylus. The cruel brilliance of Mauro's strategy was to hamper the Gramophone's commercial growth while accentuating divides within Berliner's camp. Three different companies were dividing profits: Eldridge Johnson was selling the machines to Berliner's company at a 25 percent markup; Berliner then sold the machines to Seaman with a 40 percent markup on cost price. Mauro was reliably informed that Seaman, due to his huge advertising costs, wanted to renegotiate the original deal.

When Columbia's lawsuit came to court, Mauro convinced the judge there had been a patent violation, but Seaman won time by appealing. Determined to outwit his now numerous adversaries, Frank Seaman secretly prepared to manufacture the Zonophone, a shameless copy of Berliner's Gramophone, except heavier and given extra decorative detail. He set up a new company in March 1899 with the same name but registered in a different district. Then, in October, he stopped ordering Gramophones from Berliner's factory, throwing Berliner's and Johnson's companies into a financial crisis.

Berliner was stunned by Seaman's move. His partners were, too, but as outside investors could do little more than initiate a legal response. The one person for whom Seaman's shenanigans spelled imminent bankruptcy was Eldridge Johnson. Sitting on $50,000 worth of Gramophone stock, he had just borrowed heavily to build a four-storey factory.

The plot thickened when Seaman's appeal came to court. In a complete about-face, Seaman accepted Mauro's claim that the Gramophone did copy Bell and Tainter's floating stylus. The judge upheld the injunction, which effectively closed down Berliner's business in America. Just two weeks later, Seaman and Mauro struck a deal for legal protection and commercial advantage.

With Berliner barred from conducting business in America, Eldridge Johnson had no choice but to sell his stock or go bankrupt. Although he had no patents of his own, he did have one card up his sleeve; for three years he had been secretly examining Berliner's discs under a microscope. Jagged defects in the groove, he felt, were causing a raspy, metallic timbre. By using waxy compounds instead, Johnson developed his own superior, smoother-sounding disc. His lawyers, however, advised him against applying for a patent, believing his compound infringed the Bell and Tainter wax cylinder.

Determined to pay off his creditors, Johnson recruited a talented salesman, Leon Douglass, who came up with an unbeatable commercial plan. In the autumn of 1900, Douglass spent half of Johnson's last $5,000 on double-or-nothing advertisements, "Gramophone records FREE." The eye-catching campaign invited Gramophone owners to apply for a free sample of Johnson's new, improved disc. It was enough to get momentum building.

Seaman hit back with advertisements claiming the Zonophone was the only legitimate disc player and threatened Gramophone buyers with prosecution. Making every effort to throw doubt on Johnson's reputation, he also sent letters to dealers. While Berliner's three separate lawsuits against Seaman snailed through the legal system, the German was dealt a personal tragedy. His newborn daughter, Alice, was wasting away due to severe intestinal disorders. By Christmas 1900, she was eight months old yet weighed less than eight pounds and was close to death.

As Berliner sat by his daughter's bedside, the complex web of litigation spun around him. With Mauro in the shadows, Seaman tried to get injunctions put on Johnson's business, claiming Johnson's new operation was just a front for Berliner's old company. In his first show of steel, on March 1, 1901, Eldridge Johnson personally addressed the judge, whose ruling was swayed by Johnson's compelling testimony exposing the deceit and greed of his adversaries. He stepped out of the courtroom in the strongest position he'd ever been in. He had to refrain from using the Gramophone trademark in America, but he was free to sell his various products.

Johnson's next decisive move was to hammer out a durable deal with Berliner. A complex but soundly conceived contract was drawn up, under which the Consolidated Talking Machine Company gained control of Berliner's patents and traded under a new brand name, the Victor Talking Machine. Johnson's new Camden factory began working twenty-four hours; 7,570 Gramophones were sold in Victor's first year of trade.

Then came Philip Mauro's next coup de théâtre. In the early days, an errand boy named Joseph Jones was working for the summer inside Berliner's secret laboratory. Watching Berliner struggle with his zinc masters, the young man realised that wax was the ideal material for making disc records. In November 1897, Jones filed a patent application for wax discs, which remained in administrative no-man's-land until Philip Mauro entered the building.

Joseph Jones had since taken Berliner's trade secrets to a shady entrepreneur, Albert Armstrong. Jones and Armstrong had set up a small phonograph company, Standard Talking Machine, making dual-horn players that used Berliner's laterally cut disc system despite having no patent. Berliner, of course, sued, but with Easton and Mauro's discreet guidance, Jones and Armstrong folded their company and set up a new one while Mauro tended to Jones's patent application. To break into the rapidly growing disc market by the back door, through a complex string of companies, Columbia began distributing laterally cut discs, stamped with a *Climax* logo at a casino chip factory. As such, Columbia wasn't directly producing discs, just distributing them.

Thanks to Mauro's legal prowess, the Joseph Jones patent was approved on December 10, 1901. Easton and Mauro celebrated. Their alliance with Jones meant Columbia could start legitimately pressing disc records embossed with its own logo.

Johnson and Douglass came up with a brilliant riposte. Hearing that the manufacturers of the bootleg discs were feeling used, Johnson bought them out and had their discs embossed with a Victor Talking Machine logo. When Easton was handed a copy of his new discs with a VTM logo, he hit the roof and called in Mauro – precisely what Johnson and Douglass were expecting. In the subsequent legal exchanges, it was negotiated that Victor would sell the factory to Columbia for the original $10,000. In return, Columbia and its various proxies would drop all other legal proceedings against Victor.

The four-year drama ended with a cross-licensing agreement signed on December 8, 1903, whereby Victor and Columbia pooled their patents, creating an effective monopoly over the laterally cut disc format. Edward Easton was happy with the outcome; his arch-rival, Thomas Edison, had been excluded from the new format. Eldridge Johnson could celebrate, too. Having started out as a sewing-machine repairer, he had ended up in a relatively secure position, effectively inheriting Berliner's invention.

Even the biggest loser in the saga, Emile Berliner, could be philosophical. Against such crafty operators, he could easily have lost everything. In the bitter end, Eldridge Johnson would develop the Gramophone exactly as he dreamed and it would pay dividends for the rest of his life. Throwing away the stone in his shoe, Berliner bought out Frank Seaman's American operations for $135,000 and duly closed them down.

The sensitive Emile Berliner, meanwhile, had been spared from tragedy at home. Sensing that bacteria in raw milk was causing his daughter's intestinal problems, he dismissed the doctors and began boiling the milk before feeding it to her. Slowly but surely the baby put on weight; she was almost twenty pounds on her first birthday in April 1901.

Berliner walked away from the whole experience a changed man. For the rest of his life, he spent a portion of his Gramophone-related wealth printing and distributing milk-hygiene leaflets in American schools. Lobbying health organisations and politicians in Washington, the inventor of the disc record became a key campaigner for milk pasteurisation.

The golden age of inventors had reached a conclusion. Thomas Edison and Emile Berliner had been left behind by faster, shrewder players. The infant record industry was now healthy and walking steadily. Lawyers, salesmen and musicians were taking over.

3. HIS MASTER'S VOICE

AROUND THE WORLD AND DEEPER INTO THE URBAN EXPERIMENT, RECORD BUYERS began travelling with their ears. American culture had long been forged by waves of immigration, but the new century experienced a marked increase in the numbers arriving. Nine million foreigners entered America in the first decade of the new century. This vast and ever-growing melting pot in and around New York created some great opportunities for ethnic satire.

Columbia was the leader in Jewish comedy, notably its "Cohen on the Telephone" caricature of a Yiddish immigrant talking on a telephone in ridiculous English. There were also funny American accents to tease, especially the Southern redneck. Len Spencer, for example, scored a hit in 1902 with "Arkansas Traveler." "How far is it to the next crossroads?" the traveller asks the Southern fiddler.

"You just foller yer nose and you'll come t'it."

"How long have you lived here?"

"See that mule? It wuz here when I got here."

The traveller asks why he doesn't fix the leak in his roof, to which the redneck replies that it's been raining. The traveller asks why he doesn't fix it when it isn't raining.

"It doesn't leak when it doesn't rain."

The most frequently satirised ethnic group of them all was what society then called *the Negro*. By the turn of the century, the minstrel format was turned on its head by (Bert) Williams and (George) Walker – two black men mimicking white minstrels pretending to be black. Originally called *Two Real Coons,* they had spent years developing their comedy routine in vaudeville theatres. Once hits on Broadway, they were invited by both Victor and Columbia to record songs from their musicals. "Black-faced white comedians used to make themselves look as ridiculous as they could when portraying a '*darky*' character...", explained Walker in 1906. "The one fatal result of this to the colored performers was that they imitated the white performers in their make-up as '*darkies.*' Nothing seemed more absurd than to see a colored man making himself ridiculous in order to portray himself."

In this spirit of improbable culture clashes, white songwriters were playing with the *coon song* tradition from black vaudeville. One such number that was popular in the sheet-music market, "I Wants a Ping Pong Man," gave the Victorian fashion of table tennis an absurd twist with a black maid's saucy innuendo. Such experiments, however, including Scott Joplin's 1899 sheet-music hit "Maple Leaf Rag" went under the radars of the major record companies. Their classically trained music staff, busily emphasising talking machines as luxury domestic entertainment, were simply unaware that a Southern wave was brewing in the creative world.

As Emile Berliner had predicted, the single biggest genre boom of the new era would be grand opera. In 1902, Victor's Fred Gaisberg sailed to Italy to hear a twenty-eight-year-old opera tenor making waves among European audiences – Enrico Caruso. In a hotel room in Milan, Gaisberg immortalised Caruso's voice on what are still considered some of the most important recordings of all time.

In Caruso, Victor found the first monumental star to showcase its revolutionary disc format. After his debut in New York, Victor signed an exclusive deal with the Metropolitan Opera, which evolved into its hugely successful *Red Seal* series, featuring all the biggest operatic and classical stars of the day.

Emphasising its ambitions, Victor moved its recording facility from Carnegie Hall to luxurious premises on Fifth Avenue. Here, Victor's chief recording engineer, Raymond Sooy, witnessed how *laboratories,* as recording studios were then called, became intense places. Huddled around a sound trumpet, the art of recording was a difficult craft. Not only did every musician have to stand at a particular distance from the trumpet, violinists played bizarre-looking Stroh violins fitted with horns. Because playback was limited during recording, after every take the sound engineer rapidly examined the master with a magnifying glass, visually examining volume levels and able, if necessary, to ascertain which instruments were causing distortion.

Not surprisingly, many established singers and entertainers were terrified by this peculiar science. Sooy looked on as one opera star got "so nervous after trying to make an attempt to make a record that he picked up his hat and coat and ran out of the studio, leaving the orchestra sitting there." It was also common for comedians or theatre actors to get so frightened "they would start to tell the story backwards; in fact, they would forget their own names."

As well as supplying alcohol, Sooy recorded jittery performers in their stage costumes. "Let them don an old hat and a pair of big spectacles or their accustomed make-up and they would immediately feel in the proper atmosphere and continue the story without another falter. The make-up seems to help them although there is no visible audience," observed Sooy. Because every artist had his own particular hang-up, every session environment had to be adapted to each performer's idea of comfort. "No two artists ever face the recording instrument quite alike. Some are nervous; some confident; some cannot make records with a spectator in the studio, while others must have someone standing by constantly."

The world of classical music had its fair share of divas and eccentrics. One Victor star "accused someone in the studio of stealing his tobacco pouch. A hunt for same was taken up but it could not be found. One of the men in the studio offered the artist some tobacco from his pouch; the artist remarked, 'he would try it, but he knew it would be a damn poor substitute.'" In the end, "the artist found his pouch in his own pocket."

In another bizarre incident, a difficult artist was taken to the Victor Lunch Club. "This artist found a speck of something in the drinking water and immediately started to rave and accuse someone of trying to poison him, and as each course of the luncheon was served, declared it was the vilest food he had ever put in his mouth. After a few compliments were paid to this artist's ability, he forgot about the food, and when the luncheon was finished, he arose from the table, kissed the coloured waitress' hand, complimented her, and told her how he had enjoyed the luncheon."

Raymond Sooy contrasted all these examples with the man who, pocketing a tidy fee of $5,000 for an afternoon's singing, changed Victor's destiny. "Mr Caruso was the easiest artist who came to the laboratory to record. Nothing seemed to make any difference to him, he almost always sang perfectly and with this confidence, he had nothing to fear." With experience, Sooy came to understand that "a good recording man must be the same as a good musician. He must *feel* his work in order to get the best results out of it, as this cannot be done mechanically and prove successful."

As both export and import markets opened up, Victor's recording staff was dispatched overseas to exotic destinations such as Cuba, Mexico, Argentina and Peru to record local stars. The travel involved long journeys on steamships and trains, with their equipment packed into cases. Eldridge Johnson not only allowed them to take their wives, he actively fostered a family atmosphere, helping his key staff to buy their own houses.

The magic ingredient behind Victor's rapid growth was the brilliant marketing of Leon Douglass, a streetwise eccentric who had worked his way up through the fledgling phonograph business. Nebraska-bred, Douglass had received no schooling and provided for his family from the age of eleven onward. As a boy he had worked as a printer, telegraph messenger and telephone-exchange manager. Fascinated by new technology, he worked for Lippincott's Nebraskan distributor. Noticing that few people in the 1880s had the money to buy Edison's first phonographs, he was among the first to build his own coin-operated jukeboxes. At the 1893 Chicago World's Fair, he made his first killing as an entrepreneur, installing one hundred coin phonographs for the public.

With almost twenty years of experience, Leon Douglass knew the trade inside out – the personalities, the technology, the music and above all the audience. Eldridge Johnson, who was a relative newcomer to the game, gave Douglass free rein to formulate Victor's image and commercial plan, even paying him a higher salary than he paid himself. The trust was mutual. Douglass would say of Johnson, "He was a shy man but had the most brilliant mind I have ever known."

It was Leon Douglass who understood the iconic power of a novelty painting by Francis Barraud that Berliner had received from his London office back in 1899. Called *His Master's Voice,* it depicted a fox terrier called Nipper peering into the phonograph trumpet out of which his dead master mysteriously spoke. After the transfer of Berliner's patents to Johnson, Leon Douglass labelled all of Victor's products with a simplified logo of the dog and gramophone. In time, the image and the slogan "His Master's Voice" would be among the most striking and enduring trademarks of the twentieth century.

As well as showing off Caruso in advertisements, when the industry's first monthly trade magazine, *Talking Machine World*, began in 1905, Douglass secured an exclusive deal to put Nipper on every cover. Though very costly, it proved to be an effective way for Victor to declare its pre-eminence. "Mr Douglass was one of the ablest and most brilliant men of his time in the advertising and selling fields," wrote Eldridge Johnson. "From the outset [he] insisted on spending thousands of dollars per month for advertising. Although his policy in this respect was at first somewhat startling to me, the rapid and continued results obtained proved the soundness of these expenditures."

Then, in August 1906, Victor released an experimental model that, quite literally, turned the market inside out. What distinguished the *Victrola* from previous phonographs with protruding horns was its revolutionary "internal horn," hidden inside the elegantly carved wooden cabinet. Leon Douglass personally built the first Victrola prototype, believing "ladies did not like mechanical looking things in their parlours … Mr Johnson was afraid we would not be able to sell so many. And I was a little timid myself … They cost so much, we would have to sell them at two hundred dollars each. We not only sold those, but many millions more. [Eventually] we were obliged to use seven thousand men to make the cabinets alone."

Demand for the Victrola boomed into the hundreds of thousands, firmly establishing Victor as the world leader. Many hundreds of millions of records were sold thanks to the popularity of its homely, salon-friendly design. Between Victor's powerful advertisements, its catalogue of operatic stars and its beautiful players, Douglass and Johnson had found the perfect formula to capture the spirit of the Edwardian era.

Alas, following the birth of Leon Douglass's son – whom he christened Eldridge in honour of his boss – the Nebraskan salesman became burned-out and suffered a severe nervous breakdown. In just seven years, Douglass had navigated Victor to a position of total dominance but overworked his mind until it became a room full of voices. Illustrating the deep affection for Douglass at the top of the company, Eldridge Johnson allowed him all the convalescence time he needed on full pay, $25,000 per year. As things turned out, Leon Douglass's office would remain a dusty museum in the Camden, New Jersey, headquarters. He was nominated in absentia as the corporation's symbolic chairman.

His protégés continued to scoop up exclusive deals with the biggest stars of the day: violin virtuoso Fritz Kreisler; Irish tenor John McCormack; sopranos Alma Gluck, Nellie Melba and Luisa Tetrazzini. The humbled Columbia stepped back and let Victor create a virtual monopoly in highbrow music.

Now twenty years in the game, Edward Easton was heading for his own breakdown. With Victor charging ahead on every front, he began looking for alternative markets and foolishly returned to the idea of selling dictation machines to administrations. If the business plan was ill-considered, his timing couldn't have been worse. The expanding money supply needed to support America's economy had come from discoveries of gold reserves in Alaska, Colorado and South Africa and gold transfers from European banks. Worried by their diminishing reserves, European banks increased their interest rates, and the gold began flowing back to Europe. Also, following the previous financial crash in 1893, regulation forcing banks to maintain cash reserves had failed to include trusts. As a result, the number of trusts holding only 2–3 percent cash reserves had quadrupled. So when the stock market fell by 50 percent in October 1907, worried depositors began withdrawing their money from trusts. Unable to pay, many banks became insolvent.

Although calmed by government bailouts, the so-called 'Panic of 1907' sent aftershocks through the economy. Easton had been indulging in some wasteful investments, and Columbia found itself with severe cash-flow problems as banks postponed making loans. He was forced to lay off hundreds of staff in New York and Washington. After that, his daughter recalled, a "deep melancholy settled over Father. He could not smile. He would hardly speak in the long evenings at home. He would sit for hours staring into space." Crippled by failure and fatigue, the Columbia boss sank into an inconsolable depression.

On January 23, Easton boarded the morning train to Manhattan, accompanied by his faithful colleague William Morse. When Morse noticed that Easton hadn't come back from the dining car, he sensed danger and asked for the train to be stopped. Edward Easton was found lying between the tracks farther back down the line – alive but mentally numb. He had tried to commit suicide.

The economic recession hit everyone hard, even Victor, whose sales plummeted by 50 percent. All companies adopted the same crisis management policies; cutting prices, letting go of weak product lines and concentrating efforts where demand was strongest. Phasing out cylinders, Columbia launched its own copy of the Victrola, the *Grafonola,* and began producing its own double-sided discs. By about 1910, however, confidence returned, and Victor celebrated its best year to date with 107,000 Gramophones sold. Investing heavily in marketing, it launched its own newsletter, *The Voice of Victor,* which kept dealers up to date with new releases, merchandising ideas and corporate news. Travelling salesmen began arriving in stores giving away free Victor signs and elegant shop displays.

Edward Easton came back to work, but he was dealt another blow when his popular manufacturing chief, Thomas Macdonald, died suddenly at the age of fifty-two. After years of brooding, he sent out a message to Thomas Edison: Columbia was for sale.

"Why if you people are doing so well are you willing to turn your business into our hands?" asked Edison's label head, Frank Dyer. Easton confessed he wanted out of the business. He had lost interest; his dearest business friends were all dead. Although Dyer was tempted by Columbia's disc patent, one revealing memo from him to Edison evoked the burning issue that Columbia's competitors could never forget. "There is the feeling that has always existed against Columbia and Mr Easton personally as being unscrupulous and unreliable," he wrote. "I know that Mr Eldridge Johnson entertains the same feeling."

Though Easton's offer came to nothing, it at least provoked a reality check within Edison's camp. In 1913, the company released its *Edison Diamond Disc*, which used vertically cut grooves. Being obsessed with sound quality, Edison launched his new system with heavily publicised "tone tests" held in theatres and churches. The machine and a singer were hidden behind a curtain, and crowds were invited to distinguish between the two. In fact, it was all an absurd gimmick; the singers were all trained to sing like a record player.

Edison's Achilles' heel remained music. Stubborn, uncultured and fiercely possessive of *his* invention, he took personal control of A&R. He received excellent operatic recordings from his European partners, but his contempt for people he called "opera perverts" meant that many potential hits were never released in America. A famous put-down by the violinist Samuel Gardner held that Edison's deafness "had nothing to do with his musicality, because he didn't have any."

As Edison fought back clumsily, Edward Easton's demise was rapid. Having never won the full respect of the wider record business, he died in 1915 an unhappy millionaire at the age of fifty-nine. Although his competitors considered him a shark, he was responsible for some important precedents in the music business. In particular, through his extensive use of lawyers, Edward Easton was a taste of things to come.

As war broke out in Europe, Eldridge Johnson's musical empire was on top of the world. Celebrating its first million-unit record in 1915 with Alma Gluck's "Carry Me Back to Old Virginny," by 1917 Victor had sold half a million Victrolas and released some 7,000 titles. However, with such success came responsibilities. When America entered the war in late 1917, Johnson was constrained by the government to convert most of his factory to manufacturing rifle parts and biplane wings. Coal shortages also forced closure every Monday for eleven weeks in early 1918. In that gruelling year, Victor only managed to press 21 million records, a 40 percent drop in productivity. Fortunately, America's war effort was brief, and by 1919 Victor's annual production had risen to 474,000 machines.

By 1920, annual business rose again, and the company had its second-best year, selling 560,000 machines and 33.4 million records. In 1921, Victor sold a spectacular 55 million records.

With Victor's total dominance and the laterally cut disc now the industry standard, the talking-machine business had stabilised. A weary Eldridge Johnson, by now one of the richest men in America, observed, "Improvements come hard now-a-days. The field is no longer a virgin one. Great chunks of free gold are no longer lying around to be picked up by the lucky hunter. The old-fashioned prospector is out of the race."

Fittingly, the two creative visionaries behind Victor's success, Emile Berliner and Leon Douglass, had become the record business's first semi-retired eccentrics. Enjoying a leisurely life, Berliner undertook one last great project as an inventor. It was another spinning machine – the helicopter. Leonardo da Vinci had imagined the principle, but not until 1907 was the first flight recorded. By 1909, Berliner and his son Henry had built a prototype that succeeded in lifting them six feet into the air.

Leon Douglass never really recovered from his nervous breakdown, but even though he was half mad, Eldridge Johnson refused to let him resign from his nominal position as chairman of the board. With money flowing in every month, Douglass also found himself in the unusual position of being able to pursue his passions in life. Moving his family into a fifty-two-bedroom mansion in California, he built an underground cinema laboratory with a giant window looking into a swimming pool. In 1916, he patented a technique for colour film processing, effectively the forerunner of Technicolor, which he sold to Cecil B. DeMille. He then turned his attentions to underwater filming and once took his instruments to Hawaii to film tropical fish. He wrote a surrealist book, *Ajax Defied the Lightning*, and made the first American colour film, *Cupid Angling*.

The founding fathers of the record industry were now old enough to look back and recognise what they had contributed to modern culture. Emile Berliner's background and classical music training gave Eldridge Johnson's company a European dimension that Columbia and Edison could never match. Leon Douglass understood how to present an iconic package to the public, making high culture accessible to the masses.

Johnson, for his part, was the strongest boss in the business: fatherly, loyal, disciplined and adventurous.

Thanks to their collective work, the world adopted the disc record, the most enduring of all formats. Even Douglass and Berliner's later years daydreaming around glamorous mansions seemed to foreshadow modern-day record producers. These were the founding fathers. Almost everything they pioneered has simply been reinvented over and over again.

4. EXODUS

EVERY EPOCH DREAMS OF THE NEXT ONE. AS THE NEW CENTURY STRODE toward the Roaring Twenties, the fruits of the Victorian imagination were everywhere to be seen. Young adults inherited a world very different from the austere age of horses and corsets their parents had known. Now there were electric lights, shop signs, telephones, elevators and automobiles. Cities had suddenly become a lot noisier, flashier, denser and faster.

The Victorians had dreamed of changing the world, but nobody had imagined the Great War. As its 'doughboys' – infantry recruits – returned home with maimed limbs and shattered minds, young Americans began to reject older, European values that companies such as Victor Talking Machine had so brilliantly symbolised.

Too big, too old, too distracted by wartime obligations, Victor had become a giant corporation out of touch with the younger generation. The Victorian preference for classical music, marching bands and vaudeville was being supplanted by a newfound fascination with dancing and home-grown street culture. Not surprisingly, some record producers were quicker than others to see it coming.

As early as 1911, the novelty song "Alexander's Ragtime Band" blew up into the world's first truly global smash hit. Various versions by different performers and record labels sold over 1 million records. Although the song kept to a somewhat traditional marching-band beat, its bouncy, jubilant feel made it a real foot-tapper that physically excited audiences in a way that hadn't been seen before. Victor's recording staff knew the public wanted danceable records, but being from the classical world, the best they could come up with was tango and foxtrot.

After 1914, the combined effects of reduced shipping and the enlistment of millions of young men into Europe's warring armies had slowed down American immigration. A growing isolationist feeling culminated in the controversial Immigration Act of 1917. However, with the American economy continuing to expand, businesses were beginning to feel labour shortages. These developments coincided with another upheaval happening in the Southern countryside as racism and rural poverty pushed blacks into the Northern economic pull.

So the war accelerated a century-long process known as the Great Migration, in which Southern rural blacks moved to Northern cities in search of a better life. In 1910, three out of every four blacks lived on farms, and nine out of ten lived in the South. Over the following decade, some 2 million blacks moved north – 400,000 of them between 1916 and 1918 alone. The largest concentration of Southern black migrants was in Harlem, where about 200,000 Southern blacks moved into a neighbourhood that had been virtually all white fifteen years previously.

Chicago was the second-most-popular destination, thanks mainly to *The Chicago Defender*, a Northern newspaper distributed primarily in Mississippi, Virginia, New Orleans, Arkansas, Oklahoma, Texas and Georgia. The other new development raising Chicago's national profile was Prohibition. With so much alcohol flowing over the Canadian border into the black-market economy, Chicago was the new boomtown, synonymous with speakeasies and gangsters.

The warm tones and perfumed imagery of the South found a streetwise swagger in the bright lights of Chicago and Harlem. From this meeting point, lots of interesting music began pouring out.

Black music from the South was creeping into dance halls and music publishing houses. The first important pioneer bringing Southern black music to the big cities of the North was W. C. Handy, a black composer and bandleader who had been working in the music business for a decade.

In Handy's youth, early blues was generally played by brass orchestras, a legacy of the Victorian tradition of marching-band music that had caught on in black communities. In the late nineteenth century most towns, and even many businesses, had their own brass bands for festivals, weddings and funerals. The new *rag* style evolved as cheap surplus instruments, decommissioned in New Orleans after the 1898 Spanish-American War, entered civilian circulation. Because black marching bands learned pieces by ear and played offbeat rhythms passed down from their African tradition, the upright *um-pah* of Victorian marching bands took on a woozier, four-legged groove. The term *ragtime* evolved from this loose, unwritten, *ragged* style.

Handy was the first to study the mechanics of this "three-chord basic harmonic structure." He realised that a warbling effect later referred to as the *blue note* was the hallmark of "Negro roustabouts, honky-tonk piano players, wanderers and others of the underprivileged but undaunted class … The primitive Southern Negro, as he sang, was sure to bear down on the third and seventh tone of the scale, slurring between major and minor. Whether in the cotton field of the Delta or on the Levee up St. Louis way, it was always the same."

In 1912, Handy wrote his first hit for the sheet-music market, a tune called "Memphis Blues" – the first widely distributed 12-bar blues, credited as the inspiration for the invention of the foxtrot in 1914 by a New York dance duo, Vernon and Irene Castle. Handy was a bandleader in the big city in the summer of 1914, when "the tango was in vogue," and he recalled that one night "I tricked the dancers by arranging a tango introduction, breaking abruptly into a low-down blues. My eyes swept the floor anxiously, then suddenly I saw lightning strike. The dancers seemed electrified. Something within them came suddenly to life. An instinct that wanted so much to live, to fling its arms to spread joy, took them by the heels."

As the old expression goes, it takes two to tango. Change wasn't limited to Southern blacks pouring into the Northern cities. Marking the waning of Victorian ideals of femininity, the period also brought seismic sociological shifts for women. Although the term *flapper* has become

synonymous with the Roaring Twenties, the process of women's libera-
tion took a giant leap during the war.

The wave was strongest in Britain's four-year war effort, where an
estimated 2 million women replaced men in factories. When America
joined the war in 1917, Teddy Roosevelt endorsed American writer Harriot
Stanton Blatch's public appeal to "mobilise woman-power." Voicing a
stirring tribute, Blatch claimed the British war effort had made women
"capable … bright-eyed, happy." The political world was stirring also.
Between 1913 and 1920 women won the right to vote in Norway, Denmark,
Australia, Russia, Poland, Germany, Britain, Holland and America.

All these migrations and upheavals in black and female culture explain
why suddenly in 1917, the year America joined the war, a new dance craze
exploded in Chicago and New York – jazz, the first organically grown
musical wave to rise from the street and change the face of the record
business.

Before the war, the word *jazz*, meaning *spirit* or *fizziness*, was popular
in California, where, according to one dubious theory, it had sexual
connotations derived from the nineteenth-century word *jism*. A more
plausible explanation is that the word originated from a Gaelic word,
spelled "teas" but pronounced "*tchass*," meaning heat, excitement, vigour,
or the passion of spirit. It was also the name of an Irish superstitious cult
surrounding St. Bridget's tomb, where a fire was kept burning, and as such
it had long been invoked by gamblers. The Irish imported the term into
American gambling halls, from whence it spread to other domains, first
sport, then music. The fact that Gaelic is an ancient language whose
artificial spelling in Latin letters differs greatly from its true pronunciation
might explain why at least four spellings of the Americanised word – jass,
jas, jazz and jaz – appeared between 1913 and 1918.

In 1913, an Irish American sports journalist, Scoop Gleeson, used the
word *jass* to describe the spirit and pep of baseball players. The word was
already on the street; Gleeson's newspaper, the *San Francisco Bulletin,* ran
a piece in April 1913 entitled "In Praise of Jazz, a Futurist Word Which
Has Just Joined the Language." Its author, Ernest J. Hopkins, explained
that "a new word, like a new muscle, only comes into being when it has
long been needed. This remarkable and satisfactory-sounding

word ... means something like life, vigor, energy, effervescence of spirit, joy, pep, magnetism, verve, virility ebullience, courage, happiness – oh, what's the use? – Jazz. Nothing else can express it."

In Chicago, the popular new word was pinned onto an older yet increasingly popular flavour of Southern brass-band music. The *Chicago Daily Tribune*'s editor, Fred Shapiro, wrote an excited piece in the summer of 1915 explaining: "Blues is jazz and jazz is blues ... The blues are never written into music, but are interpolated by the piano player or other players. They aren't new. They are just reborn into popularity. They started in the South half a century ago and are the interpolations of darkies originally. The trade name for them is *jazz*."

Ironically, the word arrived in the South last. In November 1916, the New Orleans *Times-Picayune,* previewing a parade, noted, "Theatrical journals have taken cognisance of the *jas bands* and at first these organisations of syncopation were credited with having originated in Chicago, but anyone ever having frequented the *tango belt* of New Orleans knows that the real home of the *jas bands* is right here ... Just where and when these bands, until this winter known only to New Orleans, originated, is a disputed question. It is claimed they are the outgrowth of the so-called *fish bands* of the lake front camps, Saturday and Sunday night affairs. However, the fact remains that their popularity has already reached Chicago, and that New York probably will be invaded next."

The first jazz record "Livery Stable Blues" and "Dixie Jass Band One Step," was released on Victor in February 1917. The performers were a white group called the Original Dixieland Jass Band – Southern musicians playing in the Chicago dance halls. Three months later, Columbia invited them to record two more tunes, "Darktown Strutters Ball" and "Back Home Again in Indiana." Even Edison jumped on the bandwagon with "Everybody Loves a Jass Band" by Arthur Fields. By the end of 1917, there appeared to be a consensus that the spelling "*jazz*" carried a nicer ring.

In 1919, the Original Dixieland Jazz Band took London by storm and was commissioned by Columbia's British company to record no less than thirty sides. In a private concert at Buckingham Palace, the bandleader ,recalled Marshal Philippe Pétain, peered ominously through his opera glasses, "as though there were bugs on us." When King George V began clapping excitedly, his motionless guests let go and began enjoying themselves. After four rapturous months, the Original Dixieland Jazz Band was forced to leave England abruptly. According to rumours, they were chased to the Southampton docks by a furious Lord Harrington. One of the musicians had romanced his daughter.

Feeling the generational chasms opening up between youngsters and their Victorian parents, Victor's senior managers were urgently rethinking their entire image and product line. Highbrow values were becoming unfashionable, which meant unprofitable. Victor's contract man, Calvin Child, was assigned the delicate task of convincing all the company's operatic and classical artists to accept new terms whereby, instead of exorbitant flat fees, they would receive a percentage of net profits, with a guaranteed minimum annual income. Caruso, of course, obtained the most generous deal, with a minimum guarantee of $100,000 per year for a term of ten years. Less lucrative names obtained minimum guarantees of around $15,000 per year. The age of percentage-based royalties had tentatively begun.

Once all Victor's artist contracts were renegotiated, in July 1919, *Talking Machine World* announced "the democratisation of music." The price of Victor's classical and operatic records was being slashed to as low as $1. Even the cost of Victor's most exclusive limited editions, which had retailed at $7, were being cut in half. In the accompanying visual campaign, operatic icons were photographed in boxing gloves, in kitchens and on bicycles. Every effort was made to take the haughtiness out of classical music.

What Victor hadn't anticipated was the loss of its virtual monopoly on laterally cut discs. Perhaps the single biggest upheaval of the postwar years was a legal battle between Victor and Starr Piano Company, owners of a new record label called Gennett. In 1919, Gennett had dared to release a laterally cut disc and was, as expected, promptly sued by Victor. However, Starr's lawyers were able to convince the court of a number of grey areas surrounding Victor's patents. In January 1920, the U.S. Circuit Court of Appeals rejected Victor's injunction and opened the floodgates to mass competition.

Accelerating a process that had started during the First World War, the record business grew dense and vibrant. The industry's monthly trade magazine, *Talking Machine World*, which contained about a hundred pages in 1916, doubled to over two hundred pages in 1920 with listings for about two hundred manufacturers. Many of these new talking machines were named after their founders: Cheney, Emerson, Heintzman, Wilson, Steger, Crafts, Onken, Weser. Other brands copied the sound of "Victrola" with names like Robinola, Harmonola, Tonkola and Saxola. In record production, interesting new labels entered the market, including Brunswick, Aeolian-Vocalion, Gennett, Okeh, Paramount and Black Swan.

It was into this complex, rapidly evolving market that the period's most progressive record man, Otto Heinemann, launched Okeh, arguably the first example of the alternative record label.

Jehuda Otto Heinemann was born in the north German city of Lüneburg in 1877, the sixth son of sixteen children. At thirty-seven years of age, Heinemann was the managing director of one of Europe's biggest record empires, Carl Lindström AG. Based in Berlin, it owned a vast record-pressing plant as well as three large labels: Odeon, Parlophon and Beka. Its factory in Berlin employed thousands and pressed 100,000 records per day. With distribution operations in France, Britain, Austria and Holland, the company was one of the first majors in continental Europe. It had just opened an office in Argentina, Disco Nacional, which produced the first recordings of tango legend Carlos Gardel.

In the summer of 1914, Heinemann was sailing to New York to investigate industrial conditions in the American record market. War broke out when he was at sea, and as a result he was briefly interned in the British port of Southampton before eventually arriving in America. As European countries began declaring war on each other through pact arrangements, borders closed, telegraph lines were severed, and shipping became hazardous. Watching events in Europe unravel from New York, Heinemann realised he was stuck in America and had to make money.

Although starting from scratch, he was experienced and adaptable, and he had been studying the American record industry since his first trip in 1909. He registered an import-export business in New York, the Otto Heinemann Phonograph Supply Company, and set up a small factory in Ohio. His business plan was to supply motors to the blooming market of smaller independent phonograph manufacturers. As he hoped, Heinemann quickly found clients among the scores of newcomers sprouting up during the boom of the First World War.

Heinemann wanted to move into record production but patiently observed the rapidly changing music market around him. In 1918, with the war drawing to a close, he bought out a bankrupt record company, the Rex Talking Machine Corporation, and hired its former musical director, Fred Hager. Symbolising Heinemann's fascination with America's indigenous culture, his Okeh logo was an Indian warrior's head wearing a lone feather.

Heinemann visited Berlin in 1920 and was shocked to find currency turmoil, massive national debt, food shortages and political instability. After six exciting years setting up his own small business in boom-time America, Heinemann returned to New York eagerly anticipating the final outcome of Starr Piano Company's landmark case against Victor. With capital investment from his former employer, Carl Lindström, he reorganised his company and opened Okeh dealerships in Chicago, San Francisco, Atlanta, Seattle and Toronto.

With Lindström's European catalogue at his disposal, Heinemann began importing German, Swedish, Czech and Yiddish-language records for America's ethnic minorities. This niche marketing approach led Heinemann and his staff to ask themselves two simple questions: Was the Negro population the most potentially profitable ethnic market in America? If so, why should black music be considered any differently than the other ethnic records Okeh was selling?

The initial question in fact came from a black composer and theatre producer Perry Bradford who had made a name for himself on the black vaudeville circuit. In February 1920, he strolled around to Okeh's studio at 145 West Forty-fifth Street to see Fred Hager. He presented some songs he had written for a thirty-six-year-old singer called Mamie Smith, the star of a recent black vaudeville production, *The Maid of Harlem*. Bradford argued, "There's fourteen million Negroes in our great country and they will buy records if recorded by one of their own, because we are the only folks that can sing and interpret hot jazz songs just off the griddle."

On August 10, 1920, Okeh organised a session supervised by a sound engineer named Ralph Peer. The song produced was "Crazy Blues," in which Mamie Smith bellowed a catchy melody over a 12-bar arrangement in the woozy, stomping style of New Orleans brass bands. Swelling into a smash hit, it sold an estimated 1 million copies – many of which went into white parlours. Realising they'd struck a gold mine, Hager and Heinemann then invited W. C. Handy to record more brass-band blues for Okeh.

Jealous of Okeh's knockout success and determined to create the first genuine black record company, Handy's publisher, a former insurer from Georgia, Harry Pace, established Black Swan. From his home on Striver Row in New York City, he borrowed $30,000 and released a string of disappointing records. Fortunately, his talented musical director, Fletcher Henderson, found a lifesaver in Ethel Waters, a young blues singer from the Harlem clubs. Her first record on Black Swan, "Down Home Blues"/"Oh Daddy," sold 500,000 copies within six months.

Harry Pace's masterstroke was to send his artists off on a nationwide tour of vaudeville theatres. Between November 1921 and July 1922, the *Black Swan Troubadours* visited twenty-one states and performed in at least fifty-three cities. A black newspaper columnist, Lester Walton, took charge of road management and persuaded the *New York Age, The Chicago Defender, Pittsburgh Courier* and *Baltimore Afro-American* to cover the tour with constant reviews. Some white newspapers even started to take notice.

The lovely Ethel Waters, whose contract with Black Swan restricted her from marrying for a two-year period, performed in elegant feather costumes, the new style in Chicago and New York clubs. A North Carolina newspaper, the *Tribute,* reported, "Ethel Waters and her jazz masters have come and gone but their memory will linger for months … The crowd was left wide eyed and gasping with astonishment … Her act, including shimmies and shivers, … sent the crowd into paroxysms of the wildest delight." After seven months of sold-out concerts, Black Swan's mail-order business was employing thirty people and had shipped some $100,000 worth of records to about a thousand dealers.

With growing demand for so-called *race records*, new distribution networks opened up around the black newspaper circuits. Paperboys began selling blues records at newsstands; Pullman porters peddled copies at whistle stops; salesmen went door to door. The editorials in *The Chicago Defender* encouraged "lovers of music everywhere and those who desire to help in the advance of the Race" to buy these new records.

Meanwhile, Okeh was busy signing a roster of black artists and formulating its own ambitious plans. As well as alternative distribution, Otto Heinemann initiated a quiet revolution inside the mainstream industry. From October 1921, Okeh took out advertorials in *Talking Machine World* showing its advertisements in black newspapers – a conscious strategy to reassure white dealers that *race music* was a wide-open, lucrative market.

As demand grew in white parlours for danceable music with a modern American identity, jazz and blues moved towards the mainstream. Blacks may not have been treated equally in real life, but in the otherworldly sphere of music, the potent mix of streetwise slang and Southern imagery seemed to express an American dream. A new wave was breaking – as an even bigger one rolled in behind.

5. THE INVISIBLE WAVE

THERE WAS ONE OTHER SHADOW ON THE HORIZON. IT WAS HAPPENING OUT at sea – but only teenaged boys could see it coming.

A tidal wave was about to crash over the record industry and wash away much of what the founding fathers had built. Compounding the cultural changes like a perfect storm, in 1922 radio suddenly hit and sent the record industry into its first serious prolonged recession, in total some twenty years of contraction and soul searching.

Way back in the 1880s, there was a third Menlo Park project going on as Edison's phonograph and light bulb were being developed. Edison demonstrated, as a few others had before him, that it was possible to transmit electrical pulses through the air. *Wireless telegraphy*, as it was first called, had been one of the great dreams of the Victorian age, but compared to telephones, electric lighting and talking machines, the science required huge investment. Even Edison, with all his money and stubbornness, gave up and sold his patents.

Eldridge Johnson, by far the most powerful man in the record industry, was one of several observers reading articles about this fledgling sector with disinterested bemusement. Radio had yielded more investment scams and fantastical predictions than any other field of research. It was probably unimaginable that a system based on transmitting Morse code messages between ships might be so spectacularly improved that entire sonic pictures could be transmitted across great distances with arguably better sound quality than talking machines.

The tragic hero of the saga was the Italian inventor Guglielmo Marconi, who in 1895 had acquired Edison's patents. Once articles reported Marconi's long-range tests, popular interest grew, and in May 1899, *The New York Times* ran an eye-catching feature predicting that "all the nations of the earth would be put upon terms of intimacy and men would be stunned by the tremendous volume of news and information that would ceaselessly pour in upon them." In 1905, a comprehensive report published in the *World's Work* magazine speculated that one day "a lone ranch-man in Arizona might set up a pocket-receiver and learn the latest news."

With the public's imagination aroused, unscrupulous entrepreneurs began taking out advertisements to attract small investors, describing their companies as "the nest eggs of fortune" or saying that "for every $100 invested it will return thousands." In 1907, however, an investigative journalist, Frank Fayant, writing a stock-fraud series entitled "Fools and Their Money" for *Success Magazine,* included a damning report on "the wireless telegraph bubble."

Following his revelations, a string of companies was prosecuted for fraud, clearing the field for the most legitimate players. Apart from Marconi, the other genuine contender was Nikola Tesla, a genius Serbian mathematician and physicist who in the 1880s had worked at Edison's Menlo Park laboratory.

Since his falling-out with Edison over money, Tesla had been working on X-rays, radiation, remote controlling and radar. Unquestionably one of the most respected minds in the research community, Tesla predicted in 1908 that "it will be possible for a business man in New York to dictate instructions, and have them instantly appear in type at his office in London or elsewhere … An inexpensive instrument, not bigger than a watch, will enable its bearer to hear anywhere, on sea or land, music or song, the speech of a political leader, the address of an eminent man of science, or the sermon of an eloquent clergyman, delivered in some other place, however distant. In the same manner any picture, character, drawing, or print can be transferred from one to another place."

Nikola Tesla may have been the most brilliant mind in the domain, but he was also showing signs of obsessive-compulsive disorder. In the luxurious hotels where he lived, for instance, he always demanded everyday objects, such as towels and bars of soap, in multiples of three. Another problem was that his research relied too heavily on European funding. Recklessly accumulating bills in the Waldorf Astoria, he was forced to hand over his half-built radio towers to the hotel's owner once the war cut off his sources.

Marconi, in contrast, was a pragmatic businessman. With stations built in Newfoundland and Galway, he wisely chose to focus all his commercial development on the shipping industry, which immediately understood the life-saving importance of radio. His other core market for early radio equipment was teenagers, colloquially referred to as *amateurs* or *boys*. Radio operators on ships were the first to complain about these young pirates of the airwaves disrupting maritime communication with foul language and pranks.

In 1909, teenaged radio amateurs on Rhode Island sent out false reports of a shipwreck, resulting in a U.S. Navy ship spending all night sailing around in circles. Later that year, after a real accident when a steamboat collided with the SS *Florida,* the navy vessel on scene was given four different false positions by eavesdropping pranksters, the rescue was delayed by twelve nail-biting hours. The Radio Act of 1912 officially restricted amateurs to certain defined wavelengths, as newspaper articles raised the question of teenagers' addiction to radio.

The game changer was the sinking of the *Titanic* in April 1912. The ship's radio operators were Marconi employees whose distress signals were picked up by a ship just sixty miles away, also equipped with a Marconi radio station. Once the *Carpathia* arrived at the *Titanic*'s last known coordinates at 4:00 A.M., it found 706 dazed survivors freezing in lifeboats on an ice-covered sea. In the coming days, as news of the *Titanic*'s fate spread through the radio networks, and the *Carpathia* sailed back to New York with the survivors, the U.S. Navy repeatedly tried to contact the *Carpathia*'s radio master on behalf of President William Howard Taft. Marconi is believed to have initiated messages to his radio operators ordering them not to send out any information to third parties. His motives became clearer upon the *Carpathia*'s arrival in New York. Marconi was waiting at the dock with *New York Times* journalists with whom he had negotiated a deal for the radio operator's exclusive story.

Already alarmed by his socialist fantasies, the U.S. Navy's top brass was not impressed with Marconi's opportunism, and in the ensuing inquiry, his radio operators were duly grilled. However, in a *Titanic* inquiry in London, Britain's postmaster general emphasised, "Those who have been saved have been saved through one man, Mr Marconi … and his marvellous invention." Marconi's technology was acquiring a geopolitical dimension; his business experienced a growth spurt of 2,000 percent.

Then came the tipping point: as war broke out in Europe, Britain cut Germany's telegraph lines to America. Stunned by Britain's belligerence and noting the strategic importance of radio technology in trench warfare, the U.S. Navy, AT&T and Westinghouse joined together in a covert project to urgently develop long-distance radio. Their discovery of vacuum-tubed radio transmitters marked the giant leap that in October 1915 enabled AT&T scientists to transmit signals from a navy station outside Washington, D.C., to Honolulu and the Eiffel Tower in Paris.

With thousands of young teenage boys reading war stories about radio operators luring Zeppelins to their death, amateur radio traffic exploded. Then, in April 1917, America entered the war, and for reasons of national security the government banned all radio broadcasts – even listening. In a deliberate move to take over radio, the U.S. Navy used wartime security powers to annul Marconi's patents and seize Tesla's German-funded radio towers. All manufacturers of radios were ordered to manufacture exclusively for the U.S. Navy.

At the end of the war in 1918, the U.S. Navy tried to have its monopoly continued, but Congress rejected the motion. In April 1919, however, U.S. Navy Captain Stanford Hooper and Admiral William Bullard met with General Electric executives to persuade them not to sell their long-distance transmission tools, termed *Alexanderson alternators*, to Marconi. They suggested instead that General Electric could set up its own American-run radio business and secure a commercial monopoly of long-distance commercial communication. Recognising the rare opportunity, General Electric bought out Marconi's American operations and created RCA in October

1919. For his work masterminding the operation, Admiral Bullard was given a seat on RCA's board of directors. AT&T was awarded a monopoly in long-distance telephone.

RCA promptly took over General Electric's and Westinghouse's manufacture of radio devices, began buying up most of the radio-related patents on the market, and set up radio stations. With the public ban on amateur radio finally lifted, a new radio craze exploded with better equipment and far bigger numbers than before.

Blindsided by this giant tsunami of teenaged excitement, record companies experienced a sudden drop in sales as retailers converted larger portions of their stores to radio equipment. Shop owners noticed how these excitable boys, accompanied by their sceptical fathers, would happily show up the salesmen's ignorance of radio equipment given half a chance. Father, of course, would only pull out his wallet if satisfied his son's questions were adequately answered. To earn a living, retailers now had to catch up with the kids.

The initially high cost of radio equipment explains why the boom witnessed a strange upsurge in pay-phone vandalism across America. Receivers in public phone booths were being ripped out on a massive scale; teenagers were using the parts to make headphones.

By the end of 1922, about 2 million radio sets had been sold in America. Of the 20,300 radio stations that were licensed, 15,780 belonged to amateurs, many of whom were youngsters clogging up the airwaves with music.

When the first National Radio Conference was convened in 1922, of the thirty-one speeches allocated to industrialists and politicians, three were given to members of the American Radio Relay League – the organisation that issued amateur licences. "We are trying to get away from the idea that our radio is a play-thing," explained this watchdog, which named and shamed radio rogues in its magazine. "When we speak of 'citizen wireless' we convey a picture – no longer of little boys in short trousers playing with toys ... but a vast field in which the private citizen of this country may enter and carry on useful communication." U.S. Secretary of Commerce Herbert Hoover emphasised in his opening speech the need "to accommodate the most proper demands [of the commercial industry] and at the same time to protect that precious thing – the American small boy, to whom so much of this rapid expansion of interest is due."

Compounding problems for record companies, the radio boom coincided with an economic downturn as the wartime economy experienced deflation due to returning soldiers disrupting the labour market. Bizarre as it seems, the biggest boom in record sales, in and around 1921, was immediately followed by the biggest slump in the industry's thirty-year history.

The first of many casualties was Columbia. Because it had built up debts overproducing stock in the boom, the sudden downturn spelled immediate danger. At the close of 1921, Columbia reported losses of $4.6 million; its deficit had ballooned to $15.7 million, and it was unable to pay notes on its debts of $22 million. Several stockholders filed an application for receivership.

Victor's downward spiral was delayed as a result of Caruso's death in August 1921, which provoked an abnormal spike in record sales. By late 1922, Victor's sales tumbled by a third, and the following year, Red Seal record sales slumped to 6 million, beginning a gradual decline that would last throughout the twenties.

Edison Records had once employed ten thousand people; by February 1922, its factories had been downsized to just three thousand workers. In one internal exchange illustrating that some of Edison's senior staff were not blaming radio as the sole source of their misfortunes, Walter Miller dared to tell the half-deaf autocrat, "A one-man opinion on tunes is all wrong. Last year when you were the only picker of tunes, you refused to let us record the four biggest successes of the year."

Throughout 1921 and 1922, many of the new independents that had sprouted up since the war simply went bust. Harry Pace, founder of Black Swan, recalled that "radio broadcasting broke and this spelled doom for us. Immediately dealers began to cancel orders ... Records were returned unaccepted, [and] many record stores became radio stores." In December 1923, Black Swan Records filed for bankruptcy. In stark contrast to the record industry's misfortunes, the net earnings of RCA rocketed. By 1924, RCA had outgrown Victor, with gross sales of $55 million compared to Victor's $37 million.

Dealers saw the tide change in their stores; the radio set made the talking machine look old. After almost forty years of growth, the once awe-inspiring Victrola had finally been overtaken by a more powerful and interactive piece of technology. The richest mogul in the business, Eldridge Johnson, suffering from depression, took to his bed and simply ordered Victor's stars to boycott radio. With its founder absent, a vacuum enveloped Victor; its senior management stood immobilised.

Hundreds of new radio stations sprouted up across the land, all broadcasting new entertainment formats – boxing matches, political events, comedy shows, children's stories. America, fascinated by its own imagination, was becoming more American than ever before.

6. SURVIVORS

FOR YOUNGER PLAYERS WILLING TO ADAPT, CUT CORNERS AND TAKE RISKS, the radio age offered the chance of becoming a bigger fish in an admittedly smaller pond. The 1920s, despite being a harsh climate for record sellers, would prove to be a unique era for music. As demands became more niche-oriented, a new breed of talent hunter was emerging from the fringes – the wheeling, dealing record man.

Through the ambient noise of radio interference and teenaged pirates, two legal precedents pointed the way forward. In January 1922, the American government banned radio amateurs from broadcasting "entertainment," an ambiguous term amended in September to "mechanically operated instruments": in other words, teenagers broadcasting records.

Then, in the summer of 1923, the nine-year-old composers and publishers union, ASCAP, filed a lawsuit against L. Bamberger & Company, the owners of a large department store in New Jersey and radio station WOR. Because the radio station had refused to pay ASCAP royalties for the songs it broadcast, the Newark court ruled in ASCAP's favour. Seemingly, music publishers were supportive of radio, even if it meant suing for their slice of cake.

Columbia was the one major company that, unlike Victor and Edison, didn't have the cash reserves to sit around debating boycotts, lawsuits, or the raspy timbre of radio. Thinking pragmatically, Columbia's cash-strapped staffers recognised radio as free promotion. Ultimately, however, Columbia's precarious situation needed a visionary leader. Enter the short, witty Louis Sterling, Columbia's London boss, who stepped up to the challenge while grey-haired tycoons like Eldridge Johnson and Thomas Edison grumbled around their mansions.

Lithuanian-born of Jewish origin, Sterling had sailed to America with his family when he was a baby. In 1903, Sterling left New York for a new life in the Old World. When his ship docked in Southampton, he frittered away his last $5 and slept his first night on the floor of an English jail. The next day, he dusted himself off and found William Barry Owen, boss of the Gramophone Company, whom he had previously met in New York. As promised, Owen took on the twenty-four-year-old as a travelling salesman – a formative experience in which Sterling learned about cultural diversity and purchasing patterns all over Britain. Moving through a number of small phonograph companies, by 1910 Sterling was Columbia's U.K. sales chief, and by the end of the war he was running the whole company. Thanks to commissions, Sterling had amassed a personal fortune, much of which he reinvested in his greatest passion of all, collecting rare books.

When radio took off in America, Sterling convinced his investors in London that records were far from obsolete. Continuing his habit of going against the traffic, in November 1922, for a cool £500,000, Sterling bought out his employers, Columbia's British company, including all of Columbia's European and Asian trademarks.

He then set his sights on America, where despite being in receivership, Columbia was still managing to score hits. Following Okeh's lead, Columbia talent scout Frank Walker signed blues diva Bessie Smith, whose "Gulf Coast Blues" sold 750,000 copies. In a curious twist of fortunes, Bessie Smith, previously rejected as "too black" by Okeh's Fred Hager and too "nitty-gritty" by the bankrupt Harry Pace, was now singing Columbia out of trouble.

Shortly after, a Wisconsin label, Paramount, signed up Ma Rainey – another gutsy blues diva from the vaudeville circuits. Sixty miles away, in an Indiana factory town called Richmond, the Gennett label began documenting Chicago's vibrant jazz scene courtesy of two music publishers, Lester and Walter Melrose. The brothers had strolled into Gennett's

Chicago showroom carrying the sheet music of two outstanding jazz pioneers, Jelly Roll Morton and King Oliver – both New Orleans migrants now playing in Chicago's clubs.

As a result of this lucky introduction, King Oliver's Creole Jazz Band, featuring Louis Armstrong on cornet, recorded sixteen sides for Gennett, officially launching the *hot jazz* genre on record. Jelly Roll Morton, sporting diamond-studded teeth, had begun his career in the Storyville brothels, then rambled around the South as a gambler, pool shark, pimp, vaudeville comedian and pianist. Not only was he composing his own tunes, he was exploring the French Creole and Caribbean rhythmic influences of New Orleans – what he called *the Spanish tinge*.

Despite these seminal records from the Midwest, Okeh remained the most progressive in the business. Singled out by the magazine *The Wireless Age* as the most radio-friendly record company in America, Okeh began field trips to Atlanta, St. Louis, Detroit and Chicago. One pioneer record man to emerge from these expeditions was Ralph Peer, the sound engineer who had supervised Mamie Smith's "Crazy Blues." While driving across America in Okeh's truck, Peer saw nothing but opportunity.

Now in his thirties, the wily Ralph Peer was a white Southerner, originally from Independence, Missouri, who began his music career in Columbia's Kansas office. While recording blues, gospel and folk songs in hotel rooms, warehouses and ballrooms, Peer began to realise that out in the virgin plains, a cornucopia of unsigned talent lay waiting.

His main contact in Atlanta was the nineteen-year-old Polk Brockman, who from one end of his father's furniture store was selling so many race records that he convinced Okeh to grant him a wholesale distributorship for his region. On a business trip to New York in June 1923, Brockman was killing time in the Palace Theater on Times Square watching a newsreel of a fiddlers competition in Virginia. Struck by a brain wave, he pulled out his notebook and jotted down the words "Fiddlin John Carson – local talent – let's record." The fiddler in question was a fifty-three-year-old white farmer from the Blue Ridge Mountains. Brockman convinced Ralph Peer to include Atlanta on his road trip.

Recording the Appalachian fiddler in a loft, Peer winced, describing the screechy sounds as "pluperfect awful." However, Brockman knew that

Carson had a loyal following among all the "rednecks" and "wool hats" who had flocked to Atlanta's mill industries. To ensure the recording wasn't shelved, Brockman begged Peer to press him 500 copies "right now."

Four weeks later, a box of unlabelled records arrived in Atlanta by Railway Express. A few days later, Fiddlin' John Carson performed his two songs at a local festival where Brockman began selling the all-black discs to enthusiastic spectators. "I'll have to quit making moonshine and start making records!" exclaimed Carson when he saw the frenzy.

As Brockman ordered more records, Peer included the fiddler in Okeh's catalogue. He remembered that earlier that spring, he had shelved a test pressing of a certain Henry Whitter singing "The Wreck of the Old 97," a folk song about a tragic train crash in Virginia. He sent a copy to Brockman, who confirmed it would sell in the Tennessee and Virginia market. Okeh had another rural hit, and Peer began to smell something in the air.

It didn't take long for the competition to catch on. Columbia's Frank Walker turned his attentions away from Bessie Smith to what was now being termed *hillbilly*. Then, in August 1924, Victor commissioned balladeer Vernon Dalhart to perform a syrupy rendition of "The Wreck of the Old 97." Tailor-made for popular audiences, the Dalhart version snowballed into a nationwide monster. As many as 7 million copies were sold, making it the biggest-selling record in the industry's forty-year history.

Such statistics were a welcome blessing in an otherwise shrinking market. An even bigger lifesaver came that year from Bell Labs researchers who developed a sonic medicine for the phonograph's technological irrelevance. Combining carbon condenser microphones, matched-impedance vacuum tube amplifiers, and a new method of electromagnetic disc cutting, they invented electrical recording. Thanks to microphones and amplifiers, both high and low frequencies could now be picked up with higher definition. Singers didn't have to bellow, diction was clearer, and instruments like guitars and banjos could be heard for the first time.

Once the technology was patented, Bell Labs presented its Westrex system to Victor. However, because Eldridge Johnson had fostered among his senior managers such disdain for radio, when they heard the distinctive timbre of tube amplifiers, they held off their answer.

Having observed all these interesting developments from London, Louis Sterling sailed into New York precisely at this juncture and bought out Columbia Phonograph for $2.5 million, then immediately signed on to the Westrex proposal. When Victor followed suit, both companies privately agreed to embark on a massive sell-off of acoustic records while their technicians refurbished studios with dampening partitions and separated amplification rooms.

Agreeing to phase out acoustic records was an important step in Eldridge Johnson's gradual, albeit grudging, acceptance of radio. In a poignant symbol of the generational rupture, Johnson's son was convinced Victor should manufacture new models combining radio sets and electrical record players. Earlier that February, Eldridge Johnson wrote a thoughtful memo back to his son. "I do not believe ... that the scheme of broadcast music will replace talking machines; it may, however, slow up our expansion. But there is the feature of privacy, selection, repeat and the sense of proprietorship in a talking machine that no general broadcasting scheme can hope to substitute."

Victor could do no better than raise its advertising budget to a record $5 million in 1924, making it America's second-biggest spender on magazine advertising behind Campbell's Soup. By 1925, the shrinking leader announced its first-ever deficit. Eldridge Johnson looked on helplessly while, one by one, senior executives who held 15 percent of the company's stock left the business. He lamented the fact that "I must reconstruct the organisation from men who are not so heavily financially interested."

Abandoning his fruitless boycott, Johnson followed Brunswick's lead by hosting a live radio broadcast from Victor laboratories on New Year's Day 1926. Starring tenor icon John McCormack, the hugely successful media event aroused renewed enthusiasm for the singer's records. The less adventurous Thomas Edison, however, continued scowling, having only once allowed a radio station to play some of his favourite Edison Diamond Discs. He personally telephoned the station after the broadcast, blasting, "If the phonograph sounded like that in any room, nobody would ever buy it.

Why do you give people a laboratory experiment? I give people a finished product, and you're a long way from having one. I don't want any part of it."

With the old moguls drifting further into irrelevance, Otto Heinemann continued charging ahead. As radio stations opened in far-flung locations, his field-recording trucks ventured to St. Petersburg, Cleveland, Buffalo, Kansas City, Annapolis, Asheville and Dallas. *Talking Machine World* ran a distinctly musicological editorial in 1925 about Okeh's Cajun recordings. "As portraits of bayou life they are real poetry, connoisseurs say, telling stories of the strange water creatures that inhabit the bayous and the uneventful life of the fisherfolk." Thanks to field recording, Okeh was exploring America's folk consciousness and the epic story of migrations into the New World.

It was perhaps inevitable that Louis Sterling couldn't resist buying out Okeh's parent company, the Carl Lindström group, in 1925, simultaneously giving Columbia a stronger foothold in continental Europe and rural America. However, by far the biggest corporate event of the period was Eldridge Johnson's capitulation. In 1926, the financial consortium Seligman & Speyer bought out the Victor Talking Machine Company for $400 million – a decision Johnson would regret to his grave.

Spotting a career opportunity, Ralph Peer jumped ship to the confused but modernising Victor. He travelled down to Bristol, Tennessee, set up a studio on the second floor of a hat warehouse, and placed advertisements in local newspapers asserting that "in no other section of the South have the pre-war melodies and old mountaineer songs been better preserved than in the mountains of East Tennessee and Southwest Virginia ... and it is primarily for this reason that the Victrola Company chose Bristol as its operating base." Peer knew how to sweet-talk a musician; the articles were careful to mention that hillbilly Ernest Stoneman had just received $3,600 in royalties. As singers and string bands began descending from the hills, Peer discovered both Jimmie Rodgers and the Carter Family, whose *Bristol sessions* would in time be revered as a seminal moment in country music.

The motivation behind Ralph Peer's defection became quickly evident. According to a Victor staffer, Nathaniel Shilkret, a senior executive, Walter Clark, met Peer to review his remuneration as a talent scout. In this meeting, Peer sold Clark a novel idea, "no raise, but a royalty of one cent per record side that he would divide with the artist." Shilkret remembered the shock it aroused. "When I heard of this I was stunned. No one on the musical staff had been offered a royalty for his arrangements or compositions, and here was a man collecting royalties with other men's compositions!"

In the second quarter of 1927 alone, Peer collected $250,000 in royalties. He duly set up the Southern Music Company, requiring his artists to sign both management and publishing contracts. Peer may have been a ruthless opportunist, but he understood the market he was working in. In these uncharted musical territories, most rural musicians were happy to accept a $25 or $50 flat fee. He even claimed that paying performers was "unnecessary, as most of them expected to record for absolutely nothing."

With talent scouts such as Ralph Peer and Frank Walker turning their attentions to country music, the less lucrative market for rural blues was left wide open for a legendary blues hunter based in Jackson, Mississippi.

Henry Speir was another white store owner. Inside his big warehouse he stocked Gramophones, musical instruments and about three thousand records. He allowed his mainly black customers to listen to records in booths, and upstairs musicians could record on a metal disc for $5. Oblivious of how important his discoveries would become, Henry Speir was personally responsible for finding nearly all of the major *Delta blues* singers of the late twenties and early thirties.

The neglected market for rural blues had been illustrated by the Wisconsin label Paramount, which scored a niche hit in 1926 with Blind Lemon Jefferson – sparse, rusty, real-deal blues evoking one man playing a beat-up guitar on his own porch. In need of follow-ups, Paramount sent out a call through its commercial networks. Because Speir was ordering his stocks from regional distributors in St. Louis or directly from the companies by mail order, he had a connection with Paramount.

Speir knew Mississippi had musicians as good as Blind Lemon Jefferson, and he knew the blues customer. On Saturdays, blacks converged on Jackson in old cars or on wagons to hear street musicians or buy records for parties on the plantations. In summer, Speir would often stay open till ten, selling up to 600 records a day. The vast majority of his customers were black women, typically maids and cooks for wealthy white families. Sharecroppers, especially cotton pickers, could only afford these 75-cent records at harvest time.

Having grown up around blacks in the hill country, Speir could pick up all the slanguage in blues lyrics. He knew that blues songs were about gambling, drinking, adultery and violence – black men really did get shot or stabbed at jook houses. In this religious land, to sing gospel was to serve the Lord. Those who played blues and lived a life of sin knew they were serving the devil and were going to hell.

In search of compelling bluesmen, Speir drove around the region listening to street singers and railway station announcers and attending barn dances on plantations. He drove across state lines and stayed overnight at full-moon parties. Although talent popped up anywhere, he soon noticed it usually gravitated to Memphis or New Orleans.

When Speir heard potential, he would record two songs himself, using his metal disc cutter, then send this demo to the appropriate record company. Supplying alcohol was an integral part of getting a good performance. During Prohibition, the popular poison among blues singers was either antiseptic or canned heat, a solid cooking fuel that became a potent liquid when melted.

For a $150 finder's fee per artist, Speir brought William Harris to Gennett, then supplied Ralph Peer with Tommy Johnson. On a plantation in 1929, he stumbled on "*The father of Delta blues,*" Charlie Patton. Speir instantly recognised the exceptional musical power of this small man with a booming voice – Patton had written more songs than he could play in one sitting. For Speir, a body of original material was as important as style, and there was a simple reason why. The lucky musicians would be sent by train to mobile studios in nearby cities. To recoup the cost of Speir's fee and the musician's $50 payment, the record companies needed at least four copyrightable original compositions. If the first record sold, follow-ups would be pulled from the same session.

Henry Speir's discoveries include most of the early legends: Charlie Patton, Robert Johnson, Son House, Jim Jackson, Bo Carter, Skip James,

Ishmon Bracey, Blind Joe Reynolds, Blind Roosevelt Graves, the Mississippi Sheiks, Robert Wilkins and Geeshie Wiley. He also found jazz bands, white string bands and Choctaw groups and once brought Mexican musicians over the border to record in San Antonio. Apart from Paramount, his other clients included Victor, Columbia, Okeh, Brunswick-Vocalion and Gennett.

During this decade of American self-discovery, the sound of the city was getting less bluesy and more jazzy. More than just a musical genre, jazz was synonymous with a whole new culture. First came a dance craze, *the Charleston*; then came a Hollywood sensation, Al Jolson, who starred in the first full-length talkie, *The Jazz Singer* – the box-office smash of 1927.

The urban poetry of jazz fit the times like Cinderella's lost shoe. As flapper fashions changed women's silhouettes, speakeasies were generously pouring slang onto the streets. For being drunk, the jazz generation invented a new lexicon: *blotto, fried, hoary eyed, splifficated, ossified, zozzled*. Nasty bootleg booze was *coffin varnish*; to "*pull a Danny Boon*" meant to vomit, hangover sensations were referred to as the *heebie jeebies* or the *screaming meemies*. A *vamp* was a seducer; a *lollygagger* was a loose woman; a *cake eater* was a playboy; a *face stretcher* was an older woman trying to look young. Engagement rings were *handcuffs* or *manacles*.

In New York's blooming jazz scene, the shrewdest operator of the pack was taking the same route as Ralph Peer in country music. Part shark, part visionary, Irving Mills also understood that in the nascent radio age, publishing and management were more lucrative than record production.

Irving Mills was accustomed to survival. He was born in an East Side ghetto in 1894 to Jewish parents who emigrated from Odessa, and his father died when he was just eleven years old. Leaving school to sell ties and wallpaper, he got his first glimpse of the bright lights while working as a page boy at Shanley's Restaurant near Broadway. It had a great orchestra, and young Irving was fascinated by the theatrical characters who tipped him for errands.

By the age of fourteen, he was a theatre usher just a few blocks away from Tin Pan Alley, working two showings a day. Actors tipped him to run around to the publishing houses and procure copies of the latest hits. One publisher eventually asked him to be its song plugger. Although Mills couldn't read music, he had a good voice and would simply sing his product to actors.

As a young man Mills sang with orchestras, set up his own publishing company, and began to produce cheap jazz records for department stores. His life-changing moment happened in 1926 when, having been tipped off about a new arrival in town, he walked into the Kentucky Club to check out the Washingtonians, whose leader was a certain Duke Ellington. Hearing genius, seeing stars and smelling dollars, Mills signed Ellington's band up the very next day; he would be both manager and Ellington's publisher. Within a gruelling year of performing and making records for department stores, Mills then secured Ellington's band a residency at the Cotton Club.

As well as organising live broadcasts from the Cotton Club, Mills masterminded a record blitzkrieg. Between 1927 and 1930, Ellington's band made over two hundred recordings under eleven different names for twenty record companies. Duke Ellington became America's greatest jazz star as Irving Mills's publishing company ballooned into a multi-artist powerhouse complete with magazines and a booking agency. The jazz equivalent of a salami machine, Mills was slicing cuts off every side – even writing lyrics for his biggest hits or, depending on who you believe, registering other people's creations in his own name.

As the curtain descended on the Roaring Twenties, the splintered remains of the phonograph industry had been utterly transformed. The new generation of record man, unlike his predecessor in the classical era, was a wheeling, dealing song hunter. As radio and music publishing became the growth areas, a new age of autobiographical music was being born.

A nationwide survey conducted by the American government in 1929 concluded that the radio had been the single biggest boom of the decade. The hardware alone was generating $842 million annually. About 41 percent of American homes were equipped with a radio.

The inventor of the Gramophone, Emile Berliner, died on August 3, 1929, with an estate estimated at $1.5 million. The founding father of the disc left a note for his grieving family. "When I go I do not want an expensive funeral," he wrote. "Elaborate funerals are almost a criminal waste of money. I should like Alice to play the first part of the 'Moonlight Sonata' and at the close maybe Josephine will play Chopin's 'Funeral March.' Give some money to some poor mothers with babies and bury me about sunset. I am grateful for having lived in the United States and I say to my children and grandchildren that peace of mind is what they should strive for."

7. DEAD SEA CROSSING

AS IF THE ARRIVAL OF RADIO HADN'T BEEN PAINFUL ENOUGH, WITHIN A FEW months of the stock market's collapse on October 24, 1929, only a few crooked structures were left standing in the dust. While film and radio corporations experienced continued growth throughout the Great Depression, public demand for records simply evaporated into a puddle.

In America, record sales were decimated from 104 million units in 1927 to 10 million in 1930, the worst collapse in the industry's forty-year history. By 1932, the entire production of records in America slid farther downward to just 6 million. With the sale of record players plummeting from 987,000 to 40,000, in those five years, the entire American record industry, both hardware and records, shrank to about 5 percent of its former size. Even by the cruel norms of the Great Depression, few industries have ever experienced such a catastrophe. It was as if the record industry had keeled over and died.

In the so-called Dirty Thirties, it was no longer enough to be a foxy survivor. From here on in, the last remains would have to rely on the charity of strangers. Whether motivated by philanthropy, vanity or misguided investment strategy, a number of wealthy outsiders, mainly eccentrics and tycoons from neighbouring industries, turned up at various fire sales to salvage what they could from all these old brand names and catalogues. Amalgamated, downsized, restructured and renamed, the new landscape was desolate and unrecognisable.

The long-declining Edison Phonograph Company understood that the crash had sounded its death knell. Edison duly closed its doors for business. "From the very first, Mr Edison himself regarded the phonograph as merely a machine," concluded a damning epitaph in *The Phonograph Monthly Review*. "Has he ever had any understanding of music: how could he hope to succeed in a musical venture?"

Before the crash, in January 1929, Seligman & Speyer had sold Victor for just $160 million to its nemesis, RCA, which in September 1930 held a ceremony rechristening Victor's headquarters as "the *Radio Center of the World*." As Eldridge Johnson writhed in his sleep, his son Fenimore, unable to stomach the new regime, decided to take a trip into the interior of Africa.

With talkies booming and television looming, RCA emperor David Sarnoff hailed a new era of "electrical entertainment in the home and in the theatre." Following his lead, Hollywood giants saw the record industry's collapse as an opportunity to expand into sound. One such entrepreneur, Herbert Yates, owner of Consolidated Film, bought out Pathé's American division and merged it with a collection of bankrupt independents – Cameo Records, Lincoln Records, Emerson Records and Plaza Music – to form the American Record Corporation, better known by its abbreviation, ARC. Then, in April 1930, Warner Bros. bought Brunswick for $10 million. As better sound technology arrived in Hollywood, Warner licensed the Brunswick back catalogue and brand name to ARC and kissed $8 million goodbye.

Columbia's fate was more complex. In Britain between 1929 and 1932, consumer spending on music halved, a mild plunge compared to the American record industry's virtual wipeout in the same period. Under pressure from its major shareholder, the bank of J. P. Morgan, the English branch of Columbia joined forces with HMV, the English branch of Victor, and became EMI in 1931.

It wasn't a happy marriage. HMV executive Alfred Clark was appointed EMI chairman, while Louis Sterling served as managing director. The two men rarely spoke and instead communicated through letters. Learning from Victor's mistakes in America, EMI began investing in the relatively tardy growth of British radio. The company refurbished a studio on Abbey Road for orchestral recordings. It also sold record players at a loss in order to flood the market with cheap machines, reasoning that consumers with new record players would buy records. Another of EMI's clever tricks was to establish societies for the recondite works of composers, then market recordings of those works by mail to subscribers to these niche clubs, so the recording and pressing costs could be absorbed by a nucleus of diehard record collectors. Amazingly, Britain exported more records during the Great Depression than America produced.

In another indication of Britain's growing importance, in 1929 Decca Records was established by Edward Lewis, a former banker who had been advising a talking-machine manufacturer, Decca Gramophone Company, to diversify into record production. Lewis argued that "manufacturing gramophones but not records is rather like one selling razors but not consumable blades." Having failed to convince his clients as a consultant, Lewis rounded up a consortium of investors and bought out the company.

Despite these positive movements in London, Louis Sterling was forced to withdraw into Europe and abandon his American acquisitions to a cruel fate. In 1930, Okeh closed down as an independent company; its catalogue and trademarks were absorbed by Columbia, which in 1931 was sold to the Grigsby-Grunow Company, manufacturers of radio consoles and refrigerators.

The only healthy music company in America seemed to be Irving Mills's publishing, management and booking empire, then happily enjoying the top two success stories of the period, Duke Ellington and Cab Calloway. Representing sixteen orchestras, Mills took over an entire floor next to Brunswick's head office at 799 Seventh Avenue. Knowing record companies had no budgets to produce jazz records, he underwrote their recording costs on the condition that his publishing catalogue be used. With a few thousand sales per record, everybody walked away with a small profit. The records were calling cards for his bands and repertoire, and as songs like "Minnie the Moocher" amply illustrated, the occasional smash hit flew out of the salami machine.

Apart from Irving Mills, New York's music industry fell deathly silent as the American economy hit rock bottom around 1932 and 1933. Yet it was from this dead sea that probably the greatest-ever record man landed some giant fish. Enter a young writer by the name of John Hammond.

While Irving Mills symbolised the caricature of the cigar-puffing entertainment impresario, Hammond was an entirely different breed of jazz adventurer – eloquent, bohemian and fiercely principled. The names of the most respected jazz masters of the era – King Oliver, Earl Hines and Duke Ellington – suggested that a jazz aristocracy was forming, and Hammond really was an aristocrat. His mother, Emily, was the great-granddaughter of Cornelius Vanderbilt, the Dutch tycoon who built America's railroads. As everyone knew, the Vanderbilts were among the richest, most powerful WASP dynasties in the land.

Although his father was the son of a Civil War general and a success-ful banker in his own right, the Hammonds were benefactors of Vander-bilt trust funds and property holdings. Summers were spent in the idyllic surroundings of Lenox, Massachusetts, which they visited in their very own train carriage. His parents had been given a luxurious five-storey metropolitan palace on Ninety-first Street, just off Fifth Avenue and Central Park. It had a domestic staff of sixteen and contained marble staircases, elevators, a library, a squash court and a ballroom big enough to comfortably seat two hundred.

Born in 1910, John Hammond was the only boy following four sisters, which may have explained his solitary tendencies. Classical music constantly poured through the mansion's many oak-panelled rooms, decorated with all the opulence of European Baroque design. Virtuoso teachers regularly came to give lessons to the family, and the latest Victro-las played Beethoven, Brahms, Mozart and all the European masters.

His sisters often found their younger brother hiding downstairs in the servants' quarters, legs dangling from a chair, listening to popular records on a battered Grafanola. Although young John was taught classical viola, he developed a fascination with black people and their reaction to music. The family servants would break into dances and sing along, and they were never afraid to cry over songs. He also observed with a sense of injus-tice how they stiffened as they walked upstairs. John devoured all of New York's entertainment magazines, notably *Variety,* and avidly collected records. "In the grooves of those primitive early discs I found in my house, I discovered a new world," he would write.

As was standard for a boy of Vanderbilt lineage, he was sent off to the respected boarding school Hotchkiss, where, under the guidance of a particularly inspirational English teacher, his communication skills were carefully groomed. After Sunday church, his English teacher would invite John and other promising students to his house, where they would lunch with his family, then adjourn to the drawing room to discuss poetry and books.

Taking the train in and out of New York, once old enough to get past the door, he began frequenting restaurants and speakeasies where he'd retreat into a quiet corner, order a non-alcoholic beverage and diligently observe the musicians. In his young mind, jazz, politics, writing and religion seemed to be interconnected in one all-encompassing destiny.

Typically, Vanderbilt sons were expected to study law at Yale and be groomed for a successful career in big business. John tried Yale for a while, then dropped out and began floating. In 1931, at the age of twenty-one, he set sail for a short vacation in London, where a chance meeting brought him into contact with the music publication *Melody Maker*. Invited to submit articles about the American jazz scene, Hammond returned to New York – using a pen as his divining rod.

His controversial articles, openly championing the supremacy of black jazz musicians, provided only pocket money. At a time of 30 percent unemployment, he was receiving $12,000 per year from the family trust fund – more than enough to pay for his new apartment in Greenwich Village and his car. Hammond wasn't good at holding down a job, but then again, he didn't have to be.

Duke Ellington recommended Hammond to Irving Mills, who called one day offering him a job on one of his house magazines. He went to Mills's office to discuss it. "How much do you want to work for me, John?" asked Mills.

"One hundred dollars a week."

"I'll hire you half time for fifty dollars a week," concluded the notoriously skinflint impresario. In the ensuing conversation, Mills asked, "You know what we're going to put there?" He gestured with his cigar toward a space on the wall. "Muriels."

In a pattern that would become familiar, the erudite journalist was quickly fired for not plugging the house catalogue with adequate bias. He also lost an interesting job as a jazz deejay at a Jewish station on the top floor of the Claridge Hotel. Following complaints from the hotel management about black musicians walking through the lobby, Hammond refused to force his musicians to take the freight elevator.

Because his apartment on Sullivan Street was within walking distance of Columbia's offices, he began running into Columbia's musical director, Ben Selvin. One night in the Hofbrau House, Selvin explained that he'd been getting requests from England for jazz records and asked Hammond for an opinion. Realising his articles for *Melody Maker* had earned him legitimacy, Hammond suggested Fletcher Henderson's band and offered to produce four sides on union rates. To his delight, Selvin agreed.

On the morning of the planned session, the musicians trudged into the studio almost three hours late. Feeling guilty, they banged out three numbers, but there was no time to record a fourth. Columbia was furious. Apparently, Henderson's lateness was due to the poor deal he was getting. "Most Negro bandleaders were discouraged, if not defeated, by the Great Depression," explained Hammond. "Duke Ellington and Cab Calloway were making it. No one else was." Fortunately, that first record sold well enough for Columbia's ill feelings to be quickly forgiven. Now welcome to drop by Columbia's offices, Hammond caught the itch for producing.

At the beginning of 1933, he dropped into Monette Moore's place to find a replacement, a pretty seventeen-year-old black girl by the name of Billie Holiday. Hearing her unusual rendition of "Wouldja for a Big Red Apple?" Hammond fell under a spell. "This was the kind of accident I'd dreamed of, the sort of reward I received every now and then, by travelling to every place where anyone performed. Most of the time I was disappointed, but every now and then it all became worthwhile."

Hammond began following Billie around the Harlem speakeasies where she performed for tips. Her real name was Eleanora, he learned. She had arrived from Baltimore, got caught up in prostitution and served a jail term. Notoriously moody and already a moderate marijuana smoker, she sang popular songs in a distinctive manner that made everything her own. Unable to play an instrument and often accompanied by a solo piano, Billie didn't fit the description of jazz singer, but Hammond heard something unique in her voice. He dragged his jazz friends along to hear her. "All I could do was talk and write about her," he would recall.

In the spring of 1933, as the Great Depression hit rock bottom, it was once again the London connection that opened new doors. When he arrived back in England, Hammond was pleasantly surprised to find that he was something of a celebrity among *Melody Maker* readers, thanks to his inspirational work as a jazz writer. Hanging out with editor Spike Hughes, who had recently begun working as a recording director for the newly established Decca Records, Hammond asked for an introduction to Louis Sterling.

As well as managing EMI, Sterling was among Britain's most committed supporters of culture. Victor's well-respected music director, Fred Gaisberg, noted that Sunday evening dinners at the Sterlings' grand home on Avenue Road "had become a regular feature of bohemian London … At the Sterlings' one always met agreeable colleagues in the theatrical, film and musical worlds. On [one] occasion Schnabel and Kreisler were soon deeply engrossed in discussing the political situation in Germany and were joined by ex-Mayor Jimmy Walker and Lauritz Melchior, greatly to the discomfort of a bridge party in the next room, which included Chaliapin and Gigli." The rise of Hitler was of particular concern to Louis Sterling, who over the coming years would sponsor the immigration of Jewish employees of his labels in Berlin. Supporting Charles Lahr and his Progressive Bookshop, he was also building one of Britain's most valuable book collections.

In their brief meeting, Sterling explained that he needed someone to make American jazz records for the English market directly. The young Hammond pounced on the opportunity and secured his first contract, for a total of twenty-four recordings with four artists: Fletcher Henderson, Benny Carter, Joe Venuti and Benny Goodman. As usual, in all the excitement Hammond forgot to negotiate any payment for himself.

He returned to New York on a new mission. His first port of call was Benny Goodman, who he knew often hung out at a speakeasy called the Onyx Club. At about ten thirty, sure enough, Goodman walked in. Tightening his gut, Hammond introduced himself and offered the clarinettist a Columbia recording contract.

"You're a goddamn liar," snapped Goodman, who the previous week had heard from Ben Selvin, the label was bankrupt.

"But this isn't American Columbia," pleaded Hammond. "This is with English Columbia, which has money."

Goodman presumed Hammond was a weirdo, but he was earning only $50 a week, so he forced himself to calm down. Hammond then explained his plan to recruit a band of master musicians capable of improvising free-flowing jazz.

Checking out Goodman's band the next day, Hammond squirmed in his chair. "The English public will laugh us off the turntable," he told the insulted but ambitious Goodman. Swing was not just a genre term for Hammond; it meant a certain rhythmic spirit. At the suggestion of hiring black musicians, Goodman put his foot down. "If it gets around that I recorded with coloured guys I won't get another job in this town."

"It can't be that bad."

"John, you don't know. It's *that* bad."

Fortunately, Benny Goodman was a born dancer who had spent many nights out in Hammond's favourite clubs and he would graciously accept that yes, black musicians were by far the best rhythm conjurers in the craft. For the time being, Hammond rounded up an all-whites band; Artie Bernstein, Dick McDonough, Joe Sullivan, Charlie Teagarden and Manny Klein. He even drove to Boston to convince the master drummer Gene Krupa to join in. The musicians each earned a meagre $20 for the three-hour session, but one of the three recordings, "Ain'tcha Glad," caught the attention of Ben Selvin, who persuaded Hammond to sign it directly to American Columbia with a full artist contract for Benny Goodman. More than happy to do what was good for Benny's career, Hammond altered his own plans. The record sold 5,000 copies – a modest hit by the bleak standards of 1933. Eager for a Benny Goodman follow-up, Hammond got his chance to call in Billie Holiday as a guest vocalist. They were her first recordings, "Riffin' the Scotch" and "Your Mother's Son-in-Law."

Hammond questioned Ben Selvin about Bessie Smith, who had been left adrift during the early thirties. Columbia's defeated staff didn't believe Bessie had a future. With persistence, Hammond succeeded in getting their approval to try out a cheap experiment. He tracked her down to a club in Philadelphia where she was working as a hostess. When he arrived, she was drunk and appeared depressed. "What would it pay?" asked Bessie. All Hammond could offer her was a deal with almost-bust Columbia to make a 35-cent record on the Okeh label. Hammond did, however, offer to pay for her trip to New York out of his own pocket. Bessie agreed without enthusiasm, concluding, "Nobody wants to hear blues no more. Times is hard. They want to hear novelty songs."

As feared, the record didn't go anywhere. Bessie Smith, once hailed as "the Queen of the Blues," took the train back to Philadelphia with $37.50 in her pocket. What the young, enthusiastic Hammond had failed to understand was the wider economic picture. Bessie Smith's core audience was rural blacks – the hardest hit by the Great Depression.

The only person recording rural blues at the time was a Texan song hunter by the name of John Lomax, whose motivations were anything but commercial. More of a musicologist, Lomax was a sixty-year-old professor of English literature and author of an anthology called *Cowboy Songs and Other Frontier Ballads*. His mission was to "gather a body of folklore before it disappeared and to preserve it for the analysis of later scholars."

Still grieving his wife's death, throughout 1933 Lomax set off with various briefs from the Library of Congress, Macmillan Publishing and the American Council of Learned Societies. His eldest son, Alan, accompanied him in a car equipped with a 315-pound acetate-disc recording machine in the trunk, and they toured the South in search of work songs, blues, ballads and reels. Lomax was particularly interested in prisoners because "thrown on their own resources for entertainment, they still sing, especially the long-term prisoners who have been confined for years and who have not yet been influenced by jazz and the radio, the distinctive old-time Negro melodies." That year, Lomax discovered the likes of Lightnin' Washington and Lead Belly.

The very day Bessie Smith was in the studio with Hammond, American Columbia's new owners, Grigsby-Grunow, went into equity receivership, and in April 1934 the record company was declared bankrupt. With another fire sale announced, Edward Lewis, head of Decca in London, sailed to New York to jointly buy American Columbia with ARC owner Herbert Yates. While Lewis was at sea, however, Yates made a solo run – scooping up American Columbia, its offices, studios, catalogues, artist contracts, trademarks and Bridgeport, Connecticut, factory for the laughable sum of $75,500.

When Lewis docked in New York and heard the devastating news, he called Jack Kapp, an experienced record man running one of Yates's labels, Brunswick, and they shared ideas about how to do business in such hard times. Lewis had the money, while Kapp had excellent credentials as a producer. Best of all, Kapp had been careful to place a top-man clause in his biggest artist contracts, including Brunswick's new hopeful, Bing Crosby. Screwing Yates royally, Kapp and Lewis moved everything over to an American branch of Decca, poaching Columbia's sales and promotion chiefs. As a result of all the buyouts, mergers and licenses, by 1934, only four small majors – RCA, ARC, EMI and Decca – controlled virtually every label, master and artist contract in a pitifully diminished market.

The most unexpected market development of all came as an indirect result of Prohibition being lifted in 1933. Although America had never really stopped drinking during its fourteen years of statutory abstinence, speakeasies turned into legitimate bars and were officially allowed to make noise again. Wurlitzer spotted an opportunity and in 1933 launched its ten-disc *Debutante* jukebox. By the end of 1934, some 25,000 jukeboxes were in operation all over America. Decca fought its way aggressively into this new market head-on with ARC, both its arch-enemy and its direct competitor in 35-cent records.

One other important development came in 1934 courtesy of Victor's imaginative new president, Edward Wallerstein. Like Louis Sterling in London, Wallerstein understood that the obstacle to recovery was the obsolete status of record players. With 20 million American households now using the radio as their main source of entertainment, anecdotal evidence suggested that record players had long been relegated to the attic. His audacious plan was to commercialise a cheap adapter to play records through a radio's amplifier. Called the *Duo Jr.*, it was an electrically powered turntable with a magnetic pickup encased in a compact wooden box. It retailed at just $16.50, but special offers gave away a *Duo Jr.* free with the purchase of several RCA Victor records.

In September 1934, just as Roosevelt's New Deal began injecting some urgently needed capital into the economy, Wallerstein announced to his demoralised troops, "We'll grant you, that back when depression was hitting rock bottom, phonograph records were perhaps a dead item. Them days are gone forever … It's time we told the world what's happening in the record business – that sales of phonograph records jumped up 100 per cent last year – and that they're still going up."

Hard times were also forcing musicians to take risks. Benny Goodman's metamorphosis happened when Hammond introduced him to an inventive black pianist, Teddy Wilson. The result of their jamming was a strange but hypnotic sort of chamber jazz. Their harmonic virtuosity turned into pure magic when Gene Krupa joined in on drums. A veritable milestone, this racially mixed touring trio was later widened to a quartet with another Hammond discovery, black vibraphonist Lionel Hampton.

In 1935, when Hammond returned to London, his suitcase was packed with the interesting jazz treasures he had produced over the previous year. Among them, on the Brunswick label, were two test pressings of an as yet unreleased experiment by Teddy Wilson's Orchestra featuring Billie Holiday. As illustrated by catchy tunes like "What a Little Moonlight Can Do" and "Miss Brown to You," the chemistry between Wilson and Holiday marked the beginning of a long adventure – in total, ninety-one songs recorded together, including most of her finest, early performances.

Hammond left London with a new contract, but rather than return to New York directly, he decided to fulfill a lifelong dream to visit Moscow. Through his family connections, Hammond met film-maker Sergei Eisenstein, who was in the process of making a film about *kulaks* – rich farmers opposed to collective farming. Visiting the giant film set, Hammond was stunned to find that an entire farm and wheat field had been built inside a brightly lit hangar. Eisenstein showed Hammond around Moscow and admitted, in a loud restaurant, that he was no longer convinced by communism. Just as Hammond was leaving for America,

Stalin decided to relax his propaganda war against *kulaks* and shut down the film. Hammond sailed back to New York with diarrhoea, smallpox and no illusions about the socialist experiment in Russia.

Upon his return, Hammond joined the NAACP (National Association for the Advancement of Colored People) board of directors and stumbled upon his next big discovery. While probing through the frequencies in his car radio, he chanced upon an experimental station broadcast out of Kansas City. Live from some ballroom, the crackly station featured Count Basie and his band. Every night for weeks, Hammond sat in his car in awe of how modern this jazz sounded. He even began writing about Basie's style in the jazz magazine *Down Beat*.

When his curiosity became too great, he drove down to Kansas City and walked into the Reno Club, a seedy dump that operated what it called *spook dances* – all-night music, 5-cent beer, 10-cent hot dogs, homemade whiskey (a "spook" was a poor tipper). Behind Basie's band, some kind of transaction, presumably marijuana dealing, was going on through a window. The place was unreal and so was the music. Hammond was particularly struck by the ever-smiling drummer, Jo Jones, who had a witty technique of playing the high hats half open. There were important spaces in the music, creating a sense of excitement that sent the solos into free flow. Within this sound, Hammond saw another glimpse of the future.

When Hammond introduced himself to Basie, the bad news hit. Jack Kapp, having read Hammond's articles in *Down Beat,* had just talked Basie into signing an extortionist deal: an exclusive three-year term requiring Basie to record twenty-four recordings per year for an annual flat fee of $750 – an average of $31 per side to be shared among all nine musicians. Basie hadn't realised the contract offered no royalties whatsoever.

The next day, Hammond filed a complaint with the musicians union but only managed to get Basie's contract amended so that all session work would be paid on union scale. He did, however, persuade Benny Goodman's promoter, Willard Alexander, to get Basie out of Kansas and making better money in big hotels around the country.

On record, Count Basie was an instant sensation, in large part thanks to the jukebox market, which, being oriented toward bars, was perfect for jubilant swing. As jukeboxes continued spreading, ARC began using its Vocalion imprint to job low-quality 19-cent records to jukebox dealers. With fierce competition from Decca, Vocalion moved to a porous shellac compound to undercut Decca with 10-cent records, which in the case of regularly played hits wore out after just three days.

Shocked by these standards, Hammond wrote a damning article in 1937 about Decca's shadier practices. Written under the pseudonym of Henry Johnson, it was published by the Communist magazine *New Masses*. In it he exposed how Jack Kapp's privately owned State Street Music Publishing acquired other people's compositions at a flat fee and even copyrighted the term *boogie woogie* to collect on other composer's titles. With the threat of a $100,000 lawsuit against him, Hammond visited Decca's office armed with a copy of Basie's contract and other irrefutable evidence. "Jack, you have a lot to answer for, and your suit will never stand up in court," asserted Hammond. Hearing the shouting from a nearby office, Edward Lewis barged in and began quizzing Hammond. In a fateful exchange, Lewis turned his head to Kapp. "Jack, if you want to sue on your own, it's perfectly all right with me, but I will not permit Decca Records to be party to the action."

Hammond then wrote an exposé on the deplorable conditions in the major companies' factories, notably the ARC labels, which then included Columbia's crumbling Bridgeport factory. Describing a torrid, soot-covered hellhole where he could barely breathe, Hammond revealed that Bridgeport workers earned just $16 a week and endured fourteen violations of the state's sanitary code. "Obvious why the pressed records sounded so much worse than the masters made in the studio," he concluded. In the bitter end, even the union-hating Herbert Yates was forced to improve sanitary conditions and quality control.

John Hammond's giant contribution to the music scene culminated in a crowning moment. In Carnegie Hall on December 23, 1938, his *From Spirituals to Swing* concert documented the story of Negro music in America. To find acts, Hammond had been driving around the South accompanied by a young Englishman with a giant destiny in the record industry, Goddard Lieberson. Hammond's archive research even brought him to some fascinating records by a then unknown Delta blues singer called

Robert Johnson. Hoping to book him for the show, Hammond learned that the singer had been murdered just months previously.

Hammond pieced together the mysterious story and wrote about Robert Johnson in *Down Beat*. In 1936, the young blues singer walked into Henry Speir's store in Jackson, Mississippi. Speir liked what he heard, sent off some demos, and got Johnson a date with Brunswick's Ernie Oertle. In a hotel room in San Antonio, Texas, over three days, Johnson recorded sixteen songs, facing a wall with his back to the engineer. The songs included "Come On in My Kitchen," "Cross Road Blues," and "Terraplane Blues" – a Texan hit selling 5,000 copies, mainly on jukeboxes. Five months later, Johnson was invited to Dallas for another session in which he recorded his more introspective compositions.

Hammond's show opened with African drums recorded in West Africa. Live acts then featured blues singer and guitarist Big Bill Broonzy, harmonica player Sonny Terry, gospel singer Rosetta Tharpe, boogie-woogie pianists Albert Ammons and Meade "Lux" Lewis and jazz clarinettist Sidney Bechet, and finished with a stomping swing number courtesy of Count Basie and his gang. *The New York Times* and the *Herald Tribune* hailed the event as nothing they'd seen or heard before.

Hammond's big night also inspired a legendary Greenwich Village club, Café Society, built inside the basement of a century-old building on Sheridan Square. Its owner, Barney Josephson, watched Hammond's rehearsals, exclaiming, "I don't have to look anywhere for talent, it's all here!" As the club's unofficial music director, Hammond invited Billie Holiday to headline the opening night. Josephson wanted "a club where blacks and whites worked together behind the footlights and sat together out front, a club whose stated advertised policy would be just that." He launched his venture with the motto "The wrong place for the right people."

It was right here where Billie Holiday first performed "Strange Fruit" to a stunned audience. The song was always her closing number and she asked that lights be dimmed, waiters stop serving and patrons refrain from making noise. Just one spotlight illuminated Billie's face as she sang in the breathless silence. All lights went out on her final note. When the lights came back on, Billie was gone.

Integrated and artistically daring, thanks largely to John Hammond, jazz had acquired a bohemian, left-wing dimension. The evolution from entertainment to art also mirrored what field-recording musicologist John Lomax set out to achieve in academic circles. Slowly replacing pejorative terms like *race records* and *hillbilly,* a precise nomenclature began creeping into journalistic language: bluegrass, cowboy songs, reels, work songs, field hollers, gospel, string bands, jug bands, spirituals, hot jazz, Dixieland, swing.

As confirmation that a thaw was under way, 33 million records were sold in America that year, three-quarters of them by Decca and Victor. In an indication of how important the jukebox had become, there were approximately 225,000 jukeboxes in operation across America, consuming 13 million discs annually. Within just five years of trading, Decca had become the biggest record company in America, producing 19 million records annually, a spectacular success story considering the desolate industrial conditions.

In the corporate sphere, 1938 also witnessed the welcome departure of Hollywood autocrat Herbert Yates and his bargain-basement ARC operation. Thoroughly outmanoeuvred by Jack Kapp, Herbert Yates sold up, retreated into Hollywood and was never missed. He at least made a juicy profit off-loading his catalogue for $750,000 to media giant CBS, at the time the third-largest American broadcaster and the one pursuing the most cultural editorial line. Under the capable leadership of its founder, Bill Paley, CBS aggressively hit the ground running by poaching RCA Victor boss Ted Wallerstein to resurrect America's sleeping beauty, Columbia.

Although he had just suffered a heart attack, Wallerstein moved Columbia's headquarters to Brunswick's former offices on Seventh Avenue, a happening centre of musical activity next to Irving Mills's offices. Rightly sensing that middlebrow classical music was the next big thing, he leased two new recording studios from NBC and CBS, big enough for recording orchestras. He then slashed the retail price of Columbia's classical *Masterworks* series to $1, about half the price of Victor's *Red Seal* records.

Wallerstein's most clairvoyant gamble was to invest in technology. Convinced that records were too short, he hired two engineers to experiment with longer-playing discs. In another bold move, he hired John Hammond as Columbia's popular-music recording director. Hammond in turn convinced Wallerstein to hire Goddard Lieberson as a junior assistant in the classical department – another fateful choice.

Hammond's first test as recording director came when Billie Holiday asked to record "Strange Fruit." Wallerstein was busy trying to rebuild Columbia's distribution networks and knew there would be resistance to the song's shocking imagery, particularly in the South. Hammond had his own musical reservations. Although he recognised the power of the original poem graphically depicting a lynched black man's corpse hanging from a tree, he felt the song adaptation had no melody. He even found Billie's rendition somewhat pretentious. For Hammond, who loved Billie's swinging side, her snarls, sultry silences and wailing finale on "Strange Fruit" seemed like a detour into melodrama.

There was also a background saga straining relations. Billie's drug problem was an open secret in the jazz fraternity. Hammond, who tolerated marijuana but drew the line at heroin, eventually made the mistake of discussing the issue with her manager, whose family his family knew well. Fearing that Billie's association with dealers, addicts and criminal gangs might lead to embarrassing problems or even blackmail, the manager eventually abandoned her and she never forgave Hammond for having interfered.Approaching thirty and a little more career conscious than in his early twenties, Hammond chose to reason like an insider and went along with Wallerstein. They did at least allow Billie a once-off contractual exemption to release "Strange Fruit" on another small label, Commodore Records.

The episode signalled a milestone in his own career. Like Billie Holiday, John Hammond was about to spend a number of years in his own private wilderness. Although demand for records was clearly picking up, Hammond found it difficult to adapt to life as an employee in a large, multi-genre company. "To be called upon to work with artists for whom I had little enthusiasm, many of whose previous records I had blasted in my reviews, was not easy for them or for me," explained Hammond. "It was no longer possible to be candid; to be dishonest was painful; still, I had accepted a full time job in the commercial world of recorded music. I could no longer record only my favourites."

As an older and wiser man, the great John Hammond would discover a skyline full of stars, but for the time being, as war broke out in Europe again, his happiest years were in the rear-view mirror. For Hammond and many other jazz musicians in his circle, world events were about to intrude.

8. HOMESICK MEDICINE

THIS TIME AROUND, PEOPLE KNEW WHAT WAS COMING. ANOTHER WAR WAS poised to plunge the world into years of darkness and upheaval. Separating entire populations of women and men, the scale would be biblical. Across four continents, 100 million military personnel were sucked into a killing system sustained by entire economies.

In the year of Pearl Harbor, some 127 million records were sold in America – levels not seen since the twenties. After fifteen years in which records seemed to be obsolete, music was becoming important again. However, not even the wildest optimists could have expected what lay just around the corner. Wartime solitude was about to spectacularly resuscitate demand for disc records – to a level that only the First World War had seen.

What made the renaissance in demand even more astonishing was the peculiar industrial context. From 1941 to 1944, America's music business experienced its first general strike, significantly reducing the supply of new recordings, but so psychologically unsettling was the war that any music, even old records, became a vital daily medicine. Just as hunger is the best sauce, in music there is no ear as receptive as a broken heart.

The music industry's own war began brewing throughout the thirties. As radical ideology stirred through the surrounding political world, impoverished musicians began taking a greater interest in their own trade unions. An industrial census in 1933 calculated that revenues from radio advertising in the United States represented about $60 million, a figure that was rising annually. This tidy treasure chest allowed the broadcasting industry to employ some 12,000 people.

Since its creation in 1914, the composers and publishers union, ASCAP, had grown into a powerful lobby. On the other side of the battlefield, radio stations grouped together under the NAB (National Association of Broadcasters) lobby. In 1937, ASCAP announced that it would be seeking a review of its licence agreement with radio stations once it expired in 1940. As the deadline loomed, ASCAP was pressing for radio stations to pay airplay royalties relative to their audience size. NAB retorted that no radio station in the land could accurately quantify its audience size.

In 1940, the U.S. federal courts finally ruled that radio stations were entitled to broadcast records they had purchased. The precedent cleared the way for the modern radio format – disc jockeys playing records. ASCAP responded by boycotting the airwaves in January 1941. For ten long months, all stations in the NBC and CBS networks were formally denied the right to play any records containing any of the 1 million compositions registered with ASCAP.

In 1942, a union representing session musicians, the American Federation of Musicians, led by James Petrillo, unleashed a second strike against record companies, which at the time were synonymous with radio corporations like RCA and CBS. By a unanimous vote at its annual convention, musicians agreed to shut down recording studios until record companies agreed to pay royalties into a union trust fund for out-of-work musicians. As war plunged the world into its biggest crisis in modern history, music production in America ground to a halt.

At first, radio stations remained defiant, while record companies began releasing back catalogue. The plot thickened as another rights organisation, Broadcast Music, Inc. (BMI), set up in 1939 by radio executives to weaken ASCAP's monopoly, stepped up its market presence to provide stations with non-ASCAP-affiliated material. Because ASCAP was dominated by the bigger Tin Pan Alley publishers, the outsiders of the publishing industry, particularly those centred around Nashville, spotted an opportunity to get more airplay.

Not only did ASCAP's strike prove to be a disastrous failure, it was forced to accept an even worse deal. The recording studio strike, known colloquially as the *Petrillo Ban*, proved more successful. With studios paralysed and musicians drafted into military service, the period would be a quiet one for most record companies.

The one record man with his finger firmly on the pulse of popular demand was Jack Kapp. In 1937 he had spotted the Andrews Sisters, a trio of country girls who had developed their own style of three-part vocal harmonies. Their early body of recordings, including the international smash hit "Bei Mir Bist Du Schoen," continued selling like hot cakes throughout the Petrillo Ban. Recruited as Uncle Sam's lady mascots, they travelled tirelessly through America and the Pacific, performing nonstop in camps, hospitals, munitions factories and military bases. They were dubbed "the Sweethearts of the Armed Forces," and part of their morale-boosting show was to invite three lucky soldiers to dine with them.

Back home but separated from loved ones, civilian audiences were also hearing music in new ways. For the third time in the record industry's fifty-year life, a new boom was being provoked largely by women. Perhaps because the horrors of the First World War were within living memory, women this time weren't particularly jubilant about working in factories. In this vacuum of uncertainty, songs brought invaluable solace.

John Hammond's personal experiences summed up what was happening to many young men and their families. By 1942, as Columbia's recording studios lay idle, he was married and the proud father of a baby son. Suddenly, in early 1943, he was drafted while his wife was six months pregnant with their second child. Filled with dread, he boarded a train in Manhattan surrounded by a sorry-looking troupe of draftees, all visibly fearful about what lay ahead. He had heard that most of Count Basie's band had been ordered to report to Fort Dix the same day, but unlike his familiar surroundings in Greenwich Village, the military base turned out to be segregated.

Within days, Hammond realised that his whole life had been swallowed up by the war. Now simply Private Hammond, following orders from a number of Southern bigots who took pleasure in bullying him for his airs and graces, he was reassigned to Fort Belvoir, Virginia, to become a combat engineer. Enduring daily marches with an eighty-five-pound pack, Hammond began rapidly losing weight as depression locked down his mind.

As a result of his passing out in physical exercises, he was kept on American soil throughout the war and assigned tedious clerical jobs in race relations and camp entertainment. He was given leave to see his newborn son in a New York maternity hospital, where he watched the baby die on his ninth day. Heartbroken and in shock, Hammond was ordered to return to Fort Belvoir. His wife would have to overcome the tragedy alone while looking after their first-born son. As she descended into grief and lethargy, Hammond's letters home were all screened by military security and arrived with censorship stamps. The war against Hitler and Hirohito was necessary, but the war effort was a terrible upheaval for families.

While popular memory and perhaps the lingering effects of propaganda tend to paint those years as heroic, music reveals a different story. In England, Vera Lynn's 1939 smash hit "We'll Meet Again" was a tragic sort of anthem revealing the uncertainty people were feeling in Britain. Glenn Miller's sumptuous "Moonlight Serenade," with its woozy clarinet and saxophone harmony, seemed to express both tears and yearning at the same time. Also recorded in 1939, it snowballed into one of the nostalgic theme tunes of the war years.

Granted an exemption by Petrillo, the U.S. Army launched its V-Discs in 1943. Some 4 million records were distributed throughout the military networks, a not inconsequential quantity considering the grooves were worn out by entire companies of servicemen. Uncle Sam shaped popular memory with a certain style of homely music – comforting songs capable of unifying diverse social groups.

Illustrating how fear heightened emotions, bandleader Artie Shaw remembered an unforgettable scene aboard the USS *Saratoga,* an aircraft carrier patrolling the South Pacific. Having been bombed seventeen times by Japanese planes in the previous weeks, the ship's inhabitants were feeling more than a little homesick. To boost morale, his orchestra was called aboard to play a concert. For dramatic effect, the band was lowered on a hydraulic platform into the vast aircraft hangar below the deck where three thousand marines awaited in full dress uniform. When the band appeared, a huge roar went up like Shaw had never heard in his life. "It really threw me. I couldn't believe what I was seeing or hearing, I felt something extraordinary. These men were starved for something to remind them of home and whatever is mom and apple pie. And the music had that effect."

The true musical icon of the war was another Decca star, Bing Crosby, whose crooning style would influence several giants in his wake. *Yank* magazine, a weekly army publication for wartime servicemen, which broke sexual barriers at the time by featuring suggestive pictures of glamour models, certainly had a handle on its audience. In a telling reminder of how important music can become in a time of extreme crisis, *Yank* made the bold but plausible claim that Bing Crosby had done more for GI morale throughout the entire war than any religious leader or any other celebrity.

In particular, among his long and impressive string of smash hits for Decca, Crosby broke all existing sales records with a crooning interpretation of an Irving Berlin song, "White Christmas," the biggest-selling record in America for eleven weeks in the winter of 1942–43. "White Christmas" was even rereleased before war's end, hitting the No. 1 spot again. Its simple lyric about "dreaming of a White Christmas, just like the ones I used to know" struck a poignant chord in the depths of war. To this day, by most accounts the recording stands as the best-selling single of all time.

One spectacular new arrival into the record business was Capitol, the first significant record label to emerge in Los Angeles. Hollywood tycoons had attempted to buy into New York's record business, but Capitol was founded by an experienced trio of music-business veterans – in particular, Johnny Mercer, a prolific songwriter and a frequent collaborator with Hoagy Carmichael. Originally from Georgia, the thirty-three-year-old had written a string of hits for Bing Crosby, Glenn Miller, Fred Astaire, Jimmie Lunceford, Cab Calloway, the Andrews Sisters and just about every other big name in the game. Like an early bird catching the worm, he wrote words in that dreamy stillness just after dawn – never toiling beyond lunchtime.

His partner Buddy DeSylva, then a Paramount Films executive, had written the musical *Blue Monday* with George Gershwin and had served on ASCAP's board of directors. The third man in the Capitol story was Glenn Wallichs, owner of Music City, the biggest record store in Los Angeles. Wisely convincing Mercer and DeSylva not to seek investment from Paramount Pictures, he put up $15,000 to keep Capitol independent.

Johnny Mercer's first big discovery was Nat King Cole, whom he signed but was unable to record. Fortunately, Jack Kapp hammered out a deal with James Petrillo whereby Decca agreed to pay the union trust fund and even throw open its accounting books, supplying serial numbers for every record pressed. In return, Decca could, in the event of another strike, lock in the artists it had under contract. Aching to record the King Cole Trio, Capitol followed Decca's lead a month later. Cole's first recording, "Straighten Up and Fly Right," was a musical reinterpretation of one of his father's favourite sermons. It sold 500,000 copies – a windfall that financed much of Capitol's early development.

Among the crooners, the most dazzling young star would belong to Columbia. Frank Sinatra was a handsome, blue-eyed Italian American who had first appeared on record as a singer in a swing band lead by Harry James. From there he was spotted by another bandleader, the tough-talking, smooth-playing trombonist Tommy Dorsey, who talked the twenty-six-year-old into signing a management contract. By May 1941, Sinatra was not only topping the male singer polls in both *Billboard* and *Down Beat,* he seemed to be gathering his very own fan base among teenaged girls. What would later be termed *Sinatramania* started in the winter of 1942, when Sinatra sold out New York's Paramount Theater for eight solid weeks. One witness, the comedian Jack Benny, claimed, "I thought the goddam building was going to cave in. I never heard such a commotion … All this for a fellow I've never heard of."

Columbia pounced on the opportunity to sign him up. In fact, it was John Hammond's superior, Manie Sacks, who convinced Sinatra to sign with Columbia and eventually untangle himself from Dorsey. With

Sinatra signed, in high demand, but unable to make records, Columbia simply repackaged the 1939 Harry James record and rereleased it as a Sinatra solo record. Although the original version hadn't sold well, with a new sleeve it sold a million copies throughout the summer of 1943. Sinatra quickly woke up to his management contract with Dorsey, which siphoned off 43.3 percent of his royalties. Under Sachs's guidance, he bought his way out of it in exchange for a $25,000 cheque. Columbia advanced Sinatra the money.

As the war raged in the Pacific, in North Africa and across Russia, conscription intensified in 1943. That December, Sinatra was classified 4-F, "registrant not acceptable for military service," on the grounds of a perforated eardrum. With the press full of photographs of the handsome playboy either surrounded by pretty women or being screamed at by adoring *bobbysoxers*, the young Sinatra became one of the war's most controversial celebrities. According to one rumour, his handlers had paid a bigwig $40,000 to keep Sinatra out of the service. It surfaced years later that a recruitment psychologist deemed him "neurotic" and "not acceptable material from a psychiatric standpoint." The journalist William Manchester, serving his country at the time, confidently observed, "I think Frank Sinatra was the most hated man of World War II, much more than Hitler."

The final years of the war transformed the music business. Due to the size of their orchestras, swing bands were the most severely affected by drafting. Glenn Miller was killed flying over the English Channel in 1944. *Down Beat*'s "Killed in Action" column had been documenting fallen jazzmen since 1942.

Although swing was given mass exposure by the army, its roots were being cut. A 20 percent entertainment tax in 1944 closed struggling ballrooms. The rationing of rubber and petrol made touring by bus difficult; trains were often block-reserved for migrating servicemen. For black musicians, because of institutional racism, the war was particularly cruel. Lester Young, Basie's legendary saxophonist and Billie Holiday's closest friend, was drafted in 1944 and sent to an Alabama training base. Caught with marijuana and promptly court-martialled, he spent a year languishing in a detention barracks. Many black musicians dodged conscription by claiming psychosis, drug addiction, or homosexuality or simply by moving around with no fixed address. Horn player Howard McGhee cleverly won an exemption by requesting to be trained in the South so that he could organise black soldiers to shoot whites. He raved with psychotic logic to a bemused army psychiatrist, "Whether he's a Frenchman, a German, or whatever … how would I know the difference?"

It was from this mindset that a more abstract, militant branch of jazz began to thrive. *Bebop*, as it became termed, was the vibrant new movement among a younger generation of jazz players connected to Earl Hines's band – in particular Charlie Parker and Dizzy Gillespie, who explained, "The enemy, by that period, was not the Germans, it was above all white Americans who kicked us in the butt every day, physically and morally … If America wouldn't honour its Constitution and respect us as men we couldn't give a [damn] about the American way. And they made it damn near un-American to appreciate our music." For some, bebop strove to expose the limitations of the white bandleaders who, they felt, had robbed black musicians of their rightful music. As Thelonious Monk put it, "We wanted a music that *they* couldn't play."

Bebop was the hungry new beast of the underground. A new wave was in motion and bebop's radical departure into abstract harmonic complexity undoubtedly contributed to jazz becoming more of an elitist and peripheral niche genre in the postwar period than it had been in the twenties and thirties.

During the recording ban, Billie Holiday drifted further astray, still sore from the "Strange Fruit" episode and falling deeper into heroin addiction. Her contract with Columbia simply expired. After one disappointing recording with Capitol in 1942 under the pseudonym Lady Day, Billie would have to wait until the end of the Petrillo Ban to record twelve new songs on Milt Gabler's Commodore label. Jack Kapp, however, hired Gabler as a producer, probably in the hope of luring Billie Holiday to Decca. The gamble worked and with bigger resources at his disposal, Milt Gabler organised some of Billie's biggest standards on Decca.

One of the most beautiful creations of the wartime repertoire was surely her exquisite 1944 classic "Lover Man," with its risqué yet melancholy lyric,

"I go to bed with a prayer that you'll make love to me." Between 1944 and her eighteen-month jail sentence in May 1947 for heroin possession, Billie recorded twenty-one lushly orchestrated jazz ballads including many of her finest moments: "That Ole Devil Called Love," "Don't Explain," and "Good Morning Heartache."

With Decca's and Capitol's recording studios open and scoring hits, Ted Wallerstein was itching to convert public demand for Sinatra into dollars. Despite President Franklin Roosevelt's personal intervention, Petrillo didn't budge an inch, comparing CBS and RCA to "the slave owners of the Civil War days" and warning that his union "will not hesitate to break off relations with these companies and leave them to die by their own nefarious schemes." Forced to capitulate, Wallerstein chose Armistice Day to issue his humiliating surrender. "We must now either sign or go out of business," he said.

In January 1946, after three long years in different military bases around America, John Hammond was discharged. Like many disoriented servicemen, "I returned to a son I did not know, to a wife with problems – and to be sure, good reasons for them. Another baby was due in a month and I faced responsibilities I felt unable to cope with. I was a stranger in my own home and I knew I needed help."

Musically, Hammond tried to find what he'd left behind. Returning to the Greenwich Village scene where in 1941 he had produced the seminal *Chain Gang* recordings by Josh White, he was happy to see that thanks to Café Society's influence, Washington Square had become a Sunday meeting point for folk singers, banjo pickers and balladeers. His old friend and sponsor Eric Bernay, owner of *New Masses,* had even set up his own cutting-edge jazz and folk label, Keynote, whose Almanac Singers included Pete Seeger, Woody Guthrie, Josh White and Burl Ives.

Alongside Guthrie, Bernay and ethnomusicologist Alan Lomax, Hammond joined Pete Seeger's People's Songs organisation, whose aim was to provide labour movements around America with protest songs. Naively thinking he could combine his day job at Columbia with producing cutting-edge jazz for his friends at Keynote, Hammond overestimated Ted Wallerstein's patience. Once again, he was fired and began roaming the underground, surviving on odd jobs.

With the Petrillo Ban still a raw nerve, Ted Wallerstein had no time for trade unions or musicology. Between 1946 and 1947, record sales in America rocketed spectacularly from 275 million to 400 million. Capitol alone had sold 42 million records in its first four years of trade. Feeling this miraculous renaissance, in April 1948, Ted Wallerstein's long-awaited secret project was prepared for launch – the 33⅓ rpm 12-inch long player.

In a historical meeting in the CBS boardroom, on one side of the table sat the group chairman, Bill Paley, flanked by Ted Wallerstein, CBS president Frank Stanton and their engineer, Peter Goldmark. The guest was David Sarnoff, accompanied by his eight engineers. For the demonstration, Stanton set up two turntables, a standard 78 and a prototype LP.

When Stanton touched down the stylus on the second turntable, the effect on the guests, according to Goldmark, "was electrifying, as we knew it would be. I never saw eight engineers look so much like carbon copies of tight-lipped gloom." Sarnoff pulled the cigar from his mouth and glared down his side of the table. "You sonsabitches got caught with your pants down again!" He could not "believe that little Columbia Graphophone invented this without my knowing."

CBS chairman Bill Paley suggested he was open to a licensing deal to share the technology. Sarnoff courteously congratulated his hosts for their impressive work and replied he would consider their offer. Although, he added, there was probably no reason to do so because Columbia's system utilised nothing patentable, just the tools at hand.

Sarnoff's legal instincts were on the money. There was no intellectual property as such, except the name "*LP,*" which CBS-Columbia copyrighted. Symbolically, on the summer solstice of 1948, the LP was publicly showcased to forty journalists at the Waldorf Astoria. For visual effect, a wobbling tower of 78s was stacked alongside a squat pile of LPs containing the same amount of music.

As Columbia basked in the limelight, RCA Victor retaliated in February 1949 with its 45 rpm 7-inch – allowing up to eight minutes of audio space. With the birth of two new disc formats, the record business was truly back from the dead.

This miraculous renaissance was, of course, being fuelled by the postwar spirit of rebuilding. With 70 million people dead and entire countries in ruins it was obvious – to young parents, at least – who would really inherit all that had been fought for. They say the Second World War marked the end of American innocence. The next age in American music would be a sort of adolescence.

9. SUNRISE

THEN THERE WAS ROCK 'N' ROLL. THE LOCATION WAS MEMPHIS, THE VERY crossroads that for years had attracted blues kings and hunters alike: W. C. Handy, Harry Pace, Henry Speir, Robert Johnson. As far as music was concerned, this nineteenth-century city, named after the ancient capital of Egypt, seemed to be built along a cultural fault line, exactly where the redneck and Afro-American continental plates were precariously interlocked.

Memphis was a major port along the Mississippi and effectively the only big city for a hundred miles in every direction – attracting farmers, black and white, from the Delta and the Tennessee plains. Its famous black neighbourhood was centred around Beale Street, a legendary stretch of bars, brothels and pawn shops leading from the heart of the city all the way down to the river.

Although R&B had many key players throughout the late forties and early fifties – Atlantic, King, Chess, Specialty, RPM, Duke, Imperial, Excelsior, Liberty, VJ – there was one label at the very epicentre of the imminent explosion. Marking the dawn of a new musical age, even its name and logo couldn't have been more appropriate: Sun Records.

The supposedly contradictory ingredients that went into early rock 'n' roll make sense when viewed through the childhood of Sun's founder. Sam Phillips was a poor white Southerner whose cotton-picking parents grew up on a 300-acre farm in Florence, Alabama. As a boy working in the blistering heat, Sam Phillips dragged heavy canvas sacks between the rows and filled them with the fibres plucked from the prickly twigs. "I was right in the middle of people who worked hard, black and white," explained Phillips. "And even though I lived in the South, we didn't see the colour line like a lot of people. We weren't better than anybody.

"There were two types of downtrodden people back then. There were the black field hands and the white sharecroppers. It was impossible in those days not to hear and grow to love all the music of oppression and the music that uplifted people – blues, country, gospel, all of it … The only hope they had was to sing the blues and to sing religious songs, and to hope and pray that times would be better … One man in particular, Uncle Silas Payne, an old black man, taught music to me. Not musical notes or reading, you understand, but real intuitive music … Did I feel sorry for them? In a way I did. But they could do things I couldn't do. They could out-pick me. They could sing on pitch."

Education, they say, begins at the kitchen table. "I was raised to respect black people," continued Phillips. "My father and mother made us understand who was Uncle Silas and who was Aunt Minnie, and how they were to be treated with respect. I never for one time – and I think this had great influence on me – I never heard my father ever abuse a black person. That, to me, showed a sense of kinship. It ensconced in me a type of feeling for the South; although we had all sorts of segregation, we also had a great amount of integration in spirit and common problems."

Phillips had caught his first glimpse of Memphis in 1939 when his father took his five sons in their Dodge coupe to see a Baptist preacher in Texas. When they passed through Memphis it was four o'clock in the morning and raining. Cruising down Beale Street with the roof down, the sixteen-year-old Sam watched bug-eyed as the Negro thoroughfare moved past – crowds pouring out of bars, hotel signs flashing, hookers, people walking in the middle of the street. Although he didn't know it yet, the dreamlike passage would replay through his mind for years, eventually drawing him back as a young man.

Thanks to his older brother Jud, he secured a hobby-job, presenting a religious radio show, *Hymn Time,* mixing up white quartets and black spirituals. He was also fascinated with justice and spent afternoons at the local courthouse admiring the "almost evangelical" style of lawyers. "A lot of the time it didn't matter what the facts were," thought Phillips watching from the gallery. "All you had to do was sway the jury."

When his father suddenly died in 1942, he dropped out of school to support his mother and profoundly deaf aunt. Working at a mortuary, he learned how to handle the bereaved and how to respect silences. In December 1943, he headed to Nashville in the hope of landing a job at the famous station WSM, which broadcast *The Grand Ole Opry*. He didn't get the job, but was told that a presenter at a smaller Nashville station had just been drafted; they needed an urgent replacement. Here he spent eighteen formative months working as a full-time deejay, until he learned of a job vacancy in Memphis. Without a moment's hesitation, he drove to Memphis and walked into the WREC radio studio in the Peabody Hotel. "Just down the block was Beale Street, and I thought, Wow."

Working as a spotter at the Peabody Hotel, Phillips had to relay technical information to the radio control room where live performances from the opulent Skyway Ballroom were fed to the nationwide CBS network. At age twenty-two, he was given his own show, *Saturday Afternoon Tea Dance,* on which he played eclectic rarities, usually with a rawer sound than was popular in the late forties.

By 1949, he began dreaming of his own recording studio. Phillips had a family of six to support, so his motivation was partly financial. Many of his radio colleagues predicted failure, citing a previous Memphis studio that opened and closed within a year. The one person to believe in his dream, however, was a talk-show host, Marion Keisker, the divorced mother of a nine-year-old son. Like so many, she was hypnotised by something magical in Sam Phillips's eyes – "swirling pools of insanity" as another associate described them.

He leased a store at the corner of Union and Marshall avenues and named his business the *Memphis Recording Service.* With a budget of just $1,000, both Phillips and Keisker refitted the old store, while a third WREC employee lent them the money for two domestic standard reel-to-reel tape machines, a four-channel mixing table, and his prized possession, a portable Presto PT 900 tape machine. The studio opened for business on

January 3, 1950. Its motto read "we record anything – anywhere – any time." So Phillips got to work chasing down odd jobs, recording bar mitzvahs, weddings, funerals, political speeches, civic functions, anything that paid.

Phillips was struggling to pay the $150 rent and Keisker's $25 salary, but his luck began to roll thanks to an R&B label based in Los Angeles, RPM. Its owners, the Bihari brothers, sent down their latest R&B hopeful, B. B. King. When King described his sessions in Memphis to a disc jockey in Clarksdale, Mississippi, by the name of Ike Turner, Phillips got another fateful call. An audition was arranged for which Turner's band wrote an energetic number called "Rocket 88." However, along the road to Memphis on March 5, 1951, the band's amplifier fell off the roof of the car, breaking the speaker cone on impact. When the musicians arrived, Phillips couldn't fix it, but stuffing it with paper, reduced the rattling to a tolerable fuzz. In the end, Phillips judged that the electric guitar played through a broken amplifier sounded a little like a saxophone.

Written with car radio in mind, the song described cruising for women in a big steely V8 Cadillac and made a cryptic reference to amphetamines. Phillips sent a copy to Chess Records in Chicago, whose owner, Leonard Chess, released it in April 1951. By June, it was No. 1 on the R&B charts; by December, it was the second-biggest-selling R&B record of the year. Phillips had produced his first hit. It was a major confidence boost, but Sam Phillips was working eighteen hours a day, holding down two jobs. Exhausted, broke and the object of racist jibes from radio colleagues, Phillips experienced a nervous breakdown and was administered electro-shock treatment while hospitalised.

Phillips slammed the door on his radio job to concentrate on the record trade. Unfortunately, he was about to taste its cruel side. Noticing the buzz in Memphis, both Leonard Chess and the Bihari brothers began poaching his best artists – first Ike Turner and then, saddest of all, his most treasured discovery, blues shouter Howlin' Wolf. Measuring "six foot six with the biggest feet I have ever seen on a human being," the Wolf was a Delta farmer whom Phillips noticed singing on a local radio station. "He had no voice in the sense of a pretty voice, but he had command of every word he spoke," observed Phillips of this shamanistic blues man. "When the beat got going in the studio, he would sit there and sing, hypnotising himself. Wolf was one of those raw people ... God, to see the fervor in that man's face when he sang. His eyes would light up, you'd see the veins in his neck and, buddy, there was nothing on his mind but that song."

Phillips realised he had no choice but to set up a proper label of his own with exclusive contracts and direct sales channels. He admitted, "If I'd had my way, I'd rather have done only the creative end and left the business to other people, but once you set up in business you have to carry it through." It was time to start anew and do everything better. "I had chosen the name Sun right at the beginning of 1952 when I had determined to try to start issuing my own recordings. The sun to me – even as a kid back on the farm – was a universal kind of thing. A new day, a new opportunity."

Getting Sun off the ground would prove a monumental task. Marion Keisker was dipping into her savings to feed the company with cash flow when, just in time, an experienced record business entrepreneur from Nashville, Jim Bulleit, offered guidance. "He gave me most of the early insight into what I was confronted with – and that was frightening," Phillips said of his business crash course. Introduced to forty regional independent distributors, Sun scored its first hit in March 1953 with "Bear Cat" by Rufus Thomas. It sold 100,000 copies, and Sun had a seat at the R&B table.

At the time, Atlantic, having to move 60,000 records every month to break even, was probably the hottest of the pack. Unlike the competition, it was staffed with well-connected New Yorkers with a hotline to the national media. Atlantic's founder, Ahmet Ertegun, was the son of a high-ranking Turkish diplomat whose family had moved between embassies in Paris, London and Washington. His background provided the cosmopolitan spirit that imbued Atlantic's epic life.

His love affair with black music began at the age of ten watching Duke Ellington perform at the London Palladium. "This was my first encounter with black people," recalled Ertegun. "I was overwhelmed by the elegance of their tuxedos, their gleaming instruments and their sense of style ... I fell under the spell of black music." When his father was transferred to an influential post in Washington, D.C., young Ahmet began hanging out at a local record store, Waxie Maxie Silverman's. While studying philosophy in college, he also made himself into an authority on jazz. With the help of a fellow jazz lover, Herb Abramson, and funding from his family dentist, he set up Atlantic Records in 1947.

By 1953, Ertegun had recruited a formidable new partner, Jerry Wexler, the *Billboard* journalist who coined the "*rhythm and blues*" moniker. "The hip of my generation, who were teenagers in the thirties, had always been drawn to Afro-American culture," the Bronx-born Wexler explained. "In fact, I had always known *White Negroes*, not pretenders or voyeurs but guys who had opted to leave the white world, married black women and made Harlem or Watts their habitat. These guys *converted*."

Eloquent and crusading, the hulky Jerry Wexler believed his chief editor at *Billboard,* Paul Ackerman, was one of the great unsung heroes of these renaissance years. Thanks to Ackerman's ethic, *Billboard* offered more than just charts, trade pulp and advertising space; its editorial line actively supported independents exploring the margins. "In Jewish lore, in every generation the hope of the world rests on ten pure souls – *tzaddikim* – without whom the universe would fragment. Paul was one such soul," claimed Wexler with due solemnity. "Nothing would offend Paul more than to be asked to print verbatim the handouts of the record companies. He drew a hard line between puffery and news. Not that he was averse to helping a friend with a harmless plug, but his kindness was leavened with righteous intolerance. Ackerman believed in true editorial content."

Above all, Ackerman actively transmitted to writers and readers alike the spirit of enlightened record men. "His heroes were Ralph Peer and Frank Walker, explorers who went with portable equipment to the Smokies, the Delta, the Savannah, the Piedmont and the cotton bottoms to find Ma Rainey and Bessie Smith, Jimmie Rodgers and Robert Johnson and Hank Williams. That's the stuff that Paul loved best – the beginnings, the earliest strain. He also identified with the pioneers who started the independent blues and country labels. He introduced me to many of these men, later to become my competitors – Herman Lubinsky, Syd

Nathan, Leonard Chess, Saul Bihari. He dug them because they broke the stranglehold of the pop record labels."

When Jerry Wexler joined Atlantic, Ahmet Ertegun explained to him, "Here's the sort of record we need to make; there's a black man living in the outskirts of Opelousas, Louisiana. He works hard for money; he has to be tight with a dollar. One morning he hears a song on the radio. It's urgent, bluesy, authentic, irresistible. He becomes obsessed. He can't live without this record. He drops everything, jumps in his pick-up and drives twenty-five miles to the first record store he finds. If we can make that kind of music, we can make it in the business."

Getting records to rural audiences relied on airplay. Most of the urban markets had at least one R&B maverick on the airwaves: Alan "Moondog" Freed in Cleveland; Zenas "Daddy" Sears in Atlanta; Hunter Hancock in Los Angeles; Hoss Allen, John Richbourg and Gene Nobles in Nashville; Clarence "Poppa Stoppa" Hamann in New Orleans; Daddy-O Dewey in Memphis.

Wexler soon began noticing a sea change. "The rhythm and blues of the late forties was adult in flavour and often spiked with booze," but suddenly, what was being colloquially termed *cat music* began creeping into the traditional R&B market. "A picture was beginning to emerge: Kids, especially kids down South, were taking newly invented transistor radios to the beach," noted Wexler. "White Southerners, I believe, in spite of the traditional aura of racial bigotry, have always enjoyed the most passionate rapport with black music, itself a Southern phenomenon. And in the fifties, white Southern teenagers started the charge towards ballsy rhythm and blues. As the Eisenhower decade became more conformist, the music became more rebellious, more blatantly sexual."

In 1953, Atlantic found its game changer in Ray Charles, whose slick musicianship took R&B into a new sound. For obvious reasons, the same task was trickier for Sam Phillips, operating as a lone ranger in Memphis. Everywhere Sam Phillips took his rougher-sounding R&B records, he'd hear the same refrain from storekeepers, café proprietors and small-town deejays: Black music was corrupting the children of decent, white folk. Avoiding any moral arguments, he'd just lean on the counter and listen. Phillips knew these prejudices ran generations deep.

Whether it was a reward for persistence or simply good luck, one Saturday afternoon in August 1953, a strange-looking kid walked in off the street to record a ballad for his mother. Spotty, nervous and sporting a big mop of greasy blond hair, the eighteen-year-old was dressed up in a pink and black outfit bought on Beale Street.

Keisker invited him to take a seat. "What's your name?" she asked.

"Elvis Presley."

As she misspelled his name and settled the $3.98 fee, the teenager tried to strike up a conversation, with a twitchiness that betrayed his best efforts to appear nonchalant.

"If you know anyone that needs a singer?"

"What kind of a singer are you?" asked Keisker.

"I sing all kinds."

"Who do you sound like?"

"I don't sound like nobody."

"What do you sing, hillbilly?"

"I sing hillbilly," said Elvis, nodding.

"Well, who do you sound like in hillbilly?"

"I don't sound like nobody."

Phillips appeared and ushered the young man into the studio, where Presley sang two old ballads. Within less than half an hour he was led back to the reception with an acetate under his arm. "We might give you a call sometime," said Phillips, running off to his next job.

Over the next ten months, Presley kept dropping by, almost making a nuisance of himself but remaining sufficiently polite – almost pitiful – for Phillips to joke as they watched him cross the street, "Here's ol' Elvis, coming to see what kind of a star we can make of him today!" Phillips kept his distance inside the studio while Elvis would always ask, "Ma'am, if you know anyone that needs a singer?" Keisker's answer would always be a gentle no, followed by a few courteous niceties. Presley would close the door behind him, trying to conceal his dejection.

Then one day in May 1954, while Phillips was visiting a Nashville prison, a black inmate presented him with a ballad that made him think of Elvis. When Keisker found his number and called him up, Elvis literally ran across Memphis so fast she got a shock to see him burst in the door so soon after putting the phone back on the cradle. The ensuing experiment didn't gel, but Phillips was curious to see what Elvis had in his belly. He stopped taping, and for three hours, Elvis sang everything he knew.

At the time, Phillips had a kindred spirit in a local electric guitarist named Scotty Moore. In their discussions of music over coffee in a nearby diner, Phillips had come to the conclusion that R&B records "appealed to white youngsters just as Uncle Silas Payne's stories and songs used to appeal to me … but there was something in many of those youngsters that resisted buying this music. The Southern ones especially felt a resistance that they probably didn't quite understand. They liked the music, but they weren't sure whether they ought to like it or not."

Everyone had noticed Bill Haley, who recorded a softer cover of "Rocket 88" in 1951, omitting its references to pills. In 1954, Haley scored two massive hits for Decca, "Rock Around the Clock" and a version of Atlantic's "Shake, Rattle and Roll" by Joe Turner. Jerry Wexler was so intrigued by the phenomenon that he picked up his pen and wrote an essay for *Cash Box* exclaiming, "It happened in the twenties when Perry Bradford and Spencer Williams were as hot as Irving Berlin; it happened when Bessie Smith and Ethel Waters sold their records into millions of white parlours. Now it's happening again."

It proved to be Sam Phillips's conversations over coffee with Scotty Moore that led to the eureka moment. When Phillips started mentioning Elvis Presley as an example of this unfathomable white youth, Moore got curious and invited Elvis to a jam. Moore called Phillips to give him his thumbs down, but Phillips persuaded Moore and bassist Bill Black to try Elvis out in a proper audition at Sun. One Monday evening in July 1954, the three musicians arrived. Sam Phillips sat waiting in the control room. The session began awkwardly with the Bing Crosby ballad they had been jamming at Moore's apartment. Feeling they were stuck in corny territory, Phillips stopped the session and came into the studio.

Beginning to loosen up, Elvis suddenly began goofing around in a very unfamiliar direction, strumming into a jiving version of an old blues song, "That's all right mama, that's all right with me …" Black perked up at the bouncing energy and joined in. Scotty followed with some darting riffs in the Bill Haley style. Phillips was amazed that Elvis even knew the 1946 number by Delta blues singer Arthur Crudup.

"What are you doing?" Phillips asked excitedly.

"We don't know," the musicians laughed back.

"Well, back up. Try and find a place to start and do it again."

Moore and Black worked out a structure while Phillips advised Elvis to sing it raw, warning that if he was too fake, he wouldn't be able to keep it up for the whole take. Phillips hit the red button, and the musicians launched in.

Listening to the playback, nobody knew what to think. After two evenings of tighter, more polished renditions, Phillips came to the conclusion that the very first take possessed a magic that outshone all the others. It was time to consult the wildest character on the Memphis airwaves, Daddy-O Dewey – tastemaker, verbal acrobat, disc addict.

At around midnight, Dewey strolled in. As "That's All Right" played over and over, the two men sat drinking beer, brooding in an uncharacteristic silence. The song made Dewey visibly uncomfortable, even wary, but he kept listening. "It's not black, it's not white, it's not country," thought Phillips, "and I think Dewey was the same way."

Next morning, Phillips was awakened by a call from Dewey, who hadn't slept all night. Whether it was because of amphetamines or Elvis, he wanted two copies of "That's All Right" sent to the station before his show. When Phillips telephoned the Presley house to warn that the legendary deejay would be playing the song that night, Elvis went into a fit of panic. He set the station on his mother's radio, asked her to listen in, and ran out to a movie theater – too frightened to hear his own voice all over Memphis.

Kicking off at ten o'clock, even by his own pumped-up standards Daddy-O Dewey was in flying form. He predicted to his listeners that local boy Elvis Presley would be a star. He played "That's All Right" seven times in a row as calls flooded the station's switchboard. Theatrically, Dewey then demanded, live on air, that Elvis come to the studio right away. He phoned the Presley home and spoke to Mrs Presley. When Elvis returned from the movies and saw the pandemonium, he ran to the radio station. Shaking with fear, he was asked which high school he had attended. Dewey's question was, of course, loaded; the answer would tell the audience the singer was white. Dewey thanked the young man for coming in. "Aren't you going to interview me?" wondered Elvis, who didn't realise he was already on air.

Sun received six thousand preorders. Two nights before the record's release on June 19, Phillips asked Moore to give Elvis a slot with his Starlite Wranglers. The venue was at a run-down roadhouse, but the awkward experiment showed Phillips that even put up against a hostile adult audience, the petrified Elvis could belt it out. In the stage light, his neck sweated profusely, his pimples glistened, and his tatty blonde hair looked like it hadn't been washed in weeks. Realising that to reach young people, they were going to have to find venues that didn't serve alcohol, Phillips telephoned a booker and deejay, Bob Neal, who found Elvis a more appropriate slot at a show headlined by a hillbilly yodeller. When Elvis arrived at the venue and saw the size of the crowd, he experienced another rush of terror. Ushered onstage, he broke into "That's All Right" as his legs went into a nervous spasm. The more he shook, the louder the kids screamed.

Sucking all the youth hysteria into his whirlpool eyes, Sam Phillips saw stars. Sure enough, despite plenty of hostility from local deejays who thought the record was an ugly mutant, by the end of August "That's All Right" appeared on the *Billboard* charts. To win over the small-town stations, Phillips needed some kind of blessing from the old guard. Carrying some Elvis records under his arm, he paid a visit to the biggest power broker in Nashville, Jim Denny. "I've heard it, Sam," Denny said. "I just better not put him on right now because we might do something to *The Grand Ole Opry*, and it's *so* traditional."

"But these people used to drive to town in a wagon," implored Phillips. "The world has changed – we got jet airplanes!"

"The door is not closed," conceded Denny like a true pro. "I think it's an interesting record, but I don't want to get sponsors cancelled."

Inevitably, as Elvis grew too big to snub, he was cordially invited to play on *The Grand Ole Opry*, followed by *Louisiana Hayride*, the most popular show among Southern youngsters. With nonstop live performances and a further single, Elvis fever was spreading through the South.

Unlike in his R&B years when he struggled to keep up with the genre leaders, Sam Phillips was by now an all-around record man with his finger firmly on the pulse of the nascent rock 'n' roll wave. Drawn to his corner shop, rockabilly hopefuls began knocking on his door. Johnny Cash, Carl Perkins, Roy Orbison, Jerry Lee Lewis – all of Sun's biggest stars *chose* him as midwife. Unlike any of his competitors, Phillips spent hours, even days, auditioning, experimenting, looking for that little flash of magic. As Johnny Cash explained, "Phillips was very smart, with great instincts, and he had real enthusiasm; he was excitable, not at all laid back. When he'd put something on tape he liked, he'd come bursting out of the control room into the studio, laughing and clapping his hands, yelling and hollering, 'That was great! That was wonderful. That was a rolling stone.' His enthusiasm was fun. It fired us up."

Phillips demanded anything up to forty takes from his artists. When it came to picking *the one,* Cash said, "we both felt that if the performance was really there at the heart of the song, it didn't matter much if there were some little musical error or glitch in the track somewhere. There are mistakes on several of my Sun records – Luther fumbling a guitar line, Marshall going off the beat, me singing sharp – and we all knew it. Sam just didn't care that much: he'd much rather have soul, fire and heart than technical perfection."

When it came to sound, however, Phillips *was* technically conscious. Despite his rudimentary equipment, having spent years running PA feeds from a ballroom to a radio network, he understood room acoustics. He constantly moved the musicians around and even placed cardboard boxes over the amplifiers, directing the sound through a hole into the corners. These techniques, topped off by his hallmark slapback delay (a short, single-repeat echo), created an itchy, churchlike atmosphere that pushed the record industry into a new age of sound manipulation. "You have to have a good song, of course, but atmosphere is nearly everything else," said Phillips. "With great artists, almost fifty percent of something good they might do happens because of an almost instant reaction to what is taking place around them … There is so much psychology in dealing with artists … Sometimes you can be too cocky around people who are insecure and just intimidate them … I tried to envelop them in my feelings of security … Atmosphere is so important."

The fateful encounter with Colonel Tom Parker happened in February 1955, just before a show in Memphis. Huddled with Elvis and Phillips around a table at a nearby restaurant, Parker set the tone by confidently lecturing Phillips on why Sun Records could never break Elvis nationally. The streetwise Phillips saw Parker was a shark – a bigger shark – and sat glumly over his coffee, knowing the crushing analysis was correct. Sun was broke. Elvis, visibly impressed by Parker's spiel, was about to get snatched.

Because Elvis was legally underage, Parker charmed Gladys Presley, even persuading country legend Hank Snow to explain to her the harsh realities of the music business. So Gladys Presley signed the extraordinarily convoluted "special adviser" contract on her son's behalf, effectively giving Parker total managerial control. Turning his attentions to the Sun contract, Parker asked Phillips to name his price. The telephone call descended into shouting. Phillips spat out a figure of $40,000, in two weeks, then slammed down the receiver.

Parker pitched Elvis to Ahmet Ertegun and Jerry Wexler, who considered picking him up, but as the deadline neared, Parker had just one firm offer, $25,000 from RCA Victor. On the final day, Parker convinced RCA's singles division manager, Bill Bullock, to find another $15,000. The relieved Parker sent a telegram to Memphis confirming he'd raised the money.

Although the seemingly puny sum of $40,000 has long been questioned, in late 1955, it was nonetheless an expensive deal for a Tennessee boy. Truth is, Phillips urgently needed a cash injection. He was nervously sitting on a sure-fire hit from Carl Perkins. As soon as the cheque from RCA cleared, he scheduled "Blue Suede Shoes" for release on New Year's Day 1956 – the year rock 'n' roll exploded nationally. Sam Phillips got his timing right.

As RCA's better-equipped producers struggled to get Elvis sounding as good as he had on his final Sun record, the haunting "Mystery Train" – even offering Phillips a fee to produce him – "Blue Suede Shoes" hit the big cities like a freight train. A million copies sold that year. With Presley covering his own version on the B-side to "Heartbreak Hotel," Phillips was even collecting publishing points on both records through his Hi-Lo publishing company.

Touring, crowd violence, car crashes, nonstop amphetamines, painting hotel rooms black – Sun's rock 'n' roll explosion was as dazzling and fleeting as a shooting star. Fuelled by Phillips's fascination with the diabolic Jerry Lee Lewis, the defections began. First, the estranged Marion Keisker resigned. Then tensions erupted with Carl Perkins over the $26,000 he received for "Blue Suede Shoes." Told by seasoned vets that a gold disc should have earned him about $100,000, Perkins waded through his royalty statements and noticed, among other abnormalities, that his "gift" of a Cadillac was a deduction. When it came to sharing the spoils, as Rufus Thomas later quipped, Sam Phillips was "tighter than the bolts on the Brooklyn Bridge." In the end, both Perkins and Cash, feeling short-changed and burned-out, jumped ship to Columbia's country music label in Nashville.

Although Sam Phillips would never again have a magical run of hits the way he did between 1954 and 1957, his record company generated about $2 million, allowing him to invest in the hugely successful Holiday Inn hotel chain and set up WHER, the first all-female radio station.

As a cultural event, not since the wartime outbreaks of Dixieland jazz and Frank Sinatra had there been such hysteria. Unlike jazz, however, which emphasised virtuosity, three-chord rock 'n' roll popularised the idea that *anybody* can be a star. Sam Phillips found boys from down the road and let their inner lunatics loose on record, confident in the knowledge that the youth of America were craving raw characters they could identify with.

Sam Phillips also proved to wannabe producers that small, unfunded independents in small towns could conquer the world and create millions. All these themes, echoing the David and Goliath parable, form the very essence of rock 'n' roll – both as art form and entrepreneurial model. For decades since, generations of nobodies driven by a religious sense of entitlement have ventured out and heroically banged their heads against the edifice – the lucky ones releasing a dammed-up river of dollar bills and pretty girls.

10. LUCKY CHILDREN

EVERYONE WANTED AN ELVIS. IN ENGLAND, DECCA AMASSED AN ENTIRE ROSTER
of copycats complete with shaking legs and fake Memphis accents: Tommy
Steele, Billy Fury, Eden Kane. French Elvises with anglicised pseudonyms
like Johnny Hallyday, Eddy Mitchell and Dick Rivers invented foreign-
language versions. Elvis impersonation was becoming such a global industry, Colonel Tom Parker should have patented the formula.

Thanks to this wave, RCA's 7-inch format came into its own and by
1960 accounted for 20 percent of overall industry turnover. Economically,
the 7-inch single was ideal for independents; costing relatively little to
make, a smash hit was the musical equivalent of a winning lottery ticket.

In this three-chord gold rush, there was one conspicuous absentee:
Columbia. Throughout the late forties and fifties, Columbia had grown
into a highbrow label whose impressive catalogue was based largely
around the company's great technological discovery, the LP – which, it
should be noted, was by no means welcomed by everyone at the time.
After fifty years of four-minute sides, the LP represented a niche format
that, beyond classical music and cast recordings, had not yet explored
its full potential. One famous jazz fanatic, the poet Philip Larkin,
wrote that he was "suspicious" of the LP at first; "it seemed a package
deal, forcing you to buy bad tracks along with good at an unwontedly
high price."

With formats following generational chasms, the record industry was splitting into different markets. Singles were flutters and could sell by the millions in short spurts, whereas costly long-playing albums, although selling smaller quantities, yielded the highest profit margins and typically stayed on shelves longer. Formats aside, Columbia's unwillingness to blindly jump on the Elvis bandwagon was ultimately an issue of corporate culture. Its editorial line throughout the late fifties was marked by a number of influential characters, especially Ted Wallerstein's chosen heir, Goddard Lieberson.

Having started out as an assistant, thanks to his warmth and rapier wit, Lieberson had become everyone's favourite – janitors and artists included. An English-schooled, classically trained composer with the gift of perfect pitch, he wrote poetry and spoke four languages. Jewish, dapper, handsome and light-hearted, he had won the hand of the stunning German ballerina Vera Zorina. In the forties and fifties, anyone who was anyone in New York either knew or wanted to know him. For a start, once you'd heard it, you couldn't forget such a bizarre name. Groucho Marx once telephoned a musician friend and asked, "Would you like to dine out with a man named Goddard Lieberson?" The friend accepted enthusiastically, to which Marx quipped, "Okay, I'll find one."

In New York's community of musicians, film stars and producers, Lieberson was a living legend for his telegrams and memos, which he signed "*God.*" They read something like this. "Sunday, at Andre Kostelanetz and Lily Pons home, I met – I don't know if you can stand it, so prepare yourself – I met – GRETA GARBO! You will want to know that her feet are not big, that she has very charming speech, is curiously (for a movie star) intelligent, and she has the chest of a small boy, which I know because she went swimming only in her man's type linen shorts … I went swimming too, but in the most embarrassing bathing suit of this century, a little number which Andre brought back from Hawaii – very Pago-Pago and very large for me, with the result that everybody looked at me as though I were a dirty French postcard – which I was."

The ageing Ted Wallerstein, recognising Goddard Lieberson as a natural-born star magnet, respectfully passed over the reins in June 1956. Beginning a golden age in Columbia's long history, as president Lieberson chose to retain his A&R functions in the classical and original cast recordings department. Lieberson had been the one who convinced the parent company, CBS Inc., to finance the entire production of *My Fair Lady*. Opening in March 1956, the show netted $66 million at the box office, while the original cast recording sold 6 million copies. The sale of film rights raised a further $5 million. "Musicians make the best businessmen," quipped Lieberson to *Time* magazine in 1959. "I'd much rather be represented in a business deal by Stravinsky than any lawyer you could name."

Columbia was also a leader in jazz, thanks to in-house producer George Avakian, who arranged and supervised a string of classics: Dave Brubeck's "Take Five," three stunning Miles Davis albums and Louis Armstrong's brilliant tribute to W. C. Handy. The ultimate in prestige, Columbia attracted most of the old legends like Edith Piaf, Duke Ellington and Billie Holiday. Lieberson frequently reminded his producers never to yield to the pressure of sales departments, whose contributions to staff meetings generally cited the latest hits on other labels. He firmly believed it was smarter to make unique records and hope for the best.

He also believed that Columbia had certain responsibilities as cultural guardian. When he bumped into Alan Lomax in a New York diner, Lieberson commissioned a seminal sixteen-volume series called *Columbia World Library of Folk and Primitive Music*. With liner notes written by Lomax, the logistically complicated project showcased traditional music from around the British Isles, continental Europe, Venezuela, India, Japan, Indonesia, New Guinea, Australia, French Africa and British East Africa, as well as music of the Sioux and Navajo Indians. Although it wasn't a commercially successful operation in itself, when George Avakian played the Spanish recordings to Miles Davis, two traditional airs inspired *Sketches of Spain*.

Flying high above the clouds, it was no wonder that Columbia was not too concerned about Elvis and rock 'n' roll. One exception was Mitch Miller, Columbia's pop A&R man, who produced the likes of Frank Sinatra, Tony Bennett and Johnny Mathis. At the first-ever disc jockey convention – in Kansas City in March 1958 – Miller gave a vitriolic speech, asserting that "Much of the juvenile stuff pumped over the air waves these days hardly qualifies as music!" Although this speech was warmly applauded, Lieberson wasn't so categorical. He was receiving calls from his superiors at CBS Inc. to invest in youth sectors and began noticing the ebbing numbers on Broadway. A generational shift was in motion. These bubblegum-chewing youngsters were tomorrow's adults. A company as old and as large as Columbia could not ignore them indefinitely.

In a remarkable twist of fate, it would be Columbia's long-lost producer John Hammond who would find the ideal candidate to rejuvenate Columbia while retaining its elitist aura. Having been persona non grata at Columbia for over a decade, Hammond was formally pardoned by Goddard Lieberson in 1959 and offered a modest salary of $10,000 per year. "God" announced to the staff in nuanced language, "John Hammond is one of the deans of America's recording industry and we are happy to welcome him back to Columbia, where he made his first discs twenty-seven years ago."

Hammond was about to turn fifty and the lines in his face revealed the private wilderness he'd traversed – divorce, psychotherapy, his father's death. His sons had been all but disowned by his mother, who gave away his father's prize farm to a dubious charity before passing away herself. Neither he nor his four sisters could afford the upkeep of his parents' estate. The privileged world of his childhood had all but evaporated. It was as a divorced loner battling through middle age and paying monthly alimony that Hammond found his soul mate, Esme Sarnoff, the ex-wife of Robert Sarnoff, son of the fearsome RCA mogul. The two ageing divorcés began a new life, spending weeks in Manhattan, weekends in Westport.

Still trawling through the papers, snooping around clubs and producing records for independents, Hammond hadn't wandered far from the cutting edge. In fact, his time at the bottom brought him to a new underground. In November 1953, he had published a hard-hitting article in *The New York Times* blaming modern production methods for compressing the sound on jazz records, thus killing the genre commercially. His purism caught the attention of Vanguard Records, which invited Hammond to conduct some jazz experiments.

Vanguard was run by a pair of perfectionist brothers, Maynard and Seymour Solomon, who were determined to offer the discerning buyer better-sounding records than the majors. Its discs, mostly LPs, were recorded in a spacious Masonic temple in Brooklyn that had the best acoustics in New York, and the Solomon brothers were meticulous in their mastering and duplication techniques. On the heels of some thirty-five cult jazz records produced by Hammond, in 1957, Vanguard began branching into folk music, first recording the Weavers. Maynard Solomon explained, "We had to find different niches, one of which was folk. Any small company had to have its wits about it in order to survive against the majors. We had to see the cracks where you could make a contribution that the majors didn't see."

Thanks mainly to the period's rapidly growing student population, engaged songwriters provided a welcome reaction to the rising tide of juvenile pop. The folk scene was centred around Hammond's old stomping ground in the Village. From the Sunday gatherings on Washington Square, various folk haunts had sprung up that hosted open-mic nights called *hootenannies* – the Actors' Playhouse, Cherry Lane, Gerde's Folk City, the Village Gate, the Village Vanguard. By the late fifties, Greenwich Village was teeming with folkies feeding off spare change from passing tourists.

One of several homespun folk labels in the Village was Elektra, operating out of a tiny store called the Record Loft. Its owner, Jac Holzman, was another sound and musicology buff producing high-fidelity albums of mainly traditional music. Growing throughout the fifties, Elektra amassed an impressive catalogue including flamenco master Sabicas and Israeli folk singer Theo Bikel. Another young folk label in the Village was Tradition Records, financed by Guggenheim heiress Diane Hamilton (her pseudonym) and run by three Irish folk musicians, the Clancy Brothers.

In the late fifties, the historical links between the jazz and folk scenes were still strong. Five years after George Wein and Elaine Lorillard began the Newport Jazz Festival in 1954, folk figures including Pete Seeger and Theo Bikel joined with Wein to create the Newport Folk Festival. Both festivals attracted the same kinds of academics. Jac Holzman explained, "People who were intellectually alert loved the idea of reconnecting to roots. Then there was the political aspect … The Almanac Singers, Pete

Seeger and Woody Guthrie were generally liberal, or left-leaning. People who bought folk music were middle-class – schoolteachers, bohemians, professionals – who, in what were still quite austere times, could afford to have interests outside of themselves."

When Hammond returned to Columbia in 1959, he was coming in from this academic corner of the music world – effectively an old man who'd stayed close to where he planted seeds in the late thirties. Except for "the superlative Miles Davis," Hammond didn't like the druggy intro- version of bebop. On the other hand, the innocence of folk embodied many of the ideals he'd written about for years, including civil rights, social justice, multiculturalism and the transmission of old repertoire.

At Lieberson's behest, Hammond's principal task at Columbia was to supervise the reissue of old Columbia and Okeh repertoire in album format. He was also given tacit permission to prospect for young talent. "Goddard knew me well, my weaknesses as well as my strengths. He did not think me much of a business man. He knew that my standards for judging talent were, and are, based primarily on on artistic rather than commercial poten- tial, although in many cases the two go together."

He made his first big find for Columbia one day when a black composer, Curtis Lewis, presented a demo of his latest compositions. Although Hammond was supposed to listen to the songs themselves, he was distracted by one of the voices singing "Today I Sing the Blues." Struck by something eerily familiar, he asked, "Who is she?" Lewis gave the details: Aretha Franklin, eighteen years old, from Detroit, daughter of a famous Baptist minister. "An unknown?" Hammond thought. Shortly after the meeting, he got a phone call from the owner of a small recording studio on Broadway. "I know you're interested in Aretha Franklin," said the voice. "If you want to meet her she'll be in my studio today." Hammond picked up his coat and headed over.

Watching her sing, Hammond heard the makings of a star potentially as important as Billie Holiday. Because RCA Victor was also interested, Hammond arranged a contract with a favourable royalty rate and an advance. In January 1961, while producing Aretha's debut album as gospel-jazz crossover, Hammond wrote her manager a diplomatically worded message. "There hasn't been a singer and performer like this in

20 years," he said. "The talent is all there, but of course it still needs very close supervision."

Despite encouraging sales and reviews, Hammond was frustrated by what he viewed as Aretha's immaturity. Distracted by her personal struggles as a single mother, she was proving unreliable, claiming throat problems and even failing to turn up for shows at the Apollo and Village Gate. By early 1962, Hammond was openly fed up. "Here is your royalty statement …," he wrote to her. "If you don't straighten up soon you will be a legend in the business and not one of the nice ones."

While on vacation in Europe, Hammond was replaced as Aretha's producer. Not only was the artist sick of *him*, Columbia's younger producers felt she wasn't being produced right. It was argued, in Hammond's absence, that the old man could find talent but didn't know how to cook up hits. As one colleague, Robert Altshuler, explained the consensus inside Columbia, "Although he had these incredible ears and the ability to recognise talent at its earliest stage, at its embryonic stage, he was not very good at producing." Columbia's young guns, however, made the fatal mistake of adding new orchestrations to old recordings without the artist's permission, thus giving Aretha's manager grounds to sue and obtain a costly out-of-court settlement. By then, Hammond was happy to see her jump ship to Atlantic, where Jerry Wexler guided her to superstardom. Although Wexler was an "agnostic Jew" himself, his winning formula couldn't have been simpler – "I put her in a church!"

Hammond's second key signing in 1961 was Pete Seeger, by no means a discovery, but a signal of Columbia's commitment to becoming the leader in folk music. In September, Hammond tried to sign a striking young folk diva called Joan Baez whom he noticed at the Newport Folk Festival. She came to Hammond's office accompanied by her tough-talking manager, Albert Grossman. The meeting fizzled out uncomfortably, and Baez signed with Vanguard. Feeling sore, Hammond instead signed up Carolyn Hester, another folk princess but perhaps lacking Baez's presence.

Coincidence or design? It was at this crossroads that a twenty-year-old by the name of Bob Dylan wangled his way into opening for Carolyn Hester at a Club 47 gig. The next day, Dylan met with Hester and explained his difficult financial situation, practically begging to get more gigs as her warm-up. Unfortunately, she wasn't planning on performing while preparing for her record, but because Dylan looked so dejected, she asked him to tag along in her studio troupe as harmonica player. Dylan pounced on the opportunity. "I'll be there, and here's my number," he said.

To get a taste of the songs she intended to record, Hammond and Hester arranged a preproduction session at her apartment. Hester had rounded up a small band with stand-up bass, guitar and the baby-faced Bob Dylan on harmonica. They all sat around a table picnic-style and the musicians went through several swinging numbers for Hammond's perusal. Dylan, seated next to Hammond, played his guitar on a few numbers and even sang some harmonies. Even though Hammond saw that Dylan wasn't much of a musician, he nonetheless sat there thinking, "What a wonderful character, playing guitar and blowing mouth harp, he's gotta be an original." As Hammond was leaving, he asked Dylan, "Have you recorded for anybody?" Dylan simply shook his head.

When the studio date rolled around, Hammond was lost in his daily ritual of trawling through the newspapers when, lo and behold, he stumbled on a concert preview in *The New York Times*. Profiling Dylan for a show at Gerde's Folk City, the piece concluded, "Mr Dylan is vague about his antecedents and birthplace, but it matters less where he has been than where he is going, and that would appear straight up."

Looking up, Hammond thought, "I gotta talk contracts right away!" As soon as Hester arrived with Dylan in tow, Hammond whisked the young man up to his office, where Dylan played "Talking New York Blues." When Hammond produced a contract, Dylan read its first two words, "Columbia Records," and asked, "Where do I sign?" Although inexperienced, Dylan knew who Hammond was. "There were a thousand kings in the world, and he was one of them."

In a moment of hesitation, Hammond asked Dylan his age.

"Twenty."

"That means you have to have your mother and father sign the contract, too. The New York state laws don't allow a minor to sign a legal agreement without his parents' approval."

"I don't have a mother or father."

Well, then, did he have any relative who could sign for him Hammond wondered.

"I've got an uncle who's a dealer in Las Vegas."

"You're trying to tell me that you don't want anyone to sign for you, do you?"

"John, you can trust me."

The deal was duly sealed in ink despite the lingering question marks. The *New York Times* journalist had observantly noted Dylan's reticence to reveal his background. Little did Hammond know that the young man was concealing his middle-class background and his real name, Robert Zimmerman, from his girlfriend. It was Hammond's turn to get a taste of this "most complex human being." Over the next fifteen years, Hammond would come to believe that Dylan lived "in a fantasy world which he is powerful enough to impose on the real one the rest of us inhabit. He has created his own persona and put it to the service of his art. The combination is irresistible."

As Dylan was leaving Columbia's offices, Hammond gave him a present of a blues reissue he was about to release. The young man walked home through the streets of New York with a contract in one hand and a Robert Johnson record in the other. When he got back to his third-floor walk-up, Dylan examined the record. Called *King of the Delta Blues Singers,* it was a remastered compilation of recordings from 1936. He put the needle on the record and out poured "Cross Road Blues." "From the first note, the vibrations from the loudspeaker made my hair stand up," Dylan remembered of that fateful day.

In a few hours in late November 1961, Dylan banged out his debut album – mainly traditional songs, only two original compositions. The *Village Voice* journalist Nat Hentoff remembered how Hammond "really wanted me to listen to [it]. He wanted me to listen to the lyrics. I saw something there, but it was only after John made me listen to the album that I started paying attention. The characteristics that John Hammond looked for in an artist were feeling and passion. He heard these things in Dylan. He heard something distinctive in Dylan – the message that came through the sound."

Hammond's younger superior, Dave Kapralik, would have happily shelved the album had anyone but Hammond been behind it. Even Dylan himself wasn't so sure. By the time the finished product was pressed, he wished he could rip it up and start over.

Only thirteen hundred copies were sold, earning Dylan the title of "Hammond's folly" inside Columbia. The unpleasant experience, however, seems to have intensified Dylan's creative ambitions. His love life was also in a precarious state. When his girlfriend, Suze Rotolo, found out he hadn't told her his real name, her mother packed her off to Italy to study art. Dylan suddenly found himself isolated in a crummy apartment, disliked by many other folk singers, and socialising only through his concert appearances and love letters to Italy. From this lonely place, songs began pouring out in abundance.

Apart from Hammond, Dylan had two other key allies on his side. Pete Seeger saluted him on radio that summer as "the most prolific songwriter on the scene." The other sympathetic helper inside Columbia was a young staffer in the publicity department, Billy James, who managed to get Dylan reviewed in a number of youth magazines. It was just enough support to get Dylan a second chance. When Hammond called his folly back to the studio, Dylan was eager to silence his many critics. Crucially, this time around, he would be given considerable time and space to put together a much stronger record.

Hearing Dylan's new compositions, Hammond was confident that his next release would make an impact – it *had* to. Dylan understood the challenge and was arriving at every session with giant-sized songs, most of them written through Woody Guthrie's "*talkin' blues*" technique – a trance-like process of strumming a guitar all day, looking inside and out, letting words fly out arbitrarily. In total, Dylan recorded over thirty songs in eight sessions spaced out over a year. Treated as a sort of research and development process, Dylan was growing into the artist he later became, as Hammond sat in the control room reading his newspapers. Even by Columbia's artist-driven standards, this was a generous second shot.

Then Albert Grossman entered the building as Dylan's manager. The bug-eyed folk impresario was the archetypal showbiz crook and everything Hammond hated. For his part, Grossman saw in Hammond a potential obstacle to controlling Dylan. Predictably, Columbia received a formal letter, supposedly written by Dylan, asserting that the artist's contract was null and void because he was a minor upon its signature. It demanded that all masters be returned to Dylan. In the middle of an arduous second album, it landed like a bombshell on Hammond's desk.

The original contract gave a royalty of 4 percent to Bob Dylan, and Hammond, of course, knew Grossman was after better terms, either with Columbia or at another label. When Columbia's in-house lawyer, Clive Davis, advised Hammond to settle the matter amicably without Grossman present, Dylan was called in. Hammond said straight out what he thought of Grossman's tactics.

Dylan was caught between two titans. Although he wanted to make records on Columbia for John Hammond, he needed Grossman to get regular gigs. In a second meeting with Hammond, Grossman, Dylan and Davis present, the manager made a conciliatory yet solid legal case pointing out that in New York state law, there is a statutory limitation of three years' duration on contracts signed by minors. Grossman was reminding Hammond and Davis that Columbia could lose Dylan in 1964.

A new five-year contract was duly written up with a higher royalty rate. Dylan signed it with relief as Grossman stood up having won something for his shenanigans. The problem, however, was that Hammond had to get the new deal countersigned by Columbia's senior management. "I have enormous faith in Bob Dylan and think he will be the most important young folk artist in the business," he wrote to his sceptical superiors. Fortunately, Hammond had Lieberson's support.

Grossman had succeeded in manipulating the situation to embarrass and alienate John Hammond, who was replaced by a young black producer, Tom Wilson. By the end of 1962, Dylan was churning out so much interesting material, all Wilson had to do was stand over the engineers and stay out of Grossman's way.

In May 1963, the year-long experiment titled *The Freewheelin' Bob Dylan* was released to critical acclaim. Featuring eleven original compositions, it was an unusually autobiographical album for the period. At the civil rights event on Capitol Hill on August 28, 1963, where Martin Luther King, Jr., gave his "I have a dream" speech, the twenty-two-year-old Dylan performed "Only a Pawn in Their Game," about the racially motivated shooting of Medgar Evers. If there was a crowning moment in Bob Dylan's early years, this was probably it.

Once again, the Vanderbilt rebel had pointed Columbia to a gold mine. A 1963 Pete Seeger live album containing the hymn "We Shall Overcome" sold hundreds of thousands of copies, and the song became the anthem of the civil rights movement. Goddard Lieberson, eager to ensure Columbia had a future with younger audiences, could learn about this vast generation courtesy of the students and brooding teenagers who appreciated folk music's engaging lyrics.

Once again, the oldest tree in the vinyl jungle was in bloom. Thanks to the towering reputation of this prolific war baby named Bob Dylan, younger Columbia producers, such as Tom Wilson, were introduced to a network of singer-songwriters whose autobiographical long-playing records would, in time, outsell and outshine all of the throwaway pop singles of the early sixties. As the old proverb goes, fortune favours the brave.

11. NUMBERS

SOMETHING WAS STIRRING IN THE MODERN WORLD – BUT WAS IT REALLY political awareness?

The elephant in the room was sitting on the floor watching television. Across the land, babies had boomed from an average of three per family in 1950 to over three and a half by 1960. Road-weary adults who'd grown up through the Great Depression and World War II were gratefully spending their unfamiliar prosperity on the 76 million American children born between 1945 and 1965.

Just as colour television was poised to replace black-and-white, kids were voting in unstoppable numbers for the end of segregation in pop music. In 1963, as a result of so many crossover hits making separate listings unworkable, *Billboard* suspended its R&B chart. Thus began a new era of multiethnic, televisual American pop. While several labels and producers contributed to the phenomenon, the most interesting was Tamla-Motown, the only black-owned R&B pioneer selling millions of records to white teenagers.

With big cars symbolising the era, it was perhaps fitting that Detroit provided the setting for this historical event. Behind this self-confident music was the story of a clan whose *can-do* philosophy was neither political nor religious. The Gordy family were devout followers of Booker T. Washington's philosophy of personal advancement through education and hard work. In his 1901 autobiography, *Up from Slavery,* Washington argued, "Nothing ever comes to me, that is worth having, except as a result of hard work." A controversial thinker among NAACP adherents, he had advised cooperation with white society, predicting that confrontation over what later became known as "civil rights" could spell disaster for the vastly outnumbered black population of America.

The Gordy family covenant reached three generations deep to a time before the Civil War. The personal mission for Motown founder Berry Gordy was simply to do in the record industry what his father and grandfather had achieved in other businesses.

The amazing legacy traces back to a cotton plantation in Oconee County, Georgia, where the first Berry Gordy was born in 1854, the illegitimate son of slave owner Jim Gordy and his lover, Esther Johnson, a black slave. As was common in that time and place, the mulatto boy was given better chances than a black child would have been; he was even taught to read and write. Working his way out of servitude, Berry Gordy grew cotton, corn, potatoes, peanuts, okra, cabbage, collard greens, sugar cane and fruits. While most of his illiterate tenant-farmer neighbours spent their entire lives in debt – and even relied on white crop buyers to keep their paperwork, Berry Gordy was such an assiduous bookkeeper, he filed every receipt, loan statement, invoice and deed – enabling him to purchase a 168-acre farm in the 1890s.

He married a half-black, half-Indian woman, Lucy Hellum. Of their nine children, Berry II, born in 1888, was a solitary soul who preferred to hang around the kitchen listening to conversations about crop prices. From the age of ten, he began accompanying his father into town; his job was to calculate the value per pound of the family's cotton. Berry senior bought his chosen heir a law book and regularly quizzed the boy on its contents.

The hardworking family's well-run business was generating sufficient profits to buy another 100-acre tract of land with a big house, a general store and a well-stocked barn. Becoming a local entrepreneur, Gordy senior even set up a blacksmith shop in town, earning himself jealousy and admiration as a "big dog." One spring day in 1913, the sky turned black over the farm. Sprinting back to the house as an electrical storm hit, the fifty-nine-year-old was struck down by a bolt of lightning. His funeral was attended by both blacks and whites from the area.

Barely twenty-four and lacking the sharp eye his father possessed, Berry II took over the family business. The tradition in the South was for a bereaved black family to appoint a white administrator to handle succession, but wisely, the Gordy family appointed themselves. Within days, Berry II was being hounded by salesmen of all descriptions trying to get him to sign on to various purchase schemes with monthly repayments. He consulted his law book and learned that if he failed to honour monthly payments, debtors could seize assets, in particular the farm. Vultures were hovering over the family estate. Understanding his father's obsession with detail, Berry II realised that just one rogue clause in a contract could lose you everything. Thanks to their impeccable records, in the months after his father's death, he and his mother even won a court case against a white businessman. Gradually, the dubious salesmen stopped dropping by.

Berry II took another leaf from his father's book by marrying an educated girl – a schoolteacher, Bertha Ida Fuller. Their romance was interrupted by America's entry into the First World War when Berry II was conscripted and sent to a training camp in Newport, Virginia. He was so worried his family would be dispossessed of their farm, he faked walking as if he had palsy, went to sick call all the time, and pretended he could neither read nor write. His muscular spasms were so convincing, he was discharged within three months. Once he got home to the farm, he was relieved to find that all the surrounding farmers had held firm to the agreed plan to maintain a high cotton price. With wartime demands so high, the bumper harvest of 1917 enabled the Gordys to pay off their mortgage.

In 1922, the Gordy family made a deal so big it jolted the family destiny right out of Georgia. When they sold a load of timber stumps for $2,600, suddenly, out of nowhere, white businessmen began coming around with investments and other proposals. Afraid even to deposit it in the local bank, Berry II hid the cheque, but the fear of being burgled, or even lynched, proved too great for the entire family. At church one Sunday, they convinced Berry to cash the cheque in Detroit, where his brother John had already moved.

So Berry II, the grandfather of Motown, was driven directly from the church to the station and boarded a train. Seated in the black compartment, he gazed out the window, realising that a chapter was being turned. Past Memphis, around Lake Erie, and northward to Michigan – this route had been taken by so many black families before him, millions fleeing poverty and racism in the South. The Gordys were leaving Georgia because they had become too wealthy for their own safety.

When the train arrived in Detroit and Berry II glimpsed its giant factories and black faces everywhere, it was love at first sight. Nevertheless, adjusting to city living proved difficult. The big dog became a hapless lamb; he was ripped off on a property investment, then struggled to find a job. Realising he needed a useful new trade, he agreed to work as a plasterer's apprentice for a meagre $2 a day. Gradually "Pops," as he now liked to be called, began to replicate his father's methodical progress in Georgia. In honour of the family's intellectual guide, he opened the Booker T. Washington Grocery Store. During the Depression, he also set up a plastering and carpentry business and eventually a printing shop. Even in hard times, Berry II was able to accumulate wealth and provide jobs for his many children – one of whom was Berry III, born in 1929.

Pops was almost religious about teaching the merits of hard work and family values. Listening to his stories around the kitchen table about Georgia and the Depression, the third generation of Gordys grew up with a deep sense of history and a belief in entrepreneurship. Leading by example, when the teenagers no longer needed full-time mothering, Bertha Gordy enrolled in various universities, studying retail management and commerce until in 1945 she cofounded an insurance company and became actively involved in the Democratic Party.

Compared to his brothers and sisters, Berry III at first struggled to find his path – boxing professionally, joining the army, then getting married too young. Musically inclined, he began hanging out at Detroit's many jazz clubs and in 1953 set up his own record shop, 3-D Record Mart, dedicated entirely to bebop. It was too much of a niche business for Detroit and it had to be closed within two years. Berry Gordy III found himself with no job, no money, and a wife and baby to support.

He took a job in a Ford factory for $86 a week fastening chrome strips and nailing upholstery to Lincoln-Mercurys. The backbreaking tedium troubled his marriage almost immediately. Although Ford was once considered the best employer in the land for African Americans, by the 1950s jokes circulated that if you saw a black man asleep on the bus in the evening, he was a Ford worker. There was even a genre of jokes about the sexual infidelities of Ford workers' wives. In Gordy's case, his wife, Thelma, filed for divorce in 1956 claiming he stayed out late, refused to speak for evenings on end when he was home, and had once struck her in the face.

Hitting rock bottom, the boxer found salvation in music. He hummed melodies on the factory line and began going out to a happening club, the Flame Show Bar, where his sisters Anna and Gwen had just landed the photo and cigarette concession. "He's a songwriter," they'd tell the local big shots. Night after night, the beaten-down factory worker lugged around his homemade tapes, in search of that elusive life changer.

After more than a year getting nowhere, but at least getting better at songwriting, a door opened. In 1957, he heard through the grapevine that a talent scout who frequented the club, Al Greene, was looking for material for R&B singer Jackie Wilson. When Gordy realised he had boxed against Wilson in the forties and told him so, he won the artist's immediate trust. Gordy duly provided Wilson with a hit, "Reet Petite," No. 11 on the R&B charts. Then, through Wilson's manager, one summer's day in 1958, Gordy met a group led by the seventeen-year-old Smokey Robinson.

They met in a café, and Berry went through Smokey's poetry notebook. Although the writing lacked structure, Berry saw the makings of a poet. More importantly, the human chemistry clicked. Smokey's mother had died when he was ten years old, and because his father was a truck driver, he had been largely raised by his older sister, who had ten children of her own. When Smokey was first invited to the Gordy home, he was adopted as a member of the extended family. A father-son relationship formed that endured for decades.

Through their showbusiness connections, Berry's sisters, Anna and Gwen, had just set up a record label, Anna Records, complete with a distribution deal with Leonard and Phil Chess in Chicago. Not only were they careful to retain full ownership of their masters, their first hit, "Money (That's What I Want)," was penned by Berry. Crippled by financial problems and encouraged by Smokey Robinson, Berry Gordy III arrived at the daunting conclusion that he had no choice but to set up his own label.

He got considerable help from Pops, Anna, Gwen and his eldest sister Esther, who now had Anna Records to learn from. The family's brainstorming was helped by an independent producer called Harvey Fuqua whom Gwen was dating and would marry in 1961. Fuqua had extensive experience in music production, having sung in the Moonglows and worked for Chess Records as a talent scout and recording supervisor. Now back in Detroit, he was making extra cash as a radio plugger for Anna Records while continuing his own projects as an independent producer. Like many other people who orbited the family, Fuqua was fascinated by the Gordy clan, in particular how Esther was grooming her husband, George Edwards, to be a state legislator. In equal measure, Berry Gordy, whenever he spent time at his sister's house, admired Fuqua's discipline as a talent coach. In Esther's basement, he would force his artists to rehearse to the point of exhaustion.

Ultimately it was Fuqua's labours as a lone record man that inspired Tamla-Motown's complex business plan. Fuqua's problem was always cash flow. Too small and too black to borrow money from banks, he was stuck between record pressers, who insisted on being paid up front, and distributors, who operated on ninety-day consignment as standard, though it was generally longer by the time they actually paid. As a result, one of Fuqua's 400,000-copy hits had almost put him in the hospital. Pops, Esther and Gwen understood that the only solution was to set up various interrelated companies – records, publishing and management. They also felt that Berry's label would probably be better off with a white-skinned insider to schmooze these all-powerful distributors.

Set up with family capital, Berry Gordy found a house at 2648 West Grand Boulevard. The plan was to use upstairs as a residence, the basement for offices, and the back garden for a studio. The studio was called Hitsville U.S.A.; the record company was Motown Record Corp., owner of the Motown and Tamla trademarks. Jobete Music Publishing would handle author/composition royalties, while a separate company, International Talent Management Inc. (ITMI), would cover a range of artist management and booking functions. Needless to say, the lucky artists would have to sign with all these companies.

Not surprisingly, Motown became a family affair. The hard-headed Esther took on the group's business administration, while brothers George and Fuller and sister Loucye joined the administrative staff. Loucye's husband, Ron Wakefield, a saxophonist, joined as staff arranger. Another brother, Robert, became a sound engineer. Harvey Fuqua handled radio plugging and recruited an old friend, Marvin Gaye, who in due course married Anna Gordy and became the in-house drummer.

Their industry insider was Barney Ales, a sales representative formerly at Capitol and Warner whose job involved chasing down cheques from distributors. Although he was the only white face in the office, Barney Ales fitted right in. Like Berry Gordy, he was a high-powered street fighter who loved playing the game. When he wasn't selling theatrically over the telephone, office hours were spent with Gordy battling it out over table tennis. Enjoying a salary of $125 per week with a company Cadillac and the title of vice president, Ales never had it so good.

Commercially, Tamla-Motown was quick to take off. In early 1961, a Smokey-Berry composition, "Shop Around," went to No. 1 on the R&B charts and No. 2 on the pop charts. Their first No. 1 pop hit was "Please Mr Postman" by the Marvelettes, a catchy ditty that skipped happily along to Marvin Gaye's doo-wop drumbeat. A string of Marvelettes hits rolled off the production lines, in large part thanks to a prolific songwriting trio, Brian and Eddie Holland with Lamont Dozier – otherwise known as *H-D-H*.

With little else happening in Detroit, Hitsville held weekly auditions to screen the steady flow of local singers. Dropping in every day after school with an annoying persistence, "the girls," as they became known, included a sixteen-year-old Diane Ross, accompanied by her friends Florence Ballard, Barbara Martin and Mary Wilson. Another visitor was an eleven-year-old blind prodigy, Steveland Morris – signed up and renamed Little Stevie Wonder. As the stakes grew, Gordy ran competitions; to pick songs for the studio, a panel of A&R judges would be augmented by kids invited in from outside. In many instances, Gordy's own songs were outvoted by the creations of his employees. A religious believer in meritocracy, he would always accept defeat with a fatherly smile.

When the weather was good, Berry Gordy would organise picnics for office staff and musicians on Belle Isle, an island park in the Detroit River, where they'd have sack races and games of football. Such was the sportive competition that A&R man Clarence Paul once broke an arm, and Marvin Gaye fractured a foot. On weekends, Berry would arrange get-togethers where they'd drink, eat barbecue, listen to records, and play marathon sessions of poker. Marvin Gaye remembers that Gordy would pick out two raindrops on a windowpane and bet against a bemused employee which drop would trickle to the bottom of the windowpane first – an early warning sign that Gordy's playful side hid an addiction to gambling.

Launching their dormant ITC management company, Esther Gordy came up with a novel idea, *The Motortown Revue,* a rolling tour throughout the winter of 1962 showcasing all of Motown's acts. She spent hours on the phone wearing down a dubious black promoter until he agreed to organising nineteen dates over twenty-three days. With Motown's sales manager, Barney Ales, appointed tour manager, forty-five people were squeezed into one bus and five cars. The older, more experienced session musicians, generally in their twenties and thirties, carried the shows, but Ales, wincing in the wings, saw that Motown's young singers simply couldn't command a live audience.

Although it was a baptism by fire, which saw Ales hospitalised after a serious car crash, the revue was a turning point for the label. Realising that thousands of cash dollars could be generated from live shows, Barney Ales and Esther Gordy returned to Detroit with a plan. Thus began Motown's ambitious artist development programme, complete with trainers, stylists and motivation coaches. In particular, Gordy's favourite, Diane Ross, was enrolled at an expensive finishing school; glamorously dolled up in sequins and mascara, the giggling schoolgirl strode out a dark princess, renamed *Diana.*

As money poured in, the Gordys even took control of personal finances. "We try to help artists personally with their investment programs so they don't wind up broke," Berry Gordy explained to a journalist in 1963. "We are very much concerned with the artist's welfare." Employing some sixty-odd staffers in 1963, Motown was a booming business. Supervised by the prickly Esther Gordy, in-house lawyers were adding provisions for every imaginable circumstance. The contracts grew to over one hundred pages in length, among the most complex in the entire record business.

In 1963 – the defining moment when this new variety of R&B-flavoured teen-pop reached its peak – Motown's primary competitor was a twenty-three-year-old named Phil Spector, who, despite his Napoleonic height, packed the biggest sonic punch. Such was the young man's disdain for the market he wished to conquer, he barely regarded his singers and musicians as artistes. Modelling himself on classical composers, *he* was the genius. Clad in velvet suits, he conducted his puppet orchestra with a silver cane. In a vast marketplace where it was nearly impossible to keep track of all the one-hit wonders, his mad-scientist aura ensured the "produced by Phil Spector" stamp got his records delivered straight to the deejay's turntable.

Few noticed at the time that behind Phil Spector's arrogance lay a haunted soul. When he was eight, his severely depressed father, crippled by financial worries, ran a hose from his exhaust pipe into the car and slowly asphyxiated himself on a Brooklyn street in broad daylight. Bullied, small, overweight, suffering severe asthma, Phil grew up troubled by his mother's maiden name, Spector. Feeling a dark secret hanging over his house, he realised his parents might have been cousins.

Success came early for the "*Tycoon of Teen.*" Aged seventeen, he woke up from a nightmare of seeing the epitaph on his father's gravestone, "To know him is to love him." Picking up his guitar, he weaved the words into an interesting chord sequence. The ensuing 1958 single, performed by the Teddy Bears, snowballed into a No. 1, selling a total of 1.4 million copies. Too nervous to perform live, within a year Spector became a record producer. He eventually relocated to New York, where he came into contact with R&B through the hit-writing duo of Jerry Leiber and Mike Stoller. With the financial assistance of Los Angeles producer Lester Sill, Spector then formed Philles Records.

Having produced on both coasts, Spector felt that the brightest sound in America was inside Gold Star, a Los Angeles studio whose recording equipment and acoustics had been custom-designed by its talented co-owner David Gold. The pure tone of the echo chambers was due to their trapezoid-shaped rooms, about twenty feet long, built in a specially formulated cement plaster. Incoming sounds entered through a two-foot-square trapdoor and were miked back into the control room. Another of David Gold's handy innovations was a small radio transmitter, enabling producers to hear their mixes on any car radio parked outside.

The term *wall of sound* had first been used by American journalists at the turn of the century to describe the sonic totalitarianism of Wagner – Spector's greatest musical influence as a boy. Spector packed the studio full of musicians – as many as five guitarists, two bass players, two drummers, three pianists and various strings. He was obsessed with percussive feel, often squeezing up to ten percussionists into the crowded room to play shakers, chimes, castanets, bells, tambourines, maracas, any kind of high-frequency sparkle. Before rolling any tape, he would usually spend hours moving between the control room and studio suggesting subtle changes. As the musicians got tired and began trundling along in unison like migrating caribou, Gold Star's echo chambers created a sonic picture as widescreen as classical music.

In awe of Spector's massive-sounding hits with the Ronettes, Motown retaliated in the summer of 1963 with Martha & the Vandellas, whose lead singer, Martha Reeves, was a Motown secretary. By January 1964, the Supremes finally got their first pop chart appearance.

Culturally, it's hard to say for sure when *the sixties* really began. Television imagery, flashing between JFK's assassination, Martin Luther King's "I have a dream," and the Ronettes singing "Be My Baby," always suggests that somewhere around that *pop-crossover* year of 1963, a sea change was under way. As Bob Dylan saw it, "the early sixties, up to maybe '64–'65, was really the fifties, the late fifties. They were still the fifties – still the same culture."

What's for sure, this wasn't really about Vietnam or miniskirts. America had seen it all before – Korea, flappers, you name it. What was different in the sixties was the underlying baby boom. Never before did pop music fit so neatly into age strata. Viewed from a demographic angle, it's easy to see why early-sixties pop was so juvenile and why it matured so rapidly throughout the decade. That sacred cow of the postwar memory, *the sixties,* was in fact the diary of a lucky generation – growing up and taking over.

12. THE INVASION

AFTER TWO WORLD WARS THAT NEVER REACHED ITS SHORES, AMERICA WOKE up on February 7, 1964, to the sound of screaming. Just four months after JFK's assassination, the door of Pan Am flight 101 opened – then *Beatlemania* swept across the land like the outburst of a deadly virus.

Wearing helmets made of hair, the four invaders were quickly reinforced by the Dave Clark Five, Manfred Mann, Herman's Hermits, the Animals, the Rolling Stones, the Kinks, Them, and the Who. In several successive waves, British bands came, conquered and changed American tastes forever.

Phil Spector, ever the client prospector, accompanied the Beatles on their historical flight across the Atlantic. Who knows what he was hoping for? The beat boom abruptly ended his brief reign over the teen kingdom; the Beatles made the Ronettes as cold as an old toy on Christmas morning. From here on in, only Motown would be strong enough to hold back these lovable pranksters from Liverpool, who at one point in April 1964 held all of the Top 5 positions on America's *Billboard Hot 100*.

Although a surprise attack for American record companies, the British Invasion woke up the market from a period of relative cooling. Industry sales figures had risen sharply from $213 million in 1954 to $603 in 1959, thanks to the combined success of LPs and rock 'n' roll. That spurt had levelled off to below $700 million in 1963, suggesting that early sixties teen-pop hadn't been able to maintain the same public excitement as Elvis. Now, as tens of millions of American teenagers entered their most turbulent years, *Beatlemania* spun the record business faster than ever before.

To this day, the Beatles remain holders of arguably the greatest achievement in pop music: twenty-seven No. 1 singles in America. Behind this extraordinary phenomenon was an unusual kind of record man, more than a studio producer – George Martin. Having joined Parlophone in 1950 and signed the Beatles in 1962, he's the key eyewitness of the British record industry's mutation from insular classical to global pop. Needless to say, most of George Martin's studio exploits have become museum exhibits, especially in Britain, where he is a national hero. For some reason, though, even the British have largely ignored his personal story – a humbling tale of self-becoming that makes the Beatles legend all the more providential.

For all his gentlemanly mannerisms, George Martin was born, in 1926, on the wrong side of Britain's class divide. A family of four, the Martins lived in a two-room apartment in Drayton Park – no electricity, no bathroom, no kitchen, no water. His mother cooked on a stove on the landing and gave him baths in a tin tub. One toilet on the ground floor was shared by all three families in the building. Martin senior was a carpenter, a simple craftsman, who in the Great Depression was without any income for eighteen long months until he found a job selling newspapers in Cheapside. In later years, George Martin vividly recalled the sight of his forlorn father standing in the rain at his newsstand. The Martin family, to put it bluntly, barely fit the description of working class.

As a boy, however, George Martin understood he had a special gift. Although there were no musicians in his family and no instruments at home, he began playing on any piano he could find, teaching himself scales, chord progressions and diminished chords and their inversions. Born with perfect pitch, he could recognise notes and figure out Chopin pieces by ear.

His first quasi-religious awakening occurred at a school concert at which the BBC Symphony Orchestra performed Debussy's *L'après-midi d'un faune*. Its abstract textures lifted George Martin's young imagination into the heavens. For the rest of his life, the French piece brought him back to that old school hall where he was first kissed on the head by the gods of music.

Chasing his muse through his teenaged years, he formed his own dance band, the Four Tune Tellers, and reinvested his earnings into classical piano lessons. However, with the outbreak of war and his school's move to the north of England, he was forced to work as an errand boy in the War Office. At the age of seventeen, in summer 1943, he broke his mother's heart by joining the naval air force. While training in the south of England, he had his first of several lucky encounters. At the end of a concert in Portsmouth given by a pianist called Eric Harrison, he waited for the crowd to disperse and, when nobody was left in the hall, began playing on the piano. Eventually he felt a presence in the room.

"What was that you were playing?" asked the musician.

"One of the things I've been writing myself," replied Martin with embarrassment.

"Oh, you compose, do you?"

"Well, I try to, though I haven't had much training."

"I think you should do something about it," the musician suggested while writing down the name of a contact at a state-funded music organisation called the Committee for the Promotion of New Music.

Throughout these formative years moving from base to base, Martin was teaching himself how to read and write music. Sailing across the Atlantic on a Dutch liner with three thousand German prisoners locked in the hold, he briefly saw the skyscrapers of Manhattan before being dispatched to Trinidad. In the suffocating heat, while being taught how to operate amphibious aircraft, he began writing a Debussy-like symphony. As part of his pilot training, he was taught social etiquette at banquets in the beautiful Painted Hall in Greenwich. During the two-week course, one eccentric officer constantly reminded the trainees that a true gentleman imposes strict hygiene and regularity on his bowel movements. Undisciplined eating habits were the slippery slope to slobbery.

Back in England as the Allies closed in on Berlin, Martin received a three-page letter analysing the composition he had mailed to the mysterious address. "You must write more of this," concluded its author, Sidney

Harrison, professor of piano at the Guildhall School of Music in London. "Keep sending it to me and we'll correspond." George Martin had found the man he later called his "fairy godfather."

The musical correspondence continued. "You really must try to take up music seriously," Harrison repeated.

"But look, I'm twenty-one, can I really take up music now?" wrote Martin.

"Of course you can," assured Harrison. "You can go and study for three years at a music college. I'll tell you what to do. You come along to the Guildhall and play your compositions to the principal, and if he likes them as much as I do, you're in."

Martin was unsure, but as the war ended, he woke up to a frightening realisation: he had no qualifications, no employable skills. So in February 1947, he cycled to the Guildhall and played piano for its principal, Eric Cundell.

"Very well. Come and start next year," said Cundell.

"How on earth do I pay for it?" asked Martin, blushing with embarrassment.

"As a man serving in the navy, you're entitled to further education. We'll apply for a grant."

Martin plunged into the otherworldliness of classical music as his mother died of a brain hemorrhage and his wife, Sheena, began suffering from agoraphobia. Surviving on a grant of £160 per year, he learned the crafts of orchestration, musical theory, harmony, counterpoint and conducting. After three years, he got a job at the BBC Music Library archiving sheet music. There, in 1950, he received another mysterious letter.

Invited to meet a certain Oscar Preuss, Martin parked his bike on Abbey Road and entered the impressive mansion. In a large office with a coal fireplace and a grand piano, the old man explained that through a mutual friend, Sidney Harrison had made the recommendation. For the modest sum of £7 4s. per week, George Martin, aged twenty-four, was hired as a recording assistant for Parlophone, an EMI sublabel.

Although EMI Records had fallen into a dark age under the poor management of its chairman, an Australian cycling fanatic named Sir Ernest Fisk, Oscar Preuss turned out to be an inspirational mentor who, conscious of nearing retirement age, acquainted Martin with record industry history and the mean-spirited machinations of EMI's bureaucracy. Things began to change, however, when a new EMI chairman, Sir Joseph Lockwood, was appointed in 1955. Astute, adventurous and gay, Lockwood thought little of his predecessor's conservatism. Identifying America as the heartbeat of the musical world, Lockwood made his first big move and acquired Capitol for $9 million. It was in this spirit of rejuvenation that Preuss and Lockwood handed Parlophone over to George Martin, who chose as his niche "the label for humorous people." Setting up mobile equipment in theatres, Martin recorded sketches and novelty songs from a new generation of daring comedians, including Peter Cook, Dudley Moore, Spike Milligan and Peter Sellers.

Rock 'n' roll landed on EMI's plate thanks to a licensing deal with RCA. Clocking up fifteen Elvis smash hits, EMI's 7-inch sales rocketed from 1 million to 7 million during 1957. George Martin looked on jealously as his colleagues at Columbia sold 5.5 million Cliff Richard records between 1958 and 1960. He was desperate for his own pop star. In a moment of ill-judged honesty, he admitted to Lockwood that he had stupidly turned down Elvis clone Tommy Steele, who went on to sell millions of records for Decca. Haunted by the blanched disappointment on Lockwood's face, Martin remained desperate – until in April 1962 he got a fateful telephone call.

"George, I don't know if you'd be interested," said Syd Coleman, a veteran publisher, "but there's a chap who's come in with a tape of a group he runs. They haven't got a recording contract, and I wonder if you'd like to see him and listen to what he's got?"

"Certainly," Martin replied. "I'm willing to listen to anything. Ask him to come and see me."

"Okay, I will. His name is Brian Epstein."

The Beatles had been turned down flatly by Pye, Phillips and Columbia; Decca had given them two auditions before passing. A disillusioned Epstein had dropped into the HMV store on Oxford Street to get his tape copied onto an acetate. Listening to Epstein's sob stories, the technician suggested he walk upstairs to see Syd Coleman, who in turn suggested, "Why don't you go round and see George Martin at Parlophone? He deals in unusual things. He's had a big success with the most unlikely recording acts. I'll give him a ring and make an appointment, if you like."

At Martin's new office on Manchester Square, Epstein launched into his pitch and even feigned surprise when Martin admitted he'd never heard of the Beatles. Seeing straight through Epstein's routine, Martin had to stop himself from asking, "Excuse me, *where is* Liverpool?" When Epstein played the acetate, though, Martin warmed to the harmonised vocals – which, despite the weak songs, were promising enough to justify a test recording.

Because the Beatles were performing in Hamburg at the time, it wasn't until June 1962 that they turned up at Abbey Road. George Martin instantly liked the musicians. Devout fans of Peter Sellers, they laid on the humour, knowing George Martin was a close friend and collaborator. As they performed, Martin's sensitive ears were disturbed by the drummer, Pete Best; despite being the most handsome, he couldn't nail the beat. Taking Epstein aside, Martin warned, "I don't know what you're going to do with the group, but this drumming isn't good enough for what I want. If we do make a record, I'd much prefer to have my own drummer." Martin's grave judgment validated what the other three Beatles already wanted, to replace Pete Best with the much more fun and engaging Ringo Starr.

A contract was drawn up – a one-penny royalty, four singles per year, for a five-year term, allowing Parlophone a yearly get-out option. It was by no means a generous deal, but after so many refusals, Parlophone was their last chance in London. Hoping to identify the band's star, George Martin took the train to Liverpool and descended into the Cavern, a revolting dungeon where sweat dripped from the ceilings onto cramped youngsters who regularly passed out in the heat. As he observed the Beatles in their natural habitat, Martin realised there was no front man – their offbeat gang format was the whole appeal.

Success wasn't going to come easy. When "Love Me Do" was released in late 1962, EMI's promotions division ignored it. Thanks mainly to the Epstein family's record shop, NEMS, heavy sales in Liverpool got the record a chart position at No. 17. Relations between manager and producer got off to a frosty start, however, when even NEMS couldn't get reorders. "What on earth is happening with EMI?" barked Epstein into the phone. The only way forward, Martin argued, was a brilliant follow-up and the help of an aggressive, well-connected music publisher. Martin suggested an old friend, Dick James, who had just set up his own company and urgently needed a hit.

Dick James convinced Brian Epstein to set up a separate company, Northern Songs, owned 50 percent by James with the other 50 percent divided between the Beatles and Epstein. It was a clairvoyant move; he even added a 10 percent handling fee to run the company from his main company, Dick James Music. Grateful for the introduction, James quietly offered Martin a cut. "It's very kind of you to think of me like that," Martin replied. "But on the other hand it isn't ethical … I think it would be wrong to split my interests."

For their follow-up, the Beatles speeded up a ballad called "Please Please Me," with George Martin adding its opening hook and triumphant finale. When the winning take was in the can, Martin pressed the intercom button. "Gentlemen, you've just made your first number-one record!" Dick James secured the Beatles an appearance on Britain's only music-oriented TV show, *Thank Your Lucky Stars*. EMI staffers, waking up to the record's potential, ensured it was regularly aired on their flagship station, Radio Luxembourg.

As soon as "Please Please Me" went No. 1, Martin called the band into Abbey Road. "Right, what you're going to have to do now, today, straight away, is play me a selection of things I've chosen from what you do in the Cavern." By eleven o'clock that night, an entire album was on tape and, as hoped, the LP went straight to No. 1. One title from the album, "Twist and Shout," seemed popular, so Martin released an additional EP with three other titles. It, too, went to No. 1. From that dream launch, original songs just kept pouring out; "From Me to You" and "She Loves You" sold 750,000 copies in four weeks. "We had opened the vent," says Martin, "the oil had started gushing up, and the well, which I had originally thought might soon dry up, simply kept on producing more and more." Just four months after their debut LP, they rushed out a second, *With the*

Beatles, containing eight original songs and three Motown covers. It stayed at No. 1 in Britain for twenty-one weeks.

Apart from the Beatles, Epstein managed other Liverpudlian acts – Gerry & the Pacemakers, Billy J. Kramer and Cilla Black – all signed to Parlophone. In 1963, the Epstein/Parlophone roster occupied the No. 1 spot for a total of thirty-seven weeks. Copying the formula, London's record industry embarked on a gold rush into the north of England. Pye found the Searchers; English Columbia found the Animals; Martin's new assistant found the Hollies in Manchester. Suddenly anything northern became chic – singers, comedians, writers. It's an often-forgotten fact that the British invasion of America in 1964 began as a Northern invasion of London in 1963.

The next problem was America. Although EMI owned Capitol, the Beatles' first singles had to be licensed to independents, VJ and Swan. According to rumour, even Atlantic's Jerry Wexler turned down the Beatles as "too derivative." Capitol's Dave Dexter replied rudely, "I got 'em in, they're a bunch of long-haired kids. Forget it. They're nuthin'." When "Please Please Me" was No. 1 in England, Capitol president Alan Livingston sent a curt reply to George Martin, "We don't think the Beatles will do anything in this market." Capitol rejected two more Beatles singles, "From Me to You" and "She Loves You." When Beatlemania began bleeping on the radars of the American media, Livingston conceded, "We'll take one record and see how it goes." The record was "I Wanna Hold Your Hand" – which went on to sell 15 million copies.

The game changed in January 1964, while the Beatles were in Paris playing two weeks of shows at the Olympia. Early one morning, Martin was awakened by a ringing telephone. It was Brian Epstein, audibly drunk. "I've just left the boys celebrating, and they're as thrilled as I am." A brief silence for theatrical suspense. "We're number one in America on next week's charts. It's quite definite. I've just been on the phone to New York." Martin sank back into his pillow and laughed at the ceiling. The adventure was entering a whole new dimension.

When they landed in America, Capitol's handlers kept George Martin as far away from the action as possible. Stepping into camera view wearing a big grin, Alan Livingston personally greeted the Beatles at the now legendary press conference at JFK Airport. Despite the pungent aroma of hypocrisy, Martin was nonetheless happy to be there witnessing such a historical event. Middle-aged men were walking down Fifth Avenue wearing Beatles wigs; television stations were covering the latest scoop from the Beatles' arrival. In front of the Plaza Hotel at Fifth Avenue and Central Park where the Beatles were staying, an enormous crowd had gathered. On virtually every station, Beatles songs played over and over.

As in England, audiences in America were instantly seduced by the Beatles' humour and spirit. "That enjoyable charisma came through to the world at large, which was seeing something it had not seen before," says Martin. "It was an expression of youth, a slight kicking over of the traces, which found a ready response in young people. Curiously, it was a response that the parents, though they might not have liked the music themselves, did not seem to begrudge."

At their first concert, in a boxing ring in Washington, D.C., Martin looked around and studied the crowd. "The audience, despite the various parental presences, was mostly teenage and very hot. In the seat next to me a little girl was bouncing up and down and saying, 'Aren't they just great? Aren't they just fabulous?' "

Martin replied, "Yes, they are."

"Do you like them, too, sir?" she inquired.

"Yes, I do rather," Martin said with a smile.

Although at the age of thirty-eight he felt somewhat old, Martin joined in when the entire crowd sang along to "I Wanna Hold Your Hand." "In that situation it was all too easy to scream, to be swept up in that tremendous current of buoyant happiness and exhilaration."

That year, the Beatles rang up six No. 1 singles and three No. 1 albums, occupying the top spot for about seven months of the year. With other British groups scoring No. 1s in their wake, the statistics were without precedent. Never before had the American market been so completely bombarded with British pop. Despite rejecting smash hits from the Beatles, the Dave Clark Five, Herman's Hermits and the Animals, Capitol's turnover jumped from $50 million in 1963 to $70 million in 1964. EMI's British turnover in the same period grew 80 percent to £9 million.

The one person who wasn't any richer was George Martin. Having joined EMI in 1950 as an assistant, he had been on a basic salary of £3,000 per year. EMI, in general, was a dusty bureaucracy whose senior managers and low-ranking staff all seemed to actively perpetuate the tradition of meanness. The Beatles were shocked to find the canteen fridges fitted with locks. Sound engineer Geoff Emerick had to get written permission to place a mic close to Ringo's bass drum for fear of being docked wages if it blew.

At the end of 1963, Parlophone staffers were rewarded an extra four days' pay as a special Christmas bonus – a shameful reward under the circumstances. Worse still, as boss, Martin was exempt. Studying the terms of his contract, he saw that a clause required him to give a year's notice before resigning. So Martin informed his superiors that he would be leaving in twelve months.

Suddenly senior managers began inviting him out to lunch. If it wasn't the "oh, c'mon now" approach, he'd get quizzed. Was he being poached by another label? Did the Beatles know he wanted to leave? Would he be available to produce the Beatles as a freelancer? Eventually a crunch meeting was called with Len Wood, head of EMI Records.

"Look now, you're being very stubborn about this," began Wood, "but I'm determined to keep you on."

"Okay, what have you got to offer?" asked Martin.

"Well, you're definitely going to get a commission on sales. What I propose is that you get three percent of our profits, minus your overheads."

"Well, that's a bit vague. Can you tell me what it amounts to?"

"Yes, yes, hold on … Let's take last year, for example. If this had been operating last year, 1963, you'd have ended up with a bonus of £11,000. How does that sound to you?" Wood smiled confidently.

"It sounds very good," replied Martin, "but how did you arrive at that?"

Adding up the label's four salaries and the previous year's musician fees and multiplying by two, Wood calculated that Parlophone's overhead was about £55,000. Subtracting that figure from a 3 percent commission of £66,000, the EMI Records boss arrived at an £11,000 bonus.

Martin's mind grappled with the numbers as a wave of anger surged through his veins. "Wait a minute," he insisted. "That must be turnover you're talking about, not profits. Because £66,000 is three percent of … £2.2 million!"

"That's right."

"But that must surely be turnover!" pressed Martin, now raising his voice.

"No, no, that's the profit."

The last sinew of trust Martin had for EMI snapped. The company was making millions out of Parlophone – not to mention the tens of millions Capitol was set to make in America.

"Thank you very much," Martin announced. "I haven't changed my mind at all. I'm leaving."

Of course, with a mortgage and a family to support, George Martin didn't have the means to just slam the door behind him. On £3,000, he would have to sit out his bitterness for another year. It was a tricky situation to be in while the Beatles were conquering the world, but financial struggle had always been present throughout his life. Walking out of that fateful meeting, George Martin started a quiet revolt inside EMI – unaware that the idea of independent production was spreading through London's rapidly mutating music scene.

13. ACTS

SHOWBIZ CHARACTERS AROUND LONDON WERE DREAMING UP THEIR OWN fantasies. In the very eye of the storm, a tall strawberry blonde by the name of Andrew Loog Oldham sensed the potential for an alternative to the Beatles.

If anyone knew such a thing was possible, it was him. Andrew Loog Oldham was a PR agent who had peddled the Beatles to London's columnists throughout the spring of 1963. Although barely nineteen years of age, Oldham was a seasoned hustler – well connected, imaginative, irreverent, and driven by an anarchic desire to disturb Britain's cosy record business, which he saw as a type of colonial civil service dominated by boring old men.

As the Beatles were swept away on a wave of adulation, he found himself standing at a perfect vantage point. With the onset of *Beatlemania*, appetites had just been whetted. Britain's entire entertainment industry now had to feed a hungry beast.

Oldham was a game changer who operated on youthful instinct. When he wasn't working his magic on the telephone, he was swanning around London in flashy chauffeur-driven cars, popping pills and scheming his next moves. With his taste for the wild life, he seemed to personify the sixties before they really started to swing. Andrew Loog Oldham remains one of the great unsung pioneers of British pop music, from whom so many bands, managers and indie labels are descended.

Although an enigma to his peers, Oldham was the sum of his various parts. Conceived in 1943, he was the love child of an American airforce pilot named Andrew Loog and an English mother, Celia Oldham. When she was just three months pregnant, his father-to-be was killed over the English Channel on a bombing mission. As a fatherless child, Andrew Loog Oldham inherited an elusive connection to America. A student of Hollywood movies, he reasoned with, bullshitted and motivated others with the self-confident swagger of a Manhattan entrepreneur. His peers were all products of England's class culture, but Oldham's dream world was a *can-do* meritocracy where the young, beautiful and daring would be kings. Charlie Watts once joked that Oldham was the first American he'd ever met.

In 1960, aged just sixteen, he quit school and secured a job at one of his favourite stores on King's Road, fashion designer Mary Quant's Bazarr. Arriving for the opening of her second store, in Knightsbridge, he caught his first glimpse of press agents stirring up interest in the national newspapers. At the time, Quant was pioneering the daring new look of the sixties: knee-high boots, miniskirts, high-waisted tweed tunics, tweed knickerbockers and bobbed hairstyles.

For Oldham, Mary Quant's modernist wonderland "was akin to being in the right movie. They knew they had recognised the right moment and turned a London cult into a worldwide success, retaining control through independent production. I was getting an education and call to arms that would cause and effect my later work with the Stones and Immediate Records." Rather than head home to suburbia after work, Oldham got a second job at Ronnie Scott's, a legendary club where beboppers like Ahmad Jamal, Dizzy Gillespie and Thelonious Monk performed. Working in the cloakroom from seven to midnight or 1:00 A.M., he also escorted customers to their seats and delivered meals from the Indian restaurant across the street.

It was during these hectic months working two (and sometimes three) jobs that Oldham started showing signs of irrational behaviour. One night when he paid a visit to his girlfriend, Sheila Klein, her psychoanalyst father opened the door and announced she wasn't allowed out until she washed the dishes. Furious, the sixteen-year-old Oldham pulled a starting pistol from his pocket and placed it against Dr. Klein's head. "Analyse this!" he said before disappearing off to the south coast.

Although he didn't understand the mechanics of his mood swings, Oldham suffered from manic depression. He was experiencing his first of many sudden encounters with a suicidal blankness. Instead of cracking up around those who knew him, he preferred to disappear to France, writing letters to Mary Quant and Ronnie Scott apologising for his absence. In the Mediterranean towns of St. Tropez and Cannes, he began hustling rich English tourists for money. He spent nights in jails and hung out with Vince Taylor, the self-destructive performer who later became the inspiration for David Bowie's *Ziggy Stardust* character.

Once the Mediterranean sunshine had chased away his inner darkness, Oldham returned to London, with his mind made up to break into the record business. In 1961, former Shadows drummer Tony Meehan, then working in Decca's A&R department, introduced Oldham to R&B records and pointed him to a tiny network of independent producers such as Shel Talmy, who later produced the Who, the Kinks, David Bowie and Manfred Mann. Joe Meek, another pioneer independent, produced perhaps the biggest hit of the period, "Telstar." Oldham began freelancing for them and others, mostly doing PR tasks.

Oldham's flair made him particularly well suited to escorting American artists around London. For example, in 1962, he was paid £5 to keep the press informed about Bob Dylan's appearance in a London theatre production called *Madhouse on Castle Street*. He also met Phil Spector during his first trip to England accompanying the Ronettes. Watching how Spector insulted hotel staff and pranced around London like a prince, Oldham's inner devil was tickled. "Little men in red corduroy jackets and shades simply did not alight from large Rolls-Royces in Mayfair," Oldham reminisced. "Phil set the example and I was infatuated with him. I'd spent my time till now being polite, and now I had the opportunity to model myself after a perfect little hooligan."

Oldham happened to be in the TV studio when the Beatles performed "Please Please Me." Observing their dapper, smiling manager in the shadows, Oldham reasoned that Epstein's being "somewhat to the manor born gave him both a self-assurance and an entrée with the stubbornly middle-class label managers he had to deal with. At *Thank Your Lucky Stars,* Brian merely stood watching his boys, yet his belief and their talent permeated the room and would soon, thanks to TV, permeate the isles, north to south."

Wangling his way into a Beatles rehearsal, Oldham approached Brian Epstein. As the well-dressed youngster pitched his PR services, Epstein sized him up. Luckily, Epstein at the time was furious with EMI for not plugging the Beatles with more determination, and he sensed that yes, maybe they should have their own representative "in … LON-DON," which Epstein pronounced "like a man getting rid of phlegm in his throat." In those days, it would have been unthinkable that even the most motivated manager based in Liverpool would spend afternoons hounding newspapers and radio stations by long-distance telephone.

So Oldham found himself, just eighteen, presenting the Beatles to London's media. Although there weren't any screaming girls yet, there was a momentum building. Oldham rented his own small office for £4 a week in the premises of an agent by the name of Eric Easton and started wearing make-up, realising that the more he camped up his persona, the more people seemed to take him seriously. When he got the Beatles into *Vogue,* Epstein was so delighted that he re-engaged him to plug a fifty-two-date tour on which the Beatles were supporting a young star named Chris Montez. It was during this multi-artist ballroom tour that the Beatles started to explode. By the time the tour got to Bedford, the screaming began.

As he stood backstage with Brian Epstein, everything seemed to change in the stillness of absolute noise. The girls were so hysterical they smashed every window into the backstage area. Oldham remembered, "The roar I heard was the roar of the whole world. You can hear something without seeing it, in the same way as you can have an experience that is beyond anything you've had before. You don't have to be clever, you only have to be a member of the public. The noise that night hit me emotionally, like a blow to the chest. The audience that night expressed something beyond repressed adolescent sexuality. The noise they made was the sound of the future ... When I looked at Brian, he had the same lump in his throat and tear in his eye as I."

After the Bedford show, Oldham knew the Beatles were on a path to giant things. His mind was racing. He felt a calling, but, bizarrely enough, not to serve the Beatles – he had to get his own group. Phil Spector had given Oldham some useful advice that took months to compute: if you ever find a group to record, never let the group sign directly to a major, nor use the record company's own studios. By using your own studios and licensing the masters to a record company, you'll keep control and earn much more money. Oldham was too young to care about money, but he was attracted to the idea of control. Just as it was for Brian Epstein, the thrill was to hold a giant chick magnet on a leash.

At the time, a pub in Soho called De Hems was where all the music-business characters hung out. Nursing an orange juice all afternoon, Oldham would watch the door and hustle for jobs. One afternoon, shortly after the Beatles tour, Peter Jones, editor of *Record Mirror,* tipped off Oldham about a fledgling R&B band called the Rollin' Stones. Jones knew Oldham was looking for a band of his own and assured him that dirty, old-school R&B was going to be the next big thing. So, just weeks after his realisation backstage at the Beatles show, in Bedford, Oldham took the tube to the Station Hotel in Richmond.

Walking towards the entrance, he saw a young couple having a violent argument by a wall outside the venue. Oldham passed by and exchanged a penetrating look with the angry young man, who later turned out to be the band's singer, a seventeen-year-old Mick Jagger. "There are no accidents," asserted Oldham, "and Peter Jones was the conduit to my destiny. I was probably forty-eight hours ahead of the rest of the business in getting there, but that's the way God planned it. I met the Rollin' Stones and said hello to the rest of my life."

As the six young musicians performed, Oldham studied the faces. The drummer looked like a jazz beatnik. The dark-haired guitarist was a thick-mouthed hunchback. The bassist had a medieval-looking head. The strawberry blonde guitarist had "a face that already looked as though it had a few unpaid bills with life. His head, having forgone a neck, slipped straight into a subliminally formed Greystoke body." The singer, whom he'd already seen outside, "moved like a Tarzan, plucked from the jungle, not comfortable in his clothes." There was just one problem – a sixth musician who looked all wrong, Ian Stewart, the piano player.

They were rough and loose, but they had a sound. Above all there was a feeling in the air. Too stunned to approach the Rollin' Stones after the show, Oldham took the train home sensing this gang was his ticket to bigger things. Unfortunately, he didn't have any money and was even too young to get an agent's licence. Having called Brian Epstein and some other potential investors, he realised his only viable option was to collaborate with the agent down the hall, Eric Easton. So, after a Stones gig at the Crawdaddy, Oldham and Easton approached Brian Jones, then the official leader of the band.

Although Eric Easton was old-school, he was shrewd. Accepting Oldham's novel idea to cofound a production company, he discreetly registered the supposed joint venture 100 percent under his own name. The plot thickened when Brian Jones admitted the Stones had recorded a demo at no cost, in return for their management rights. The studio in question, IBC, had unsuccessfully shopped the demo around to the usual labels but legally still had a right to the Stones for another six months – an eternity in 1963. So Oldham and Easton convinced Jones to drop by the studio, pretend he was joining another band, and politely request a release. Whining about himself came naturally to Brian Jones even when the details were all bogus. Better still, his parents had lent him £90, which he dangled as a courtesy gesture. The trick worked. IBC took the money, and because Jones was the sole signatory, the entire contract became worthless.

Oldham's next smart move was targeting Dick Rowe at Decca. Having turned down the Beatles, he signed up the first Stones single from Oldham's production company – an obscure Chuck Berry cover called "Come On," recorded for just £40. For their first photo shoots with photographer Crispian Woodgate, the band blankly refused to doll themselves up. Oldham quickly realised their anti-look was itself a slant to pitch to the media. "That look, that just-out-of-bed-and-fuck-you look – the river, the bricks, the industrial location – was the beginning of the image that would define and divine them," said Oldham, who came to understand that in a market dominated by the smiling, buttoned-up Beatles, the fastest way in was to stand out.

Broke but resourceful, Oldham obtained lists of which stores reported sales to the charts. He sent in friends to buy copies on Thursday and Friday, then had them return on Saturday knowing the store was out of stock and would order five more copies on Monday. This scam got "Come On" a chart position at No. 49.

The corny American apostrophe on the end of "*Rollin'*" had always irked Oldham. "How can you expect people to take you seriously when you can't even be bothered to spell your name properly?" he asked. They added the *g*. He then convinced Jones and Jagger to ditch Ian Stewart. "Five is pushing it, six is impossible. People work nine to five and they couldn't be expected to remember more than four faces. This is entertainment, not a memory test." Ian Stewart held back his tears as the band broke the news.

Pumped up by Oldham's theatrical sense of entitlement, the five brutish, correctly spelled Rolling Stones were repackaged just in time for their first TV appearance on *Thank Your Lucky Stars*. While they were nervously hanging around the studio waiting for their slot, Keith Richards walked past an Irish show band dressed up in blue uniforms and joked, "Oh the Irish fucking navy." The Irish musicians got so frisky, the producer rushed in to keep a fight from breaking out. "Look, boys, let's pull together," he implored, as Keith Richards persisted, "Well, they shouldn't be in the Irish fucking navy, should they!" Once things settled down, remembering Epstein's confidence-building effect on the Beatles months earlier in the same studio, Oldham ordered one of the stagehands to move the drum set four inches to the right, "daaaarling." Feeling invincible, the Stones mimed with attitude.

With a major TV appearance scheduled for broadcast the following Saturday, Oldham urgently needed a major newspaper's endorsement. Because the *Daily Mirror* had a circulation of 5 million, he begged for help from a powerful PR agent, Leslie Perrin, who reluctantly arranged a meeting in a Fleet Street pub with *Mirror* columnist Patrick Doncaster. With an unnerving smirk, Perrin introduced Oldham to Doncaster and duly left. Wearing the same smirk, Doncaster got straight to the point.

"When Leslie called me about you, we both laughed and said you should be able to get into the column on cheek alone, so you can relax, I think you'll be very pleased with next Thursday's *Mirror*."

When the article appeared, the Stones not only got the headline – BAD NEWS IS GOOD NEWS FOR THE STONES – but Doncaster played along with Oldham's bad-boy strategy. For the better part of a page, he showered praise on the band, which in fairness didn't deserve such exposure. In Oldham's own words, "That Thursday when the Rolling Stones rolled over England's breakfast tables and bus queues with Doncaster's stamp of approval, the nation – had it been listening closely – would have heard the distant sound of thunder."

Then came the bizarrest of coincidences. At a rehearsal in search of a new single, Oldham and the Stones were getting nowhere. After hours trudging through their repertoire of blues and R&B covers, Oldham started feeling depressed. Stepping outside to take a breath of fresh air, he began walking aimlessly toward Charing Cross Road. Suddenly, two familiar faces stumbled out of a taxi. It was John Lennon and Paul McCartney – drunk and trying to pay the cabby with fumbling fingers. They were coming from a luncheon where the Beatles had received *Melody Maker*'s Best Vocal Disc of the Year award.

Oldham sauntered over, and they exchanged hellos. Despite their state, they noticed Oldham wasn't looking himself. "What's wrong?" they asked. Oldham explained he was at a Stones rehearsal just around the corner and they couldn't come up with a suitable song for their next single. Lennon and McCartney exchanged twinkling glances. "C'mon, take us there," they said. The three pairs of Cuban-heeled boots strutted back down the road and into the basement where the Rolling Stones were sitting around glumly. Borrowing their instruments, Lennon and McCartney offered the Stones one of their own previously unreleased songs, "I Wanna Be Your Man." The two Beatles were, however, in a rush to get somewhere and were gone almost as quickly as they came. As the door shut behind John and Paul, the Stones smiled at each other, jaws dropped. They had their first potential hit single for the taking.

Although relieved their lucky star had shone, Oldham was feeling a familiar sensation. Another depression was rolling down its iron curtain.

He took the ferry from Dover and walked his suicidal thoughts around Paris for a few days until he felt like himself again. He missed the recording session for "I Wanna Be Your Man" but at least returned to London with a spring in his step. The Stones couldn't understand why he'd disappeared. Eric Easton didn't care.

Thanks to the older agent, the Stones embarked on their second tour in the autumn of 1963 – thirty-two dates with just three days off. Although the Stones were at the bottom end of the bill, the tour promoter began noticing that his headliners, the Everly Brothers, Little Richard and Bo Diddley, were not selling out. Then Oldham organised a Rolling Stones stage rush when the tour was in London, with all his friends' girlfriends and all their friends feigning Beatles-style hysteria; the *NME* reporter went home thinking the Stones had provided the highlight moment of the star-studded line-up. Another journalist, Sean O'Mahony, remembered, "At Hammersmith, the bouncers dragged girls out of the audience and parked them along the wall backstage. There were about seventy girls sprawled on the floor showing their knickers – it was an appalling sight."

With a buzz growing, "I Wanna Be Your Man" reached No. 30. Unfortunately, Eric Easton and Brian Jones, who saw themselves as the rightful leaders of the enterprise, were getting greedy. Easton had been pocketing kickbacks from the tour promoter; Brian Jones demanded special hotel rooms, alternative transportation, and £5 more per week than his bandmates.

As the smell of success grew stronger, a serious rift was forming – further accentuated by Oldham's moving in with Jagger and Richards. Getting to know the secretive, brooding Mick, Oldham had less of a relationship with Keith, who spent his whole time either sleeping or practising the guitar. Although most of their waking hours were spent in vans, it was at this address that Oldham put Jagger and Richards in the kitchen and warned, "I'm not letting you out or giving you any food until you write something."

Apart from their own material, the other vital ingredient they didn't have was a suitable, cheap studio. Oldham found Regent Sound, one of the smallest and filthiest dumps in London's Tin Pan Alley district near

Denmark Street. It was where songwriters came to record their demos. The place probably hadn't been cleaned since the day it was built; there were, according to witnesses, "stains on the stains." The control room was so small you could barely fit a chair between the console and back wall. Because the studio had no baffling and fed into a two-track mono machine, all the instruments bled into what Oldham described as his "wall of noise." Inside this dump, the Stones recorded a four-track EP featuring "You Better Move On," which, thanks to BBC airplay, got to No. 11 in the singles charts.

It was with these early successes that his contacts at the *Record Mirror* reported, "Andrew Loog Oldham predicts he will be the most successful independent producer in the country by autumn." He was going to have to move fast. Throughout January 1964, the Stones went on their second ballroom tour, supporting the Ronettes, meaning Oldham and Spector were again getting into trouble all over London. The Stones also headlined their own privately run shows, supported by the Detours, a mod group who later became the Who. Brian Jones even appeared with the Yardbirds, still resident at the Station Hotel in Richmond, where Oldham first saw the Stones play.

At Regent Sound, they recorded a shuffling number, "Not Fade Away." Their first major hit, it reached No. 3. Oldham's next brilliant move, in the spring of 1964, was the Stones' first album cover. Recorded in January and February 1964, the album was mainly cover versions of old blues and Motown, with one song credited to Jagger and Richards and two to "Nanker Phelge," a collective pseudonym for the band. The sleeve photo by Nicholas Wright was dark, ominous and stylish. Oldham was convinced that for maximum visual impact, the sleeve should not include any title or even the band's name, just five faces. When Decca refused the idea, Oldham refused to hand over the masters. The stand-off continued until Decca, sensing that Oldham just might be right, finally relented.

The effect was instant. While the Beatles were breaking all records in America in April 1964 with songs that had been hits in England the previous year, the Rolling Stones' nameless album was released and shot to No. 1 on the U.K. album charts, where it stayed for twelve weeks.

"The Stones' role in music is a powerful one," announced Oldham's press release. "They have the anger of the parents on their side. Young fans now realise that their elders groan with horror at the Rolling Stones. So their loyalty to the Stones is unswerving." The Who guitarist Pete Townshend, who witnessed the Stones' ascension up close, felt that generational rupture; "the Stones finally cemented the huge fucking wall that we wanted to build between the previous generation and everybody who was to follow."

Decca producer Tony Meehan remembered, "The Stones were in one studio, and I was in another doing some mixing, the first time I met them. They looked very sort of wild, like beatniks. They were having great trouble tuning up. And I said to Andrew, 'That's out of tune.' He looked at me and just laughed – his inimitable sense of anarchy. He said, 'Yeah, it's great, isn't it?' He couldn't give a shit. It was *great,* people were fooled by it. It was the image – he was selling an image and he did it very well. It was almost like punk."

The other joke was that the Rolling Stones had a much better deal with Decca than the Beatles had with Parlophone. One of Oldham's associates in his PR agency, Tony Calder, believed that "even if Andrew was operating more on instinct and luck than suss [knowledge] the deals the Stones got on paper were absolutely sensational – they had the greatest deals, fair to this day. The Beatles were on a shit deal, probably because they came first. The pioneers always get the arrows in the back."

With a hit album under his belt, Oldham was determined to fulfill his own prophecy of becoming the biggest independent producer in England before autumn. He was working on his experimental Andrew Oldham Orchestra, a sort of baroque pop that reworked Stones hits with wacky orchestral arrangements. He had also discovered a seventeen-year-old beauty called Marianne Faithfull, for whom he reworked the lyrics of a Jagger-Richards composition into "As Tears Go By."

Needing money to bring all his dreams to life, he presented his projects to Dick Rowe, then talked his way into a meeting with Sir Edward Lewis, the mogul who set up Decca in 1929. In an impressive antique office overlooking the Thames, Oldham studied the old man's wrinkled face. So this was the dinosaur behind the colonial civil service that was Decca.

Everyone in London's record business knew Sir Edward loathed rock 'n' roll and hoped it was just a passing fad.

Sir Edward took a newly pressed copy of "As Tears Go By" and placed it on an antique Gramophone. Oldham watched his reaction as the English horn announced the song's baroque-pop melody. As the sun shone down on the Thames, Andrew Loog Oldham, just nineteen years old, stood glowing, as if all of London were smiling back at him through the window. When the song faded out, Lewis picked up a telephone and asked to be put through to Dick Rowe. "Give the boy the money" was all he said.

14. A SLOW ECLIPSE

IT WAS IN JANUARY 1964, JUST BEFORE THEY EXPLODED IN AMERICA, WHEN the Beatles first heard *The Freewheelin' Bob Dylan*. As John Lennon put it, "For three weeks in Paris we didn't stop playing it. We all went potty about Dylan." Later that momentous spring, Lennon was interviewed in London by an American journalist, Al Aronowitz, who happened to be a friend of Dylan's. In their conversations, Lennon admitted he wanted to meet this enigmatic songwriter from Minnesota.

In August 1964, the Beatles returned to America. They had just released the film *A Hard Day's Night* to critical acclaim and were on the cover of *Life* magazine. Back in April, Lennon had even published his very own book of drawings and stories, *In His Own Write*. It had been an eventful few months in Lennon's life as an artist. Feeling buoyant, he sent out a message to Aronowitz to arrange the meeting.

The year had also been a transitional one for Bob Dylan. He had lost interest in writing "finger pointin' songs," and much of his new material was autobiographical. In February, he and three friends had embarked on a twenty-day adventure driving across America; typing away in the backseat, Dylan completed the material for his June 1964 album, *Another Side of Bob Dylan*. He started writing "Mr Tambourine Man," his most ambitious lyric of the year, at the New Orleans Mardi Gras and first performed the song at the Newport Folk Festival that summer.

The meeting was set at the Delmonico Hotel in New York on August 28, the evening after a Beatles concert. Aronowitz, Dylan and his road manager, Victor Mamoudas, drove down from Woodstock and parked their station wagon around the corner from the hotel, pushed through the crowd of Beatles fans and gained access into the relative calm of the hotel lobby. Once official contact had been made with their hosts, two policemen escorted them up to the Beatles' floor. When the lift opened, Dylan was ushered past more policemen posted along the corridor. Beyond them, a group of journalists, disc jockeys and musicians poured out of an open room where drinks were being served. Dylan was led into a closed suite where Brian Epstein and the four Beatles had just finished eating dinner.

As he came through the doorway, the Beatles were first struck by Dylan's small stature and hooked nose. Trying to break a palpable tension, Epstein invited his guests into the living room, asking them what they'd like to drink.

"Cheap wine," replied Dylan.

Unsure if Dylan was joking, Epstein dispatched his assistant Mal Evans to procure some cheap wine. During the wait, it was suggested that amphetamine pills were available. The guests declined, but Dylan seized the cue to suggest they all smoke some fantastic grass he had brought down from Woodstock.

Stuck for words, Epstein and the Beatles looked at each other. "We've never smoked marijuana before," admitted Epstein with embarrassment.

"But what about your song?" Dylan asked. "The one about getting high?"

"Which song?" asked Lennon.

"You know … 'and when I touch you I get high, I get high,'" sang Dylan in reference to "I Wanna Hold Your Hand."

"Those aren't the words," explained Lennon. "The words are 'I can't hide.'"

Epstein spent half an hour securing the hotel suite before Dylan was even allowed to produce the grass from his pocket. The doors were locked; then towels from the bathroom were stuffed into every crevice around the door frame. The blinds were shut tight and the curtains drawn, obscuring the majestic views of Park Avenue. Once Epstein felt they were securely airtight, a bemused Dylan was allowed to roll a joint.

Dylan lit up, passing it first to John Lennon. Too apprehensive to take a puff, Lennon passed it on, joking that Ringo was his royal taster. Unaware of joint etiquette, Ringo proceeded to smoke the entire joint himself. So Dylan and Aronowitz rolled half a dozen joints and passed them around. As the other Beatles began smoking the strong-smelling herb, they thought, "This isn't doing anything," until Ringo started laughing uncontrollably.

Within minutes, the hotel suite was a madhouse. Epstein was clutching his seat repeating, "I'm so high I'm on the ceiling. I'm up on the ceiling ..." At the centre of this bedlam, Dylan kept his hosts in convulsions by pretending to answer the telephone, "Hello, Beatlemania here!"

The Beatles' weapon against stress was humour, and on this historical night, everyone had a sore belly from so much laughter. When Dylan and his friends eventually left, they all promised each other to meet up at the end of their tour. For the Beatles, and especially John Lennon, the encounter marked the beginning of a bizarre relationship with the musician every interesting songwriter in the business was starting to notice. These little events, hidden from the public eye, sowed the seeds of what in time would grow into a brand-new musical genre, *psychedelia*.

Something was in the air. Just a month later, a British group from Newcastle called the Animals scored a smash-hit No. 1 in America with "House of the Rising Sun," a traditional air that Dylan had recorded for his debut album, cleverly reworked with electric guitar, bass, ride cymbals, and some stirring organ playing by Alan Price. Then *Beatles for Sale,* released in December 1964, contained the first of many audibly Dylan-inspired songs by John Lennon – "I'm a Loser," complete with a harmonica solo. By the time the Beatles started filming *Help!* in the new year, John Lennon had become such an unashamed Dylan freak that he wore a Greek fisherman's hat and a suede jacket and even traded in his Rickenbacker for an acoustic guitar.

Always one step ahead of the posse, Dylan himself was exceptionally prolific in this period. As the brilliant *Bringing It All Back Home* hit the streets in the spring of 1965, a cover of "Mr Tambourine Man" by a young

Californian group called the Byrds was climbing the charts, eventually reaching No. 1 in June. Signed to Columbia at the end of 1964, the Byrds were originally billed as an American answer to the Beatles but quickly cultivated their own image. David Crosby crafted distinctive harmonies; Roger McGuinn contributed the bright sound of a twelve-string electric guitar.

Dylan's own breakthrough came with "Like a Rolling Stone," a six-and-a-half-minute sledgehammer describing a Greenwich Village hipster's decline. Columbia's sales and marketing staff had been cautious about releasing it as a single due to its length and raucous sound. Fortunately, before condemning the recording to a lesser fate as an album track, release coordinator Shaun Considine took an acetate to a happening club, Arthur, whose in-crowd of deejays and journalists duly wore it out. Lo and behold, the next morning, a programming director from a Top 40 station telephoned Columbia for copies. So, on July 20, 1965, Columbia released all six-plus minutes of "Like a Rolling Stone" – a precedent in pop music.

Andrew Loog Oldham was so impressed, he was moved to write a review in *Disc and Music Week*, saying, "Whether he likes it or not, this man is so commercial and has his finger on the pulse just that little bit ahead of everybody else, which makes him unique. 'Like a Rolling Stone' is the most fantastic thing he's done, a Dylan version of 'Twist and Shout' with a little Tamla-Motown thrown in." Although Dylan wasn't in the same sales league as the Beatles or the Stones, he knew he was ahead of his contemporaries in that other contest for artistic resonance. He would repeat to his journalist friend Al Aronowitz, "You've got to be psychically armed," taunting him, "Why don't you ask Mick Jagger if he thinks he's psychically armed?"

Just five days after the release of "Like a Rolling Stone," Dylan performed his now-legendary electric set at the Newport Folk Festival of 1965. The first to understand the significance of this little event were, not surprisingly, the professional record men watching backstage.

A case in point is Jac Holzman, owner of Elektra, which had become a leading force in folk music thanks to Theo Bikel, Judy Collins and Tom Paxton. Holzman had spent the day hanging out backstage with Pete

Seeger, Bikel and the Solomon brothers, who headed Vanguard. He was particularly excited as evening neared because members of the Paul Butterfield Blues Band, one of Elektra's newest signatures, were providing the backbone of Dylan's band. Holzman recalled, "I had attended the rehearsal, so I knew what to expect. But what I did not expect was the negative reaction from the folk fans."

As Holzman took photos from the crowd of Dylan performing "Maggie's Farm," "the hair on the back of my neck stood up and it was real clear to me you had to go here. That was the point at which I got it as religion … It was of such intensity that it almost lifted me off the ground. I started tingling all over … A thing clicked in my head because his lyrics were so mature – you can think and you can boogie at the same time … So, I just made up my mind. I was gonna go more aggressively after rock. I saw the future for Elektra."

Interestingly, the man who provided Holzman with an inside track was Elektra's new producer Paul Rothchild, the concert's sound man. "That night at Newport was as clear as crystal," said Rothchild. "It's the end of one era and the beginning of another." Having been poached by Holzman from a folk label called Prestige, Rothchild not only spotted the Butterfield Blues Band in Chicago but added its fiery electric guitarist, Mike Bloomfield. "Paul Rothchild was on the street more than me," admitted Holzman. "Paul came from the Boston area, had broad and deep music smarts, smoked dope, and was exactly the right guy at the right time … He carried himself well – the Borsalino hat, the leather coat … He was the perfect choice to attract artists – he was one of *them*."

Tension between the traditionalists and the modernists had begun brewing earlier that day when festival organiser Alan Lomax walked onstage and introduced the Butterfield Blues Band. "Today you've been hearing great music from the great blues players. Now you're going to hear a group of young boys from Chicago with electric instruments. Let's see if they can play this hardware at all." As Lomax left the stage, Butterfield and Dylan's manager, Albert Grossman, snapped back, "That was a real chicken-shit introduction, Alan." Lomax pushed Grossman, provoking an ugly altercation that Jac Holzman described as "two overweight and out-of-shape growlers rolling in the dirt."

Enraged, Alan Lomax tried to ban Grossman from the festival, claiming he was the source of drugs in the artists' lodge. However, the supreme boss, George Wein, halted Lomax's efforts, wisely arguing that the super-manager could plunge the festival into chaos. When Bob Dylan launched into "Maggie's Farm," Paul Rothchild's stagehand, Joe Boyd, found himself running messages between both camps. Backstage, Alan Lomax, Pete Seeger and Theo Bikel ordered Boyd to "tell them the sound has got to be turned down. That's an order from the board." Boyd jumped over the fence to the mixing desk, where Rothchild, Grossman and folk star Peter Yarrow were guarding the volume control.

"Tell Alan the board is adequately represented at the sound controls and the board member here thinks the sound level is just right," responded Yarrow, raising his index finger. Grossman and Rothchild erupted into laughter as Dylan launched into "It Takes a Lot to Laugh, It Takes a Train to Cry."

The young messenger, Joe Boyd, would move to London later that year, working for a while at Elektra's British office and bringing the Incredible String Band to Jac Holzman's attention. From there, as an independent producer, he began the seminal UFO psychedelic concerts in London's Blarney Club, which, in 1966–67, launched Pink Floyd, Procol Harum and Soft Machine. Writing his memoirs, the well-travelled Joe Boyd asserted that "the Birth of Rock" was that night at Newport. "Anyone wishing to portray the history of the sixties as a journey from idealism to hedonism could place the hinge at around 9:30 on the night of 25 July, 1965."

Inside Columbia, Bob Dylan's producer at the time was Bob Johnston, a Texas-born musician who had grown up bathed in hillbilly and country music. Recognising that Dylan's output was bordering on the superhu-man, "I heard him, and I wanted to work with him," said Johnston of that milestone summer. "He was a prophet, and in another few hundred years, they'll realise he stopped the [Vietnam] War."

"Why do you want to work with him?" Columbia executive Bob Mercy asked Johnston. "He's got dirty fingernails and he breaks all the strings on his guitar."

Determined to ensure Byrds producer Terry Melcher wasn't assigned to Dylan, Johnston petitioned John Hammond and Bill Gallagher, the head of sales, until everyone agreed.

On the morning of Johnston's first session on *Highway 61 Revisited,* a German sound engineer was waiting in the control room.

"Vot are ve vorking on today?" asked the technician.

"Bob Dylan."

"Do ve haff to?"

"Hell no," replied Johnston, who found a more enthusiastic engineer.

Johnston quickly figured out that the best service he could provide Dylan was getting absolutely everything on tape. Perhaps a sign of total self-confidence, it never seemed to bother Dylan that some takes were plain terrible. He tried out songs in different grooves, and if something didn't work, he moved on swiftly and without any self-flagellation. "Dylan was fast, and you never knew what he was going to do next," said Johnston. "I figured Dylan knew something none of us knew, and I wanted to let him get it out."

The logistical problem was that Columbia's tape machines "were way down the hall. We had union engineers, so one would be in the control room at the console with me, and I'd say, 'Roll tape,' and he'd tell his assistant near the door, 'Roll tape,' and he'd yell down the hall to a guy at the other end, 'Roll tape,' and then they'd start all over again yelling, 'Is tape rolling?' God, it took twenty minutes to get those damned machines going. It was like a *Three Stooges* short." After an impromptu jam was lost because the machines weren't turned on in time, Johnston installed two tape machines in the studio and kept them rolling.

That August, Dylan's former producer, Tom Wilson, sensing the folk-rock wave, attempted an unusual stunt. Back in March 1964, he had supervised an acoustic record by one of Columbia's folk duos called Simon & Garfunkel. The album, *Wednesday Morning, 3 A.M.,* was a commercial flop that resulted in the duo breaking up and Paul Simon emigrating to England. However, on that album was one promising song, "The Sound of Silence," which had aroused some interest among radio disc jockeys. Wilson found the tapes, overdubbed drums, bass and electric guitar, and released the song in September 1965 without even the artists' knowledge. It grew into a smash hit, eventually reaching No. 1 on the *Hot 100*. Utterly delighted, Simon & Garfunkel re-formed while another Columbia folk-rock smash hit, "Turn! Turn! Turn!" by the Byrds, hit No. 1 for three weeks just before Christmas 1965.

Columbia's lucky run, like Motown's five No. 1s that year, was a rare American success in a general pattern of British influence. In total, half of America's No. 1 singles in 1965 were by English acts. The Beatles alone clocked up four No. 1 albums for a cumulative stretch of thirty weeks. Getting rawer and edgier, the British Invasion's second year carried in the Rolling Stones, who scored two No. 1s in America with "Satisfaction" and "Get Off of My Cloud." In their wake were the Who, the Yardbirds and Them.

Back in England, EMI's tight-fisted culture was provoking a mutiny. In August 1965, George Martin resigned and set up his own production company, AIR. No fewer than seven other disgruntled colleagues followed him, effectively all of EMI's youngest talent scouts. Embarrassingly for EMI, AIR had secured production contracts with several hot acts: the Beatles, Cilla Black, Manfred Mann, Adam Faith, the Hollies, Gerry & the Pacemakers, and Billy J. Kramer.

Martin's first project as an independent producer was the Beatles' most ambitious body of recordings to date. Although predominantly folk-rock in spirit, *Rubber Soul* also signalled the beginnings of a second musical subplot that would alter the course of pop music. At the time, Paul McCartney, by far the most technically capable Beatle, was living in the family home of his girlfriend, Jane Asher – a large, beautiful town house where classical musicians and interesting characters from London's cultural world regularly stopped by. He had begun writing increasingly complex compositions like "Yesterday" and "Michelle" in a room that Asher's mother used for classical lessons.

As coincidence would have it, George Martin knew Jane Asher's mother, who was a professor of oboe at the Guildhall, where he had studied. In recording sessions, McCartney first began taking an interest in George Martin's hidden talents. As his muse reached toward higher-brow inspirations, McCartney was wondering if he should study classical music. George Martin wisely dissuaded him, arguing that his unorthodox melodies benefitted from his self-taught naivety.

Still, the race for a new brand of classically infused pop music was in the air. It was while stoned, listening to *Rubber Soul* on headphones, that the Beach Boys' creative force, Brian Wilson, vowed to outwit the Beatles – as such, declaring a creative war against Paul McCartney and George Martin. Like Andrew Loog Oldham, Brian Wilson was a disciple of the Phil Spector school of independent production, except that it was his father and manager, Murray Wilson, who had negotiated the contract by which the Beach Boys' production company would lease finished masters to Capitol.

Drawing from Phil Spector's pool of session musicians, Wilson began mixing honky-tonk pianos, organs, harpsichords, French horns, giant-sized bass harmonicas, anything with an unusual texture. Like Spector, Wilson relied on drummer Hal Blaine for happy-feeling rhythms – chimes, bells and childlike percussive sounds, with occasionally some snare and timpani rolls for dramatic punctuation. However, where Phil Spector had a rather sloppy method of cumulative layering, Wilson, despite the handicap of a deaf right ear, sought a sonic clarity that conjured up images of California sunshine through a psychedelic lens. Above all, Wilson was a highly inventive composer who, like his other guiding reference, Burt Bacharach, had a gift for unusual chord changes held together by catchy melodies.

On this logistically complex project that became *Pet Sounds*, Wilson also began using Columbia's eight-track facilities for recording vocal harmonies. Byrds front man Roger McGuinn remembered how, at the time, "the eight track was in Columbia's L.A. studio [but] the engineers were afraid of it – they had a handwritten sign taped on to it that said BIG BASTARD." The fiercest sceptic of Wilson's experimentation, both sonic and chemical, was fellow Beach Boy Mike Love. "Don't fuck with the formula" were his fateful words.

Due to Wilson's laborious perfectionism, *Pet Sounds* was not released until May 1966, and by then, unashamedly trippy sounds were popping up with increasing frequency. In January 1966, the Byrds recorded their unambiguously titled "Eight Miles High," featuring drones and a dissonant guitar solo inspired by John Coltrane's free jazz saxophone on "India." In spring, Bob Dylan's *Blonde on Blonde* lurched into town with its now-famous opening gambit, "Everybody must get stoned!"

In the first of several clues that Dylan's effortless roll was coming to an end, at the end of 1965, five recording sessions backed by his touring band had yielded only brash, nervous material. Watching from the control room, Bob Johnston suggested Dylan start anew in the quieter surroundings of Nashville. Dylan got curious and took down just two trusted band members, Al Kooper and Robbie Robertson. Rounding up local session musicians, Johnston put everyone in a tight space without baffles, though according to Kooper, "Johnston pretty much stayed out of the way and let the magic happen."

Whether it was the friendliness of the local musicians or just a change of scenery, the Hammond organ came out silkier, the guitar parts were sweeter and not always electric, the drums had better shuffle and tone, and Dylan's voice was grainier and sitting more confidently in the centre of the mix. Long criticised for his grating sound, Bob Dylan found a resonant timbre in Nashville. One key factor may have been the piano in his hotel suite. As Kooper explained, "I acted as Bob's live cassette player and played the song over and over for him on the piano in his hotel room so he could work on the lyrics. It also helped me, as music director of the album, to *know* the songs and teach them to the band before Bob would arrive each day."

The final result was a dense double album, which shone thanks to its beautifully written moodier ballads scented with Southern air in the small hours. Dylan's proudest creation was an eleven-minute epic, "Sad-Eyed Lady of the Lowlands," recorded in just one take at 4:00 A.M. Specially written for Dylan's biggest fan, there was even a poisoned arrow. "During the recording of '4th Time Around,'" said Al Kooper, "I asked Bob if he was worried about the melodic similarity to 'Norwegian Wood.' He said curtly, 'I think they will be more worried about it than I am.'"

Whether out of courtesy or mischief, Dylan played the song to John Lennon in person just before the album's official release. As expected the perverse game of Dylan copying Lennon copying Dylan, almost like those black minstrels, proved to be too much for the adoring Beatle, who later admitted, "I was very paranoid … I remember he played it to me when he was in London. He said, 'What do you think?' I said, 'I don't like it' … I thought it was an out-and-out skit."

At the time, the Beatles were finishing *Revolver,* another unashamedly druggy body of recordings whose daring finale, "Tomorrow Never Knows," was a live performance of tape samples complete with Indian drone, tribal drumming, and Lennon singing surreal imagery through a Leslie amplifier. Released in August 1966, in an experimental sleeve mixing illustrations and photographs, *Revolver* was a resounding hit among British critics and fans. Curiously, in America, Capitol was proving to be unsupportive of all this psychedelia. Not only were the American versions of Beatles albums butchered into compilations, Capitol was so convinced *Pet Sounds* had been a mistake that within just eight weeks of its release, the company put out a Beach Boys greatest-hits album featuring all their older surfing anthems.

Realising that London had become the centre of musical innovation, Brian Wilson hired Beatles publicist Derek Taylor to promote the U.K. release of *Pet Sounds* in the summer of 1966. Taylor's tack was to deconstruct the public preconception of the Beach Boys as a surf band and instead communicate Brian Wilson's genius as a writer and producer. Articles began appearing in the British press about this fascinating, seminal album, Brian Wilson's personal masterpiece.

The Beatles had first heard a test pressing of *Pet Sounds* at the Waldorf Astoria in May 1966 just before embarking on their last world tour, all summer long. Physically chased out of the Philippines and symbolically burned by Southern evangelists, in autumn 1966, they took a long-overdue sabbatical in which Paul McCartney got to know the album intimately. He was regularly brought to tears by his favourite song, "God Only Knows." "It was *Pet Sounds* that blew me out of the water," he confessed as an older man. "I've just bought my kids each a copy of it for their education in life … It's the classic of the century." George Martin shared his enthusiasm, declaring, "If there is one person that I have to select as a living genius of pop music, I would choose Brian Wilson."

The years between 1964 and 1966 had been a period of rapid transformation in which the world's most powerful hit machine – John Lennon, Paul McCartney and George Martin – had become obsessed with America's prodigal sons, Bob Dylan and Brian Wilson. Respectively the lyrical and musical innovators of the day, like Icarus, they were venturing dangerously close to the sun.

Although Brian Wilson would crash hardest, Bob Dylan was the first to catch fire. Due to impossible workloads maintained by amphetamines, Dylan's relations with the shady Albert Grossman were souring. Gaunt and booed by audiences for his electric transformation, he withdrew into the bosom of Sara Lownds, his wife, who in January had given birth to their first baby, Jesse. Whether by accident or on purpose, Dylan jumped off the roller coaster on July 29, 1966. "I had been in a motorcycle accident and I'd been hurt, but I recovered," admitted Dylan forty years later. There may have been a road accident resulting in a minor injury, but there was neither an ambulance called nor any hospitalisation. "Truth was that I wanted to get out of the rat race."

15. TERRA NOVA

INSIDE THE AMERICAN RECORD INDUSTRY, A QUIET MIGRATION FROM EAST
Coast to West Coast was gathering momentum. Los Angeles already had
its own record industry, of course – in particular, Capitol, then getting fat
on Beatles hits pouring in from its parent company, EMI. Since the fifties, various independents had sprouted up around Hollywood, notably
Warner Bros. Records and its sister label, Reprise.

Throughout the sixties, a colourful new community of migrant record
producers was forming. One character with a big future was Jerry Moss, a
twenty-five-year-old promotions man from the Bronx, who in 1960 left
the Brill Building in search of sunnier adventures out west. "The plane
landed, my aunt picked me up, the weather was fantastic," remembered
Moss, who found work as an independent promotions man. Hungrier
than the local competition, "I believed in working a full day!" Because
he had no friends, he ended up hanging out with disc jockeys day and
night. "It was a dreamy time in California. You could park your car in
front of the radio station and walk right in. It was not like New York,
which was high buildings and going through people. Here was a frontier
feeling."

In those years, Jerry Moss befriended a musician and struggling actor
named Herb Alpert with whom he began listening to the exotic jazz-samba
records of Stan Getz, João Gilberto and Brazilian bossa nova genius

Antonio Carlos Jobim. Launching their long and illustrious career with Alpert's Tijuana Brass band, "we gotta be able to make money while we're sleeping," vowed Moss to Alpert. "I don't care if this record is six months old, we gotta keep letting radio stations know this is a hot act." Right time, right place, right sound. By 1966, their four-year-old label, simply called A&M, was in orbit, selling 13 million Tijuana Brass records – more than the Beatles. Thanks again to their Brazilian inspirations, Alpert and Moss spotted and signed Sergio Mendes & Brasil '66, who scored a hit with "Mas Que Nada" while supporting Alpert on tour.

Herb Alpert's former business partner Lou Adler was another happening indie who had relocated from Chicago to Los Angeles. It was Adler, working as manager and producer, who guided the local folk group the Mamas & the Papas to their national breakthrough in early 1966 with "California Dreamin'." In fact, even Byrds front man Roger McGuinn, the bespectacled face of California cool at the time, was actually a blow-in from Chicago.

When it came to pioneering uncharted musical territory, pushing the wagons deeper into the wild west was Elektra founder Jac Holzman. In the spring of 1965, "I thought I had the Lovin' Spoonful, and [losing them] really put me on edge," Holzman recalled. Then came Bob Dylan's electric set in Newport. "So I just pulled up the stakes and went to California because I thought everybody's picking over what there is in New York." Holzman already had a local promotions office in Los Angeles, but by the summer of 1965, was looking at ways to develop it into an A&R unit.

The claustrophobia of New York's folk scene contrasted with the expansive effect of marijuana, which was radically altering Elektra's musical tastes and company culture. Beyond his official job in the studio, Elektra producer Paul Rothchild had a profitable side business selling grass among his circle of musicians and hipsters. Jac Holzman began hosting sessions in his Manhattan apartment, equipped with his high-definition stereo sound system, where guests would be served space cookies, then played the latest wow.

In his many visits to Elektra's Los Angeles office, Jac Holzman shot the shit with local players and noticed how "in California, musicians were finding each other naturally rather than being cobbled together by managers – big, big difference. You'd hang out there, you could get loaded, you'd bond – it was a lot more fun." With its sunny climate and liberal atmosphere, California was also home to a booming marijuana culture. In these innocent days before baggage inspections and sniffer dogs, Holzman began flying back to New York with large bags of grass packed in his suitcase.

Then, in the autumn of 1965, Paul Rothchild was busted and imprisoned for nine long months. Paying half of Rothchild's salary throughout, Holzman tightened his gut and intensified his A&R reconnaissance missions into the unfamiliar underground of Los Angeles. "Colleges were really important in the folk scene, but rock was different," he explained. "It wasn't smart college kids sitting around in coffee houses. This was a different kind of audience; much more racially integrated … There were dozens of clubs in the heart of Hollywood, near Vine and on the Sunset Strip, from La Cienega on the east to Doheny on the west … I'd pick up a copy of the *Los Angeles Free Press,* I'd go through every listing of every band playing and check off the ones I've heard. The ones that seemed interesting to me, I'd check around with friends who'd say 'oh yeah they're interesting' or 'don't waste your time.'"

Eventually, in late 1965, Holzman's first eureka moment struck at a club called Bido Lito's, where a folk-rock ensemble called Love was performing. Accompanied by his wife, Nina, he stood among the "silken-clad girls with ironed blonde hair moving the kind of shapes you didn't see in New York." Nina Holzman recalled how "Arthur Lee got up, and he had these boots with the tongues hanging out, no laces, and his eye glasses had one blue lens and one red, and a funny shape. He was the most bizarre person I'd ever seen in my life, by far." The Elektra boss was instantly hooked. "When there's an element of danger, when you don't know what a band is going to do next, that attracts me," he explained. The next day, he set in ink a three-year, six-album deal for a $5,000 cash advance. That very day, the drug-crazed Arthur Lee bought a flashy convertible and gave his bandmates the change – $100 each.

As the cookie crumbled, Love's debut album and accompanying single provided vital experience for Holzman's next discovery, Elektra's biggest ever – the Doors, one of the most important acts of the late twentieth century. In early 1966, as Love was fast becoming the new noise in L.A., the Doors, fresh-faced and building up a repertoire, were playing in a Sunset Strip dive called the London Fog. "We were doing it for ourselves," recalled keyboardist Ray Manzarek of those formative months before bleeping on anyone's radar. "Most of the time there were about seven people in the club, the four Doors, the waitress, the bartender … , and Rhonda Lane, the go-go dancer."

Shopping their self-produced demo around town, they visited Lou Adler, who skidded the needle through the first five seconds of every song, then showed the Doors to the door. They took their acetate to another local indie, Liberty Records. When Jim Morrison's voice sang, "Once I had a little game, I think you know the game I mean, the game called Go Insane," the label boss ripped off the needle, shouting, "Get outta here! Take this record and get out! You guys are sick!"

They eventually found a more receptive ear in Billy James, Bob Dylan's former publicist, who was now working as an A&R man in Columbia's Los Angeles office. "Their music was different," said James. "It had an insidious quality, not just moody, almost threatening, a quality of implied danger. 'The Game Called Go Insane,' what an odd idea for a three-minute song that you want to get on AM radio and have little girls dancing to. Go insane – that's an option we hadn't considered in rock 'n' roll."

"I like what you guys are doing," he announced to the delighted youngsters. "You guys are now signed to Columbia Records."

A record contract was signed; however as James would later find out, "Columbia did nothing. Weeks went by, months, and then they put the Doors on their drop list." Despite this crushing let-down, the four young men simply dusted themselves off and continued gigging, until, as so often happens with giant destinies, luck intervened. The very night the London Fog's owner laid off the Doors due to lack of interest, a lady dropped in – Ronnie Haran, the booker for the hippest club in town, the Whisky a Go Go. Bowled over by Jim Morrison's sex appeal, she announced, "I want you guys to be the house band."

It was at this crossroads that Jac Holzman bought his lucky ticket into the pantheon of record men. "In May 1966, I had flown to L.A. and was picked up at the airport by Ronnie Haran in her white convertible," he explained. "Arthur Lee was playing the Whisky and expected me to drop by. It was 11:00 P.M. L.A. time, 2:00 A.M. New York metabolism time. I was beat, but I went. Arthur urged me to stick around for the next band." At the time, Holzman was feeling jittery as the race to sign up California's folk-rock bands intensified. "There was another group that played the Whisky that I had fallen in love with and tried desperately to sign, Buffalo Springfield, but Ahmet Ertegun of Atlantic was far more convincing. We were a smaller label without Atlantic's amazing track record of hit singles. Love had gotten my foot in the rock door, and now I needed a second group to give Elektra more of that kind of credibility."

The young band onstage wasn't grabbing him. "Jim was lovely to look at, but there was no command. Perhaps I was thinking too convention- ally, but their music had none of the rococo ornamentation with which a lot of rock and roll was being embellished – remember, this was still the era of the Beatles and *Revolver* circa 1966. Yet, some inner voice whispered that there was more to them than I was seeing or hearing. So I kept returning to the club. Finally, the fourth evening, I *heard* them. Jim generated an enormous tension with his performance, like a black hole, sucking the energy of the room into himself. 'Alabama Song,' which I knew thoroughly, but what they did with it was pure Doors. And then I got it … And when I heard – really *heard* – Manzarek's baroque organ line under 'Light My Fire,' I was ready to sign them."

Getting their four signatures on the dotted line was no foregone conclusion. Following their eye-opening disappointment with Columbia, they had turned down offers from independent producers Terry Melcher and Frank Zappa. Luckily for Holzman, Doors guitarist Robby Krieger was a devout fan of Elektra's flamenco and blues records – he already considered the label a mark of quality. Keyboardist Ray Manzarek, not necessarily the natural leader of the band, but the eldest and most musically capable, instantly connected with the Elektra boss, later joking that Holzman was the first person he'd met in the record business who spoke in full sentences. "He was an intellectual," said Manzarek, "the cowboy from New York. He was like Gary Cooper riding into town, but with brains. Jac even knew 'Alabama Song' was written by Kurt Weill and Bertolt Brecht."

Besides being bohemians from liberal Jewish families, Manzarek and Holzman, along with Jim Morrison, shared a passion for movies. Originally from Chicago himself, Manzarek was in L.A. to study cinematography at UCLA – where he met Jim Morrison. Among this gang of kindred spirits, music was discussed in cinematic, literary and musicological dimensions. "We loved Orson Welles and the music of Howlin' Wolf, in other words darkness," Manzarek said of the Doors' inspirations. "Or Muddy Waters singing 'Hoochie Coochie Man.' Or listening to Miles Davis's music, with its dark overtones. Music that had a deep psychological poetry. Allen Ginsberg's opening line in *Howl* was very influential: 'I saw the best minds of my generation destroyed by madness.' That's where the Doors come from: *City of Night, Raymond Chandler's Los Angeles*, Nathanael West's *Miss Lonelyhearts* and *The Day of the Locust*."

The shoe fit perfectly. "They liked me," Holzman recalled, although "they were reticent because they had just been burned by Columbia. I finally realised what the closure might be: not to guarantee that I would release a record, but to guarantee I would release three albums. I knew they had enough [material] for two full albums, and I would give them what no other label would." Although the basic terms of the contract were fairly standard for the period -- a $5,000 advance, a 5 percent royalty on record sales, and a 75/25 percent split on publishing in favour of the artist – it was the long-term commitment that clinched the deal.

The next problem was production. "At my insistence, Paul went to L.A. and watched one of the Doors sets," explained Holzman, "and told me I was nuts. I said, 'I don't think so.' I looked at other producers, but kept coming back to Paul … The group needed a force they couldn't push around, someone who could earn their respect, and Rothchild was all of that. And once Paul made a commitment he stuck to it. With great reluctance I finally said, "Paul, I never thought I'd say this to you, but you owe me. You've got to do this band. You are the only person for the job." And Paul said … 'Well, if you put it that way.' "

Holzman had to meet Rothchild's parole officer and sign documents guaranteeing Rothchild's good conduct. True to his reputation, the tough

Bostonian got the band practising hard for two weeks solid before any recording began. Once in the studio, "we nailed the sound on the first day," said sound engineer Bruce Botnick. "And after that, no one touched a knob, an amplifier, or a microphone. It was all recorded live. Even tape delays on the voice were done in the moment."

Among these capable musicians, Jim Morrison was clearly the odd man out – being unable to play an instrument and relatively ignorant of music. "Jim was a huge Elvis fan and an even bigger Sinatra fan," Botnick noticed with a little bemusement. "Jim had this enormous vocal range and could go from a whisper to a scream, from zero to sixty in two seconds. He could croon and then scream … [But] Jim wasn't a musician." Paul Rothchild noticed that Morrison's "timing was terrible – whenever he picked up maracas or a tambourine, myself or someone in the band would try to take it away from him."

Like all great artists, though, Morrison instinctively knew from which well to drink. One key influence turned out to be Van Morrison, front man of the Belfast group Them. Robby Krieger explained, "In the early Whisky days [Van Morrison] was a terror. I mean you'd be afraid to come anywhere near that stage – drunk as hell, throwing the mic around, screaming and railing and stuff. He had some real devils inside." Jim Morrison carefully studied the Belfast singer's brand of bewitched R&B, and the principle of trance carried much of his subsequent career. One of his friends, Digby Diehl, confirmed, "Jim would work himself into these frenzies. I would arrive with him and sit backstage and watch him in an hour or so drink or toke himself up into the performer that went on stage. Often he'd arrive as the shy poet, and he would become that wild, theatrical, sexual figure."

Recorded in just one week, the Doors' debut album was a treasure trove of timeless classics. Although "Light My Fire" would later provide the commercial breakthrough, it was the album's closing track that would resonate longest. "We were in the middle of recording 'The End,' a landmark composition," Paul Rothchild recalled. "I got chills top to bottom … And at the end of the take, I was drained as anyone out in the room from the experience."

To faithfully capture the spirit of this organically written epic, Jim Morrison had dropped some acid before arriving at the studio. After the tension of the first take, Rothchild called a break, whereupon Morrison wandered off to a nearby church, tripping intensely. Staring at a statue of the Virgin Mary, he got so worked up about the song's hidden meanings that his second take contained a thunderous performance of the song's latter section where "the killer awoke before dawn, he put his boots on," then "walked on down the hall" to his Oedipal catharsis. Rothchild spliced the silky intro of the first take with the powerful finale of the second to create the now-legendary masterpiece. "And at that moment," said Rothchild, "I knew the band was going to be famous."

The only lingering question mark was Jim Morrison's volatility. After "The End" session wrapped up, Morrison went back to the empty studio, still tripping, and sprayed a fire extinguisher around the facilities, actually covering a harpsichord in foam. Although Holzman had to write a cheque for damages, he was pleasantly surprised with the Doors' subsequent professionalism. When he suggested they wait four months for a January 1967 release to avoid being drowned out by the usual glut of pre-Christmas products, the band accepted without any tantrums. Also, despite the fact that Jim Morrison and Robby Krieger were the main songwriters, "all monies from performing, writing and publishing were split equally and all copyrights were listed in the name of the entire band."

While they waited for their album launch, Holzman secured them a month's residency in New York at Ondine on Fifty-ninth Street, a hot spot whose sophisticated crowd Ray Manzarek described as "all the Andy Warhols and plastic inedible kinds of chicks and mod guys." This October 1966 reconnaissance mission deep inside New York's velvety underground provided the Doors with a glimpse of the very cutting edge of the art and music scene. "When it came to their visual image," said Holzman, "the Doors knew what needed to be done – they put their personal egos aside and Jim upfront. During the photo shoot for the first album cover they said ... , 'Let's make Jim a little bigger.' They knew he was the draw."

One famous write-up in *Rolling Stone* mused that "Morrison is so pretty he looks like he was made up on the phone by two fags." Inspired by Marlon Brando's biker costume in *The Wild One,* Jim Morrison found a clothing designer, Mirandi Babitz, to work up his black-and-white silhouette, including his now-iconic belt and tight leather trousers.

Elektra's head of promotions, Steve Harris, noticed that "he knew how to look at a camera, better than any rock star I've ever known. He posed … Jim had a degree in film from UCLA." As another perceptive witness, promoter Bill Graham, put it, "Watch him just move, the way he goes toward the microphone, what he does with the microphone stand, but mainly how he gets from one space to another, how he prowls the stage, and there's that, if you want to call it, snake, panther, slithery whispery movement to him that exuded sexuality, sensuality. Especially dressed dark, the black leather pants … No underwear. Jim Morrison doesn't wear 'em. Very powerful statement."

Both band and record company were thinking along the same lines. By shooting a video for "Break On Through" – a novel idea at the time – Elektra supplied TV networks with a striking image of the band's true personality. "We could not afford to tour the Doors at the beginning," Holzman explained. "And I didn't want them performing in front of distracted teenagers on shows like *Bandstand* and *Hullabaloo*. I thought it would shift the focus away from the music. I wanted the exposure, but in a controlled situation." Still thinking in widescreen, Holzman also rented Doors billboards along Sunset Strip.

Despite its title, the album's accompanying single "Break On Through" only peaked at No. 106 on the *Billboard* charts – a resolute flop under the circumstances. However, an encouraging momentum was gathering behind the album, whose most instantly popular track seemed to be the seven-minute "Light My Fire." Realising they'd probably backed the wrong horse, Paul Rothchild made a three-and-a-half-minute radio edit by chopping out a large chunk of the swirling instrumental section. Hearing it, Ray Manzarek and Robby Krieger looked at each other, skin crawling. Rothchild made his case. "Just imagine you're a kid in Minneapolis, Minnesota, you're seventeen years old, and you've never heard of the Doors. You love rock 'n' roll – and this comes on the radio."

Then Morrison tipped the vote. "Well, if you hear it on the radio like this, and you like it, and go out and buy the album, then you get the bonus of a seven-minute 'Light My Fire' that you never expected."

The band finally agreed. "Call New York and tell Jac it's a go."

At the end of the day, as Holzman points out "they really wanted to make it, and Jim wanted the ride." Elektra's PR chief, Steve Harris, also began noticing Morrison's deft ability to hypnotise, even manipulate, those around him to facilitate his climb to the summit. "Jim had a way of knowing who was important and who was going to be important in his life, and conquering that person – man or woman," said Harris. That applied even to the women in the Elektra entourage – both Jac Holzman's and Steve Harris's wives admitted that Jim Morrison would gaze into their eyes, determined to win their admiration and support.

As the short version of "Light My Fire" began rolling through the radio networks, the Doors were being carried by an entire West Coast wave, gathering in size and momentum throughout the spring of 1967. Making it happen was a handful of Los Angeles impresarios, in particular Lou Adler, who, having noticed the signals on the street, seemed to be making all the right moves – right time, right place. The Mamas & the Papas' smash hit "California Dreamin'" earlier that winter had seized the spirit of the moment. So, together with the group's front man, John Phillips, Adler began planning the crowning moment of West Coast flower power – the Monterey International Pop Festival. Its hypnotic invitation floated on American airwaves throughout that magical spring – "if you're goin' to San Francisco, be sure to wear some flowers in your hair."

With the Beatles and the Stones taking a sabbatical from live shows, Andrew Loog Oldham convinced Lou Adler that the Who would amply suffice as ambassadors of London rock. Both Oldham and Paul McCartney then convinced Adler to take a blind gamble on Jimi Hendrix, at the time just a London phenomenon. Reprise boss Mo Ostin, with admirable prescience, had just signed Hendrix's American rights from Track, an indie set up by Who managers Kit Lambert and Chris Stamp.

The shy but determined Mo Ostin was another rising force on the West Coast. Having learned the business at the mythical jazz label Verve, he had been quietly navigating Frank Sinatra's label into the swinging sixties thanks initially to a licence agreement with British indie Pye Records. That one deal secured Reprise the North American rights to the Kinks and Petula Clark. Assiduously thumbing through trade magazines ordered from London, Ostin watched as Jimi Hendrix's first single, "Hey

Joe," entered the U.K. top ten in February 1967, followed in March by another British hit single, "Purple Haze."

Alas, as Ostin knew, due to a licensing agreement between Atlantic and Decca, which distributed Track, Ahmet Ertegun had first call on Hendrix's North American rights. "I couldn't believe they passed on Hendrix," admitted Ostin, who learned that Ertegun, in a rare lapse of judgment, thought Hendrix was too like B. B. King. "I went after him very, very quickly. I called people in England whose opinion I trusted, and they all told me what an outstanding performer Hendrix was. And that look Hendrix had – it was phenomenal. I couldn't stop thinking about him. All of the elements were present in Hendrix to indicate that he might be something important – a major find."

Not only would Monterey soon provide Jimi Hendrix with a spectacular homecoming, his American breakthrough set up Mo Ostin's giant future. The festival's biggest challenge, however, was convincing the San Francisco underground bands to participate for free. As Warner Bros. Records executive Joe Smith already knew, the Bay Area groups were a law unto themselves. "Truthfully, I hadn't a clue as to what the Grateful Dead were all about when I signed them in 1966," confessed Smith, "but I did realise that there was a buzz on the street. The band had something like seven managers at the time. You never knew which one would arrive at a meeting or pick up the phone."

Signing them turned into a long, tedious saga of mutual paranoia. The band, having heard all kinds of horror stories, considered the Warner executives bloodsucking capitalists. The Warner executives, having heard their own horror stories, were terrified of ingesting any liquid in the band's company. Finally, "my wife and I went to the Avalon Ballroom and, wow, it was like walking into a Fellini movie," recalled Smith, who stood out like a suit at a hippie party. "The music, the lights, the drugs, the people dancing, the overall craziness – it was just overwhelming. We watched and listened with our mouths open the whole time. When it was over, we did the deal. The Grateful Dead had its recording contract, and Warner Bros. had its first big hippie band."

Still, $25,000 was a risky bet for such drugged-out, unreliable people. Realising that other happening flower-power acts such as Janis Joplin and

Country Joe were ripe for the taking, Joe Smith told his Warner boss, Mike Maitland, "I can sign every act up there for $25,000 apiece."

"Let's see how we make out with the Dead," replied Maitland with understandable caution.

"It'll be too late by then," concluded Smith.

Monterey proved his point. About 55,000 people stayed for the entire event, while the big shows at night attracted up to about 90,000. Not only was it the world's first experiment with a modern sound system, as a media showcase, Monterey was a veritable coup, in large part thanks to Beatles publicist Derek Taylor, who attracted over one thousand media personalities.

Interestingly, for the London contingent, Californian *flower power* was hard to stomach. "Haight Ashbury was like a fucking tourist dive," Who guitarist Pete Townshend thought. "What was going on in London at the time seemed to be much more interesting. I was surprised at how shallow it all seemed. The bands at Monterey were really pretty bad. I couldn't get Janis Joplin ... She was just an ugly, hard-drinking, screaming woman who to me didn't evoke Ike and Tina Turner or any of the other people whom she was compared to. Her band the Holding Company were just about the worst fucking band I'd heard. Country Joe & the Fish were on; Country Joe was interesting as a kind of political balladeer but the band put together around himself were all geeks ... When Otis Redding walked on with Booker T & the MGs, complemented by the Memphis Horns, I started to think this means something. But I thought, even Otis Redding is gonna get blown away when the Who and Hendrix walk on stage."

Andrew Loog Oldham also returned to London unimpressed by what he'd seen at Monterey. "I didn't like the bands; to me they weren't stars. They were dirtier than thou, unoriginal and totally fuelled by drugs and liquor. Although via Monterey ... these new bands seized back for America a large part of the pop 'n' rock mantle from Britain, I couldn't understand the attraction. I like my stars to behave like stars." There was little doubt about the event's general effect on the music industry. Monterey was the defining moment when counterculture went mass market, convincing independents and majors alike what type of bands to sign. Record bosses who hadn't been at Newport in 1965 now got the picture, loud and clear.

A&M founder Jerry Moss was there, feeling slightly sore he had no acts on the bill, but in equal measure resolutely enchanted by hippie culture. The man holding the winning ticket, Mo Ostin, was also watching from the crowd as Hendrix torched his guitar. "I've always wondered if I would have been able to sign Hendrix after the festival," mused Ostin. "Afterwards, I had A&R people from other labels coming up to me and asking me if I was interested in selling his contract." At Monterey, Ostin also met a hip, well-connected Englishman, Andy Wickham, who had started out under Andrew Loog Oldham's tutelage in London and was working for Lou Adler. Ostin hired him as an A&R man, and Wickham pointed him to Joni Mitchell, Jethro Tull and Van Morrison.

"When we saw the numbers that those records could sell in," explained Mo Ostin, "we said, 'Wow, there's something here.' You'd struggle with a middle-of-the-road artist to sell maybe 300,000 albums when you could sell two million Jimi Hendrix albums. Frank Sinatra never sold two million albums. Dean Martin never sold two million albums. I don't think there were too many artists who ever sold two million albums until this wave of *involving* records."

Although neither the Doors nor Love played at Monterey, Elektra was reaping the rewards. "By the spring of 1967," recalled Jac Holzman, "the Doors were smoking, and by Monterey, the label was on fire. L.A. was the place." As Californian psychedelia captured the contemporary imagination, the radio-friendly edit of "Light My Fire" provided the elusive breakthrough. "After 'Light My Fire' everything just exploded," said Ray Manzarek. "In mid-July 1967, the Doors were the number one band in America."

After seventeen eventful years chasing his muse through the wilderness, Jac Holzman had entered the major league. Already the owner of a chauffeur-driven Cadillac, he celebrated Elektra's first No. 1 single by splurging on various gifts. Doors drummer John Densmore received a horse. Robby Krieger and Ray Manzarek were given film equipment. Even the parole officer who facilitated Paul Rothchild's sojourn in Los Angeles was sent a gold disc.

"I remember the day in 1967," said Rothchild, "Jac walked up to me in the hall and said 'Paul, this is the first year we're going to break five million, gross.' There were about fourteen or fifteen of us on the payroll. And then all hell broke loose. The company got huge. Jac was running a corporation. The record part of it was tangential for a long time … I watched him study what it takes to be an executive, and that's when Elektra got into its big stride. He equipped himself and Nina with the tools of the yuppiedom of the day. You know, a nice apartment – the first co-op I'd ever been in in my life in New York – great kitchen, great food on the table, stuff on the walls … good collections."

Striking while the iron was hot, Holzman reinvested profits back into Los Angeles. "Nailing down real estate on La Cienega was the easy part," recalled Holzman, who felt that Elektra could never be a genuine presence on the West coast without its own recording facility. He spent $120,000 building a state-of-the-art studio beside the main offices – in his own words, "the fulfilment of a dream."

After eight decades of New York being the nerve centre of America's vast record industry, the psychedelic explosion put Los Angeles firmly on the musical map. Battle lines were being redrawn; networks were being rewired; the British underground had even sold an American blues guitarist back to America, via Monterey. Just three years after the British Invasion landed at JFK, a new dream was swirling across the continent from west to east, inviting the boom generation to "turn on, tune in, drop out."

16. ON BLACK CANVAS

NO ROMANCE WITHOUT FINANCE. ALTHOUGH REMEMBERED IN POPULAR CULTURE as the *Summer of Love,* when accounts for 1967 were compiled, the American record industry's annual turnover, for the first time ever, exceeded $1 billion. With various corporate events, including the buyouts of both Atlantic and Warner, 1967 in many respects marked the beginning of the record industry as we know it today.

Gazing out across Manhattan, the debonair Goddard Lieberson, president of the CBS Records group, was one key eyewitness to this giant renaissance. Having begun his long career as a young man in the Great Depression, the enlightened mogul understood the global surge in teen music as cue to start thinking about the future – both Columbia's and his own.

The only problem was that he was still having a great time being Goddard Lieberson. One of the less admirable aspects of his style of presidency was a personal aversion to team building. Maintaining an aloof distance from his senior management, he allowed vicious power struggles to run riot in the floors below. In particular, two younger bucks had been vying for position throughout the midsixties: Bill Gallagher, Columbia's sales chief, and Clive Davis, a lawyer who had been promoted to the international division.

Since Goddard Lieberson took over Columbia in 1956, he had been flying around the world, wining and dining in various languages with the best minds of his generation. The more he was out of the office, the worse the office politics got. The more they tried to outperform one another, the less they demanded from him. It was a perfect arrangement from which both company and president benefitted. Occasionally, when tempers overheated, Lieberson would step in as a peacemaker.

The only problem was that Goddard Lieberson did have to answer to the chairman of CBS Inc., Bill Paley, who was wont to throw a wrench into the gears occasionally. As the baby boom prompted corporations to buy into youth products, CBS found itself the reluctant stepfather of Fender Guitars and a toy company called Creative Playthings. It didn't take long to realise that such haphazard acquisitions were a mistake, so Paley called in the Harvard Business School to study the CBS empire. Then came an unwelcome surprise for Goddard Lieberson. The consultants advised Paley that CBS Records and its two big labels, Columbia and Epic, should combine marketing and A&R into one omnipotent department, the very thing Lieberson had always resisted. To complicate matters, Columbia's head of pop A&R, Mitch Miller, decided to leave the company.

Being the monarchical figure that he was, rather than get his own hands dirty, Lieberson decided to create a buffer between his busy lifestyle and the thankless headache of reorganising Columbia. To most insiders, the obvious contender for a major promotion was Bill Gallagher, who had been instrumental in setting up CBS's distribution system. However, Lieberson had an instinctive preference for Clive Davis, admitting, "I have a penchant for lawyers because ... I think the training they've had gives them some cultural background, in addition to a very clear way of thinking that's not too frequently messed up with emotionalism."

At this late stage in his career, Lieberson was concerned about maintaining Columbia's cultural legacy. For years, he had been investing a small portion of profits on money-losing projects he felt were of historical or artistic importance. He shuddered at the idea that Columbia might be taken over by *commerçants* who understood only warehouses and ledgers.

So Lieberson called Davis up to his office and offered the thirty-three-year-old a new post with an unusual title, administrative vice president. What Lieberson hadn't foreseen was that Clive Davis, despite being a musically illiterate lawyer, harboured big ambitions. Lieberson also underestimated the rapidity and scale of change in popular culture. In the past, fifty-six years of age was not too old to run Columbia, but by 1967, Goddard Lieberson looked like a dinosaur from a bygone age. The numbers spoke for themselves; although the company still commanded the biggest turnover in the industry, pre-tax profits had flattened to just $5 million. At a time when the record industry was rapidly expanding, Columbia was going cold.

As the court intrigue played out upstairs, throughout the spring and summer of 1967, John Hammond, then aged fifty-seven, landed Columbia a rare fish. He had stumbled on a thirty-two-year-old poet from Montreal by the name of Leonard Cohen. A friend named Mary Martin, who would later be Van Morrison's manager, called him with the tip, warning that although Cohen was a "wonderful songwriter," he was "sort of strange" and unlikely to interest the rank and file at Columbia.

Always curious, Hammond watched a documentary entitled *Ladies and Gentlemen ... Mr Leonard Cohen* that had been made by the National Film Board of Canada about Cohen's career as a young poet and novelist. His best-known works were the novel *Beautiful Losers* and *The Spice-Box of Earth*, a book of poetry. Like Hammond, Cohen was well heeled, a beneficiary of a small family trust fund. Yet, also like Hammond, Cohen wasn't interested in money. Whether flush or going through a lean phase, he always lived frugally and was generous to others.

The Cohen family had made their fortune in the clothing business, and, again like Hammond, Leonard had grown up in a world of maids, butlers and chauffeurs. Since 1961, he had been hiding away with other bohemian exiles on the Greek island of Hydra writing to the sleepless tempo of amphetamines. Cohen enjoyed a youth following in Canada, and he had just written folk diva Judy Collins a song with gorgeously embroidered lyrics, "Suzanne," which she included on her latest album and showcased on her TV show. The more Hammond found out about Cohen, the better he sounded.

Hammond decided to invite him out to lunch. They met in the lobby of the Chelsea Hotel, then walked around the corner to a restaurant on Twenty-third Street. Cohen knew about Hammond's giant legacy as a talent scout; he later remarked, "He stands, and has always stood for, a certain kind of integrity and morality, in music and his dealings with musicians. I don't think there's another man of his stature in the country." Looking across the table, Hammond saw an eccentric with an absolute belief in his destiny as an artist. Cohen was no fake.

After lunch, they headed back to the Chelsea Hotel, where, sitting on the edge of his bed, Cohen played a handful of songs: "The Master Song," "The Stranger Song," "Suzanne," and "Hey, That's No Way to Say Goodbye." Hammond sat silently, saying nothing between songs. He noticed Cohen's left hand struggling with basic chord changes, but Cohen had developed his own peculiar style of flamenco finger picking, which was hypnotic. His lyrics were genuine poetry on a par with Bob Dylan's though different, perhaps reflecting Cohen's more continental, academic background. Above all, Cohen was an enchanter whose songs drew the listener to a timeless place.

"You've got it," said Hammond, as Cohen put his guitar down. Cohen wasn't sure whether *it* referred to a talent or a record contract.

Hammond's problem, as his friend had predicted from the outset, was convincing Columbia. Hammond first petitioned Bill Gallagher. "A 32-year-old poet?" gasped Gallagher in disbelief. "Are you crazy, John? How are we going to sell him?"

In an attempt to assemble some commercial arguments, Hammond arranged to meet with an old friend who happened to be Cohen's book publisher, Tom Guinzberg of Viking Press. Over lunch, Hammond began his line of inquiry. "I'm about to sign one of your writers, Leonard Cohen."

"Well, you may be interested to know that we sold five hundred and forty copies for his last book of poems," Guinzberg replied in reference to *The Spice-Box of Earth*. "You're really crazy, John!"

"Didn't *Beautiful Losers* do well in paperback?" Hammond persisted.

"Yes, it's true. Its sexual imagery has a wide public unappreciative of poetry, and it must have sold six hundred thousand copies by now."

"Doesn't that make you believe he has something?"

"No, not really," Guinzberg concluded.

Fortunately, the complex political situation at CBS played out in Cohen's favour. Feeling circumstances sliding out of his control, Goddard

Lieberson decided to get out while he was ahead. He negotiated a semi-retirement position as chairman of the board and passed over the presidency to Clive Davis, just thirty-five years of age.

The revolution inside Columbia coincided with Clive Davis's attendance at Monterey, which, in his own words, "changed me as a person." As one of his protégés, the witty Walter Yetnikoff, recalled, "He came back transformed. He described it in lofty terms. 'I have,' he said 'caught a glimpse of the new world.' He spoke of the sweetness of the flower children and the transcending nature of their music. He put on a necklace and love beads. He became a convert ... He started wearing Nehru jackets and tinted glasses. I think Clive was sincere. And just as sincerely, inside his head I believe he saw dancing dollar signs."

When Hammond explained his belief in Leonard Cohen to the new boss, careful to mention that Bill Gallagher was against the deal, Davis signed the contract. In the studio later that summer, Hammond teamed up the nervous singer with a sensitive bass player, Willie Ruff, to record the basic tracks as a duo. As Hammond had hoped, the chemistry between the two men clicked. Cohen's haunting ballads were given structure and a hypnotic heartbeat thanks to Ruff's unintrusive yet supportive punctuation.

To create a powerful mood, Cohen demanded that all the lights be turned off. Placing candles and incense around the relatively small room made Studio E feel like an orthodox church. When Cohen explained how he had written his songs looking in a mirror, Hammond found one in the building. As Cohen sang transfixed before his own dim reflection, the only show of excitement that Hammond seems to have expressed from behind his newspaper was "Watch out, Dylan!" after one particularly powerful take.

Hearing Cohen and Ruff's enchanting simplicity, Hammond envisioned an arid album with as little instrumental arrangement as possible. As Cohen listened to the stark-sounding playbacks, however, he winced at the naked tremble of his own voice. Can I have reverberation, strings, mandolins, fairground organs, lady backing vocalists, he pleaded. The inevitable disagreement on production style led to a standoff. In a familiar scenario, a twenty-six-year-old producer, John Simon, was wheeled in to embellish the recordings with a whole host of orchestral frills, but Cohen quickly got confused when Simon suggested adding drums and syncopated piano to "Suzanne."

Cohen tried to mix the final cuts himself but struggled to nail down his ornate creations. Hammond dropped in to have a listen. "Whatever spell you've created has been lost," he told Cohen bluntly. "This isn't you any longer." Throughout his long career, Hammond had seen hundreds of efforts to make records more commercial actually turn buyers off. Imperfect as his singing performances were, Cohen had to admit his songs spoke more poignantly as naked confessions. So Hammond began paring down the mixes in a backward process he described as "like trying to take the sugar back out of the coffee." Nonetheless, by editing and reverberating the orchestral detail into the background, leaving Cohen's trembling voice prominently in the foreground, he created a stark black canvas containing just occasional splashes of abstract colour.

The unusual record by the 30-something Canadian poet went from cult phenomenon to classic, earning Cohen justified comparisons with Bob Dylan. Revered as a genius in Europe throughout his long career, Cohen would go on to sell over 30 million records for Columbia – leaving in his wake an artistic legacy that has grown cumulatively for decades. At a time when most record men were scrambling around for young rockers, Leonard Cohen was another timeless legend personally escorted into the pantheon of modern music by the great John Hammond.

Although he had countersigned the contract, Clive Davis was only moderately impressed with Leonard Cohen. To put Columbia firmly back in the driver's seat, Davis needed a roster of psychedelic rock. He drew up shopping lists of acts he'd seen at Monterey; his obsession was Janis Joplin, whose band, Big Brother & the Holding Company, was already signed to an independent but, following Monterey, had signed a management contract with Albert Grossman, who in turn succeeded in moving them to Columbia for $250,000.

As contracts were being formalised in the boardroom, Joplin suggested to Davis that they consummate the deal by having sex. Turning slightly green, Davis, with his disarming manners, managed to wriggle out of the room unscathed. Before he did, he assured the musicians that Columbia was not as formal as its boardroom looked. One of Joplin's entourage, feeling those comments needed to be put to the test, duly removed all of his clothes.

Although Clive Davis didn't really have an ear to begin with, he learned the necessary skills of the hit-making business. "Clive's upward climb was impressive and, at times, funny," Yetnikoff remembered. "One afternoon I dropped by his office and saw he was taking dancing lessons so he could shake his ass to the contemporary music he was champion-ing … 'Loosen up,' his teacher would urge. Clive tried, but rather than resemble the free-flowing free-loving hippies he'd seen at Monterey, he looked like Dr. Frankenstein's unwieldy monster."

Turning a definitive page on the Lieberson epoch, Davis ominously told Bill Gallagher's loyalists in the sales departments that if they weren't reading *Rolling Stone* maybe they were in the wrong business. "Clive was obsessed with success," explained Yetnikoff. "I'd accompany him to midtown Manhattan record stores to inspect the placement of our product. When Columbia records weren't in the front of the racks, Clive would move them there." Speaking, moving and dressing up like an entertainment don, Davis "sold like crazy," said Yetnikoff. "He fought off fierce competitors like Ahmet Ertegun and Jerry Wexler at Atlantic, seasoned vets with vast music backgrounds. By haunting concerts and hanging out backstage, Clive stayed on the scene. By carefully cultivating his persona as a hit-maker, he drew ambitious artists into his circle. He and his PR staff worked the press. Clive couldn't get enough press and soon began believing the hype surrounding his ascension. Rather than opine, he pronounced. He was the new Pope of Pop."

In the difficult art of seducing pop stars, Clive Davis's arch-rival was Ahmet Ertegun, New York's other self-ordained monarch, who was also leading his company, despite some internal resistance, into the new world of psychedelic rock. The son of a decorated ambassador, Ertegun was arguably the most deviously charming of all the great American record moguls. Wining and dining his way from London to Los Angeles, Ertegun had developed a special relationship with Brian Epstein's partner, Robert Stigwood. As well as getting the American rights to the chart-topping Bee Gees, the Stigwood connection led Ertegun to his proudest scalp of the late sixties – psychedelic blues shredders Cream.

According to Ertegun's own account, at a party for Wilson Pickett at the Scotch of St. James in London, he was struck by the skills of a twenty-year-old guitarist playing onstage. Turning to Stigwood, Ertegun insisted they develop and sign the young man by the name of Eric Clapton. Stigwood, however, claims Cream came together themselves – drummer Ginger Baker and bassist Jack Bruce had already been members of the Graham Bond Organisation, which Stigwood also managed. Ertegun "wanted the Bee Gees but he actually wasn't so keen on Cream," explained Stigwood, who became Cream's manager. "I played him their demo at Polydor in London and [Ertegun] said, 'Oh fabulous, fabulous. But not very commercial.' That's from the horse's mouth ... Part of Ahmet's charm was that he was a great storyteller but he could really [cut] many corners in his storytelling. I made him take Cream because I gave him the Bee Gees. And that is the absolute truth."

What is undeniable is that Ahmet Ertegun did a fine job guiding Cream to American stardom. Atlantic licensed Cream's American rights for the single "I Feel Free" in early 1967 and enjoyed good sales, but Ahmet Ertegun winced at its tinny, English sound. "There wasn't enough blues for my taste," said Ertegun. "Then we took over production." Fired up by a shared love for the real deal, with Ahmet Ertegun supervising operations in Atlantic's New York studios, Cream reworked an old blues song, "Lawdy Mama," into "Strange Brew." "Boy, did they play loud. I don't know how I never lost my hearing," Ertegun remembered of that session. A vibrant album of trippy blues, *Disraeli Gears,* came together in a few days, including "Sunshine of Your Love," a No. 6 smash hit that broke Cream in America. Ertegun later admitted to Stigwood, as they flew to London together, that collectively the Bee Gees and Cream constituted 50 percent of Atlantic's album turnover.

Jerry Wexler, who had a somewhat wary, competitive relationship with Ahmet Ertegun, looked on in horror as all these long-haired "rockoids" began flooding the charts. Sticking to the only music he truly loved, Wexler continued producing R&B in his favourite Alabama studio. He had no desire to accompany Ertegun chasing hippie rockers through airports. In June 1967, Atlantic had no less than eighteen singles in the *Billboard Hot 100,* including the first two slots, "Respect" by Aretha Franklin and "Groovin'" by the Young Rascals. Being conscious of history, Wexler knew his latest successes were lucky flukes defying the general flow. In the R&B landscape, VJ had collapsed, Chess was in steep decline, Stax was struggling, and Morris Levy, the Mafia-connected owner of Roulette Records, had retired.

Jerry Wexler had always been, by nature, a prophet of doom. "I never think anything is going to work out – and I think that's better than being a smarmy optimist, walking around with a happy grin while the roof's caving in over your head … Ravening fear was my motivator at Atlantic – that ran the engine for me."

For some time, Wexler had been gripped by "this feeling that a puff of wind could come along and blow us all away instantly. All you had to do was make a succession of flop records … It was either grow or disappear." Sharing Wexler's bleak prognosis, Atlantic's third shareholder, Nesuhi Ertegun began petitioning his brother to sell, even though as Wexler remembered, "Ahmet never had those feelings, or if he did he would never yield in the way I did … Ahmet had a true courage and insouciance. You know, he's always been a devout practising voluptuary. He really lived it – he gambled, took shots, and didn't worry about failure."

"I saw no reason to think that disaster was imminent," said Ahmet Ertegun. "However, they were so intent on selling, I really didn't have an option." The three partners shopped around until a potential buyer appeared: Warner–Seven Arts, neither the Warner Bros. film giant of old nor the Warner conglomerate of modern times. In 1967, Warner–Seven Arts was an unhappy marriage between the ailing Hollywood giant and a film distributor. For $184 million, Jack Warner had sold out the entire Warner Bros. group, including the two record labels Warner Bros. Records and Reprise, to Eliot Hyman, owner of Seven Arts.

For Ahmet Ertegun, Hyman was "a businessman and wheeler-dealer of questionable reputation. There was nothing about Warner–Seven Arts that enchanted us." The only remaining question was how much. "We had some Wall Street big shots come in to represent us," explained Wexler, "and they did a horrible job. We wound up selling for about half what we should have got … We sold it for $17.5 million when it was worth $35 million … I just have a feeling that our main negotiator was of a very low order of intelligence."

The ink was barely dry, in late 1967, when Jerry Wexler confessed to his partners that "we made a big mistake. We undersold. I regret it, and always will." To prove the point, the following year, Atlantic's turnover jumped to $45 million. Wexler and Ertegun tried to buy back Atlantic for $40 million, but Eliot Hyman flatly turned them down. The situation deteriorated to such a low point that all of Atlantic's top staff threatened to resign unless the deal was renegotiated. Because, as Ertegun reasoned, "the company did not have very much value without the management … they had to sweeten the deal, so to speak … We almost sold it a second time." Scared his new cash cow might keel over and die, the alcoholic Eliot Hyman kept shutting up Ertegun and Wexler with additional handouts and wisely chose to resell the company before they really did leave.

Fortunately, the messy arrangement was never intended to last. "If Eliot Hyman had continued as head of the company, I probably wouldn't have stayed on," admitted Ahmet Ertegun. Within a year, though, Hyman "made his bunch," then "ran off into the night." In the corporate marketplace, three hot independent labels, Warner, Reprise and Atlantic, were up for auction in a single lot. Fortunately, a potential buyer was hovering in the shadows – and he was of a much higher order.

Whatever the effect of psychedelic music on popular culture, in purely industrial terms, the global surge of counterculture was provoking a process of concentration in which just a few giants would emerge as market leaders. It all came back to the contradiction of Britain's musical dominance and America's market size. As independent producer Bob Krasnow observed, "In England, there was a revolution taking place … There were all these English labels whose releases could be licensed … The smaller labels in the States didn't have access to that, and therefore the independent record distributors often missed out. It was the rise of the majors in many respects."

17. FORBIDDEN FRUIT

A QUIET ROT WAS SPREADING OUT FROM THE ARTISTIC EPICENTRE IN LONDON.
In early 1967, a media debate erupted courtesy of a three-part investigation in the *News of the World* given the eye-catching title "Pop Stars and Drugs: Facts That Will Shock You."

English folk singer Donovan was named in the piece and promptly busted. Then one dawn in February 1967, during an all-night party in which Keith Richards, Mick Jagger and some friends had taken their first acid trip, police arrived and began searching the house. Alas, while Jagger and Richards laughed hysterically, the police found amphetamines and marijuana in their pockets. One other guest, artist Robert Fraser, was even found in possession of heroin. Foolishly, as the police were leaving, Keith Richards decided to play a record loudly. It was that opening track on Bob Dylan's *Blonde on Blonde* with its woozy cacophony of brass and laughter, "Everybody must get stoned!" The already notorious Stones couldn't have handled the situation worse. As if by coincidence, the very day Jagger and Richards appeared in court, Brian Jones was busted for hashish possession. A concerted judicial and media campaign against drugs was in motion.

It seemed to be a poignant symbol, later that spring, when Paul McCartney took test copies of *Sgt. Pepper* out to California, he found a noticeably strung-out Brian Wilson in a studio littered with produce, recording a novelty song about vegetables. The creative force behind the Beach Boys was another pacesetter speeding into a brick wall. His daily medicine was Desbutal, a potent combination of amphetamine and barbiturate, known for its God-like highs and dark, paranoid lows. Feeling musically invincible following the knockout success of "Good Vibrations," Brian Wilson was collaborating with another speed-freak poet, Van Dyke Parks, on a new album, *Smile*. Billed as a "teenage symphony to God," its first recordings, "Surf's Up" and "Heroes and Villains," suggested something truly grandiose. Alas, Wilson drove himself and his collaborators crazy with a never-ending pattern of creating and reworking his mixes until he got confused. Capitol eventually lost patience and cancelled the release. In fact, as well as suffering from drug addiction, Brian Wilson was descending into schizophrenia.

Throughout that turbulent spring, Andrew Loog Oldham was in California, officially helping out with Monterey but actually avoiding the Stones' criminal saga in England. Suddenly, his business associate Allen Klein flew into London and announced to the *Daily Mirror,* "Their problems are mine. I'm working my ass off to get them the best lawyers and will be in the front row of the trial every day." It was a striking PR move, especially considering Oldham hadn't been consulted. Oldham later joked, "better he'd said 'their copyrights are mine.'" The shrewder and older New York accountant, who was technically Oldham's business affairs adviser, had his eyes on the prize. Knowing that Mick Jagger was beginning to reject Oldham's artistic control, Klein spotted a fissure and forced in a crowbar.

As the astute Mick Jagger knew, the fastest way to oust Oldham was to waste his money and humiliate him into resigning. When Oldham convened the band at Olympic Studios to make their next album, Jagger would arrive hours late followed by the band and an entourage of stoned hangers-on. Ignoring Oldham's directions and usually tripping on acid, the Stones jammed shabby improvisations of finger-fumbling sludge – Mellotrons, sitars, bongos. The invisible sixth Stone, Ian Stewart, who still occasionally played piano, relished Oldham's alienation, later admitting the sessions were "the worst blues we could possibly play." After three weeks, Oldham's bill at Olympic Studios stood at £18,000.

Pacing around the control room, Oldham knew that Jagger was "stoned as a matter of convenience." While playing the part of a pouting bohemian in search of artistic freedom, the rapidly maturing pop icon was taking control of the band. The only two notable highlights of an otherwise messy album eventually titled *Their Satanic Majesties Request* were "2000 Light Years from Home" and "She's a Rainbow," whose track-saving arranger, John Paul Jones, remembered "waiting forever. I just thought [the Stones] were unprofessional and boring."

It was time for Andrew Loog Oldham to walk away. "You can't fight a witch hunt," warned his worldly-wise film star friend Laurence Harvey. "It's the nature of the beast. The artist has to rise and shine and dismiss his maker – it's as true as Adam and Eve." In the high times of 1967, ideas of revolution, self-discovery, and corporate independence were on every pop star's tongue. Of course, with habitual drug use came delusions of grandeur. Seeing how the Rolling Stones were breaking free from their former master, that other Adam and Eve combination, Lennon and McCartney, wanted their own taste of the tree of knowledge.

The Beatles' will to break free coincided with the official release of *Sgt. Pepper*, their most critically acclaimed record to date, which sold 2.5 million copies in the first three months. Although a flood of reviews hailed it as their masterpiece, many raised the issue of George Martin's giant contribution. When Martin was questioned by journalists, he aroused the seething resentment of Lennon and McCartney by admitting, "It's true to say they must depend on me a lot. They know many things – but they don't know detail."

Their other worry was Brian Epstein's management. Between 1963 and 1966, EMI, its Capitol subsidiary, and its overseas licensees had sold an incredible 200 million Beatles records worldwide. Brian Epstein, enjoying a 25 percent commission on all Beatles revenue, was also the proud owner of the Saville Theatre, one of London's trendiest venues, where he had his own royal box and side-stage bar to entertain friends and business contacts. Paul McCartney and John Lennon, however, knew they were on a shit deal with EMI – an embarrassing fact further emphasised when Allen Klein renegotiated a fantastic deal for the Stones with Decca. There was also the serious problem of Britain's tax laws in a period dominated by Labour governments. In early 1967, the Beatles' accountant warned that if they didn't invest profits in business ventures, the tax man would skim off a shocking 86 percent of their personal earnings.

Feeling the Beatles pushing him aside – in particular Paul McCartney, who appeared to be the chief instigator of the revolt – Brian Epstein had spent his last months wrestling with demons. While he was undergoing professional treatment for his pill addiction, his father passed away. Spending time with his bereaved mother kept him out of trouble, but despite his best efforts, Epstein kept lapsing back to his bad old ways, popping too many pills and prowling the streets of London for young men. Friends noticed his sweating and incessant jaw grinding as tensions with business partner Robert Stigwood were poised to end in litigation. That August, in a moment of insomniac carelessness, Epstein topped up on too many sleeping pills and expired in his sleep.

The Beatles were in Wales on a meditation retreat with the Maharishi Mahesh Yogi when news of Epstein's death arrived. "We've fuckin' had it," Lennon thought to himself. Publicly, after spiritual counsel with the Maharishi, he repeated the guru's convoluted mumbo-jumbo to a posse of journalists. "Brian is just passing into the next phase. His spirit is still around and always will be. It's a physical memory we have of him, and as men we will build on that memory." A band meeting was convened in McCartney's house that Friday afternoon. The news was daunting: Epstein hadn't left a will; so ownership of his management agency, NEMS, would probably pass over to his brother, Clive Epstein, who had no experience of the music business. The Beatles had no paperwork of their own; all their record and film contracts were filed away somewhere in Epstein's office. They didn't even know where their money was banked. As their assistant Neil Aspinal explained, "It didn't make them vulnerable, but it did make them realise that they had to get it together … They needed an office and an organisation of their own."

So they formed Apple – a multimedia corporation containing seven alphabetically progressive botanical subsidiaries: Apricot, Blackberry, Cornflower, Daffodil, Edelweiss, Foxglove and Greengage. With a £1 million treasure chest of accumulated royalties, Lennon enthusiastically announced to his friends, "We're just going to do – *everything*! … We'll have electronics, we'll have clothes, we'll have publishing, we'll have music. We're going to be talent spotters."

At exactly the same time, the BBC launched Radio 1, whose first broadcast, on September 30, 1967, was "Theme One," a baroque-pop jingle composed by George Martin. The North Sea pirate-radio ships, active from 1964 to 1967, had proved instrumental in making Britain arguably the world's most fertile habitat for cutting-edge pop. Radio Caroline came first in early 1964, quickly followed by Radio Atlanta and then the most successful offshore station, Radio London, a former U.S. minesweeper anchored off the southeast coast. As the total number of pirate-radio ships rose to twenty-one, some 15 million listeners were tuning in every day.

When Parliament began legislating to ban pirate-radio ships, with admirable pragmatism the BBC began studying the hugely popular Radio London, whose Top 40 format copied American radio. By hiring the best deejays from the ships, the psychedelic underground was given a giant vent into national broadcasting service – which in England's tax-funded system was intended to both entertain and spread culture.

Feeding these young, daring deejays was a new generation of independent labels. The Who's managers, Kit Lambert and Chris Stamp, had launched the Jimi Hendrix Experience on their own Track label. Robert Stigwood released Cream's debut on his own indie, Reaction Records. Denny Cordell had his Deram label, which produced Procol Harum. In 1968, Fleetwood Mac, then fronted by the brilliant blues guitarist Peter Green, released their debut album on Mike Vernon's blues label, Blue Horizon. Andrew Loog Oldham's Immediate Records broke the Small Faces, whose landmark 1968 album *Ogdens' Nut Gone Flake* stands as a monument to the London spirit.

Of all the new independents, there was one record man with a unique past and future: Chris Blackwell, founder of Island Records. In addition to breaking acts such as Traffic, Jethro Tull, King Crimson, Free, Cat Stevens, Roxy Music, Bob Marley and Emerson, Lake & Palmer, Island incubated two world-conquering labels, Chrysalis and Virgin. In the geology of British rock, Island Records formed around the psychedelic volcano and changed the British musical landscape forever after. Accordingly, Chris Blackwell stands as probably the most important record man in the history of British music.

Having started out importing Caribbean records into England, he had taken an unorthodox route into the rock 'n' roll business. He was a white Jamaican, athletic, handsome and well spoken, who despite being somewhat reserved stood out among his contemporaries. His unusual accent, speckled with colonial nuances, echoed a distant world that few Londoners even knew of.

Born in 1937, Chris Blackwell was a few years older than the majority of characters who made the sixties swing. He was also a rare kind of ethnic mixture, even by Caribbean standards. His father, Middleton Joseph Blackwell, was a Protestant Irishman of military stock who hailed from Westport in County Mayo. His mother, Blanche Lindo, was the daughter of a wealthy Jamaican merchant dynasty whose Sephardic Jewish origins stretched back to Portugal in the seventeenth century.

As with so many great record men, it was a bittersweet childhood that forged Chris Blackwell's personality and career. Despite his privileged, sunny, multicultural horizons, he was an only child who was dealt some unlucky cards. As a result of severe bronchial asthma, he was kept at home with the house servants, meaning he could not read or write at the age of eight. He also witnessed more than his fair share of domestic drama; both of his parents were socialites who entertained the likes of Errol Flynn, Noël Coward and James Bond author Ian Fleming, in what Blackwell described as "great dinner parties where [my father] used to play Wagner and Strauss very loud."

When he was twelve and struggling at school, his parents divorced in unpleasant circumstances, causing both an emotional and geographical upheaval for their son. Chris was shipped off to Harrow, a prestigious English boarding school – both thousands of miles from his estranged parents and far behind his classmates academically. His father relocated to a town near Chicago, meaning Blackwell's teenaged years were spent migrating between England, Jamaica and Illinois. While visiting his father in the early fifties, he travelled the forty miles into Chicago to see his first jazz club.

In these formative years, Blackwell learned to be independent, but academically, he remained easily distracted, lagging through Harrow for five years until his education was cut short at the age of seventeen when he was caught peddling alcohol and cigarettes to fellow boarders. He was flogged in front of the pupils and expelled. "Christopher might be happier elsewhere," his headmaster wrote to his mother. Floating without any qualifications, the young man briefly tried accountancy and even professional gambling but eventually returned to Jamaica in 1958, where he found a job as a water-skiing teacher at the luxurious Half Moon Hotel in Montego Bay.

For an heir of almost aristocratic lineage, Chris Blackwell was off to a disappointing start in life, but his destiny was about to change thanks to a series of freak incidents. One hot Jamaican afternoon in 1958, he headed out to sea on a motorboat excursion with some friends. Departing from the former pirate haven of Port Royal, they headed down Jamaica's southern coast. Carelessness got the boat stranded in a swamp. With no other options, the athletic Blackwell headed for help. After four hours struggling through swamps in the tropical heat, he arrived at a beach and fell down, gasping from thirst and exhaustion. Weak and dizzy, he heard a voice overhead; dreadlocks were hanging down over him. The Rastafarian pulled Blackwell to his feet and helped him to an encampment. He drank the water they gave him and collapsed into sleep.

When he woke up sometime later, the Rastas were reading from the Bible. They fed him traditional Ital food and continued their prayers until he came to his senses. Although Blackwell was too confused to understand what was happening, the memory would stay with him for life. This was the late 1950s, a time when even the tough characters in downtown Kingston steered clear of these strange-looking tribal creatures, then called "beard-men."

Shortly after his potentially fatal experience, Blackwell set up Island Records, which within a year scored a string of Jamaican hits. In 1961, when scenes of the first James Bond film, *Dr. No,* were shot in Jamaica, he briefly worked as a production assistant. The movie producer offered him a permanent job, prompting the twenty-three-year-old to consult a fortune-teller, who confidently advised him to stay in the music business.

In 1962, a new wave began dominating the Jamaican charts. Termed *Sound System*, these were producers of Jamaican R&B who deejayed their records through the streets of Kingston on the back of trucks. Rather than compete, Blackwell wisely moved to London, where he set up an import business distributing *Sound System* hit records from Sir Coxsone Dodd, Duke Reid and King Edwards. He simply drove his Mini Cooper to shops and market stalls, selling records out of the trunk. The move proved quickly lucrative; big sellers like Jimmy Cliff's "Miss Jamaica" and Derrick Morgan's "Forward March" sold 30,000 copies each.

Much to Blackwell's surprise, among London mods, the step from R&B to Jamaican rhythms wasn't all that difficult. In clubs such as the Ram Jam in Brixton, Blackwell noticed mixed crowds, all dressed alike, moving in the same manner to the infectious beats of ska. London's most happening mod club at the time was the Scene, a small basement club in Soho run by Ronan O'Rahilly, the Irish entrepreneur behind the first pirate ship, Radio Caroline. There, Blackwell noticed the in-house deejay Guy Stevens, who was such a brilliant researcher of obscure R&B records that the Rolling Stones and the Who were visiting his apartment to rummage through his collection.

In April 1964, while the Beatles were invading America, Blackwell began delivering Jamaican records to fashionable record stores in Soho. He also persuaded Guy Stevens to augment Island's catalogue with an R&B imprint, Sue Records, which quickly scored a string of British hits: "Mockingbird" by Inez & Charlie Foxx; "Land of a Thousand Dances" by Chris Kenner; "Harlem Shuffle" by Bob & Earl; "Night Train" by James Brown; and "Shotgun Wedding" by Roy C. "Guy Stevens took us out of West Indian reggae music with Sue Records," attested Island's first employee, David Betteridge. "He was buying in tracks from America, and that gave us the knowledge of how to break bands into the mainstream."

Blackwell's first major hit as a producer was the international smash "My Boy Lollipop" by Jamaican teenager Millie Small. While accompanying Millie to an appearance in Birmingham, Blackwell checked out a local band called the Spencer Davis Group which featured a fourteen-year-old prodigy, Steve Winwood. Repeating the same recipe, he signed a management deal with the band and persuaded them to rework a Jamaican song, "Keep On Running," with a pop beat and fuzzy guitar reminiscent of "I Can't Get No Satisfaction." He pitched the recording to Fontana, a Philips sublabel whose A&R man advised Blackwell to improve various aspects of the mix. In an indication of how charmingly devious Chris Blackwell could be, he waited two weeks and returned to Fontana with the exact same master. With elegance, he thanked the A&R man for such great advice. "Listen to how good it sounds now!" The flattered A&R man fell for Blackwell's trick and arranged a release. By January 1966, the smash-hit record knocked the Beatles "Day Tripper" out of Britain's No. 1 spot. Chris Blackwell, approaching thirty, was entering the big time.

When the Spencer Davis Group broke up after two albums, Island Records was big enough for Blackwell to sign Steve Winwood's new group, Traffic. Released in 1967 with the recently redesigned pink label, Traffic's first album, *Mr Fantasy,* was a jazzy, psychedelic hit, complete with elaborate sleeve artwork. Another key sign of Island's growing legitimacy arose from Blackwell's belief that "a proper label has to have a studio," which he duly built on Basing Street.

Of all the unique features that made Island boom, Blackwell's knack of attracting artist magnets was spectacular. He recruited Joe Boyd, the American émigré who had been running the seminal UFO club parties where Pink Floyd, Soft Machine and Procol Harum first got noticed. Through Boyd, Island picked up Fairport Convention, whose *Liege & Lief* probably represents the very pinnacle of English folk. Boyd also discovered and produced for Island the genius Nick Drake, whose superlative (but at the time ignored) debut album, *Five Leaves Left,* included such enduring gems as "River Man" and "Way to Blue."

To lure the highly solicited Jethro Tull to Island, Blackwell set its ambitious managers, Chris Wright and Terry Ellis, an irresistible challenge. "When you have made ten hits which go top thirty, I'll switch everything over to your own label." Chris Wright later surmised, "I would imagine at the time, Blackwell being pretty smart, as he is, would have said to himself 'They won't have ten top-ten singles anyway, so I can easily agree to that,' and he also would have said, 'But if they do, I'm gonna be making lots of money out of it as well.' It was a win-win situation for him." Wright and Ellis fulfilled the bargain and set up Chrysalis in 1969.

Blackwell's deft touch was getting noticed by the foxiest players in the game. Because Island was licensing King Crimson's North American rights to Atlantic, it was Ahmet Ertegun who gave Chris Blackwell his legendary nickname, *the baby-faced killer.* As Terry Ellis explained, "Chris would arrive from Jamaica to New York, there could be a foot of snow, and Chris would be in jeans and flip flops, a big shock of blond hair. The fresh-faced island boy! And if you're a businessman like Ahmet Ertegun, you'd think, 'This guy's easy meat, I'll deal with him.' But then when Chris gets to the bargaining table, he's tough and *very* smart."

Another important mover in Chris Blackwell's inner circle was manager David Enthoven, who brought the pioneering progressive rock group King Crimson to Island. "Blackwell allowed you to have a vision and you stood or fell by your vision," said Enthoven. "I have an undying gratitude for the man, I think he's a genius. He's a good people's person. He was very skilled in tact. He was a leader. And I unashamedly followed him." Enthoven also pointed out that "without Guy Stevens, Island would have been a very different place … It was Guy Stevens really that found King Crimson and then took them to Chris. Guy Stevens set the palate really, he was a music maniac … He actually allowed – along with Chris, to be fair – musical freedom for the artists. That's what no other record company was allowing at the time."

Chris Wright also emphasised the role of Guy Stevens in Island's early success. "Blackwell was the overall creative presence there, but he had a great aspiring partner in Guy Stevens, who moved them into areas that even Blackwell wouldn't have gone into. Guy was obviously a bit nutty like sometimes talented people can be. He had this wildish mop of frizzy hair, a little intense, wild in a way, but he was good fun." Island's managing director at the time, David Betteridge, concurred. "Guy had a very high-intensity personality; hard and driven. Very nice man, possibly bordering on the edge of madness. He saw things before anyone else. He was really an absolute genius." Having foreseen the rising tide of progressive rock, in 1969 Guy Stevens also spotted and named the glam rock group Mott the Hoople – another scoop pointing Island toward the sound and spirit of the future.

Fittingly, the dream transatlantic alliance formed between Island and the rapidly booming A&M, which had moved into Charlie Chaplin's former film studios. "That was the beginning of a great time for me," recalled A&M boss Jerry Moss. "I met Denny Cordell, I met Chris Blackwell. I would go to England every six weeks and put my bags down in Chris's house and just start going to clubs. It was perfect: They had records they wanted distributed in America and I was looking for bands. Through Denny, I got Joe Cocker, I got Procol Harum, and through Chris, I got Free, Cat Stevens, Spooky Tooth – some great English rock 'n' roll."

Moss became so enchanted by London that he opened a British A&M company in 1969. "It did affect our relationship," admitted Moss, who, though eternally grateful to his hosts for setting him up, effectively became a competitor. Of course, by then, the race to find the next super-groups was intensifying. "Every time I turned up somewhere to see a group," sighed Jerry Moss, "I'd see Ahmet Ertegun's limo parked outside … He was *very* charming and could be *very* persuasive!" When both were chasing British blues group Humble Pie, "Ahmet kept upping the ante," said Moss. "I ended up signing them for 400,000 bucks, which was a ton of money in those days." Fortunately, "Humble Pie was a very successful signing for us. We got a platinum album and we got Peter Frampton in the net."

Artistically, there wasn't a cloud in the sky, but organisationally Island Records had been built on sand. As David Betteridge explained, "In about 1968–69, Island went from being a sort of specialist West Indian label to suddenly breaking acts all over the place. And the shock of that, although we didn't feel it in that sense because we were young guns, sort of began to spell the inevitable downfall. I just think we became too successful too quickly and didn't know where to go." Betteridge paints a portrait of Chris Blackwell in those years as a creative individual who, in the prover-bial sense, only wanted to eat his meat but not his greens.

In fairness to Chris Blackwell and his hip staff, the culture of London's record industry in the late sixties was not conducive to responsible, studious management. You shall know them by their fruit, holy men say, and in those fertile years, Chris Blackwell's private island became *the* orchard for Britain's hottest acts. He hadn't been the first artistic entrepreneur to challenge EMI and Decca, but by 1969, he had gone further than his predecessors; Island had its own studio, its own fleet of vans distributing Jamaican records directly to stores – even its own pressing plant.

By about 1969, a changing of the guard was under way. Andrew Loog Oldham was falling out of the race, while Apple had degenerated into the most comical mistake in record business history. Such was the privileged opulence of daily life inside Apple's £1 million Savile Row headquarters that those lucky enough to get a seat on the gravy train were draining the river dry. A kitchen staff cooked meals on order and even kept an ever-replenishing cellar of fine wines. Its payroll of forty was teeming with friends, consultants, and various parasites who all ran up expense bills. John Lennon's acid buddy, a crank scientist nicknamed Magic Alex, had personally wasted £300,000 trying to make flying saucers, an artificial sun, electric paint, a seventy-two-track studio, and various other mad creations. The Apple boutique supposedly selling "groovy" fashion was so badly managed that it paid more than retail for its tatty stock and recorded more thefts than sales. If the original idea had been to spend money rather than pay taxes, Apple Corps had fulfilled its purpose.

In an interview given just after the abandoned *Let It Be,* John Lennon, by now a hairy heroin addict, admitted that Apple had been "pie in the sky from the start. Apple's losing money every week because it needs close running by a big businessman. It doesn't need to make vast profits, but if it carries on like this, we will all be broke in the next six months." After reading the interview, Allen Klein began asking Mick Jagger probing questions. "Who was their natural leader?" he wondered. "John," replied the deceptively shrewd Jagger, whose girlfriend Marianne Faithfull described how "Mick called up John Lennon and told him, 'you know who you should get to manage you, man? Allen Klein.' And John, who was susceptible to utopian joint projects such as alliances between the Beatles and the Stones, said, 'yeah, what a fuckin' brilliant idea.' It was a bit of a dirty trick, but once Mick had distracted Klein's attention by giving him bigger fish to fry, Mick could begin unraveling the Stones' ties to him."

Shortly after the Beatles signed with the burly New Yorker, Mick Jagger ran down the street and burst into Apple. Panting and feigning horror, he told John Lennon, "Don't sign, man! We're suing him." Of course, it was too late. Lennon, Harrison and Starr had already handed over the chewed-up and rotting Apple Corp to Klein. Complicating matters, Paul McCartney had his own personal manager – Lee Eastman.

Innocence lost – the Adam and Eve of British pop were now speaking to each other through American lawyers as a new generation of bands and record men were happily playing on Chris Blackwell's paradise island. England's future was migrating south.

18. TAURUS

ON EVERY HORIZON, IT WAS A FAMILIAR PATTERN. IN 1968, ELEKTRA BOSS
Jac Holzman, wrestling with the record man's equivalent of a midlife
crisis, took time out on the Hawaiian island of Maui. Alone on a double
bed watching the fan revolve hypnotically, he savoured the balmy stillness and, for the first time as an adult, contemplated a life beyond the
music business.

Years of workaholism had taken their toll. He'd been feeling his age
lately – a corporate president commanding operations deep inside the
hippie revolution. His marriage was doomed; drug casualties mounted in
the artist roster. Barefoot on the beach, looking out across the glassy azure
sea, he promised himself, "In five years, somehow, I'll be through with
this. I'll move here to Maui and start over."

Despite all the commercial success, Elektra had seen its fair share of
collateral damage over the previous year. The fiery genius of Arthur Lee
had consumed Love. The angelic Tim Buckley was drifting down a path
of self-indulgence and introversion that eventually led him to heroin.
Elektra's dark star, Jim Morrison, mainly as a result of alcohol abuse, now
needed full-time care. "The Morrison storm warnings grew in volume and
frequency, including Jim passing out on the studio floor, peeing in his
pants," Holzman remembered. On Paul Rothchild's recommendation, he
hired a suitable babysitter – Bob Neuwirth, Bob Dylan's former sidekick.

"It became a matter of trying to keep him interested in making a record," recalled Neuwirth, who found that if he drank at Morrison's pace, he was able to gain the singer's trust. "It was a lot of cajoling. I represented the record company. Jim knew that I was there to try to bounce ideas around him, and he didn't want to be tricked into anything." Engaged in a dangerous game of self-destructive exhibitionism, "he knew what he was doing," Neuwirth believed. "He had a method behind all of it, he had great sense of his own image, and played it."

Beefing up, with bloated jowls, Morrison was losing interest in his own sex appeal, but experience had earned him a subtle command of the fame game. The further he took his daredevil antics, the larger the legend grew. At a concert in New Haven in December 1967, he sassed back to a policeman and was maced. Exercising his First Amendment rights through the sound system, he was arrested onstage. It was "a defining moment in pop culture," Holzman believed, and it led to a multi-page report in *Life* magazine. "Advance orders for their next album, *Waiting for the Sun,* shot up to three-quarters of a million units."

Morrison kept up the same routine until, inevitably, he went too far. Performing to 13,000 on a hot March night in 1969, he taunted his Miami audience to strip off their bras and underwear, then allegedly pulled out his cock. He was arrested onstage for indecent exposure and incitement to riot. This time, however, promoters across America cancelled dates, airplay dipped, and even the music press turned on him.

In the studio, Paul Rothchild had lost the will to pry vocal performances out of the singer, who for the previous two years had been stumbling into the studio, roaring drunk, with undesirables in his shadow. Following arguments with Jac Holzman over the inappropriately slick production on *The Soft Parade,* Rothchild reverted, somewhat reluctantly, to a raw, bluesy approach on *Morrison Hotel.* He swore to never produce the Doors again.

It was an eerie illustration of how much Jim Morrison's stage persona had become his last refuge that, despite having plenty of other places to lay his head, he stalked Elektra's L.A. office, coaxing staff to a bar across the road, and even vandalising the office after hours. When one morning Morrison was found crashed out in the adjoining bushes, Elektra's Los

Angeles manager, Suzanne Helms, grit her teeth and ordered her staff not to call any ambulances. "Just leave him there," she hissed. The boss in New York wouldn't have disapproved, later joking that he'd have put traffic cones around the unconscious star. "Over the years, I purposely held back from getting too intimate with the artists," explained Holzman. "I am not their best pal or hanger-on; I run their record company. To get too close erodes your objectivity and authority, and there may come a day when you will need both."

As the American counterculture scene radicalised, Jac Holzman, fast approaching forty, had to recruit clued-in hipsters to keep Elektra's ears on the street. Among these *company freaks,* as they were called, the new face at the New York headquarters was Danny Fields, a close friend of Andy Warhol's experimental pop-art group, the Velvet Underground. "I was a sixties kind of person," said Fields. "I had started out as a New York Weavers Jewboy, and now I was Andy Warhol and hard rock and revolution and march on Washington and marijuana galore." In contrast, the Elektra senior managers were, in Fields's opinion, "suit and tie, Martini lunch, old school, Madison Avenue, fifties kind of people." His discovery of a quasi-political rock 'n' roll group from Detroit called the MC5 was, in retrospect, a natural step from what was already happening in New York. The MC5 were in fact part of a revolutionary commune. Their manager, John Sinclair, was leader of the White Panthers, an extreme left, antiracist political organisation.

"I stayed in Sinclair's house, in the commune," remembered Fields. "I loved the whole situation, the Minister for Defense with the rifle in the dining room, the men pounding on the table for food like cavemen, and all the women running in and out of the kitchen with long Mother Earth skirts on and no bras … The men did everything but drag them by the hair … I'd never met anyone like Sinclair. He would sit on the can, taking a shit with the door open, barking out orders, like a Lyndon Johnson smoking dope … I virtually signed them myself, gave him a handshake and assured him that getting Jac's approval was a mere formality."

It was through the MC5 that Danny Fields was introduced to the Stooges, featuring a nineteen-year-old Iggy Pop. As Jac Holzman explained, "John Sinclair wanted to help his *mascot* band, the Stooges, and offered to sell them in the same package. I said, 'Not without meeting them first,' which I did on a visit to set up the MC5 live sessions. There really was never an audition, but because Danny was so hot on the Stooges, I succumbed and signed them, too. If I had heard them, I probably would have declined. Good thing I didn't!"

That leap of faith cost Holzman a $15,000 advance for the MC5 and another $5,000 for the Stooges. As Danny Fields had been careful to explain over the phone, the MC5 was a brilliant live band selling out 3,000-capacity ballrooms. To best capture that revolutionary spirit, their debut album was recorded live – *Kick Out the Jams,* a sonic thunderbolt that grew into a classic over time.

Unfortunately for Elektra's staffers, the group proved to be both unmanageable and intimidating. In-house producer Bruce Botnick described these communal warriors as "really gross ... defecating on stage, as a cultural protest. Two of the guys bared their asses and took a dump and held it up." They stole equipment, demanded Elektra organise free concerts, even took out a bogus advertisement using Elektra's logo to insult record shops. An atmosphere of mutual suspicion quickly soured the collaboration. Feeling misunderstood, the MC5, for their part, were frustrated by what they saw as the record industry's hostile reception.

Even by late-sixties standards, these were radical characters who lived their music all the way to the edge. "Iggy Pop was this demonic spirit who kept falling all over himself," said Holzman. "He's playing the Electric Circus, a major club on St. Marks Place. Covered in peanut butter and glitter, he swan dives into the crowd. And they won't catch him. Iggy crashes ten feet to the floor." Elektra's promotions man, Steve Harris, remembered one unforgettable evening driving a war-torn Iggy Pop from a concert to an address on Park Avenue. Having cut himself up merci-lessly onstage, Pop stepped out of the car, still bleeding and wearing a diaper.

"Who shall I say is calling?" asked the doorman in full uniform.

"Tell her Iggy's here."

"Send him up," said the lady's voice.

Harris stood mortified in the elevator; "all the way up, the elevator operator's looking at Iggy in his diaper, bleeding. We get there and it's this magnificent apartment, just like you see in the movies, and a girl answers in a negligee – slinky, a tall Lauren Bacall-looking woman. We had a couple of drinks, then I left and Iggy stayed." The next day the singer telephoned Harris, apologising, "I can't work tonight. I had thirty-two stitches this morning."

As it was all happening, record sales for the Stooges were modest. However, as Danny Fields accurately testified "the influence they've had on other musicians and around the world has been incalculable ... They were really the proto-punk band of the world. There would have been no punk rock without them, no Sex Pistols, no Ramones or anything that was really important in the seventies." Acknowledging Fields's clairvoyance, Holzman described the whole episode as being "like an odd piece of art that someone strong-arms you into buying, and years later it turns out to be of lasting importance."

It wasn't only inside Elektra; all record companies surfing the late sixties were struggling to comprehend what appeared to be a culture of self-destruction. Over at the rapidly mutating Atlantic Records, still torn between R&B and pale-faced rock, there was Buffalo Springfield, who, despite their artistic promise, had become a sorry saga of egos and vampire managers. Their fate had been sealed within the extortionist clauses of a management contract – 75 percent of their composition revenue was being gobbled up by their manager's publishing arm, Ten-East Music. While they were enjoying their first hit, "For What It's Worth," Neil Young's first royalty statement had amounted to just $292.

It didn't get much better from there. As the story goes, whenever the sensitive Neil Young failed to turn up for a rehearsal, the ambitious Stephen Stills would hunt him down to his Laurel Canyon bungalow, where, wielding a guitar over his head, he'd scream, "You're ruining my career!" When Young began having epileptic fits before shows, Stills dismissed him as "full of shit," believing the Canadian was simply a drama queen, shirking his responsibilities.

In one recording session, when Stills and Young locked horns over who should play a guitar solo, Young had a seizure in the control room. "You will have to stop this," demanded Ahmet Ertegun. "If you two guys beat each other bloody, no one cares ... Understand?" They didn't. In

May 1968, Buffalo Springfield split up while the Atlantic sultan wrestled with another smoking meteorite – psychedelic shredders Cream, whose wild-eyed drummer, Ginger Baker, had been a heroin user since his jazz days in the early sixties. "On their third tour of America, there were rows and fighting every night," said Cream manager Robert Stigwood. "Ginger was going to murder Jack. Jack was going to commit suicide. And Eric was dying and saying, 'Get me out of here. I hate the two of them.'"

Rumour has it that when Ahmet Ertegun heard Cream had split up, he begged them, "Oh no, man, you have to do one more for me. Jerry Wexler has cancer, and he's dyin' and he wants to hear one more album from you." Imagine the musicians' surprise when, after they had dug deep to deliver a swan song, Ertegun announced the good news. "Jerry isn't dying, he's much better, he's improved." Nonetheless, thanks to the decisive crisis management of Stigwood and Ertegun, Cream bowed out elegantly, performing several farewell shows at the end of 1968. Fifteen million Cream records had been sold since their debut, the majority of them in America, on Atlantic.

In this age of high stakes, Cream, Buffalo Springfield and the Yardbirds had popularised the idea of the *supergroup* – a dream team of famous musicians invariably represented by a supermanager. As the crossroads year of 1969 marked profound changes in the very structure of the record business, a young, curly-haired agent by the name of David Geffen was getting noticed. He was the perfect symbol of the new era.

David Geffen's personal Goliath was the entire entertainment industry. Called "King David" by his doting mother, he had found a role model when, still just a teenager, he read a biography of MGM mogul Louis B. Mayer. He fibbed his way into the William Morris Agency by faking UCLA qualifications, and his lowly job in the company's mail room proved to be an effective trampoline. By reading the letters he was sorting, he not only followed the agency's affairs, he learned the art of negotiation.

Clive Davis was the first record mogul to notice him. One of the flower children who had enchanted Davis at Monterey was sultry singer-songwriter Laura Nyro, and Geffen was her agent. Although Nyro failed to make a major breakthrough on CBS, the twenty-five-year-old Geffen had the wisdom to set up her own publishing company, Tuna Fish Music, taking a 50 percent equity share for his troubles. Pending the settlement of a legal dispute with impresario Artie Mogull over Nyro's publishing rights, Geffen negotiated the sale of Tuna Fish Music to Clive Davis – a contentious, messy deal that in the end earned Geffen a couple of million.

Galloping closer to the hippie sunset, Geffen relocated to Los Angeles, where he and partner Elliot Roberts set up a management agency. They tapped straight into the growing singer-songwriter community in Laurel Canyon – a sort of rural-scented mountain retreat overlooking the sprawling metropolis of Los Angeles where David Crosby, Eric Burdon, Mama Cass, Frank Zappa, Jim Morrison, Carl Wilson and Paul Rothchild all lived. Their first giant break was with Crosby, Stills & Nash, or CSN.

Although the three stars jammed and built up an original repertoire, they had a serious contractual problem. David Crosby's former group, the Byrds, was signed to Columbia. Graham Nash's group, the Hollies, was signed to Columbia sublabel Epic. Stephen Stills, through the defunct Buffalo Springfield, was still signed to Atlantic.

Thus, Crosby, Stills & Nash would be the object of one of many duels between the rival kings of the rock world, Clive Davis and Ahmet Ertegun. Although they both disposed of money, Ertegun's advantage on Davis was a more seductive charm and, crucially, far more perceptive ears. When Ertegun heard a two-track demo Crosby, Stills & Nash had recorded with Paul Rothchild, he pulled out his chequebook. "Fill in the number," he said to Rothchild. "I don't care – whatever, it doesn't matter." Although Ertegun didn't yet have a contract to release the material, he sensed this trio could be huge.

Ertegun was also quick to notice that *his* artist, Stephen Stills, was the musical force, and as such the dominant personality. When Stills came into Atlantic's offices and moaned that he didn't even have the money to go to England to jam with Nash, Ertegun opened his drawer and handed over $2,000. Knowing their contractual tangle needed an experienced manager, Ertegun suggested that Stills visit Robert Stigwood.

"Nice to meet you, let's have dinner or something," said the gruff Stephen Stills to Stigwood in London. Then came the absolute clanger. "I saw a Rolls-Royce in the window of a car shop and I liked it. Can you have it delivered to me tomorrow?"

"Well, I think we should talk about whether we're working together first," suggested Stigwood, barely able to believe his ears.

"We've decided on you," Stills announced. "Ahmet said it'd be good."

Needless to say, Stephen Stills failed the personality test. It wasn't the only disappointment awaiting him in London. Although he was spending Ahmet Ertegun's money, he and Graham Nash brought their demo to George Harrison, who turned them down. Getting desperate, Stills contacted David Geffen and Elliot Roberts, the managers of David Crosby's ex-girlfriend Joni Mitchell.

The fearless Geffen rang Clive Davis, who refused to release Crosby and Nash but instead offered the new group a deal with CBS. Geffen then went to Atlantic, where his pleas to release Stephen Stills from his contract were met by Jerry Wexler roaring, "Get the fuck outta here!" When Wexler apologised the next day, Ertegun worked his charm on Geffen, who came around to the idea that Atlantic, being smaller and more cutting-edge, was the better vehicle for the new supergroup.

Geffen relayed various possible compromises between the two moguls until he found the ideal trade-off. Davis wanted to sign a new country rock band called Poco, which included former Buffalo Springfield guitarist Richie Furay. Ertegun, of course, pretended to protest at this outrageous demand but, having sharper ears than Davis, huffed, puffed and took the swap.

In the mix, Paul Rothchild was excluded from the CSN story the minute Geffen entered stage right. Looking back in later years, Rothchild felt "that was the beginning of the end of the love groove in American music … When David Geffen enters the California waters as a manager – the sharks have entered the lagoon."

Symbolically, Geffen negotiated novel conditions allowing all three musicians unprecedented individual freedoms – which was why they chose no band name. When the two Atlantic bosses entered the cloudy studio where the trio were recording their debut album, Jerry Wexler suggested they call it *Songs from the Big Ego*. His joke failed to inspire even a wry smile. "Guess they don't have the distance to appreciate it," Wexler muttered into his beard.

Endearingly called Captain Many Hands by his bandmates, Stephen Stills was running around playing every instrument on the album, except drums. He was even dashing in and out of the control room, adjusting the mix to his liking. The album's producer, Bill Halverson, ended up working as more of a sound engineer.

In both America and England, a pattern was forming. Aggressive managers were demanding so much money and artistic freedom on behalf of their stoned divas that the few record companies able to compete were becoming mere financiers and sales apparatuses, having little or no say over the record-making process.

One could also blame Bob Dylan's former manager Albert Grossman for setting cynical precedents in business practices. Grossman had been managing Janis Joplin, and when he discovered she was injecting heroin, he discreetly took out a $200,000 insurance policy. When she overdosed, the insurers tried to contest the payout, arguing Joplin had committed a type of involuntary suicide. Grossman denied any knowledge of Joplin's heroin addiction and walked away with the $200,000 cheque.

A new breed of heavyweight bagman was on the march. A fine example – in corpulence as well as in briefcase – was Peter Grant, who represented Led Zeppelin. A former wrestler and nightclub bouncer, Grant was a hulk of a man with piercing eyes and a handlebar mustache. In late 1968, Jerry Wexler, who had previously noted the blues virtuosity of Yardbirds guitarist Jimmy Page, outbid CBS, Warner and Island to sign up Led Zeppelin, then touted inside the industry as the next supergroup. Getting Grant's and Page's signatures cost a generous $110,000, but as Wexler acknowledged, "I signed Led Zeppelin and then had nothing to do with them. Absolutely nothing. Ahmet took over their care and cleaning. I don't think I could have tolerated them. I got along fine with Peter Grant, but I knew he was an animal."

Even the record industry's heftiest tanker, CBS Records, was being pulled by the tide. Compounding the death of Janis Joplin, Simon & Garfunkel split up in 1970. Then Andy Williams's and Johnny Cash's TV shows were axed, depriving their records of free publicity. Under Clive

Davis, the CBS market share had rocketed from about 13 percent in 1967 to 22 percent by 1970. Knowing he couldn't continue producing the growth charts he presented to the parent company, CBS Inc., as "inverted lightning bolts," he began emulating the oil industry; it had now become safer to muscle in on known oil reserves rather than prospect for crude. From here on in, the major companies would be sucked into an age of bidding wars – the stakes constantly rising.

Of all the symbolic events in 1970, there was nothing as final as the Beatles' demise. With their financial and personal problems an open secret, the corporate sell-off began. First, Clive Epstein sold his 70 percent stake in NEMS to a financial company called Triumph Investment Trust. Shortly after, Henry James sold Northern Songs to ATV for £1.2 million. Investing EMI's brimming coffers in television, Sir Joseph Lockwood, for a cool £56.6 million, bought out Associated British Picture Corporation, which included Thames Television and Elstree Studios, making EMI a diverse entertainment empire unequalled in Britain. Meanwhile, in America, EMI's subsidiary Capitol Records was grossing over $100 million.

Once Paul McCartney admitted that the band had ceased to function as a working unit, John Lennon announced to fans, "And so, dear friends, you'll just have to carry on. The dream is over." Weeks later, Sir Joseph Lockwood stepped down as EMI chairman, quitting while he was ahead. His empire entered a new decade with an annual turnover of £225 million. For those at the top of the food chain, the swinging sixties had been serious business.

In America, as in Britain, a particularly colourful chapter was drawing to a close, as a new audience for home entertainment came in off the street and curled up on the sofa.

One interesting eyewitness of this whole process was independent producer Alan Douglas, who, apart from producing Jimi Hendrix's last recordings, had released spoken word records by the Last Poets, Timothy Leary, Malcolm X and Allen Ginsberg. Having learned the business in the fifties as a jazz producer, Douglas had been around long enough to know that "at the end of 1970, it was all over in a minute. I woke up and closed everything down. Our audience was gone. From 1965 it was happening on the West Coast, in San Francisco mostly. From 1966 and 1967 it moved across the rest of the country. Then we had three or four years, that's all. It was very short-lived, the whole thing – our audience had gotten off the street and gone back to work. This whole underground symphony was over."

19. KINGS

IT ALL STARTED WITH A CERTAIN IDEA OF SELF-ENTITLEMENT, ALBEIT dressed up in flares, that in time honed its craft and increased its appetite – slowly evolving into fully fledged yuppiedom. If anything, all the clichés synonymous in popular culture with the Reagan era began creeping into the rock scene of the early seventies. It was as if the camera panned back and the starry-eyed idealist sporting bushy sideburns turned out to be an ink impression of George Washington sitting on a dollar bill.

Opening a pipeline from Laurel Canyon to Wall Street, at the dawn of the new decade, three of America's hippest independents – Atlantic, Elektra and Warner – formed a corporate alliance capable of competing head-on with the behemoths. At the top of this financial pyramid was Steve Ross, the debonair operator behind Kinney National Company, a publicly traded conglomerate owning funeral homes, parking lots, limousine services and talent agencies.

Correctly foreseeing, in 1969, that home entertainment was destined for bionic growth, Steve Ross, aged just forty-two, convinced his shareholders to buy the Warner–Seven Arts portfolio for $400 million. To transform the acquisition into genuine opportunity, Ross first had to tidy up a whole host of messes left behind by Jack Warner and Eliot Hyman. Not only was one-third of Reprise's stock still held by Frank Sinatra, over at Atlantic, morale was at an all-time low.

Fortunately, a lucky accident occurred one day when a twelve-year-old friend of the Ross family happened to say, "Gee, Steve, I think it's great you're acquiring Atlantic Records. They're really fantastic, and it's run by Ahmet Ertegun, a fantastic fellow. Have you met him?"

Ross shook his head.

"Well, you've got to meet him," the boy insisted, "because they've just put together a group called Blind Faith. That's Stevie Winwood on the organ, plus the old Cream, and they haven't even cut a record yet, but they've sold out Madison Square Garden. Isn't that fantastic?"

When Ross invited the Atlantic boss to dinner, Ertegun replied cordially, "I'd be glad to, but I want you to know that I'm really not interested in going ahead with the deal." At a fashionable restaurant just below Kinney's headquarters, Ross spent hours assuring Ertegun he'd never interfere in Atlantic's operations. Ertegun reminded Ross that he'd been promised the same things from Eliot Hyman. "Let me show you how you don't, or never will be able to, understand our business," said Ertegun gravely. "We have a group called Blind Faith."

"You mean Stevie Winwood on organ plus the old Cream," interrupted Ross, "and you haven't got a record but you've sold out Madison Square Garden?"

"Yeah, yeah, that's it," responded Ertegun, with the twinkle back in his eye.

"I think that's fantastic," Ross said with a smile, knowing he'd just won Ertegun over.

Hearing of these interesting developments, Jac Holzman donned his best suit and got himself introduced to Steve Ross by Ahmet Ertegun and Mo Ostin. He had already debated common problems with Jerry Wexler and Mo Ostin, and now he laid out his industrial analysis for Ross. Because the march of the supermanagers had driven a costly wedge between label and artist, record companies had become mere financiers and distributors. "But if you don't control your own distribution," warned Holzman, "you're working through thirty-plus independent distributors around the country, which have different ways of doing things." Apart from the logistical messiness of launching albums, "if any one of those distributors went bankrupt, they could take me for up to a million dollars," gasped

Holzman. Wexler, Ostin and Holzman had already calculated they needed an annual turnover of about 100 million records to sustain a nationwide distribution system. Warner and Atlantic represented about 83 million; Elektra made up the difference.

Ross listened and was enthusiastic, but as weeks passed, Holzman visited Jerry Wexler's home wondering, "What happened? I had this terrific meeting with Ross and I haven't heard a peep since." Ahmet Ertegun forced the issue and even accompanied Kinney VP Alan Cohen in the negotiations, in which Holzman was offered $8 million. Justifying his $10 million price tag by multiplying Elektra's annual profits of $1.2 million by eight years, Holzman held out. Kinney actually paid $7 million in cash, with the $3 million balance in convertible debentures. Despite twenty unforgettable years as an independent, Holzman had no regrets. "It gave me the opportunity to compete with the majors – to become a boutique label with real power and money behind it. I wanted to solidify Elektra's future. I also knew I wasn't going to do this forever," confessed Holzman. "I didn't want to die a record guy. I wanted other adventures."

As this new major came together, inevitably it was the dapper diplomat's son, Ahmet Ertegun, who stepped into Steve Ross's court like a custom-made shoe. Imbued with the same penchant for high stakes, Ertegun had his sights on the biggest deal in the business – the Rolling Stones, whose contract with Decca expired in July 1970. Now managed by Prince Rupert Loewenstein, the Stones were returning to their bluesy roots and had recorded the catchy "Brown Sugar" in Jerry Wexler's favourite studio, Muscle Shoals in Alabama.

For almost a year, the Turkish sultan behind Atlantic Records shamelessly chased after Mick Jagger, the pouting diva Keith Richards nicknamed "Her Majesty." Experienced, musically hot and in dire need of a cash injection, Jagger had also recruited the streetwise heir to Chess Records, Marshall Chess, to run the group's own production company, Rolling Stones Records. Leaning heavily towards Atlantic but holding out for the biggest dowry possible, Jagger and Loewenstein tried to provoke a bidding war. Although Clive Davis sniffed, he balked at Jagger's demands for between $5 and $6 million as well as a "staggering" royalty rate.

In the end, Ertegun set up a meeting at the Beverly Hills Hotel, where Steve Ross got to eyeball Rupert Loewenstein and Marshall Chess. With Ross's blessing, Ertegun offered Rolling Stones Records a $1 million advance per five albums based on a $1 royalty for every copy sold. With its iconic zipper sleeve designed by Andy Warhol, *Sticky Fingers* was a transatlantic No. 1, clocking up 3 million in unit sales and comfortably recouping the advance.

Steve Ross had his eye on the bigger picture. In 1970, Atlantic, Warner and Elektra collectively accounted for 18 percent of the American albums market, higher than CBS. Wanting to keep the arms independent, yet needing a single brand name to seduce Wall Street, Ross off-loaded Kinney's funeral parlours and moved the property holdings into a separate branch. A new corporate head controlling the record and film companies was given a dazzling new name: Warner Communications Inc. Then, in late 1971, the three record labels moved over to their own distribution network, WEA. With eight regional branches from coast to coast, each with its own travelling sales force, the synergy created was far greater than the sum of its individual parts. As the corporate CFO, Bert Wasserman, explained, "Steve had this saying, if you had one office with three doors, you wouldn't have grown as fast as having three offices with doors located in different buildings."

Preparing his deals as a type of hypnosis, Ross would regularly test his pitches on his closest financial executives – if they understood, he'd keep convoluting the terms until their eyes glazed into bemused submission. In Jac Holzman's view, "Steve Ross was a smart guy who never finished college – a *bon vivant,* hail fellow well met. He had an eye for numbers and nose for bullshit. Until you got to know him a little, nobody knew how sharp and incisive and what a gambler he was. The record companies might make a few hundred million dollars a year; they sent the cash up to corporate and corporate could do whatever they needed to do. Whereas when the movie people sent a couple of hundred million dollars up, they'd be calling it back the next year to make pictures. So he realised the record business was sustainable cash flow – if you did it right. And he got to keep that money to use for other acquisitions, like buying Atari a few years later."

Rather than demand reports and projections, Steve Ross convened informal gatherings of the label barons every three months. Arousing the envy of competitors, Ross lent his private jet to any label executive who needed to impress a manager or artist. Before Thanksgiving, he sent fine turkeys to everyone's wives. Unafflicted by the frustrated-artist syndrome, Ross, crucially, never showed any desire to get invited to showbiz soirées. "Steve believed that the management of creative companies was the key," explained Joe Smith. "The artists will come and go, but Mo and Joe and Ahmet and Jerry will always be there." Accordingly, he congratulated hits and never chastised flops. Maintaining a spirit of interested laissez-faire, whenever Ahmet Ertegun would telephone talking up some new act, Ross would fib, "Ahmet, I have a long-distance call coming in." He would quiz his children, then call Ertegun back.

Although Ahmet Ertegun was cut from the same cloth, thanks to the Californian singer-songwriter wave, Warner was quietly becoming the jewel in the crown. Adding to a juicy catalogue that already included Neil Young, the Grateful Dead, Frank Zappa and Randy Newman, between 1969 and 1970, Ostin and Smith signed Jethro Tull, Van Morrison, James Taylor, Fleetwood Mac, Ry Cooder, Black Sabbath, Deep Purple, Doug Kershaw, Gordon Lightfoot, Alice Cooper, America and the Small Faces. Of the two presidents, the shy but determined Mo Ostin was cultivating a deserved reputation among artists, managers and competitors alike as the father figure of the WEA group. Although he wasn't really a music man himself, Ostin by now understood the finer subtleties of the business. "If all it took was money," he constantly told his staff, "General Motors would be in the record business."

As well as brilliant A&R, the magic ingredient that boosted the Warner beanstalk was what the company called *creative services* – the brainchild of Stan Cornyn. Realising Warner's target audience wasn't paying much attention to AM radio or the mainstream press, Cornyn swivelled his periscope towards the underground press and student FM stations. He worked, on his own admission, "usually at home, lying on my rug on my belly with a pen and yellow tablet – amusing myself." He turned advertising into a game of wacky sloganeering. Visually inspired by the spacious minimalism of Volkswagen advertisements, Cornyn and art director Ed Thrasher created Warner's stylish, saucy face. "We just kept thinking of ways to get outrageous attention," said Cornyn of those years, by tapping into what he termed "State of the Seventies" – a look, a feel, a set of values. "Nobody censored me. We just felt the rhythm and started marching out front with those who wanted out of Vietnam and into acid."

Nicknamed "the *Gold Dust Twins*" by their staff, co-presidents Mo Ostin and Joe Smith quickly understood the spin-off value. "Every manager, attorney, or artist sits down … and they talk about our advertising," explained Joe Smith at the time. "Tell me another company where people talk about their advertising. Not how much, but the quality of it." Cornyn began noticing how "Mo and Joe started doing office tours with would-be signees, entering the office doors in Creative Services, pointing at our group and saying, '*That's* them.'" The curiosity eventually spread to the corporate headquarters. "Steve Ross invited me to New York to speak to financial market analysts – an auditorium full of them," recalled Cornyn with bemusement, "as if Creative Services had found the divining rod to a whopping new market."

Meanwhile, just down the road from Warner's offices at Burbank, super-manager David Geffen, based in Hoagy Carmichael's old house, was getting noticed by Steve Ross's barons. Representing CSN, Joni Mitchell and Neil Young, the agency had a policy of no contracts that was a powerful glue among these embodiments of the hippie dream. Smoking joints on the office sofa, the artists were all kept entertained by Geffen working his telephone – squeezing promoters and record executives with a zeal that verged on sadistic pleasure.

Although few could understand the fire in his belly, David Geffen was a complex personality haunted by the professional failures of his father, confused by his homosexuality, and ashamed of his mother's lack of sophistication. If anything, he probably found handling the business of folk singers easier than sitting alone wrestling his own demons. His immense powers to persuade and even manipulate sprang from a deep reservoir of emotion that rendered him, like an iceberg, a deceptively powerful force of nature. When he wasn't in killer mode, he could be an attentive friend whose puppy eyes drew artists into a world of intimacy and comfort. Although relatively unmusical, he was sincere and discerning in his appreciation of lyrics and possessed the same dissatisfied energy as the brooding songwriters he defended. Like them, he was fleeing drabness and mediocrity – in search of gold-plated recognition.

Geffen's sugar daddy in these years was Ahmet Ertegun, an adorable rogue in his own right, with a taste for luxury and elaborate schemes. The fascination was mutual. Observing Geffen working his magic over the telephone one afternoon in the Beverly Hills Hotel, Ertegun whispered to a journalist friend, "He must be talking to an artist. He's got his soulful look on. He's trying to purge at this moment all traces of his eager greed." Sure enough, it was Joni Mitchell at the other end.

Partly grooming, partly showing off, Ahmet Ertegun berated the young man's manners and introduced him to collecting art. Ertegun even brought Geffen on a junket to the South of France, where the Rolling Stones were recording *Exile on Main St.* However, Geffen's transformation from manager to record mogul began in Clive Davis's office while shopping around his latest discovery, Jackson Browne.

"I'm sorry, but I have to interrupt," Davis apologised as his secretary made signals from the door. "There's only one person on earth that could make me interrupt your singing, and that's Goddard Lieberson, and he's on the line."

"Pack up your guitar," snapped Geffen, standing up. "Pack up your guitar, we're leaving!"

"We don't have to leave, Dave," pleaded the baby-faced musician.

"Just do what I tell you," barked Geffen.

As manager escorted artist to the exit, Davis bleated, "Wait!" He'd put the man Columbia employees still called God on hold.

Despite his bluster, Geffen skulked back to Atlantic. "Ahmet, look, I'm trying to do you a favour by giving you Jackson Browne."

"You know what, David, don't do me any favours," quipped Ertegun.

"You'll make millions with him," drooled Geffen.

"You know what? I got millions," sassed Ertegun. "Why don't you start a record company and then we'll *all* have millions."

From that fateful repartee, Geffen's rejection rose into revenge. "Fuck it!" he thought. "If I really believe in these artists I *should* start a record company." Financed and distributed by Atlantic, he found the perfect name for his very own artist sanctuary, Asylum. The company was loosely modelled on A&M – at the time, the most artist-friendly label in Los Angeles. The controversial David Geffen had gained access to the WEA banquet, albeit, for the time being, on Ahmet Ertegun's knee.

Within a year, Geffen had lined up a small but impressive release schedule including Joni Mitchell, Tom Waits, the Byrds, Jackson Browne, Jo Jo Gunne, David Blue and Linda Ronstadt. Thanks in large part to Jackson Browne's advice, Geffen tapped into an emerging country-rock scene at a Los Angeles club called the Troubadour. From that connection, various musicians at a loose end began jamming with the help of Browne and another capable songwriter, J. D. Souther. They called themselves the Eagles. Geffen signed them up and paid for Glenn Frey and Don Henley to get their teeth redone.

As their management agency expanded into a record company and publishing arm, David Geffen and Elliot Roberts were forced to delegate. Geffen moved his attentions to the label; Elliot Roberts continued handling the musicians with his humorous but deceptively shrewd techniques. "He would smoke a copious amount of fantastically great dope and then make these deals," recalled J. D. Souther, who likened Roberts to a cross between Woody Allen and Fat Freddy. "You'd see guys stagger out of his office as though they just did not know what happened."

Picking up the waxy scent of money on the California breeze, in late 1972 Steve Ross asked Geffen to name his price for the barely operational label. In a fateful meeting, Geffen pulled out a cigarette, and quick as a flash, Steve Ross extended a light. "Seven million," ventured the unprepared debutante. Without batting an eye, Ross agreed and offered Geffen an employment contract for $150,000 per year. Walking out of the meeting on a cloud, Geffen was now among the top fifteen shareholders of Warner Communications, with a personal estate worth $10 million. Or so he thought.

"Asylum was an artist-oriented label for about a minute," noted Don Henley, who, like his fellow Eagles, took a few years to realise that their publishing and record contract had been sold, effectively by their manager, without due consultation. Geffen had played his hand far too soon. He was about to pick up a game-changing joker – Bob Dylan, whose contract with Columbia had run out and ended in conflict. He was still a big name but artistically at a low ebb. "It's like as if I had amnesia all of a sudden," said Dylan of those fallow years in the early seventies when he was raising a large family while struggling to fulfil his contractual obligations. Jerry Wexler felt he was close to poaching Dylan for Atlantic when he was spectacularly outmanoeuvered by none other than Ahmet's wonder boy.

In an elaborate game of seduction, Geffen had treated Joni Mitchell and Dylan's guitarist Robbie Robertson to a dandy sojourn in Paris, rooming at the Ritz and swanning down the tree-lined boulevards. Geffen began quizzing Robertson. "Why don't you, Bob and the Band do a tour together?" When Robertson argued that Dylan fans were expecting such an obvious move, Geffen delivered a short, sharp reality check. "It's not expected *anymore*. It's been a long time. It would be amazing, and I'll help put the whole thing together."

Hesitant but hungry, Robbie Robertson eventually introduced Geffen to the man himself. Strolling down the beach at Malibu, where Geffen had just moved in near Dylan's house, Geffen's decisive brainwave was to suggest selling the tickets directly to the public by mail order. With Dylan excited, Geffen then brought in Bill Graham as tour manager to organise forty shows in twenty-one cities throughout January and February 1974. Geffen, of course, had been providing his professional assistance as a friendly favour, but as the tour approached he made his next move. "What about a live album?"

Knowing that Jerry Wexler was offering Dylan a conventional deal on Atlantic, Geffen convinced Dylan to set up his own label, Ashes and Sand Records, promoted and distributed through Asylum/Atlantic. Promising 1 million units per album, Geffen exclaimed, "You'll sell records you never dreamed you could sell." Dylan altered the plan slightly; he felt a studio album, released just before the tour, would give his comeback added punch. So an unusually loose deal was concluded for one album only.

Then came a legendary corporate lunch held in Joe Smith's Beverly Hills home. It was the record industry's equivalent of a Mafia gathering.

All of the WEA top brass were present: Steve Ross, Ahmet Ertegun, Mo Ostin, Jac Holzman, Stan Cornyn, Jerry Wexler and David Geffen. Grinning from the corner of his couch, Geffen began teasing Wexler.

"Okay, David, you've got Dylan," conceded Wexler. "Now let's just forget the whole thing."

Geffen continued to poke away at Wexler for his "old style." The stocky army veteran began berating Geffen's artist-pampering methods as "ridiculous," and once Wexler's notorious anger was aroused, the afternoon's agenda cartwheeled straight off the highway.

"Well, if we're going to follow some kind of rules, let's talk about who's fucking up the rules here!" barked Wexler. "You stole an artist that we had!"

"You're an old washed-up record man!" groused Geffen. "What the fuck do you know?"

With veins bulging in his reddening face, Wexler thundered, "David, why don't you just shut up! You don't know a thing about music. You're nothing but an *agent*! You'd stick your head in a pool of pus to come up with a nickel in your teeth."

The lunch host physically restrained Wexler from mauling the terrified Geffen. Steve Ross stood up. "We can't have this," he said, then exited to the nearest bathroom. Mo Ostin, shaking his head in disapproval, followed the boss outside.

When the party adjourned to the dining room, Joe Smith's wife, who had not heard the shouting from her kitchen, presumed her choice of menu was responsible for the deathly silence around the table. Staring into his cheese soufflé to the sound of forks and knives, Stan Cornyn "felt puzzled by the change in the room … Was it David, who seemed to bring an odd attitude to what we did, who seemed to care less for the boogie and more for the cash? After the pee-break, no one observed that, with his Dylan-signing methods, David Geffen had changed the way record deals worked … David evangelised that record companies, like his own, were to *serve* their artists … Artists became, in appearance at least, kings, queens, tyrants, though so far very little the richer for it … Only later did I realise that this day had been spent with no talk about music. Of the executives in that room, only one still spent time in studios producing music, and that day he, Jerry Wexler, had felt the least comfortable. Among these men of purpose, opportunity and spritzing, only Jerry Wexler had, for the moment, lost his way."

Whatever the personal, moral or musical permutations, for Steve Ross, business remained a game of picking winners and calculating odds. "He was a card counter," explained Jac Holzman. "He'd go to Las Vegas, he could count cards. He'd make a modest amount of money and leave the table."

Looking at the Dylan saga through gambler's eyes, Steve Ross dismissed any need for procedures or arbitration. "If *you're* going after him and *he's* going after him," Ross, grinning, told the shell-shocked faces, "we have *twice* the chance of getting him."

20. PSALMS

ON THE GARBAGE-INFESTED STREETS OF DOWNTOWN NEW YORK, A BRAND-
new species of record man planted a seed. David Mancuso was an ascetic
on a crusade to bring people together in dance-party gatherings that as
yet hadn't acquired a name.

The history of New York's dance scene is both complex and hotly
disputed. We know for sure that the original *discotheque* format was, by
then, an almost extinct French import from a bygone era. The double-
turntable, multicultural *disco* of the future drank from a different source:
David Mancuso's memories of his childhood in an Utica orphanage in
the late forties and early fifties, where every week the kindhearted Sister
Alicia threw parties for the children. They jumped around chasing
balloons to the sound of music from records on a little turntable.

Without realising the connection until much later in life, Mancuso as
a young man was drawn to *rent parties*, then popular especially among
African Americans. "I would go to the Village, I would go to Harlem, I
would go to Staten Island, I would go wherever I heard there was a party
going on," said Mancuso. "I've always had all sorts of friends, which
probably has something to do with growing up in the orphanage."

Falling under the spell of Timothy Leary in the midsixties, the introverted and intensely spiritual Mancuso first began hosting LSD rituals
around a shrine inside his spacious apartment at 647 Broadway. From

playing records on a high-definition sound system, his private gatherings got progressively bigger and more dance-oriented. Rejecting possessions, meditating naked, surviving on stolen food, even taking his front door off its hinges to provide homeless people with a place to sleep, David Mancuso by about 1969 reached so far inside the immaterial world in search of his true identity that concerned friends, seeing his weight loss, convinced him to be hospitalised. It was while standing at the edge of the sane world that he realised his mission in life.

With the help of friends, he re-equipped his apartment with Klipschorn speakers, Mark Levinson amplifiers and two turntables. The result, at what was increasingly referred to as *the Loft*, was private, balloon-filled parties like nobody had previously experienced. Mixing brilliant musical story-boards of percussive rock, psychedelia and R&B, Mancuso interlaced his records with sensory special effects – lights, moments of total obscurity, wind fans that blew up to the sounds of tropical storms. "There was something intangible – magical – that wasn't happening in other places. I hadn't taken any drugs, yet I felt like I was tripping," said one eyewitness, Danny Krivit. Although LSD and other drugs were common, Mancuso forbade dealing. It was the sound, music and collective spirit that made these nights such epic emotional experiences.

"No way did I want to be a disc jockey," stipulated the purist Mancuso, who still prefers the more socially conscious title of "*musical host*." He invited only friends and music lovers to the Loft – black, white, Hispanic, obese, old, homeless, straight, gay. "We were like a family. There didn't seem to be any conflicts. Music helped us reach that place. Music was the key to going back home."

"I think of David as the acorn that the tree grew from," said Krivit, who, like so many other Loft regulars, later became a professional deejay. At the time, there were other dancing clubs sprouting up, in particular the Sanctuary, which, despite playing the same types of records courtesy of deejay Francis Grasso, was run as a business. As a social gathering, it leaned more towards pickup joint, reliant on the requisite drugs-and-alcohol formula. These were the two blueprints for most of the clubs that followed.

In keeping with the communal, nonprofit ethic in which the hundred or so Loft members paid a token $2 at the door to eat proper meals and dance all night, Mancuso actively helped a wave of lofts and dance clubs in its wake. "It was like a good joint. You passed it," reasoned the uncompetitive Mancuso. "We were like bees and could pollinate."

From more gay-oriented imitations such as the Tenth Floor and the Gallery, all the heavyweight deejays of New York's nascent dance scene ventured forth in Mancuso's shadow – Larry Levan, Walter Gibbons, Nicky Siano, Frankie Knuckles and David Rodriguez. Competition and increasingly exhibitionist mixing techniques turned some deejays into performers. It became a "quest to find new records!" exclaimed deejay Steve D'Aquisto. "We had this thing and we had to keep moving it along."

In New York, the proliferation of specialist record stores owed a great deal to independent distributors, who, having been squeezed out of the mainstream rock market, increased their supply of imports and other jazz, soul, funk, Latin and indie rarities. This motley marketplace was centred around Tenth Avenue, where several independent distributors fed a growing network of specialist record stores. For the new generation of deejays, the main suppliers of rare, danceable vinyl were Colony Records, located in the Brill Building, and Downstairs Records, which had two outlets in the subway. Both stores allowed customers to listen to records before buying.

"It was already starting to change by the end of the sixties," noted Krivit, the son of a club owner. "There weren't any superclubs yet. This was a time when there was no admission charge, so things were pretty lax money-wise. All the places with jukeboxes were stuck with the same records that everyone else had. The company just said 'choose from this Top 100.' My father, however, who had the Ninth Circle, would go up to Tenth Avenue and they would actually cut an individual record – it wasn't an acetate or vinyl, it was a clay substance, and he could get any jazz record or album cut put on a seven-inch. So he loaded his jukebox with all this hot music. Those distributors really had a wide variety of stuff – they were opening the doors."

In 1972, disco pioneer David Mancuso experienced something strange at a place called Blue Hole near Mount Tremper in upstate New York. "There was this little stream that went into a quarry. It was maybe five feet wide, and there were these little whirlpools that looked like speakers, so I leaned over and got as close to them as possible without getting wet. The sound was incredible. It was the cleanest I have ever heard, and there was all this information. It was almost as if I could hear the history of life. Not in words, but in music."

To re-create what he called "the spirit of the babbling brook," Mancuso got a former musician and stereophonic sound engineer to construct a flower-shaped cluster of tweeters that could hang from the centre of his loft space – the idea being to transmit crystal-clear stereo in every direction. Alex Rosner was one of New York's specialists in club sound systems; as a boy he had narrowly escaped the gas chamber thanks to a musically sensitive Auschwitz commandant who recognised him and his musician father from a concert. "When I walked into the Loft," said Rosner, "I just tore off my shirt and started to dance. David was very idealistic, and that idealism caught me."

Pushing the science of club sound systems further into uncharted territory, Rosner augmented his prototype of Mancuso's brainwave by a set of Vegas subwoofers on both sides of the dance floor. When people walked in, they literally entered the music. Although still an underground wave known only to a few hundred New Yorkers, the nascent dance scene was charging forward – Mancuso out front and, compared to his numerous imitators, always that little bit closer to the very source.

A new moon was on the rise. Although Los Angeles was still, at face value, the boomtown of the music business, the superstars of counterculture were retreating into their Laurel Canyon palaces as hungrier souls were chasing their muse down the streets of New York City – by now stirring from its five-year slumber.

One Manhattan morning in May 1972, three miles uptown from Mancuso's loft, John Hammond, then aged sixty-three and occupying a leisurely position as a Columbia VP, strolled into the "Black Rock" at 51 West Fifty-second Street. As he sat down to his pile of newspapers, his secretary mentioned that a certain Mike Appel was pencilled in for 11:00 A.M. "Never heard of him," Hammond thought, unaware the manager in question had harangued his way onto his secretary's schedule.

At the appointed time, two men entered the office. "So you're John Hammond, the man who is supposed to have discovered Bob Dylan," said the less handsome face. "I want to see if you have any ears. I've got somebody who is better than Bob Dylan."

"I don't know what you're trying to prove," choked Hammond over his cold coffee, "but you're succeeding in making me dislike you. Now I haven't got much time. Who's your boy?"

"His name is Bruce Springsteen."

Turning his head to the youngster, Hammond softened his tone, but only slightly. "Why don't you take out your guitar, Bruce, and start playing before I get any more irritated."

What happened next, Hammond hadn't been expecting. Concealing his shrivelling embarrassment behind an easy smile, Springsteen took out his guitar and launched into "It's Hard to Be a Saint in the City." Hammond was immediately hooked but, not wanting to show the cantankerous manager his interest, sat poker-faced as Springsteen played two hours of original material. Eventually, Hammond picked up the phone and called Sam Hood, the owner of the Gaslight.

As a favour to Hammond, Hood agreed to let Springsteen perform that very evening during happy hour. Later, as Springsteen played his heart out to the empty club, one of Hammond's musician friends asked with visible approval, "Hey, John, where did you find this guy?"

"He just walked into my office with his soft-spoken manager," Hammond said with a smile.

Thoroughly satisfied that Springsteen had compositions and a commanding stage presence, Hammond announced, "You're going to be a Columbia recording artist," then booked the delighted singer into a small studio for the following day. Although Hammond just wanted to make some demos, he invited *New Yorker* journalist Jane Boutwell, who was writing a piece on the producer. "I've found a new artist," Hammond told her, "and I think something will happen with him, although it may take time … I'd like you to hear talent when it's really raw." After two hours of recording Springsteen's solo performances on a guitar and piano, Hammond wrote "The greatest talent of the decade!" on the session recording sheets. He presented his demos to Clive Davis two days later, and a second meeting was convened in Davis's office, where Springsteen was officially signed.

In the first proper recording sessions, Hammond urged Springsteen to stay acoustic, whereas the artist himself imagined a rock band sound. Although the final album, *Greetings from Asbury Park, N.J.,* was an awkward mix of folk and unripened rock, CBS shipped a firm commitment of 74,000 copies – most of them returning unsold. Meanwhile, another seismic power struggle began engulfing the corporation's top floors. Increasingly disliked by the ghostlike presence of Goddard Lieberson, Clive Davis's airs and graces had started to consume too much oxygen inside the CBS boardroom, which, in stark contrast to Steve Ross's court, remained an old-fashioned administration where personality politics tended to trump commercial considerations.

When the group's chairman, Bill Paley, chose a young outsider, Arthur Taylor, as corporate president, Clive Davis became unashamedly condescending in conclaves. He also felt underpaid. Earning $100,000 with a further $40,000 bonus, Davis knew his salary was puny compared to the packages, perks and private jets Steve Ross gave his barons. "Please, Arthur," Davis would berate his superior in full view of the wincing executives, "do not question my judgment. You simply do not understand the market. You do not understand the music business." As one key eyewitness, Walter Yetnikoff, put it, "Clive was right, but Clive was arrogant, and arrogance – he would learn, I would learn, everyone eventually learns – has a way of taking down the mighty."

Inevitably, the regal Clive Davis was dethroned thanks to a scandal exposed by Jonathan Goldstein, the U.S. attorney in Newark. Codenamed Project Sound, the investigation was probably a politically motivated witch hunt by Richard Nixon's administration, investigating payola in Columbia's R&B labels. Suspecting what came to be termed "*drugola*," investigators monitoring a heroin smuggler, Patsy Falcone, noticed a connection with a certain David Wynshaw, an unusual Columbia employee who, when he wasn't playing butler to Columbia's stars, handled some of Clive Davis's personal affairs. Combing through

Columbia's accounts, they found that Wynshaw had helped Davis invoice as company expenses a total of $94,000 for home renovations and his son's bar mitzvah.

Due to the massive cost of the investigation, the powers that were needed a scalp. In May 1973, the attorney's office confronted Bill Paley with their damaging, albeit petty, evidence. Due to the precarious nature of CBS's federal licence, Arthur Taylor ordered security guards to escort Davis out of the building. The stunned Clive Davis returned to his apartment overlooking Central Park – unemployed and humiliated.

In the bitter end, Project Sound indicted nineteen people including Davis, who was charged with filing false income tax returns. To maximise the political impact, the various judgments were announced the same day, ensuring news reports left an impression that the entire record business had been punished for its culture of corruption.

If institutionalised drugs were what Nixon's apparatchiks had hoped to expose, they should have been snooping around Los Angeles, where a whole generation of cowboy rockers were, one by one, checking into the proverbial Hotel California. "Decaying mansions," said former Doors manager Danny Sugerman, "an uncleaned pool, palm fronds afloat ... sunlight was out, night life was in."

There was no better symbol of the shift than the sleek new theater on Sunset Strip opened in 1973 by David Geffen, Lou Adler and Elliot Roberts, the Roxy. It was more than a deliberate attempt to put the folksy Troubadour out of business; its adjoining VIP club, On the Rox, became the scene of limousines, bodyguards and celebrities powdering their noses in the half-light. "If you want to talk about what happened to the L.A. scene in the first half of the seventies," mused local producer David Anderle, "you can sum it up with one name; David Geffen happened. A bunch of hippies had become major players and were now calling the shots. All of us stopped smoking pot and got serious."

Problem was, record executives weren't saying no to cocaine. Even Warner's resident freak, Andy Wickham, sent Mo Ostin a damning memo in 1973, lamenting within the corridors of Burbank "a looseness, a smugness, an appalling lack of civilised behaviour – secretaries using filthy language, executives shambling around in ragged jeans and dirty sweatshirts, endless silly parties in the conference room, cocaine-snorting in the lavatories." At the time, as Elliot Roberts pointed out, "no one realised that it was *totally* addictive, that it ate your cells away and made your nose fall off. Everyone was like 'wanna bump?' It was so *mainstream.*"

Cocaine was influencing the California sound in a way that Linda Ronstadt eloquently described with the image of "a tight throat and a very flat mask." The decreasingly innocent Joni Mitchell, at the time rooming in David Geffen's Malibu pad, "wrote some songs on cocaine because initially it can be a creative catalyst" – but, as she eventually learned, "in the end it'll fry you, kill the heart. It kills the soul and gives you delusions of grandeur as it shuts down your emotional centre."

Not everyone took years to realise how shallow the scene really was. One outspoken cynic on the Geffen roster was Tom Waits, who joked to a journalist at the time, that the Eagles "don't have cow shit on their boots, only dog shit from Laurel Canyon." The other group of urban cowboys being managed by the Geffen-Roberts agency was America. Waits found them vacuous. "How about," he mused, " 'I rode through the desert on a horse with no legs'?"

Asylum was rocketing into the commercial stratosphere, but behind the scenes David Geffen was spitting fireballs. "I got fucked in that deal," he realised of the Warner buyout, which "earned back one hundred percent of what the company cost on just a couple of records." Worst of all, due to a collapse in Warner Communications' share price, Geffen's theoretical $5 million had since dropped to less than $2 million. From riches to bitches, Geffen, true to his growing reputation, went berserk with Steve Ross, who, true to *his* growing reputation, bent over backward to keep the cash cow happy.

"Geffen was a gifted screamer and by sheer energy he'd usually get his way," explained Jac Holzman. "There was no ambiguity at David's core. He was right, you were wrong. Q.E.D." A practical solution was suggested by the Elektra boss, at the time both personally disillusioned and, since Jim Morrison's death, struggling to keep his label hot. Negotiating a transfer to a technological wing of the Warner empire, Holzman gave Ross his blessing to merge Elektra into Asylum. Ross offered Geffen a bumper salary of $1 million per annum and promised to pay off the agreed $5 million balance on the contentious Asylum deal. Geffen accepted somewhat reluctantly, then purged two-thirds of Elektra's artists and staff – in his own words "valueless."

With Bob Dylan, Joni Mitchell and Carly Simon scoring smash hits for the renamed Elektra/Asylum, *Time* magazine hailed David Geffen as "the financial superstar of the $2 billion pop music industry." Adding to Geffen's growing status, Joni Mitchell even wrote him a song, "Free Man in Paris," empathising with his heavy burden of "stoking the star-maker machinery."

Considering that Asylum Records and its innocently named publishing arm, Companion Music, had been envisioned a year earlier as a boutique independent, Mel Posner, one of the survivors of Elektra's mass purge, rubbed his eyes as "this Wall Street guy" from Warner Communications asked, "How come you have Carly Simon down here for three hundred thousand records when you sold a million records last time?"

"Because I don't know what this record's gonna do," explained Posner.

"What kinda business you got here?" chortled the suit.

Then came the first of several negative Geffen incidents. On the last night of Dylan's comeback *Tour '74,* the singer announced to the standing ovation, "We want to thank a legendary guy who put this whole tour together. Without him, this thing just wouldn't have happened." In the front row, Geffen stood up and began beaming proudly among his VIP guests.

"Can you give a warm round of applause," said Dylan, "to Bill Graham!"

Geffen, utterly humiliated, shrank back into his seat.

After the show, Geffen sobbed backstage as the Band rolled their eyes to heaven. The following day, Robbie Robertson, feeling a debt to Geffen, telephoned Dylan. "Whether or not he was on the road putting up lights and carrying equipment, he played a big part in this. We should thank him," pleaded Robertson. "It's the decent thing to do."

"Oh Jesus," groaned Dylan. "Okay, okay, let's do it."

After talking it over with Geffen face-to-face, Dylan sensed he wanted a public apology. After taking out full-page advertisements in the trades acknowledging "immeasurable thanks to David Geffen who made possible

Tour '74," Dylan and Robertson then consulted Cher, who at the time was Geffen's controversial fiancée. When she suggested they organise a surprise party for Geffen's thirty-first birthday, Dylan rented a grand ballroom at the Beverly Wilshire Hotel and ordered an impressive birthday cake on which the acknowledgment "For the Man That's Responsible" was pasted in sugar. Mo Ostin was given the job of luring Geffen to a bogus meeting with his favourite icon, Barbra Streisand, when lo and behold, the doors swung open and a cheer erupted from seventy-five smiling faces including Warren Beatty, Jack Nicholson and Ringo Starr. Dylan even performed "Mr Tambourine Man" for the birthday boy.

In the weeks thereafter, Dylan and the Band began doubting the handshake deal to release their live album, *Before the Flood,* on Elektra/Asylum. Not only was Dylan starting to feel queasy about Geffen's appetite for magazine celebrity, *Planet Waves* had thus far only sold 600,000 copies – below his batting average on Columbia. So Dylan and his lawyer, David Braun, consulted the out-of-work Clive Davis regarding an alternative idea to sell the live album directly to the public by way of a free phone number. In a meeting in the Beverly Hills Hotel, Davis warned such a stunt would cheapen Dylan's image and instead suggested an alternative. Liking Davis's idea, Dylan then summoned the unsuspecting Geffen to the meeting.

"David, we're not going to put the concert album through Elektra/Asylum," announced Dylan straight out. "I'm going to do it myself."

"You can't do this!" screamed Geffen. "We have an arrangement!"

"No, I'm not going to do it," insisted Dylan firmly. "Besides, it's not *your* money, David. It's Warner Communications' money."

"Whatever happened to the guy who wrote 'The Times They Are A-Changin'?" sneered Geffen, storming out.

Not wishing to see Jerry Wexler's beardy grin, Geffen in the end outbid Columbia for the live album. Speaking to an interviewer years later, however, Geffen obliquely alluded to "the biggest artist of them all, a legend … who turned out to be so mean, so jealous, so cheap, ego-ridden and petty, such an ingrate." In another confession, Geffen claimed "that Bob Dylan is as interested in money as any person I've known in my life."

It was time for Dylan to leave Malibu. Moving his family back to Greenwich Village, he began taking art lessons with a Jewish philosopher and master painter, Norman Raeben – whose novel technique was to teach students how to perceive objects from a variety of angles and even through timelines. Although the classes taught Dylan "how to see," they probably, in the long run, lost him his family. "My wife never did understand me ever since that day. That's when our marriage started breaking up," said Dylan. "She never knew what I was talking about, what I was thinking about, and I couldn't possibly explain it."

In a terrible bargain, as Dylan's wife and four children drifted over the horizon, his mojo returned. He spent a pensive summer living near his brother, David Zimmerman, by the Crow River in Minnesota, writing stream-of-consciousness songs about two lovers breaking up. Mixing up tenses and speaking in first, second and third person, Dylan applied Raeben's techniques to the songs that became *Blood on the Tracks*.

When he signed a new record contract with Columbia, Dylan returned to one of the last remaining vestiges of the old school – his discoverer, John Hammond, who was honoured to prepare the homecoming. "Our first record date happened to fall on the Jewish New Year," remembered Hammond, who at the artist's request booked the old studio where Dylan's first three albums were made. "Promptly at sundown, Bobby brought out a Bible and some wine and we drank a ceremonial toast." That evening, a bluesy number called "Meet Me in the Morning" was recorded.

"It was clear from his mood and body language that he was vulnerable," recalled the session engineer, Phil Ramone, who was fascinated by Dylan's trancelike techniques. "Bob would start with one song, go into a second song without warning, switch to a third midstream, and then jump back to the first … I saw them as a spiritual release – a letting out of the man's insides … For four days, Dylan stood at the mic and bared his soul on record."

Hammond had advised Ramone and the session musicians to give Dylan space, but two months later, a doubtful Dylan, feeling the album was too acoustic, asked to re-record certain tracks in Minneapolis with his brother taking over as producer. Columbia had to destroy pressed copies of the first draft, as the Zimmerman brothers reworked five tracks with bigger arrangements.

With critics and fans hailing *Blood on the Tracks* as a masterpiece, Dylan released, just five months later, a double album of homemade recordings from his Woodstock sabbatical in 1967 – *The Basement Tapes,* a colourful treasure trove of altered-state folk-rock. Simultaneously touring with the Band on his *Rolling Thunder Revue* throughout that busy summer of 1975, Dylan recorded another classic album, *Desire.*

Dylan's return to form was a source of immense pride for John Hammond. "His genius has been the acuity of his vision of American life, his ability to internalise his observations and experiences, and his artistry in retelling them in a penetrating and dramatic poetry that overwhelms his hearers. He helped shape the attitudes of a generation, and God knows his unique and uncompromising albums transformed Columbia Records!"

Meanwhile that summer, Bruce Springsteen was working on his elusive breakthrough: *Born to Run.* Back in September 1973, his promising second album, *The Wild, the Innocent & the E Street Shuffle,* earned him critical acclaim as "the new Dylan." Even so, as Columbia president Walter Yetnikoff bleakly concluded over the subsequent months, "that kid's not selling any records for us." Columbia A&R executive Michael Pillot confirmed that throughout 1974, "we had a lot of meetings about the artist roster, and there was a lot of talk about dropping Bruce." Fortunately, a music critic by the name of Jon Landau wrote a glowing review of Springsteen's electrifying concerts, predicting, "I have seen the future of rock 'n' roll and his name is Bruce Springsteen." It was enough to lift Columbia's hopes and convince Yetnikoff to test one last single before deciding the young man's fate. So Bruce Springsteen began writing his last-chance epic, "Born to Run." The writing was slow but the effect was instant. CBS executive Bruce Lundvall, visiting the studio, told an incredulous Springsteen, "You've just made a hit record."

The increasingly estranged John Hammond winced at its cathedral-sized rock sound, but the radio deejays who received a test pressing were unanimous in their enthusiasm. A conscious attempt to mix Bob Dylan,

Roy Orbison and Phil Spector, "Born to Run" was a blood-strirring cry for stardom that convinced Columbia to get firmly behind a third album co-produced by Landau. Splashing out $250,000 on tour support, ads, posters, and radio promotion, Columbia took full advantage of Landau's "future of rock 'n' roll" endorsement. With *Newsweek* and *Time* giving the hunky singer their front pages in October 1975, the album climbed to No. 3 – in Springsteen's own words, "the dividing line" in his life.

Managed success can be disappointing. "It's going to piss people off," Springsteen warned of the dreaded "future of rock" slogan. "It pisses *me* off." Fearing a media backlash and eager to maintain a human proximity to his audience, Springsteen turned down lucrative offers to play stadiums, even though he was still effectively broke. Hearing reports that, in one fit of rage, he tore down a hall full of "future of rock" posters at a gig in London, Columbia staffers began realising they'd overhyped their product. Walking onstage "it's like I'm ten points down," Springsteen felt. "You've got to blow this bullshit out of people's minds."

If anyone, the artist's own manager, Mike Appel, was behind the campaign's unashamed zeal. "Bruce Springsteen isn't a rock 'n' roll act," he often repeated. "He's a religion." Realising that Appel owned the masters and half the publishing, the increasingly agitated singer confided in Jon Landau, "He's robbing me blind." Freedom from Appel cost Springsteen an $800,000 termination settlement, after which Landau took over as manager. Springsteen's business arrangements would be straighter without the cantankerous Appel, even though, as Walter Yetnikoff later joked, "Landau saw Bruce as Jesus. He'd call me to report what Bruce had for breakfast."

As he listened to the latest sagas from the Springsteen circus, John Hammond was feeling his age. Having suffered a serious heart attack, the sixty-four-year-old was writing the final chapters of his memoirs. In the pampering culture of corporate rock, he observed sadly, "today so much rides on every record that even the most trivial opinion is impelled to express itself and, worse, may even have to be listened to. In the bad old days, when jobs were scarce, any musician who got a record date automatically assumed that the producer who arranged it must have his best interests at heart. Today, musicians – big money artists – are not so sure."

Hammond's old friend Jerry Wexler was in a similar place. As he wandered through Atlantic's new offices in the Warner Communications tower, "I started seeing people in the halls whose names I didn't know." When Ahmet Ertegun and David Geffen nearly merged Atlantic with Elektra/Asylum in the summer of 1974, Wexler hit the roof, warning Ertegun, "One day, you'll cry rivers of blood from this wonder boy of yours!"

In fact, the mighty David Geffen was heading for a fall of his own making. After a dinner in Los Angeles, Ahmet Ertegun, flanked by Mick and Bianca Jagger, woke up Cher at 2:00 A.M. in Geffen's luxurious Malibu residence. As Jagger tinkled on a piano and Cher sang in her billowing alto, Geffen sat there looking glum in a pair of tennis shorts and sneakers. "Look at that creep," muttered the drunken Ertegun out of earshot. "How can he dress like that?" Everyone in the room knew Geffen was gay – so was this celebrity couple some kind of PR move?

When Cher called off their wedding, Geffen's humiliation slid into depression. Despite the commercial success of Elektra/Asylum – which in 1976 shipped 2 million units of what would become the second-biggest album of all time, *The Eagles: Their Greatest Hits,* with 42 million sales to date – Geffen suddenly wanted out of the music business. Dreaming of conquering Hollywood, he convinced Steve Ross to give him a senior position in a Warner Bros. movie division. Within months, his lack of tact got him fired. A spectacular burn-out even by Hollywood standards, Geffen lost Steve Ross's patronage, was misdiagnosed with cancer, and withdrew into retirement.

Back in New York, Jerry Wexler, by now absent and excluded from Atlantic's corporate decisions, handed in his resignation to Ahmet Ertegun. "In an odd way, I was glad to be leaving," he later confessed. "The industry was going big time, entering an era in which middle executives ran companies with perfunctory approval from above, and top executives had become too involved with megamillion-dollar deals to spend much time thinking about ... what, music?" Describing his inner life as a "ballroom full of ghosts," Jerry Wexler remained a freelance producer who, like John Hammond, still believed that music mattered – culturally, intellectually, spiritually.

The adaptable Ahmet Ertegun simply boogied on into the late seventies, wining, dining and serving himself generous helpings of Steve Ross's private jet. Taking a far lighter view of the vocation, Ertegun felt compelled to remind his peers, "It is a mistake to invest the music we recorded with too much importance. It isn't classical music, and it cannot be interpreted in the same way. It's more like the old Fred Astaire movies: They're fun, but they're not great art."

21. THE ISLAND

FORTUNATELY THINGS WERE ALWAYS A LITTLE DIFFERENT IN ENGLAND. Throughout the seventies, England's comparatively homespun record industry continued to punch far above its weight. If America was the Goliath market dominated by majors, little old England was becoming the proverbial David – firing indie hits across the Atlantic with unbelievable accuracy.

In England, pop music had become such a national sport that every Thursday evening, one in four inhabitants watched *Top of the Pops,* the BBC's chart show. England was also a big spender: domestic record sales were about one-third higher than in similar-sized European countries like France or West Germany.

On the fringes of the mainstream media, England had a vibrant network of musically elitist deejays, TV hosts and journalists. Of all the BBC's former pirates, the most daring explorer of the British airwaves was John Peel, whose *Top Gear* radio show was fearless in its showcasing of experimental music. In 1971, BBC television began *The Old Grey Whistle Test,* a live music show on which the erudite Bob Harris presented the cutting edge of rock. In an indication of just how many music nuts were on the street, Britain's music publication *NME* enjoyed a weekly circulation of about 300,000.

There was one other magic ingredient influencing England's amazing capacity to keep supplying America with hot records. Since the beat boom, most of England's biggest acts had been managed by homosexuals. Along with the ambiguously camp Andrew Loog Oldham, there had been Brian Epstein, Robert Stigwood and the Who's co-manager Kit Lambert. There was also Tony Stratton-Smith, manager of Genesis and owner of the seminal indie label Charisma. Most of the major British acts had a dandy circus master commanding operations from the wings.

"Never let the music get in the way of the act," joked Kit Lambert to his boys, the Who. Beyond theatrical flair, the gay influence probably imbued a touch of eternal youth into English rockers. As Who guitarist Pete Townshend pointed out, "Gays were different. They didn't behave like other adults; they were scornful of conventional behaviour; they mixed more easily with young people, and seemed to understand them."

From about 1970 onward, Mick Jagger wore lipstick; then Marc Bolan appeared on television with glitter under his eyes. Then, upping the ante considerably, in strutted the very brilliant David Bowie – arguably the most important artist of the whole decade. Since his somewhat shy chart in 1969 with a novelty hit called "Space Oddity," Bowie had been study-ing under the gay mime artist Lindsay Kemp, himself a student of the great Marcel Marceau. Combining performance art and experimental rock, Kemp had taught Bowie about make-up, costumes, body movements, voice projection and sexual power.

With Bowie consciously approaching his music as an "actor" playing characters such as Ziggy Stardust and Aladdin Sane, the dividing line between reality and fiction became a mysterious curtain that, as the seventies unfolded, attracted artists and audiences alike to the very limits of fantasy.

Bisexual glam rock began crossing the Atlantic in about 1972, when Bowie and his classically trained collaborator Mick Ronson produced Lou Reed – at the time drifting away from his commercially unsuccessful Velvet Underground. The result was *Transformer,* a classic in which Bowie and Ronson's glittery orchestrations added a sweetness to Reed's sleazy depictions of the transvestites in Andy Warhol's factory. It became an entry-level classic through which hordes of English teenagers began delving back through the Velvet Underground repertoire, discovering New York's bittersweet underworld of syringes, whips and ermine furs.

As time would tell, thanks to glam rock, a new musical hotline was operating between the London and Manhattan undergrounds.

Transformer's iconic sleeve is said to have inspired the cult transsexual musical *The Rocky Horror Picture Show,* produced in 1973 by a group of gay actors from Robert Stigwood's and Lindsay Kemp's networks. As coincidence would have it, the first *Rocky Horror* stage performances, at a King's Road theatre, were seen by the owner of a retro clothes shop located nearby – Malcolm McLaren, then just a Teddy Boy revivalist destined for bigger things.

Moving with the glam tide, in 1972 Britain's hottest label, Island Records, signed Roxy Music, a collective of art-school bohemians whose jarring retro pop came as an unpleasant shock to the company's fainter-hearted. "Had it been left to the so-called A&R department, which was Muff Winwood, Roxy Music would never have been signed to Island Records," said their manager, David Enthoven, whose chief ally at the time was Island's sales manager, Tim Clark. "Tim got it immediately. He got the music, he got the artwork. Muff Winwood absolutely rejected it, he thought they were rubbish. And interestingly, one day in Basing Street, Tim and I were looking at the first Roxy cover, Chris Blackwell walked past and asked Tim, 'have you done the deal yet?' Once Chris saw the artwork, to be fair to him, he absolutely got what we were on about."

The cover of Roxy Music's first album, depicting a swimsuited glamour model lying on satin sheets beside a gold disc, was a deliberate middle finger to hippie fashions. Although the group has since been revered as revolutionary, David Enthoven insists that "Roxy was *not* a huge departure. I know musically it was avant-garde and arty, but King Crimson was pretty avant-garde, and in fact Bryan Ferry auditioned to be lead singer for King Crimson … The thing about Island was there was a diverse range of music in there; there was a kaleidoscope of talent, all the psychedelic stuff and all the folkies as well. Island didn't really have a musical identity, it was a whole breeding ground of musical genres, and that's what was cool about it."

Destiny or sheer luck? It was at this crossroads that Island boss Chris Blackwell stumbled on his most timeless, universal and overtly religious discovery. In the spring of 1972, a talented Jamaican songwriter by the name of Bob Marley began winding his way to Blackwell's office. Already a celebrity in Jamaica, Marley was the front man of the Wailers, who, since the early sixties, had recorded over one hundred tracks for a variety of Kingston labels. Throughout the winter of 1971, the Wailers had been in London, living out of suitcases in a crummy hotel – penniless, cold and desperately looking for a record deal. Accompanied by their tall, dapper manager, Danny Sims, the Wailers had at first tagged along behind his star act, Johnny Nash.

The previous year, a twenty-four-year-old rookie publisher by the name of Derek Green had dropped by A&M's London office, where seated "in the reception area were the most exotic-looking people, Danny Sims, Johnny Nash and some drop-dead-gorgeous black women." As they introduced themselves to each other, Sims explained "he had some great music with a story to tell." Later, in Green's office, demos were listened to and a deal was signed. "One of my biggest career moments," said Green, "was when they brought Bob Marley to my office to play me his songs on his acoustic guitar. Danny had brilliantly described Bob as a *black Mick Jagger.*"

Feeling that London's bigger record companies would be wary of black Mick Jaggers, Green shopped his Jamaican demos around Los Angeles, where "the legendary Lou Adler was the only record producer who had the foresight to recognise the potential of Bob Marley's songs. Lou gave me a cover by recording a Marley song, 'You Poured Sugar on Me,' by the Robinson Family on his Ode Records. Unfortunately, when I signed Marley, the market just wasn't ready for him yet," concluded Green, who gave both artists to Dave Margereson, an old friend in the London office of CBS. Margereson was really interested only in Johnny Nash, who provided CBS with two U.K. hit singles, "Stir It Up" and the No. 5 classic "I Can See Clearly Now." The Wailers had been signed as a favour, which partly explains why their CBS recordings were shelved.

Although the Wailers had been initially reluctant to visit Island, by the spring of 1972, they were disillusioned and desperate. With Danny Sims back in Jamaica, a promoter called Brent Clarke arranged them a meeting with Chris Blackwell. Looking at the cool but cagey Bob Marley, Bunny Livingston and Peter Tosh file through the doorway, Blackwell thought "they were nobodies but they were like huge stars, their attitude and the vibe they gave off," he recalled. "They were prepared and they were ready to work, but they wanted to do everything pretty well on their own terms."

At the time, Johnny Nash's rendition of Marley's "Stir It Up" was No. 13 in England. Chris Blackwell had heard of the Wailers anyway, but his homework suggested they might be tricky. Apart from their contract with CBS, there was the question mark hanging over their manager and publisher, Danny Sims – allegedly connected to the mob, not just in Jamaica, but in America, where he used to run a booking agency and fashionable Broadway restaurant called Sapphire's. "Marley was actually signed to CBS," said David Betteridge, "and what happened was that CBS, God bless them, just did not know what to do with him. But Chris did. Chris wanted to sign him, and did a deal with [CBS U.K. chairman] Dick Asher, basically for a two percent override that we had to pay CBS on the sales of the first two Wailers albums on Island."

The problem was, Marley harboured suspicions about Island's accounting – probably why, in this last-ditch effort to get a deal, he asked Blackwell for the cash to produce a single himself. Rather cleverly, Blackwell upped the ante. How much would it cost to make an entire album in Jamaica? Between three and four thousand pounds, replied Marley, holding Blackwell's eye contact. In the end, Blackwell handed Marley a wad of bills, wished him well, and saw him to the door. Being intuitive, he had managed to turn the situation on its head. The Wailers could have disappeared with the cash, but they returned to Kingston feeling both a moral and musical challenge to hold up their end of the bargain.

That summer, Marley returned alone to London with the tapes, and Chris Blackwell and sound engineer Tony Platt began extensive post-production. With Island's sixteen-track facilities and far superior sound-processing equipment, the Kingston recordings were enhanced and overdubbed with additional instrumentation. The sonic alchemist proved to be Texan keyboardist John "Rabbit" Bundrick, a member of the Danny Sims gang Marley had met in Sweden. Coached by Marley, Rabbit learned how to "chicken scratch" a clavinet through a wah-wah pedal, creating what became the hallmark sound of Bob Marley's Island recordings.

The album's potential hit songs such as "Stir It Up" and "Concrete Jungle" were gently hypnotic grooves tailor-made for dope smokers. Given a luxurious and suggestive sleeve evoking a Zippo lighter, the album, called *Catch a Fire,* only sold about 14,000 copies in its first year, but it earned the Wailers an appearance on *The Old Grey Whistle Test.* If the truth be known, Blackwell was bitterly disappointed at the public's lack of interest.

Simplifying the game plan, they unanimously agreed to revert to a raw, aggressive follow-up album before year-end – *Burnin',* which made no effort to Westernise the band's Trenchtown sound. More political and explosive, it contained two potentially radio-friendly tracks, "Get Up, Stand Up" and "I Shot the Sheriff." Throughout 1973, Island kept the Wailers on the road – not exactly touring, but *promoting*, a record-company euphemism for hotchpotch itineraries on which a wannabe act lugs its own show around indifferent halls and local radio stations, often providing supporting slots for established bands.

Buses, greasy cafés, dive venues – the Wailers were at a low ebb. After they were fired in Las Vegas by Sly Stone on their second American tour, the introverted Bunny Livingston, sorely missing Ital food and Jamaican home life, refused to go out on the road again. Then, in the depths of late November, a weary Peter Tosh, suffering bronchitis, trudged through a fourth tour around northern England until he, too, threw in the towel.

Despite their long history singing their way out of the Kingston ghetto, the three-man gang split up after one year on Island. Dubbing Chris Blackwell "*Whiteworse,*" "because he isn't black and he isn't well," Peter Tosh later accused the Island boss of manipulating Bob Marley into a solo career. Bunny Livingston also maintained he was mistreated and intentionally sidelined. David Betteridge, however, felt "they shouldn't have been so harsh … The breakup of the Wailers was to do with the band and nothing to do with Island. There was undoubtedly a huge amount of jealousy because Bob got all the plaudits, because he was writing most of the material and because he had a lot more money in his pocket than the other guys. Plus, of course, they were putting too much ganja up their noses!"

Paranoia generally came with the genre. "The whole of the West Indian music community, generally speaking, didn't like each other," continued Betteridge. "In the days when the Jamaican labels were producing the Wailers, the Maytals and all the others, half the time they just did not get paid. So there was a huge amount of distrust before we ever got involved with these guys."

Throughout 1973 and 1974, as the Wailers lugged their reggae around England, Island's core market seemed to be moving in the exact opposite direction. Among bohemians and art-school chin strokers, progressive rock and cerebral music were reaching their commercial peak. Handling sales for their new semi-independent label, Virgin Records, Island's senior staffers looked on in envy as Mike Oldfield's experimental *Tubular Bells* sold 2 million copies in Britain – far bigger than anything Island had at the time. In an A&R meeting, Blackwell suggested they create an Island sublabel specialising in avant-garde mood music. Guy Stevens interrupted the boss's brainwave with his Cockney drawl. "Why don't we call it Lukewarm Fucking Records?" Bursting into hysterical laughter, Blackwell let his idea gurgle gently down the drain.

Luckily, in the summer of 1974, fate threw out a wild card when an Eric Clapton version of "I Shot the Sheriff" rocketed to No. 1 in America. Although Clapton had struggled to play its offbeat groove, it was a resounding endorsement among the white-rocker demographic. For Trevor Wyatt, an Island A&R man and Marley friend, "the whole thing just came together … but certainly Clapton doing that song really opened it up for us, especially in America – well, everywhere, I think. People said, 'Hmm, who's written this?'"

Blackwell, sensing Jamaica's hour was nigh, began pouring resources into Marley. With new musicians and a token Jamaican manager, Bob Marley's touring machine travelled the world with a spring in its step. Learning from experience, Marley hired a Jamaican cook to keep the band nourished with locally sourced vegetables and fruit. The backing vocalists affectionately known as the I-Threes included his wife, Rita.

As well as providing tour support, Blackwell called in PR heavy-weight Charlie Comer, who'd previously worked with the Beatles and the Stones. Wherever Marley performed, Comer ensured the best journalists in the local media were waiting pencil in hand. Above all, Comer was a hands-on operator – managerial, fatherly, straight-talking, tireless. Famous for his unstoppable tongue, he loved the lifestyle of grooming raw talent into stars.

Chris Blackwell considers Bob Marley's crowning moment the sold-out Lyceum concerts in London in July 1975, where the now legendary live performance of "No Woman No Cry" was recorded. With the cost of tour support eating into the modest album sales, however, the financial payback was still a long way off. In the midseventies, it was Island's entire roster and affiliated labels that enabled Chris Blackwell to expand his London head office into a stunning new premises in the pretty surroundings of Hammersmith. Choosing his office directly above the studio at the back of the building, Chris Blackwell, they say, wanted to remind his company that true leadership had to retain its proximity to the creative action.

Or so the legend goes. "He's got a huge, fertile mind and imagination, but I think he got bored of things easily," reasoned David Betteridge. "He never wanted to get involved in the nitty-gritty … He was the absentee owner. He wanted to do things his way, which is fair enough; he was the majority shareholder. But ya know, you need to talk to the troops! You need to tell people, 'I wanna do this and I wanna do that!' " The company's number three at the time, Tim Clark, also admitted, "He did sort of do a disappearing act. He spent a lot of time in America: he was messing around with films and the film industry, and he wasn't very much available for us at Island Records in the U.K." As events would illustrate, Chris Blackwell and the U.K. indies in general, despite their immaculate taste, were generally not as rigorous as their American counterparts when it came to running businesses.

As with most record men's idiosyncrasies, it's arguable that Chris Blackwell's aversion to management can be largely explained by his early life. "There's no doubt about it, he is a loner," David Betteridge confirmed with audible empathy. "Sometimes I didn't get to talk to him for two months as he disappeared off doing this, that, and the other, causing all sorts of problems." For those clocking in at the office every day, ol' Chris was like the classroom rebel who regularly blew off school – and when he was there, he could barely stay seated at his desk.

In fact, the only time Chris Blackwell appeared to be fully available was when he was barefoot by the sea. "We used to have meetings in what we called *the Western Office*, which was actually a beach in Nassau called the Western Shores," recalled Betteridge. "There, we used to discuss strategy sitting under the palm trees, eating sandwiches and drinking something. But when he came back to London, trying to sit him down and have an actual meeting was extremely difficult. So you had to guess a lot. When we would have a meeting, it was in a corridor, five minutes, and away we went again. *Undisciplined* is a good description."

It all came to a head in 1976. When Virgin's three-year distribution deal came to an end, Richard Branson jumped ship, and within months, Chrysalis also left. "Island had been like the mother ship, but we could do it ourselves," explained Chrysalis boss Chris Wright. "We could cut the middleman out and go straight to the distributor. So all we needed to do was marketing and promotion, which we increasingly wanted to do ourselves anyway … There was no personal aspect to us leaving. It was just a natural progression." As they rode off into the sunset, however, Chrysalis inherited key aspects of Island's character. "Terry and I would have always ended up doing what we did. But you know, you can't reinvent the wheel that much," said Wright.

On the delicate question of emulating Island, Virgin's A&R man, Simon Draper, recalled that "we went into reggae because we loved it, too. We started out small and then got into it in a big way, and I don't think that Chris Blackwell liked us for that. We particularly fell out over Peter Tosh, who we signed … Chris Blackwell was *incensed*! I clearly remember going into a meeting with Blackwell in a pancake house in Notting Hill Gate. Richard Branson was there also. We worked out some kind of compromise in the end, even though I think Island were in the wrong. But it was all to do with whether or not they owned

Peter Tosh because he was in the Wailers. And of course with Jamaicans there's a lot of grey areas when it comes to contracts."

David Betteridge estimated that both Chrysalis and Virgin represented about 20 percent of Island's overall turnover – a loss compounded by the money they were throwing down the drain of their American company on Sunset Boulevard. "There were about seventy to eighty employees in the U.K. company," explained Betteridge. "In those days, there were only fifteen radio stations in England and five thousand in America. Everything from distribution to marketing was on a far bigger scale. The danger with America is that although the rewards are huge when you're successful, it's so much more expensive to get there ... Once our American operations became a record label, it sucked huge amounts of money out of the European company, and it was never discussed properly."

For years, Betteridge had adapted to Chris Blackwell's nomadic lifestyle, but "Island was no longer the company we had started; it had become too unwieldy and I became disillusioned," he confessed. "People began taking sides. There was a lot of backbiting going on when I left ... Three or four indies came and went quickly because the whole company was sliding around in different directions. It was partly my fault, partly other people's fault, partly Chris's fault. But a knife should have been taken to it. It should have been reduced in size. We all would have been much happier. It should have remained a smaller, tighter, creative company."

As Island's new managing director, Tim Clark, put it, "The problem for us at that time was Island had a number of retail arms, if you like. We were still distributing a certain amount of Jamaican stuff directly to retailers; we'd got into the whole thing of starting a factory because we had such terrible difficulties getting records pressed. But of course it suddenly became a machine we had to feed, both the distribution network and the factory. So when Virgin and Chrysalis left us, it meant we weren't feeding the machine enough and it started to cost a lot of money."

A perfect storm had formed over Chris Blackwell's island. "We had a real financial crunch in 1976, and it wasn't that long after I'd taken over as managing director," explained Tim Clark. "It was one evening and Chris Blackwell had just flown in from New York and he was just *drained*. And he said, 'You know, I just really don't know what to do.' We chatted a bit and I honestly didn't know what to do either. Eventually he said, 'We've got to do a licence deal with EMI,' so we got on the phone, talked to them, and we got a cheque for a million pounds."

It took a few years to restructure Island Records, and its near-death experience marked the end of its halcyon days as a gang of kindred spirits. Not only had key players left, two vital sources of talent, Guy Stevens and David Enthoven, were sliding into addiction. From that season of upheaval, though, two important British indies had stepped out into the world: Chrysalis and Virgin. With Terry Ellis moving to Los Angeles, Chrysalis as a label was determined to conquer America the way Jethro Tull had done as a band. Meanwhile, commanding Virgin's various businesses from his London houseboat, the fiercely ambitious Richard Branson began imagining ways of consolidating his foothold into continental Europe.

22. HIGH TIDE

"FUCK WARNER," READ THE SLOGAN. "FUCK THE BUNNY!" ITS ELOQUENT AUTHOR was Walter Yetnikoff, Columbia's new boss. Thus began a despotic reign that would end in rehab. "The appointment went to my head, went to my dick, and over a period of years turned me into a madman," Yetnikoff admitted to himself on a therapist's couch.

Yetnikoff's war against the market leaders, declared at a CBS sales convention, was just a humorous gimmick designed to conquer the spirits of his own troops. His real problem was that "I had a great new job, yet I couldn't help questioning my qualifications ... I was tone deaf." He knew he needed to invent a king-sized persona to fill the corporate vacuum left by Goddard Lieberson and Clive Davis. "War is exhilarating," he thought to himself. "War elicits loyalty, solidarity. War gives us purpose and drive. War was what I wanted. War was who *I* was."

Shouting into telephones in fuck-littered Yiddish, the rumpled, hard-drinking Walter Yetnikoff personified the sickness dripping out the nostrils of the American record industry. Inside the American majors, musical literacy was in steep decline. Jerry Wexler, John Hammond, Goddard Lieberson, Jac Holzman – the erudite crusaders were riding into the sunset. Although the industry's two fallen kings, Clive Davis and David Geffen, would both return from the dead, their subsequent

242 ★ COWBOYS AND INDIES

influence on the story of pop music would be as businessmen – peddling artists of little cultural significance.

Even Warner's halcyon days were over. Following Geffen's resignation, Joe Smith was transferred to run Elektra/Asylum, where he inherited the cocaine-frazzled Eagles. With Smith's transfer, Mo Ostin became California's biggest mogul, presiding over a corporation that had grown so large that Walter Yetnikoff was warning big artists leaning towards signing with Warner, "Be careful, you'll get lost in there!"

A short drive away, the last remaining bastion of purism had locked itself inside the gates of Charlie Chaplin's old film studio – A&M, for some *the* label of the early seventies. Whereas inferior imitations such as Asylum had been dressed up as artist havens, A&M was the real thing. An organically grown fairy tale, it all began with two friends listening to records – their bond forged in the fires of Herb Alpert's meteoric rise to stardom.

"Hanging out with Herbie, I got to learn a lot about artists – their moods, their temperament," explained the principled Jerry Moss, whose gentle, protective style as a label boss grew from that founding artist-manager relationship. "Herbie was smart, he came from a family of very smart people. But he was an artist. He could remain sort of aloof, dreamy or artistic – it wouldn't get in the way of his image, and I would come in and do the stuff. But I'd be talking about it to Herbie all the way, whether we were together or on the road, I'd bring him up to date. Herbie was very knowledgeable. He participated in every major decision."

As A&M evolved into a boutique label for acts as diverse as Burt Bacharach, Procol Harum, Sergio Mendes, Antonio Carlos Jobim, Joe Cocker, Humble Pie, the Carpenters and Supertramp, Alpert continued to record, tour, and produce various jazzy pet projects. A successful production deal with Creed Taylor's CTI imprint also brought A&M a treasure trove of seminal jazz and funk. With the help of general manager Gil Friesen, Jerry Moss handled company operations and generally signed the rockier acts. As A&M opened offices in Canada, London and Paris, new recruits immediately felt the atmosphere of kinship and musical excellence that gave it such a special aura. "There was that trust, that incredible trust," Moss recalled, "and I think when people work for a couple of guys where there's no question about the leadership of the company and how it functions, it just makes everything cooler and easier."

Despite his twinkling eyes and Mexican mustache, Jerry Moss was very selective when it came to picking staffers and artists. "Because Herb and I had a complete trust in each other," said Moss, "and absolutely would not tolerate corruption from anyone, we were able to make this work. The rules were very simple: If you lie or if you cheat on a deal, you don't belong here. If you're an honest person and you want to work hard, A&M was a place for you. Nobody lied. Because lying takes a lot of energy. And this way, we were able to put all the energy into the music. Therein lies the culture that Herb and I created – it became A&M."

Whenever A&M's new London boss, Derek Green, called up with a problem or doubt, Moss would repeat, "Derek, just keep signing good acts that we can sell in America," always emphasising the virtues of simplicity. Of course, such youthful innocence could not last forever. As Los Angeles became the city of decadence, the rising tide was seeping through A&M's fabled gates. By late 1976, roomfuls of A&M's promotion staffers were "visiting the bathroom" with an alarming frequency. Across the industry, the cult of crystal powder was quietly enslaving foot soldiers and record bosses alike, many of them barely thirty and ill prepared for the drug's insidious side effects – including, among other things, cocaine's thirst for alcohol.

As one recent arrival from England, Terry Ellis, explained, "L.A. is a show business town. If you're doing well, and I really was, every door opens to you. You're the toast of the town." The conventional wisdom in those days was "*work hard, play hard,*" but as Ellis recognised with the benefit of hindsight, "the free love legacy of the sixties had got out of hand. Alcohol and drugs were free flowing in a way that seemed normal. I think a lot of people did damage to their health in those years. It didn't seem abnormal to be at work drunk or stoned, because *everybody* was." Or as Jerry Moss put it, "I loved the ideals the sixties created. I was so into the sixties and seventies in a cultural way – as a nation, I felt we were on the verge of something tremendous. And then we blew it. The drugs got more serious, AIDS came in. Late seventies, early eighties; things turned."

With the big American corporations churning out music that evoked Woody Allen's gag in *Annie Hall* about mellowness making you ripen and then rot, the A&R advantage was moving back to the hungrier independents – especially those of a theatrical persuasion who hadn't got stuck in the Woodstock mud. Presenting Brett Smiley, a Broadway glam rocker, on British television in 1974, Andrew Loog Oldham predicted, "The music business has become very mundane. The music business thinks they make the stars. And I think, this year, they're gonna find out they're wrong." Oldham sensed people were fed up with the sultry dysfunction of hippie rock. He pointed to Elton John's breakthrough in America, rightly warning, "Entertainers are back!"

Sure enough, as the decade progressed, the theatrical dazzle of early seventies glam rock provided the electric shock that infused life into the rising monsters of the late seventies – disco and punk. A perfect example of Dr. Frankenstein was future Sex Pistols impresario Malcolm McLaren. Still looking for his break, he was swanning around New York in 1975 with his designer partner, Vivienne Westwood, making costumes and iconography for the New York Dolls, whose kitsch blend of lipstick, hair spray, and hard rock was almost like a transvestite's parody of the Rolling Stones.

Rough, exciting and often compared to the Velvet Underground, the New York Dolls were inspiring a crop of younger groups all playing at CBGB – a dank, windowless club on the seedy Lower East Side where regulars like Television, the Ramones and Patti Smith first performed to audiences that included Talking Heads, Suicide and Blondie. Curiously, the club owner, Hilly Kristal, was a folkie who, having previously managed the Village Vanguard, opened CBGB in 1973 to showcase country, bluegrass and blues – hence its initials. Evolving organically with the music that walked in off the garbage-infested street, the now legendary CBGB was a folk experiment gone fantastically awry.

Something was in the air. At exactly the same time, London had its equivalent; *pub rock*, the new moniker to describe small gigs, where for the price of a pint, audiences could hear back-to-basics rock songs oozing wit, energy and lager froth. Including groups such as Dr. Feelgood,

Kilburn & the High Roads, Ducks Deluxe and Brinsley Schwarz, many of the scene's central characters were former mods, now approaching thirty and increasingly bored with the hippie detour in between.

One key figure in this emerging London scene was Dave Robinson, who would found Stiff Records, Britain's most iconic New Wave indie of the late seventies. Somewhat similar to the owner of CBGB, Dave Robinson was an adventurous folkie who'd seen the sixties from a different angle. A tough nut with a soft brogue, the sharp, shifty Robinson had grown up in Ireland – then a banana republic sinking into the Holy See. Inheriting his father's eye for graphic design and slogans, Robinson started out as a magazine photographer and, like so many other restless youngsters of the Irish sixties, set off for London in search of work. He was followed by an Irish R&B band, the People, who camped on his floor and got him evicted – but, one sleepless night in 1967, helped alter his destiny.

After a gig at one of Joe Boyd's psychedelic UFO happenings, Dave Robinson, acting as manager for the People, collected the £10 fee but returned a few minutes later. "Joe, can you give me a hand? There's some nutter in the dressing room upsetting the lads. He says he manages Jimi Hendrix and he wants them to open for him on a tour." Boyd confirmed the man in the suit really was Mike Jeffery. Robinson "looked at me wide-eyed for a second," he said, "then dashed back to the tiny dressing room." So Robinson's band, renamed Eire Apparent, flew away with the Jimi Hendrix Experience to tour the world and elsewhere.

When the road manager fell ill, the lucky Dubliner suddenly found himself lugging Jimi Hendrix's amplifiers through airports. Playing fifty shows over fifty-four days on one of several backbreaking tours, the strung-out and suspicious Jimi Hendrix began quizzing Robinson about money and contracts. Robinson himself was just as puzzled by Mike Jeffery's opaque ways. "I wanted to know how the machinery worked," he recalled, struck by the sight of Muddy Waters forced to play dives in America while Hendrix sold out the best venues to white audiences.

The Jimi Hendrix job experience left Dave Robinson with a head full of ideas. As a roadie and wheeler-dealer looking at London's gig circuits through Irish eyes, he began contemplating the true meaning of folk –

not the California format that was dominating England's album charts but, as Robinson put it, "music that had a social connection to the environment that it came from." He noticed a crippled Cockney poet, Ian Dury, to whom he explained his vision, sometime around 1972, of a grassroots, anti-major movement that would bring music back to the people. "Dave sat on the floor," said Dury, "had a bowl of rice, and said he thought that music would grow by word of mouth, if you had an environment where it could develop in one locality."

So, between 1973 and 1975, Robinson set up a recording studio above the Hope and Anchor, an elegant, high-ceilinged Victorian pub in a multicultural neighbourhood in Islington, whose basement venue was perfect for unknown bands without vans or equipment. Although there were other venues in the pub rock circuits, the Hope and Anchor was London's equivalent of CBGB. "He was a hustler. And we liked him accordingly," attested Dury, who was then the singer of Kilburn & the High Roads. "I've seen him loading boxes in the back of the van and getting sweaty. For all his verbal, he still gets down there on the concrete, rolls his sleeves up, and gets stuck in. But I didn't feel for one minute that I never saw him coming."

Not only were London's pub rockers struggling financially, the bleak economic context was affecting the public mood at large. As the saying goes, when America sneezes, the world gets a cold. The costs of the Vietnam War had prompted the *Nixon Shock* of 1971, when the U.S. government unpegged the dollar from its gold standard. With the West's currencies all linked to the dollar, turbulence swept through the financial markets, provoking a global recession – particularly in Britain. By 1974, British GDP was shrinking at a rate of 4 percent per year, inflation was at 25 percent, and unemployment had spilled over the symbolic 1 million mark. With strikes paralysing the country, mounds of rubbish bags began piling up on street corners, and an international oil crisis caused penury in gas stations. Britain's malaise hit rock bottom in 1976, when Prime Minister James Callaghan was forced to call in the International Monetary Fund.

It was onto these depressed, rubbish-encrusted streets that Malcolm McLaren returned from his New York adventures – determined to shock

London out of its hippie coma. He changed his shop name to *Sex* and began specialising in hard-rocker outfits inspired by bondage. One customer, sporting his very own look made from destroyed clothes held together with safety pins, was a redheaded teenager by the name of John Lydon. A peculiar kind of streetwise intellectual who understood that Britain's so-called working class had long since turned into a welfare class, he had a gang of friends, referred to as *the four Johns*, that included two characters who later invented the stage names Sid Vicious and Jah Wobble.

As coincidence would have it, another character who occasionally dropped into McLaren's shop was Steve Jones, a kleptomaniac scavenger who had just stolen a vanload of guitars and amplifiers from a David Bowie gig and dreamed of starting a band. He consulted the well-connected McLaren, whose first suggestion was to give Lydon an audition. Standing beside the shop jukebox, Lydon contorted and wheezed to Alice Cooper's "School's Out" and got the part. For a band name, McLaren came up with the *Sex Pistols* – effectively an extension of his boutique.

More interested in the fashion than the music, McLaren suggested that Lydon study the leather-gloved cripple Ian Dury, who wore razor-blade earrings and had an imposing stage pose of arching his back over a low-adjusted microphone stand. Dury had borrowed the trick from his childhood icon, fifties rocker Gene Vincent, who wore a leg brace as the result of a motorcycle injury.

The Ramones arrived in London on July 4, 1976, like the outbreak of a virus. They had just released their debut album on Sire Records and were being managed by Danny Fields. Despite a few supporters in New York's music press, the Ramones were broke and going nowhere. Imagine their delight flying into London and performing to an enthusiastic crowd of three thousand at the prestigious Round House.

Just before the show, Clash members Joe Strummer, Mick Jones and Paul Simonon climbed through a broken window backstage and hung out with the Ramones in their dressing room. John Lydon charmed his way in through the stage door and joined this prophetic assembly. With other nobodies watching from the crowd, including members of what would become the Stranglers and the Damned, if there was a seminal moment when *punk* was born, this was it – symbolically, on Independence Day in London.

At exactly the same time, disco's rapid evolution from the New York underground to global pop phenomenon came together. Back in 1973, the first warning shot was Manu Dibango's *Soul Makossa,* a French pressing shipped into Brooklyn by African importers. Found by David Mancuso in a Jamaican store, it burned the house down every night at the Loft. With other deejays clambering for the last remaining copies in circulation, in May *Billboard* ran a piece noting *Soul Makossa* was "fetching a record price of between $2 and $3 in New York shops because of its unprecedented popularity in the black community." Observing the flood of cover versions, Atlantic secured American rights for the original.

As record labels started noticing this growing dance-floor community, in 1975, David Mancuso, with Steve D'Aquisto and journalist Vince Aletti, set up a nonprofit *record pool.* Once a week, about one hundred deejay members converged on Mancuso's new Loft at 99 Prince Street to pick up thirty to fifty new releases and prerelease promos. Record companies, both majors and indies, as yet inexperienced in the art of club promotion, only had to deliver a box of records to one address in return for precious feedback and support from all of New York's trendsetting deejays. Once again, the idealistic David Mancuso was putting the scene first.

The first record mogul to invest heavily in disco was inevitably Robert Stigwood, the Cream manager turned *Jesus Christ Superstar* bankroller, who with his booming entertainment company, RSO, had produced the 1975 film adaptation of *Tommy,* starring Roger Daltrey and Elton John. In February 1976, Stigwood's waning clients the Bee Gees had recorded their first disco smash hit, "You Should Be Dancing" – a spectacular comeback.

During that summer of 1976, just as punk was rising up in London, Stigwood read a *New York Magazine* story called "Tribal Rites of the New Saturday Night" written by British music critic Nik Cohn. Presented as real-life reporting, it described the urban struggles of a working-class Brooklyn youngster who, every weekend, went wild on the dance floor of the Bay Ridge discotheque 2001 Odyssey. Stigwood bought the screen rights for $90,000, signed a three-picture deal with

John Travolta for $1 million, and began filming *Saturday Night Fever,* whose soundtrack was in large part supplied by his Bee Gees.

Probably the most iconic disco label of them all was an independent based in Los Angeles: Casablanca, whose comical, New York–bred founder, Neil Bogart, was one of the most spectacular boom-to-bust record men the business has ever seen. He may have been straight, but like Robert Stigwood's, his career began theatrically; he attended the School of Performing Arts, which inspired the 1980 film *Fame.* From there, he ran the inexplicably misspelled Buddah Records, whose core market was *bubblegum* – low-nutrition pop rock aimed at youngsters musically disenfranchised by counterculture.

Throughout the late sixties, Neil Bogart was happily going against the hippie-rock traffic, honing his promotional techniques for the likes of Curtis Mayfield, Bill Withers and Gladys Knight. His favourite mantra, religiously repeated to staffers with a cheeky grin, was "Whatever it takes!" If a radio deejay or programme director wouldn't accept gifts or lunch invitations, Bogart and his gang would do *anything* to get their records aired on the right stations.

According to one Bogart legend, in his formative years the hardest, most incorruptible programme director was Rick Sklar from the influential WABC. Inventing a brand-new trick, Bogart got his brother-in-law Buck Reingold to hide in a stall in the station's men's room. Looking through a crack in the door, with his battery-operated record player placed on the toilet seat, he waited for Sklar to enter. When he eventually did, Reingold waited until his prey was comfortable, then played his new record from the neighbouring cubicle.

With such hilarious stories spreading through the record industry, Neil Bogart caught the attention of the humorous Joe Smith, who believed the job of record company management was simply "to keep people pumped up all of the time." To set up the inspirational Neil Bogart with his own Warner-affiliated label, Smith talked Mo Ostin into an agreement whereby if Bogart wasn't making a profit after $1 million of funding, Warner would take over.

The label was named after the classic movie *Casablanca*, and its first signature was Kiss, whose make-up and ear-splitting performances appealed to Bogart's taste for theatre and excess. For Kiss's first show in the Midwest, Bogart booked an established headliner, Rory Gallagher, to ensure the showcase would be packed to the gills. With the help of an independent promoter, they lured an influential deejay to the show and handcuffed him to his seat.

Kiss strutted out. Peter Criss's levitating drum riser went up too high for the low ceiling and knocked him briefly unconscious. Gene Simmons set his hair on fire. Guitarist Ace kept falling over in his giant space boots. As expected, when the denim-clad Rory Gallagher eventually stepped into the smoking ruins, he died a slow death. Bogart repeated the trick on the unsuspecting Aerosmith. Every time Kiss opened a show, their explosive performance left a trail of handcuffed deejays laughing with disbelief.

Larry Harris, Bogart's cousin and radio promotions man, toured stations building special relationships with radio deejays. Sitting quietly in the studio during broadcasts, he nonchalantly carved out lines of cocaine on a Kiss album sleeve. It was a convincing argument, though "I don't think I pioneered the practise," stipulated Harris. Still, "the black background of that album was perfect to do coke on."

The 100,000 Kiss records sold thus far were insufficient to cover Casablanca's heavy expenditures – the office included a pool house where rock chicks treated visitors to unmentionable surprises. But because the overstretched Warner was struggling to press and distribute orders, Mo Ostin kindly wrote off the $750,000 thus spent and allowed Bogart to battle on as an independent. It was right then, teetering on bankruptcy, in November 1974, that Bogart stumbled on his ticket to disco paradise.

He was visited by Trudy Meisel, wife of German impresario Peter Meisel, who was representing an Italian-born producer by the name of Giorgio Moroder, then enjoying some success in Germany with *mood music*. Broke, but liking the demos, Bogart secured a label deal whereby Casablanca would promote and distribute Moroder's *Oasis* catalogue throughout North America. Late one night, the Casablanca gang was listening to one of Moroder's latest creations, "Love to Love You Baby," featuring an American soul singer, Donna Summer. When somebody accidentally bumped the needle back to the start, the revellers continued rolling their drugged-up heads to the song's sensual repetition. Feeling a strange magic in the air, Bogart telephoned Germany and asked Moroder to mix an extended version.

Although it wasn't exactly danceable, the seventeen-minute version, released by Casablanca in August 1975 as a full side, started making noise in discotheques, first in Florida, then the Northeast. It was even noticed by a few late-night radio deejays who specialised in progressive rock. As a buzz gathered momentum, Bogart began planning Donna Summer's future.

When she eventually arrived at JFK Airport in 1975 for a six-week promotional campaign, Bogart had choreographed the dream home-coming. After seven long years in Germany, she stepped into a waiting limousine and sank into her seat as "Love to Love You Baby" came on the radio. When she walked into her hotel suite overlooking Central Park, nearly two dozen floral displays had been carefully arranged. When she visited her hometown of Boston, Buck Reingold had personally escorted all the way from Los Angeles a life-sized cake impression of the singer, requiring two first-class seats on the plane. Considering she'd spent several months of the previous year bedridden with myocarditis, Bogart ensured that before America fell in love with Donna Summer, she was first happily married to Casablanca.

The bankroller for Casablanca's first disco experiments was, of course, Kiss, who in November 1975 shot into orbit. Their fourth album, *Alive!*, entered the Top 10 album charts – Casablanca's first platinum album. The following spring, a studio album, *Destroyer*, went platinum, as did another studio album, *Rock & Roll Over*. In a period in which most rock bands released an album a year, Kiss was engaging in a campaign of mass assault. In just thirty months, they released six albums and toured constantly, louder, campier and more excessive than anyone else on the market.

As cash began pouring in, Bogart paid off his $750,000 debt to Warner, bought a Moroccan casbah in Hollywood, hired new staff, and moved the company into a bigger building on Sunset Strip. Both the lobby and Bogart's office were given a Rick's Café theme, complete with stuffed camels, plastic palm trees, Moroccan furniture and draping textiles suggesting Bedouin tents. Believing that envy would get him the best staff in the business, Bogart gave his people impressive titles, Mercedes sedans and expense accounts and encouraged everyone to fly first class. Everyone's birthday, even the box packers', was celebrated with a champagne party. It was the same strategy for trade fairs. At one, Casablanca constructed a Moroccan casbah whose interiors were filled with various gambling games. Veiled belly dancers moved through the aisles giving away Casablanca gambling chips – lucky visitors could actually win prizes.

Making hits was beginning to feel easy at Casablanca, and for a glorious moment, life never felt so good. The company was happy – musically, professionally, and chemically. Larry Harris, the company number two, smoked joints openly in the office, but as the sun went down, stronger drugs were taken out of drawers. In the early days, Casablanca's drug of preference was a type of legal pill called *Qualudes,* usually referred to as *ludes.*

Seeing the success Kiss was enjoying thanks to their extravagant shows, Casablanca's funk signature George Clinton began demanding tour support in "meetings" that were grass and cocaine sessions. His brainwave, described through a cloud of smoke, was the *Mothership* – a model flying saucer would swoop in from the back of the hall over the heads of the crowd, then, with the lights turned off for two seconds, a bigger version would appear on the stage. Emerging from the dry ice, suggesting cosmic energy, George Clinton would commence his "pimp walk." Fortunately, thanks to his sense of humour and brilliant rhythm section, George Clinton's self-indulgence was an instant success with audiences. The accompanying album, *Mothership Connection,* released in December 1975, went platinum.

Such lavish experiments weren't always so profitable. Casablanca was also trying to break a progressive rock group called Angel, whose attempts at so-called high-art illusions inspired several sketches in the film satire *This Is Spinal Tap.* With the hall lights dimmed, the golden face of Angel Gabriel appeared over the drum riser as a celestial voice boomed out across the audience, "And it came to pass one day in Heaven that Gabriel summoned his flock of angels …" A system of lights, dry ice and mirrors illuminated a set of pyramids. Five glass cubicles rose up from under the stage and released the band into the earthly realm. Unfortunately, musicians occasionally got trapped in their pods.

Clearly there had to be cheaper ways of promoting records. Even the heavy-gambling Neil Bogart sensed that dance-floor hit singles were the

solution in a rock world that had literally grown out of all serious proportion. In Europe, Peter Meisel's Hansa label had been the first to score
disco hits, in particular "Daddy Cool" by Boney M. It was the Bee Gees,
in early 1976, who proved the point in America. Shortly after, Bogart got
another fortuitous visit from Henri Belolo and Jacques Morali – the
French producers who had dreamed up the Village People, a sort of
gay-club fancy-dress concept depicting symbols of American life: an
Indian, a construction worker, a cop, a cowboy, a sailor, a biker.

Like the fate of so many of the label's other signatures, the Village
People's destiny was decided by the so-called *Casablanca Test,* a company
tradition of playing a demo at ear-bleeding volume to see how staffers
would react. Sure enough, as soon as Bogart rattled the building with the
Village People's demo, an enthusiastic crowd began pouring into his
meeting. Casablanca had just found its second disco-bomb, earning its
place in music history as *the* disco label.

Just as the last great party of the baby boom was about to get under way,
another important pioneer stepped into the rapidly thickening crowd on the
dance floor. Nile Rodgers was a struggling funk guitarist who, having developed his "chucking" style on the chitlin' and airforce circuits, had been
observing the signs from both sides of the Atlantic. During a long stay in
London in the mid-seventies, Rodgers had his big awakening at a Roxy
Music gig. Knocked out by their bizarre mix of suave pop and theatrical
costumes, he began rummaging through the racks at the nearest record shop.

Seeing that Roxy's album sleeves featured glamour models, he began
noticing the meteoric rise of Kiss in America – all clues suggesting to him
that pop music was becoming faceless, conceptual, glitzy. He returned to
New York and formed Chic with bassist Bernard Edwards. Their addictive
second single, "Everybody Dance," was recorded in late 1976, with the
powerful background vocals of Luther Vandross.

As coincidence would have it, the sound engineer on the demo, Robert
Drake, was a deejay at a fashionable black discotheque, the Night Owl.
Weeks after the demo had been mixed, Drake telephoned one night.
"Hey, Nile, you've gotta come over and see this!"

When Rodgers entered the discotheque, Drake said "Check this out,"
and dropped the needle. As the distinctive bass line announced "Everybody

Dance," howls reverberated through the club. "A frenzied crowd of dancers, playing air guitar and air bass on the dance floor, lasted through seven continuous plays of Robert's two lacquers – approximately an hour of the same song," remembered Rodgers. "I understood why deejays played a popular record repeatedly to keep the dance floor hopping, but this was ridiculous."

Disco was erupting like a volcano. "The movement, in every sense of the word, was as open and communal as the forces driving the hippies of my youth," Nile Rodgers believed. In fact, for downtowners like Rodgers and his friends of African, Hispanic and Asian origin, disco was *more* inclusive. "It was now cool again to touch your dancing partner. A whole slew of touchy-feely dance moves were introduced into mainstream clubs – a consequence of gay sex coming out of the closet and onto the dance floor."

Right time, right place. In early 1977, Paramount discreetly released Robert Stigwood's latest film, *Saturday Night Fever*. Nobody was expecting the movie, and its soundtrack would become one of the blockbusters of the decade. Meanwhile, at Casablanca, Donna Summer was looking at one-hit-wonder status – four syrupy singles with whispery vocals failed to break into the Top 40. Then, suddenly and spectacularly, the B-side to her fifth single on Casablanca flipped. Called "I Feel Love," it had been composed and produced by Giorgio Moroder, who had been experimenting in late 1976 with pulsating and modulating electronic sounds – no acoustic instrumentation whatsoever.

The vinyl equivalent of a flying saucer had landed. The first authority in the business to apprehend its importance was Brian Eno, the crossdressing, avant-garde producer from Roxy Music. Interrupting a David Bowie recording session in Berlin, Eno stormed in with a copy of "I Feel Love" in his hand. "I have heard the sound of the future!" he declared, beaming. "This single is going to change the sound of club music for the next fifteen years!"

23. SOURCES

IT WAS AS IF NEW YORK AND LONDON WERE DOTTED WITH WATER WELLS that tapped into a giant network of underground rivers. The oncoming New Wave wouldn't just ooze from lofts and basements; its multidimensional sound owes much to the specialist record stores that were supplying deejays, musicians, and vinyl addicts with weird and wonderful rarities. Far below the towers of the major corporations, a new generation simply began mixing up the diverse sonic and ethnic ingredients that were already being stocked and played, back to back, in happening stores.

In London, one interesting maverick was a bespectacled and bearded Irishman named Ted Carroll, who ran record stalls in the Golborne Road and Soho markets with his partner, Roger Armstrong. In 1975, they opened a shop called Rock On around the corner from the Camden Town tube station. Understanding how easy it was to press and sell records, Carroll began his Chiswick label, including "Keys to Your Heart" by the 101ers, featuring Joe Strummer in his pre-Clash days.

Stringing a thread between the progressive rock, punk and postpunk eras was a far more spectacular example – Virgin, which had opened several alternative shops in the early seventies, then took off in 1973 as an Island-affiliated indie. Although the label was synonymous with its more famous entrepreneur founder, Virgin's record man was in fact Simon Draper, Richard Branson's distant cousin from South Africa.

Born into an academic family, Simon Draper had spent his childhood in the KwaZulu-Natal highlands of South Africa, later studying in Cape Town and Durban. He kept himself up to date by reading American and English publications like *Down Beat*, *Beat International*, *NME* and *Melody Maker*. Mail-ordering records and books from a number of specialist import stores in Johannesburg, he soaked up a wide variety of influences: Soft Machine, Frank Zappa, Thelonious Monk, Jack Kerouac, Lawrence Ferlinghetti, Gregory Corso. Although it took about a month for his orders to arrive, he became so good at sourcing music that, for example, he had the American pressing of Soft Machine's debut album, long before it was available in the U.K.

Deejaying his own weekly show to the Durban region in the late sixties, the nineteen-year-old came to fully apprehend South African censorship. The national broadcasters' music library, "had quite a lot of interesting records but they were all banned," he recalled. "You'd see a Bob Dylan album, but all the tracks were scratched out with chalk. The same with the Doors' first album; most of the tracks you weren't allowed to play. So I began ordering records from SABC Johannesburg, where there was a bigger library, but that just seemed to ring alarm bells because I was always asking for the wrong records." Draper was the first deejay in South Africa to play Jimi Hendrix.

At the time, he was studying politics under an inspirational Hegelian-Marxist lecturer who was later murdered by the secret police for living with an Indian woman. "My parents were very anti-Apartheid," he says. "My mother was a member of the Black Sash, a woman's movement which organised public demonstrations against the government. But I wasn't as brave as one or two of the people I went to university with. I just wanted to get out. I felt deprived of cultural stuff. It wasn't just records that were banned, so were the books I wanted to read. Norman Mailer was banned. The library would have, let's say, William Styron's *Confessions of Nat Turner* and then someone would complain. They would actually burn the book."

Throughout his youth, Draper heard his mother discussing the latest news from relatives in England. One of them was Eve Branson, who, while her husband went back to college to study law, had set up her own business selling trays depicting scenes of country life. Their unique and dyslexic son, Richard, had struggled through school but set up a successful magazine called *Student*. Simon Draper's ears pricked up when he realised that his distant cousin had just set up a mail-order business selling cut-price records.

Accompanied by his younger brother, Simon Draper arrived in London in December 1970 with £100 in his back pocket. Once they'd set themselves up with an apartment, he tracked down Richard Branson and introduced himself as a long-lost relative who ate records for breakfast. Surprised but flattered, Branson took Draper out to lunch and explained his plans to set up a shop, a label, a recording studio and a publishing company.

The very next day, Draper was put in charge of Virgin's mail-order service and began buying stock for Virgin's first shop on Oxford Street, just opening that very week. "I found that I knew more about records and music than any of the people who were already there," said Draper. "Far more. I told them, 'We've got to have records that nobody else has. We've got to have imports. We've gotta have rare records. We've got to have bootlegs.'"

Religiously listening to John Peel's radio shows and reading letters from customers, Draper sourced rare cut-outs (remainder discs) in America and began importing experimental music from Germany and France. "When I started looking for artists to sign," said Draper of Richard Branson's decision in 1973 to start Virgin's own label, "I knew the label would have to make an impact. Obviously we wanted sales, but you looked at other labels who were significant, particularly Island, and you saw that Chris Blackwell had great judgment. He signed originals. Same with Charisma, Chrysalis, Elektra, Vanguard – always one man's taste. I wanted to be sure that our label was distinctive."

From the very outset, Richard Branson was an ambitious young businessman. He negotiated a lucrative distribution deal with Island – far better terms than what Chrysalis had started out on. Despite Virgin's promising start, "by around 1975, we realised we were overly dependent on Mike Oldfield and Tangerine Dream," explained Draper. "We were boxing ourselves into a corner." Too small to secure deals with the likes of 10cc, whom they'd chased for months, "we were still trying to find acts starting from scratch, when luckily for us, punk came along."

At the very heart of the punk explosion, a small but buzzing record shop called Rough Trade opened its doors for business in that milestone summer of 1976. Its young founder was Geoff Travis, another vinyl addict with an important destiny in the record business. As was true for so many other great talent spotters of the New Wave, markets, libraries, universities and cultural melting pots had provided a rich background to his childhood. His Russian grandparents, fleeing anti-Jewish pogroms in the thirties, had settled in the London suburb of Dalston, where young Geoff Travis spent many a Saturday hanging around their shoe shop – soaking up the sights and smells of the local market.

Geoff attended school in the multicultural neighbourhood of Islington, where "my very first experiences buying records was in an electrical shop in North London," he explained. "It was in an arcade; you went past washing machines and toasters and in the back there'd be a record counter." As a teenager in the late sixties, he then discovered London's specialist record shops, often jumping on the tube during his lunch break to go hear a new release in town. His favourite was Musicland, where one of the faces behind the counter was none other than Elton John.

After studying English literature at Cambridge, Travis got his life-changing brainwave at the end of a road trip across America. In San Francisco, he walked into City Lights and melted into the friendly, non-elitist atmosphere. "City Lights had always been a romantic thing in my mind," he explained. "I liked the Beats to a degree, but I have reservations about a lot of the writing. I prefer the Black Mountain Poets." Wondering what to do with his growing collection of vinyl, Travis began imagining a humanised record store where people could hang out, play records, and chat with the staff – without ever feeling pressured to buy something or get out.

As well as Musicland, Travis acknowledged, "the Virgin shops were definitely an influence, especially the one in Oxford Street when you went upstairs and you sat on the cushions on the floor. They also had listening booths. It made me realise that going to a record shop could be more than just going to purchase something. It could be more of a community place." What made Rough Trade unique was its location in Ladbrook Grove, London's Caribbean neighbourhood, which was also home to plenty of struggling musicians. To foster a community atmosphere, Travis looked no further than the immediate neighbourhood. Reggae, punk and avant-garde rock intermingled, as did its core customers – black, white, male, female.

The proliferation of all these alternative record shops made it possible for cutting-edge independents to reach customers. Like the disco scene in New York, the punk explosion was about to create alternative networks. London's coolest stores were all stocking punky singles from America thanks to a mail-order company – Skydog, based in Paddington. Of the new English imprints sprouting up, one mail-order indie stood out: Stiff Records, also set up in the summer of 1976 by Dave Robinson and Dr. Feelgood manager Jake Riviera. For pub rockers like Robinson and Riviera, the step into punk wasn't any kind of quantum leap. Although the punks were younger, they shared the same irreverent ethos and preference for raw sound.

In late 1976 and early 1977, the Sex Pistols were like some absurd window display attracting customers through the door. Because they were so slow to deliver actual product, others benefitted from the hype – notably Stiff, whose "New Rose" by the Damned was the first English punk record. Operating the mail-order business out of a one-room office where Dave Robinson often slept on the floor, Stiff then released "Blank Generation" by New York proto-punk Richard Hell, a former member of Television.

When "Anarchy in the U.K." by the Sex Pistols was released by EMI in late November 1976, it was a minor hit, charting at No. 38. Then came the famous incident live on British TV in December 1976, when Sex Pistols guitarist Steve Jones called the host a "dirty bastard" and "a fucking rotter." The ensuing outrage, as popularised by the *Daily Mirror* headline THE FILTH AND THE FURY, prompted EMI to fire the Sex Pistols just ninety days after they'd signed their contract.

In urgent need of a new label, Malcolm McLaren talked his way through two secretaries to obtain a meeting with A&M's London boss. "I clearly recall Malcolm coming into my office wearing a leather outfit with his knees chained together," laughed Derek Green, who also took note of the smarmy grin and intentionally wonky haircut. "I was a hippie but a rebel at heart. As is my way, I paid little attention to the story he was telling me about EMI. I just played the tape and was blown away! I couldn't stop playing it – I *had to* sign the Sex Pistols."

Closing the deal turned into a nightmare. "Those close to me pleaded with me not to sign them," admitted Green, "but the more they reacted, the more determined I became to shake A&M out of its lethargy and elitism. It was showing me just how safe and almost middle-aged we had become. I even had my hair cut and removed the beard!"

The other problem was that because Green and McLaren were intent on the Sex Pistols conquering America, the negotiations dragged on while Green flew out to California to petition his A&M colleagues. Calling McLaren long distance to progress the negotiation, Green would dial the clothes shop's number. "Hello, I'm the MD of A&M Records. Can I speak to Malcolm, please?" "Fuck off" was all Vivienne Westwood would say before the line went dead.

As Green remembered it, "I was busy explaining to Jerry Moss how important this signing was but also how difficult they were to deal with. Jerry was amazing. He just didn't get it for the U.K. punk scene, but he supported me totally to concede more points than I usually would." Green then brought McLaren out to Los Angeles to meet the Americans. "He arrived on a perfect day at the A&M lot – the home of hippie values, sweltering in his black leather one-piece with his knees chained together. Can you imagine how he was being laughed at?"

McLaren explained the ideological thinking behind punk to A&M's general manager, Gil Friesen, who politely engaged the manager. "Bullshit aside, the recordings were in my view ready to release without any further production," said Green, commending the raw, hi-fi sound producer Chris Thomas had captured. With the album ready and the contractual points finally ironed out, the parties agreed to meet in London for the official signing. "Unfortunately, in all the drama, I had not yet met any of the Pistols," explained Green. As a precautionary measure, he set up a meeting in the offices of an affiliate publisher, Rondor Music – away from his sceptical staff.

As Green entered the room, his guests were playing an obscure A&M album called *Magma* – one of Herb Alpert's weirdest pet projects. Without any handshakes or hellos, Johnny Rotten glared at Green and said, "This is the *only* A&M record I would ever listen to!" Green then noticed a new and menacing face. "To my utter amazement bassist Glen Matlock was not with them, but instead someone with the unlikely name of Sid Vicious. I was devastated, as I understood Matlock was the main writer." Taking McLaren aside, Green asked, "Is Sid proficient?" "Sid can't play at all," confirmed McLaren proudly.

Green concealed his first sinking feeling as McLaren planned probably his best-ever publicity stunt: the bogus signing of the Sex Pistols outside Buckingham Palace, which provided news networks with a powerful image of the band falling out of a car in front of the imposing gates. For the written press, A&M had booked a conference room at the Regent Palace Hotel, where Green first noticed McLaren's manipulative talents as the manager whispered into Lydon's ear to tell him to plug the tour dates. "I tried to hide at the back," said Green, "until a journalist from German TV asked me if the contract gave me any control over the group's behaviour. Before I could say anything, Sid Vicious farted."

As the day unravelled into a drunken rampage, the band's next appointment was their first encounter with A&M's staff. "The first I knew of them misbehaving," said Green, "was when my head of sales came in saying Sid was swearing drunkenly and cleaning his bleeding foot in a toilet." Green kept reminding his staff that preorders for "God Save the Queen" suggested they had a sure-fire No. 1.

That Sunday, a particularly angry voice telephoned Green at home. The previous night at the Speakeasy Club, Sid Vicious had attacked a key BBC figure – Bob Harris, both an *Old Grey Whistle Test* presenter and Radio 1 deejay. Knowing he'd be sucked into the latest Sex Pistols scandal, Harris was lying low in the north of England, utterly enraged.

"So, what are you going to do about this?" his agent demanded.

"The Pistols' behaviour is none of my business," replied Green.

In the silence of that Sunday afternoon, however, Green began to seriously wonder what he'd got himself into. "The Pistols' behaviour just wasn't sitting right in my conscience. The Bob Harris incident upset me." Having tossed and turned all night, on Monday morning Green picked up his A&R man, Mike Noble, then drove his Rolls-Royce all the way to the Brighton seafront. They sat on the stony beach as Green admitted his physical discomfort at the press conference days earlier. "I felt a hypocrite driving a Rolls, sending my kids to private school, travelling first class and trying to pretend I was some kind of punk benefactor. In truth, I felt their music but never understood the punk ethic." Throwing stones into the waves and working out his next moves, Green reached his lasting conclusion. "The whole thing had become a media circus!"

Back in the office, Green waited until breakfast time in Los Angeles, then telephoned Jerry Moss. Summoning McLaren and his lawyer, Green presented a draft press release stating that A&M was rescinding the contract. Green pointed at the blank space, then explained they had two hours to pencil in the sum of money before they sent the notice to the media. "Malcolm's first reaction was utter disbelief. Then he pleaded to work things out to stay on the label," remembered Green. "It was the only time I witnessed Malcolm off balance. But quite quickly he recognised the publicity value." In that tense meeting, McLaren agreed to a severance package of £75,000 – half of the original advance.

Apart from that one communiqué, "I had made a firm decision that I would not speak to the press," explained Green, "so I took my family [to the country] and hid out." When he picked up the next day's papers, the *Daily Mail* headline read FILTHY RICH – PUNK GROUP GET £75,000 FOR DOING NOTHING. In the accompanying article, Malcolm McLaren dubiously claimed that in the contract-signing celebrations at A&M, "a window got busted. Some people made accusations that there were attempts to rape some of the girls," to which Sid Vicious added a sarcastic disclaimer, "We wouldn't have touched the girls with a barge-pole." Each newspaper had a slightly different story; the *Evening Standard* quoted McLaren saying, "The Sex Pistols are like some contagious disease – untouchable. I keep walking in and out of offices being given cheques."

Standing tall after yet another coup, Malcolm McLaren signed with Virgin. Richard Branson's total lack of music culture has long inspired smirks inside the record business – Island's Tim Clark once commented, "Richard Branson had cloth ears" – but the Virgin boss did have an eye for media value and had been chasing Malcolm McLaren with a personal zeal since the Pistols' first firing from EMI. Because Virgin urgently needed a hot new act, "there was nothing Malcolm McLaren or the Sex Pistols could or would do to put off Richard or any of us," explained Simon Draper, who admitted he wasn't a fan himself. "Of course, there were some people in Virgin who loathed them. Sid Vicious used to come to our office and behave terribly. But there was no way we were going to be fazed by it."

Virgin's two-thousand-word press release proudly spewed out McLaren's self-righteous schlock. "The Sex Pistols have remained unrepentant and adamant. They want to shock people out of apathy. They want other young people to *do something*!" To launch "God Save the Queen," McLaren and Branson rented a barge to sail down the Thames during the Royal Jubilee celebrations – knowing they'd probably get arrested in full view of the media. By this stage, the publicity stunts were becoming so visibly staged that John Lydon was starting to feel uncomfortable.

With the Sex Pistols' American rights still up for grabs, Mo Ostin dispatched two A&R men to London, Bob Regehr and Bob Krasnow. The eloquent McLaren made a lasting impression on the visiting Americans, then led them "down four flights of stairs. We went to hell," recalled Krasnow. "Here are these scroungy, horrible guys that were just gross. It was like stepping in shit. And they can't play their instruments. The whole thing was a disaster for me." Back at his hotel, Krasnow called Burbank and left a message – "Mo, that's the worst shit I ever saw in my life!"

A confused Ostin called back an hour later wondering if Krasnow had seen the same rehearsal as his colleague. Regehr had just left a very different message – "Mo, we've got to sign them. They're gonna be huge!"

Mo Ostin flew out to London and tracked down the increasingly elusive McLaren. "I finally found him," said Ostin. "We agreed to meet, but every time we set a date, he'd break it. It was incredibly frustrating. Finally we sat down and I offered him a deal. Malcolm said yes, but only if Warner Bros. agreed to finance a film he wanted to do." Thus began the Sex Pistols mockumentary, *The Great Rock 'n' Roll Swindle*, starring Malcolm McLaren as "the Embezzler."

In a fast-moving business where timing is crucial, almost a year of red-hot demand had been spent creating hype. By the time the Sex Pistols' debut album hit British stores, it was November 1977, at which point the scene was moving on from raw punk. Malcolm McLaren's subsequent claims about masterminding a great pop heist therefore merit due questioning. As Simon Draper put it, "The Sex Pistols didn't sell that many records. But they really cemented our image." Malcolm McLaren couldn't have put it better himself.

On the question of Sex Pistols mythology, Draper thought "McLaren was a totally exaggerated figure who invented himself and invented all kinds of stuff. He liked to keep everyone on edge. He liked to keep everyone guessing. He got fun out of it. He obviously had some really good ideas, particularly his own records; the first two I thought were great. But he was an awkward person to deal with because he was always trying to subvert everything … He wanted to manipulate them. He wanted them to be *his* creation, and who knows, perhaps to some extent they were his creation – initially. But he'd chosen these strong characters, and John Lydon was not going to submit."

For Draper, there was one revealing incident when Lydon gave a radio interview in which, by picking a selection of records, he showed his musical culture. "Malcolm must have been away, but he would never have let it happen. What came across was that John not only liked reggae, he liked Van der Graaf Generator and Can and all these other groups the Sex Pistols were meant to be anti. You know, anti-prog-rock, anti-everything that had gone before – when in fact they weren't at all!"

By late 1977, two independent labels were standing out as the pace-setters of the New Wave: Sire in America, Stiff in England. Securing a distribution deal with EMI in the summer of 1977, Stiff represented a hipper, more humorous variation of the punk attitude. As well as giving away merchandise with slogans like "*If it ain't Stiff it ain't worth a fuck*," they sent out questionnaires to deejays and record shops asking, "How would you like to die?" and "What is your favourite perversion?"

Throughout the summer of 1977, Robinson and Riviera were busy launching their new hopeful – Declan MacManus, a London-Irish singer-songwriter, whom they restyled with Buddy Holly glasses and an improbable stage name, Elvis Costello. Hoping to export him to America, they talked the ambitious musician into busking with a battery-powered amp outside a CBS convention on Park Lane.

Although they didn't tell him, the plan was to get him arrested on film. As soon as he started his routine, Stiff anonymously called the police complaining that a suspicious Irishman was making a nuisance on Park Lane, then contacted news reporters. Fortune favours the brave; Lisa Robinson, the respected American journalist who had introduced the Ramones to Danny Fields, happened to be attending the conference. Struck by Costello's songs, she tracked down Walter Yetnikoff in his hotel and begged him to take a look.

"He has hits. You must sign him," she insisted.

While rushing to the convention, "I turned around," recalled Yetnikoff, "and standing on the street, his guitar hooked into a little amp, was a little gawky guy with glasses." When Costello was finally arrested later that day, he gave the police Stiff's phone number. They denied they'd ever heard of him. Meanwhile, back on Park Lane, Walter Yetnikoff was calling his A&R men in New York.

With momentum building, Costello was given the cover of the August 1977 edition of *Sounds* magazine, which emphasised Stiff's plan to present him as a cool geek. "Elvis Costello looks like a creep, a weed. The paste-on glasses, the skinny face, the pinstripe suits and executive tie. The sort of face that begs to have sand kicked into it. Elvis Costello, do you know, is a pop star. Last month he was a computer operator." Although the term *New Wave* wasn't yet the moniker for this emerging brand of jerky, ironic pop-rock, by late 1977 the so-called punk movement was entering a new phase. In New York, Sire's Seymour Stein was launching his next CBGB discovery, Talking Heads. At Virgin, Simon Draper signed up XTC – the group that pointed Virgin to its pop future.

Then, on Stiff's multi-artist revue in late 1977, Robinson's old acquaintance from the early seventies, Ian Dury, began to take off. With backup by his brilliant funk band, the Blockheads, his "Sex & Drugs & Rock & Roll" became the rousing anthem of the nationwide tour, while his first album, *New Boots & Panties,* began selling like hot cakes. And from that first lift, Ian Dury began cooking up his sizzling No. 1 English break-through, "Hit Me with Your Rhythm Stick."

As the New Wave went big-time in both London and New York, it was all happening the way Robinson and Dury had imagined it in the early seventies – through word of mouth, a grassroots movement was rising from clubs and record shops, bringing music back to the people. There was no better symbol of the anti-major phenomenon than Dury himself, aged thirty-six when he became a star. His body had been so deformed by childhood polio that his handsome face looked enormous on his emaciated torso. He had such difficulty walking, he lurched painfully with the aid of leg braces and a cane. The authentic Quasimodo of the punk eruption, Ian Dury proved that *anyone* can be star, even a cripple – or a "raspberry ripple," as he described himself in Cockney slang.

For clued-in A&R men, it was a dream harvest. At the London office of United Artists, Andrew Lauder spotted the Stranglers and the Buzzcocks. At Island, Chris Blackwell signed up the Slits and the B-52s. Dave Robinson added to Stiff's happening roster Devo, Lene Lovich, and his big jackpot, Madness.

The biggest financial winners of all were the middle-weight independents with clout in America. In May 1977, Chrysalis signed a raw, unripe CBGB band with a stage-blonde singer, Deborah Harry. "I signed Blondie," explained Terry Ellis, "because I thought they had tremendous potential to be a major pop group. And that's also what *they* wanted to be." The previous year, his partner in London, Chris Wright, had signed Generation X, technically a punk band but with a handsome, ambitious singer. "I also saw Billy Idol as a potential major pop star," continued Ellis. "The whole punk ethos that you didn't need to play an instrument to get up on a stage didn't appeal to me at the time. But there were important people who came out of that movement."

Throughout 1978, punk began to cross over into disco. Symbolically, Blondie's first global smash hit, "Heart of Glass," was a dance-floor groover complete with pulsating synths and disco high hats. Mick Jagger was another well-travelled opportunist splashing his feet in both waves. For the Stones' 1978 hit "Some Girls," "the inspiration for the record was really based in New York and the ways of the town. I think that gave it an extra spur and hardness … Punk and disco were going on at the same time, so it was quite an interesting period."

Although the term *punk* probably helped certain bands get a start, the word means little to most record men. "I saw nothing punk in the Ramones, I saw a great band," reasoned Seymour Stein, who always preferred the term *New Wave*. "To me they were a bit influenced by ABBA and Brian Wilson and the Beach Boys. I don't look at what people are wearing, I listen to the music, and their music was commercial from day one." Watching David Byrne's intense performances at CBGB, Stein rightly sensed that Talking Heads also had pop hits in their belly.

"Seymour does hear songs in any genre or style," said Byrne. "In the case of the Ramones, he saw past the image and the press and heard that they had some classic – if hilarious – pop songs. I suspect he heard something similar with the Talking Heads, as he could warble some of our material back to us over drinks and Chinese food. He wasn't making huge promises like some of the major labels were. He genuinely seemed to like some of the songs."

In much the same manner, a cash cow landed on the plate of A&M's London boss. "Following the public firing of the Pistols, I felt no credibility to look around the punk scene," admitted Derek Green, who had endured the lowest hours of his career following the embarrassing saga. "Going to the office felt like going through the motions. I started to see my workmates and record-biz contacts as outdated." Absent and depressed, Green was coasting around London in his Rolls-Royce when a pop song with a pumping synth came on the radio. Green phoned the deejay for details, then tracked down the band's manager and producer, Miles Copeland, "an old music biz hippie, who like myself had cut his hair and embraced the new scene."

It was a lucky coincidence. Because Green had helped Copeland set up his own label some years earlier, the manager happily signed over Squeeze to A&M. Then, hey presto, Copeland presented his brother's group, the Police, with their punky-reggae debut, "Roxanne." "I was back on a crusade," sighed Green, "working with my staff again in a positive way. They had shifted their positions on punk and were no longer seeing it as the end of good music. With the Police, Squeeze and Joe Jackson, we had New Wave acts that could be marketed in America … A&M was back on the cutting edge." In fact, A&M was now surfing several waves at once. Another English discovery, Supertramp, having relocated to Los Angeles, exploded in 1979 with their blockbuster *Breakfast in America*. As a new decade approached, A&M was becoming the biggest independent in the world.

Despite all the cultural changes happening in New York and London, the underlying laws of the business hadn't changed since the British Invasion. "The U.K. was really a loss-making shop window," explained Green. "In the seventies, *Billboard* was the chart that mattered most to English record men and artist managers like Chris Blackwell, Terry Ellis, Chris Wright, Tony Stratton-Smith, Bill Curbishley and myself. Our overheads and egos needed worldwide sales. We were entrepreneurs who knew how to befriend the market makers in America, unlike many of the eighties guys, whose attitude of being 'punkish' was never going to get the job done. I, for instance, would have signed the Jam for the U.S. if Paul Weller's dad hadn't been a manager who took the artist's view that touring America was unnecessary."

Another example was Ian Dury, who confessed, "You'll never find me in Malibu, darling, because I don't like America." Dave Robinson secured him an American tour as supporting act for Lou Reed – on paper an irresistible bill. Alas, with Ian Dury convinced his Cockney poetry wouldn't work on American audiences, the expedition was doomed. "I hate America," announced the long-faced Dury to his PR aide Kosmo Vinyl when they landed at JFK. Six weeks later, following a disappointing tour on which the moody Lou Reed ignored him backstage, the crippled poet boarded the plane home. "I told you so" was all he said.

24. SODOM & GOMORRAH

SNEERING PUNKS GOT ALL THE BAD PRESS, BUT BENEATH ITS GLAMOROUS veneer, disco was probably lewder and grimier. Nile Rodgers, the Chic guitarist who co-wrote "Le Freak" – the monster anthem of disco wonderland – spent those magical years in a toilet.

"I can still remember how exciting it was the first time a girl brought me inside," reminisced Rodgers of his favourite niche inside Studio 54. "I spent most of my time in the women's bathroom – which came to be known as my office." His reasons were entirely pharmaceutical. "I had lots of blow. I was never asked to leave ... All my drinks were brought to me, friends met me there ... If someone had to use the toilet, I'd let her come in and she'd just go in front of me, even if we were total strangers."

The game of influencing the charts was even dirtier. Casablanca VP Larry Harris had been assigned the job of lobbying probably the most important individual in the record industry, Bill Wardlow, the man who managed *Billboard*'s charts, which in turn determined orders from America's biggest retailers. By showering Wardlow with disco gifts, gossip and visits to the film set of *Thank God It's Friday,* starring Donna Summer, at one point even Kiss managed to get no less than four titles on *Billboard*'s album charts.

In April 1978, Casablanca treated Wardlow to an unforgettable night in the "restricted area" at Club 54. As described by anyone lucky enough to have seen it, the forbidden zone was a hedonistic underworld where party people had sex in the shadows and celebrities sat at tables covered in cocaine. Although Bill Wardlow was in his midfifties and looked completely out of place, his hosts spoiled him as if he were a sultan in a harem.

RSO's master salesman, Al Coury, also knew how to play the game. In May 1978, he was mysteriously spotted in Venice showing Bill Wardlow the magnificent aquatic city by gondola. The following week, RSO's next big single from *Saturday Night Fever,* Yvonne Elliman's "If I Can't Have You," was No. 1 on the *Billboard* singles charts. Others didn't bother with flowers. Grateful for KC and the Sunshine Band's five *Billboard* No. 1s, TK Records owner Henry Stone gave Bill Wardlow the down payment for a house in Palm Springs. "I threw him a dolla here and there," admitted Stone. "He kept me wherever I told him to on the charts."

Laughing at the top of the food chain was PolyGram, the European major then co-owned by manufacturing giants Philips and Siemens. In what at first seemed like a brilliant move, PolyGram spent $23 million acquiring both RSO and Casablanca. Throughout 1978, *Saturday Night Fever* and *Grease* yielded nine No. 1s held for a total of thirty-one weeks. Over at Casablanca, the Village People and Donna Summer provided another four platinum albums. Posting a $407 million turnover in America, PolyGram in early 1979 began planning a lavish party to celebrate becoming America's third powerhouse, breathing down the necks of WEA and CBS.

In all the excitement, it never once occurred to PolyGram's Dutch and German executives that film soundtracks are one-offs. Nor that Casablanca was a drug-frazzled liability that had just shipped a total of 5 million solo records from each of the four members of Kiss – a contractual obligation forced on Neil Bogart by Kiss's managers in the hope that solo projects might deter the strung-out band from breaking up. They were released the same day in September 1978 with a $750,000 promotional campaign, a four-way gamble that was the record business equivalent of self-mutilation. The average Kiss customer was never going to buy all four solo albums.

"Neil could snort a whole table full of coke with one nostril in one breath," Henry Stone recalled of one unforgettable party during a *Billboard* convention. As one regular visitor from PolyGram's distribution arm, Rick Bleiweiss, described the atmosphere inside Casablanca at the peak of its commercial success, "Music was blaring, twelve phones were ringing. You never could talk in that building. You had to shout. I think the average person walking in there would have been floored by the electricity and volume." Down the corridor, promotions men hit an Oriental gong every time a Casablanca record was added to a radio's playlist.

One new salesman in the company, Danny Davis, settled into his office in 1979 and could not believe his eyes. "On a Monday or a Tuesday, I'd be looking for a secretary and I'd be calling her name. I'd look all over, and there she would be with a credit card in her hand, chopping, chopping the coke on the table ... I would be on the phone with a program director, and a certain party would come in. And he would run around with a fucking golf club, squashing things off my desk. And as I was on the phone, he would take a match and torch my desk. I would say into the phone, let's say to Jerry Rogers of WSGA, 'Jerry, gonna have to hang up now, my desk is on fire.' "

Meanwhile, on the streets of New York, disco was losing its magic as cheap imitators and tourists arrived en masse. "There was just this huge influx of people," said Loft deejay Danny Krivit. "There were clubs opening up constantly. Everything was overflowing full. So there just wasn't enough space – things were getting bigger and bigger. And then you start to refer to crowds as *Bridge and Tunnel* – people from the outer boroughs coming in. And to us, they seemed a little bit in that *Saturday Night Fever* vision. You know, less hip, the basic crowd – without the flavour."

Reporting the rapidly evolving scene was a young journalist, Tom Silverman, who in 1978 started the trade publication *Disco News*. He gleaned his information from a nationwide network of deejays, record stores and radio programmers. "In 1978," he explained, "the first big station went to a disco-only format and within six months, thirty-five or forty stations followed – some in cities that couldn't justify it. Everyone was trying to cash in on the boom. Meanwhile, all these really bad disco records were coming out: 'Baby I'm Burning' by Dolly Parton, and Arthur Fiedler conducting *Saturday Night Fiedler*."

The first of several omens occurred in the summer of 1979 when an unknown radio deejay in Chicago announced a bizarre event. Steve Dahl was a disco hater who had recently been forced to walk out of a job when his station changed to a disco-only format. In his new job on rock station WLUP, he met a kindred spirit in Mike Veeck, son of the Chicago White Sox owner. With the approval of Veeck senior, the two deejays hatched an imaginative plan to figuratively smash the disco ball with a giant-sized baseball bat.

Calling their ceremony *Disco Demolition Night*, Dahl informed listeners that for the White Sox game on July 12, spectators would be admitted for 98 cents if they presented a disco sacrifice at the gate. An incredible 50,000 people descended on the stadium to see fireworks specialists exploding stacks of disco records as Dahl, wearing an oversized helmet, scrambled around in an army jeep. For thirty-five minutes chaos reigned as fans stormed the field and turned the pyrotechnics into a bonfire of the vanities. Unprepared for such mayhem, the White Sox had to forfeit the game. Outside the stadium, 15,000 rockers drank beer and chanted, "Disco sucks, disco sucks …"

Soon enough, disco was about to suck the bottom out from underneath PolyGram. Due to a combination of economic recession and disco saturation, for the first time since the 1930s, in 1979 the record industry experienced a tangible shrinkage of 11 percent. Everyone felt it. Teetering on the edge of bankruptcy, Clive Davis's Arista label had to be sold off to German giant Ariola. The most spectacular casualty of all was PolyGram's American distribution. "Between Casablanca, RSO, and smaller hits from Mercury and Polydor, we thought that we had entered the big leagues – there was no reason to think otherwise," explained Rick Bleiweiss. Then came the mother of all flops, Robert Stigwood's latest folly.

"The *Sgt. Pepper* film was a disaster for us," continued Bleiweiss. "Everyone expected it to be another *Fever* or *Grease*. We tried holding back account orders for the soundtrack, but the accounts insisted on buying tons of it. It was like the last big wave of a tsunami. First the *Fever* wave hit, then the *Grease* wave hit, and then the *Pepper* wave came. Only this one was destructive." From their royal boxes, PolyGram's senior executives looked down in horror as the dance floor imploded into a flaming black hole.

It wasn't simply returns flooding in. Over the previous two years PolyGram's distribution network in America had tripled in size. Without enough volume to pay for the company's huge running costs, all of PolyGram's international profits were sucked and burned in the disco inferno. For his crimes against accounting, PolyGram fired Neil Bogart, and by the time he died in 1982 of cancer, Casablanca had been all but shut down.

Like the house lights flashing on at closing time, reality was nigh. Cutting an increasingly dishevelled figure, in shuffled Bob Dylan with *Slow Train Coming,* a religious record produced by Jerry Wexler at Muscle Shoals. Some wondered if Dylan was undergoing Christian rehab, but the Minnesota bard hadn't lost his sense of timing. "It might be the Devil or it might be the Lord," he sang to a hall of record executives at the Grammys, closing a decade synonymous with self-entitlement and hedonism, "but you're gonna have to *serve* somebody." Cynics may have been smirking in their bow ties, but in time Dylan's award added an ironic footnote to the fateful incident seven years earlier, when he chose David Geffen's gilded asylum over Jerry Wexler's old school.

Curiously, at the time, Mo Ostin was talking David Geffen back into the music business. Flattered, interested, and wanting more, Geffen negotiated a two-sided deal that set up his billion-dollar future. Mo Ostin would finance a Geffen-run record label through Warner Bros. Records; Steve Ross, through Warner Communications, would finance a movie and theatre production company. Aged thirty-seven and very lucky not to have contracted HIV in his Studio 54 days, Geffen was back in Los Angeles to conquer the entire entertainment industry. When he was struggling to find a name for his company, his designer friend Calvin Klein suggested "Geffen Records" because "you'll get laid more!" For additonal good luck, Geffen chose an office on Sunset Boulevard right beside where his career first took off.

"David, why didn't you come back to Atlantic?" asked Ahmet Ertegun when he heard the news. "We could have worked together again?"

"Are you kidding?" gasped Geffen. "You're out of it … Atlantic is finished!"

For all his talk, Geffen had also lost his feel for the times. Convinced he needed established names to launch the label, he splashed out a $1.5 million advance on Donna Summer, who, coming down off her Casablanca high, turned out to be depressed, religious and burned-out. For the same price, Geffen then poached Elton John, also going through his own creative and commercial slump.

Geffen was still the best star seducer in the game. At the time, John Lennon had just produced his own comeback album, *Double Fantasy*. Hearing that Lennon was waiting for offers, Geffen outwitted all the contenders by addressing a telegram to Yoko Ono, politely requesting a meeting to discuss *the couple's* musical future. "He's it," Lennon said, smiling at his beaming wife. With Yoko Ono acting as manager, Geffen agreed to another million-dollar advance.

Although lukewarm reviews and slow sales greeted Lennon's midlife comeback on Geffen Records, following his assassination in December 1980, *Double Fantasy* was carried away on a wave of mourning. Fearing accusations of cashing in on Lennon's death, Geffen halted all advertising, but by then, the new label had its first profitable smash hit.

However, inside the Warner empire, Geffen's return was not greeted with equal enthusiasm. When WEA's international division, headed by Nesuhi Ertegun, offered Geffen a modest $1 million advance for the label's export rights, Geffen was furious. Hall & Oates lawyer Allen Grubman heard of Geffen's problems and positioned himself as broker in a rival offer with CBS. The timing was perfect; Grubman's mentor, Walter Yetnikoff, operating solo, had just pitched a film-company project to Warner Communications but had been turned down by Steve Ross. Yetnikoff wanted revenge.

In a New York restaurant, slurping up langoustine and mussels, Yetnikoff agreed to license Geffen's export rights if Grubman begged like a dog. For his finder's fee, the flabby lawyer slumped to his knees and whined, "Plee-eeze!" When Geffen walked off with a $15 million advance from CBS, aghast Warner executives spoke of treason. The calm-headed Mo Ostin, however, remained philosophical, arguing that CBS was only supplying Geffen's start-up with vital cash flow.

Times were hard. As the biggest-selling albums of 1980 illustrated, in the postdisco recession, the embattled majors were reverting to the hard currency of adult-oriented rock. Despite shrinking profits, CBS in particular was on a lucky roll thanks to smash hits such as *The Wall* by Pink Floyd, *The River* by Bruce Springsteen, and *Glass Houses* by Billy Joel. Now five years at the helm, Walter Yetnikoff was coming into his own.

It was common knowledge inside CBS's "Black Rock" tower that Yetnikoff never arrived at work before eleven o'clock. When he did arrive, he was already coked up and smelling of vodka. Since he'd left his wife and sons for twenty-four-hour showbiz action, Yetnikoff's natural habitat was a nocturnal office visited by lawyers, sycophants, and party girls who, according to one old friend, "revealed Walter's low opinion of himself."

Although he wasn't really a record man, Yetnikoff had earned a reputation as a formidable power broker and, underneath his blustery persona, a strangely endearing character whose sense of humour made up for any artistic deficit. Considering he'd endured regular beatings from his father, Yetnikoff's rise from Brooklyn boy to Manhattan mogul had been a remarkable tale of resilience. Maybe because he didn't take himself *that* seriously, yet possessed the tactical and legal instincts to play the game fast and hard, his boozy dictatorship, warts and all, lived long and prospered.

Not everyone *got* him, though. In the sober corridors of CBS Inc., the new, eager-to-please corporate president, John Backe, couldn't really understand how this foul-mouthed specimen had gotten where he was. Fresh into his new functions and anxious to impress Bill Paley, Backe believed the record division needed a self-disciplined technocrat to change what appeared to be a culture of overspending.

Being a former airforce commander, Backe saw an ideal candidate in Dick Asher, a former marine who had run CBS Records in London and was now in charge of the international department in New York. So Asher was promoted to a potentially awkward post – serving as Yetnikoff's deputy head, with a mandate to cut wasteful expenditure.

Studying the books, Asher quickly saw one glaring hole: so-called independents, a network of regional radio pluggers whose services could cost anything up to $100,000 per single. He found out from department staffers – and a series of damning media exposés later revealed – that this opaque system was a nationwide network headed by a certain Fred DiSipio in New York and his counterpart in Los Angeles, Joe Isgro. Suspecting a giant payola scam, Asher added up the invoices and calculated that CBS was forking out a total of $10 million to these independent promoters every year.

Then came the eye-opener. In February 1980, Pink Floyd was in Los Angeles preparing for seven quadraphonic shows complete with inflatable pigs, giant animations, and a four-storey wall that was built and demolished during the performance. Knowing L.A. was gripped by Floyd hysteria, Asher withheld the usual payments to local radio promotion, presuming that under the circumstances L.A. stations would play the hit single "Another Brick in the Wall." Mysteriously, the city's four biggest stations, with a cumulative audience of 3 million, never played the record. When Pink Floyd's manager complained, the necessary payments were made and the radios began playing the single.

Asher was stunned. Yetnikoff was almost laughing. "I like street characters. DiSipio was one," confessed Yetnikoff, who a few years earlier had invited the bespectacled radio promoter to Patsy's Italian restaurant on Fifty-sixth Street. During that dinner, Yetnikoff had asked straight out if his service was disguised payola. DiSipio assured him it was nothing of the sort and he would happily sign Yetnikoff's legal disclaimers. "If the labels had promo men who knew what they were doing, you wouldn't need me," argued DiSipio. "Radio is hit with so much product they need to weed. Radio knows I can weed. Radio respects me. Radio listens to me. What I bring them they play. I'm the maître d' who decides who gets in the restaurant. Give me a hit record, I'll make sure it's played. I don't handle anything but hits."

With the recession biting, Steve Ross's corporate supervisor, David Horowitz, began making his own investigations and calculated these indie promoters were costing Warner, Elektra and Atlantic a total of $6 million each year. In November 1980, *Billboard* reported an unnamed source at Warner announcing a boycott. "The reason independents have not been dropped before now is because each company wanted the next company to do it first. The lead had to be taken by the Warner Communications labels or CBS."

As *Billboard* began quizzing all the major labels about independent promotion, a picture slowly emerged. MCA was also considering dropping independents, whereas Capitol's head of promotions, Bruce Wendell, admitted, "there's no reason in the world I should drop indie promo men … Why should I give up one of my strengths because somebody else does?" Interestingly, *Billboard* also revealed that Atlantic, despite the Warner Communications boycott, was secretly continuing to use independents.

Ignoring these dissenters, Dick Asher began petitioning his superiors. In a crunch meeting with Yetnikoff, Asher wisely avoided any moral diatribes and stuck to tactical arguments. Here was a rare opportunity to break independent promoters who had grown too expensive. Feeling the eyes of Bill Paley and John Backe peering down from above, Yetnikoff yielded, though without sharing any of Asher's zeal. In early 1981, CBS joined the boycott.

What Asher and Horowitz had failed to foresee was the reaction from artists. As red-hot records mysteriously failed to get airplay, managers began throwing toys out of prams. As Paul Marshall, lawyer for the Boomtown Rats and Adam Ant, explained, "My kids were getting injured, and I thought Dick was wrong. I thought he was right morally, assuming there was a moral issue, because I never knew of payola. But you cannot ride a white horse when artists who are giving you your job are the ones suffering the lance." Maurice White of Earth, Wind & Fire told Asher to his face, "Look, man, I have only one career. So don't make me your crusade."

"The ban was a joke," concluded Walter Yetnikoff. "When certain songs didn't hit, it became clear that the indie promo guys knew what they were doing. Given the fiercely competitive nature of the business, an industry-wide boycott never held … Artists hunger for hits with as much, if not more, desperation than the labels. To get around the ban, the labels – including our own – would give extra money to the artists or their managers so that they, and not us, would hire the indies. Any way you looked at it, independent promoters were in the game. If you wanted to play the game – and win – you couldn't ignore them."

A&M promotions man Charly Prevost recalled that despite their subsequent depiction as mobsters, in his own experience indie promoters wouldn't take on a record they didn't believe in. It probably was an opaque system of "greasing the palm," but Prevost always felt "these guys *were* record men."

Casablanca's number two, Larry Harris, agreed, attributing their growing power to the chart and station valuations in *Radio & Records* magazine. "These indie promoters were for the most part into the music and took pride in helping to break a record," said Harris, who saw their rise in the seventies. "They all came from the industry at one point and had decided to work for themselves instead of a corporation. We had people on retainer in Chicago, Portland, Seattle, etc., who had close relationships with their market's programmers. It was well known in the industry who was able to 'take care of business,' but it always bugged me that big business used bribes daily and hardly ever got in trouble, yet we were the ones who got the government on our case. What about payola in the defense industry, the drug industry? Bottom line, the indies had a great service and did it well. If you got the inkling that you had a hit, you could then spend money to bring it home."

"You just gotta remember, it's all done by people," explained another seasoned practitioner of payola, Henry Stone, then the owner of several labels and Florida's biggest independent distributor. "And people like booze, drugs, hookers, expensive meals, and nights on the town. Especially deejays." Living by the philosophy that it takes a dollar to make a dollar, Stone's trusted promoter, Fred Rector, would drive around the Florida stations with a suitcase full of records and money, even though, as Stone always understood, "you can't *buy* a hit record. If it's not a hit and the public don't want it, you can play the hell out of it … but it'll just pass. But a hit record will stick … People still remember those records, to this day, which hadda mean something."

Tested and strengthened by the failed boycott, America's regional independent radio promoters were gradually becoming the official gatekeepers to hitland. They even dared to raise their fees when Warner came back with its tail between its legs. In an industry that admires mischief, most onlookers couldn't help but smirk. As every veteran knew, payola had been around since the late forties when getting R&B records on air meant slipping $50 into the paw of some underpaid jock. The big difference was that now, influential deejays were expecting as much as $10,000 to spin records all over a key region – a fee unaffordable to small record labels. These so-called promoters couldn't turn shit to gold, but even in a time of recession, theirs was a proven system, which, by keeping out the poor, made it easier for the big labels to stay on top.

25. SHADOWS

AS FAR AS THE MOGULS WERE CONCERNED, THE DISCO BUBBLE HAD BURST like a septic boil. Still, right under their runny noses, New York nightlife continued to foreshadow the future of pop music.

In Harlem and the Bronx, thanks to a new generation of club deejays, the turntable had become an instrument in its own right. In 1979, Sugar Hill Records was opened by a former soul singer, Sylvia Robinson, with the financial help of the notorious Morris Levy. Her first release was the seminal "Rapper's Delight" by the Sugarhill Gang. A few months later, Blondie mixed postpunk and rap ingredients into an eerie six-minute groover, "Rapture" – their first No. 1 in America, complete with a video featuring graffiti artists. Although what we now call *hip-hop* had yet to find its name, the last child of the New Wave was officially born.

"By 1979, disco had a negative connotation, and it took the blame for the recession," explained Tom Silverman. "So we changed our name from *Disco News* to *Dance Music Report*. We didn't really like the word *disco* anyway because it was just the place, not the music itself. We trademarked the term 'DOR,' dance-oriented rock, and began reporting *any* kind of music that people were dancing to in clubs. That's when I made my calls to retail and discovered *break beats*."

Silverman telephoned Downstairs Records, a popular deejay store on 6th Avenue and Forty-third Street, and was informed about their new

Breaks Room. "I went down. It was a separate room about the size of a closet. There's just a guy at a desk, and behind him is this strange selection of records: Bob James, the Monkees, Kraftwerk, the Incredible Bongo Band, Cerrone, Billy Squier, a certain record by the Eagles – all these records that seemingly had nothing to do with each other. But there's this line of seventeen-year-old kids out the door – waiting to buy two copies of each!"

Knowing they were amateur deejays too young to have seen these records come out, Silverman asked, "How do you know which ones to buy?"

"We buy what Afrika Bambaataa plays," replied a customer.

Bemused but curious, Silverman tracked down the mysterious name to a club in the Bronx.

"It was this crazy mélange of music: James Brown, Sly & the Family Stone, George Clinton – all this funk mixed with rock and disco and other things. But they were only playing four or eight bars and looping them." Coming in as a reporter, Silverman was equally fascinated by the background story of Afrika Bambaataa, a reformed Black Spades gang member who began Zulu Nation, a community culture movement aiming to pacify and uplift New York's ghettos. "There was still a lot of segregation back then and kids were getting killed. But break-dancing, graffiti, rapping, deejaying," noted Silverman, "these were forms of expression available to people without any money." Wanting to get Afrika Bambaataa's electrifying performances on record, Silverman borrowed $5,000 from his parents and set up Tommy Boy in 1981. "I looked at Sugar Hill Records and realised you didn't need to be a major label. You didn't even need to be smart!"

Meanwhile, in downtown Manhattan, a new dance scene was rapidly evolving from where disco and punk had started. One eyewitness was Craig Kallman, who became the CEO of Atlantic Records in 2005. Kallman was a teenager at the time, sniffing around New York's record stores, determined to get a deejay residency. "When the disco era died, it all moved downtown," he explained. "It had been uptown with Studio 54, Xenon and Copacabana, which were driven by the jet-set, celebrity crowd. But because living in New York City was more affordable back then, you had all these pockets on the Lower East and West Sides." Multicultural, sociologically diverse and distinctly seedy at the edges, these new hot spots were "black, white, Hispanic, gay, straight, transvestite. There were musicians, poets, painters, drug dealers, actors, journalists, you name it."

In addition to clubs like the punky Hurrah on West Sixty-second and the Loft-inspired Paradise Garage downtown, there was a new superclub on West Thirty-seventh Street capturing the very essence of the moment. Opened in 1979 by an adventurous German impresario named Rudolf Pieper, "Danceteria was the ultimate melting pot," according to Kallman. Mixing European artiness with New York multiculturalism, "it had different deejays and musical themes on four distinct floors. I became a resident deejay on Friday and Saturday, trading nights with my compatriot, the legendary Mark Kamins."

Scouring Manhattan's coolest record stores every Saturday, Kallman, like most other deejays of the nascent dance scene, moved between Downstairs Records, Vinyl Mania, 99 Records, Downtown Records, Rock & Soul and Rocks in Your Head – a whole network of genre-specific vinyl hives. "I was buying everything from Fela Kuti to James Brown, New Order to Lee Perry, Eric B. & Rakim to Sylvester, Jorge Ben to Parliament-Funkadelic, Kraftwerk to the Clash. I wanted to be known as the guy that whatever night you were having – reggae, punk, funk, disco, hip-hop, Brazilian, or krautrock – you called Craig."

Apart from its diverse mix of dance floors, Danceteria was also showcasing live bands from the cutting edge. Citing Talking Heads, Tom Tom Club, Depeche Mode and Soft Cell as the pacesetters of New York's nascent dance scene, Kallman concluded with audible nostalgia, "This was the post-punk, Sire Records era. Seymour Stein was king!"

From its Ramones-fuelled liftoff in the late seventies, Sire Records had become New York's most happening record label. Bohemian in spirit but plugged into the WEA machinery, the Brooklyn-bred Seymour Stein had sold half the label to Warner Communications in 1978. Just thirty-six, Stein had begun his career as young as fifteen compiling overseas charts for *Billboard*'s Paul Ackerman, the erudite editor who had also been so important in Jerry Wexler's education. "When I first started working at *Billboard,* more hits were coming out of Germany, France and Italy than the U.K.," said Stein, who never forgot the lesson. "When I got into the business on my own, one of the first sources of repertoire I would look at is music from other territories."

Having learned the actual business as an apprentice for Syd Nathan, the Cincinnati pioneer behind King Records, Stein gained a foothold in the American indie business by negotiating dirt-cheap licences from EMI. From there, he and Sire cofounder Richard Gottehrer invested in a promising British indie, Mike Vernon's Blue Horizon, whose classics included the original Fleetwood Mac. "When I first started coming over to England in the early sixties, I stayed in people's houses," explained Stein. "To save money, Mike Vernon insisted I stay with him. He lived in a Hampstead Garden suburb and his wife cooked a lot. I would have spaghetti on toast and beans on toast. If my mother knew that I was eating that kind of food, I would have been whipped!"

Stein's trips to London became so frequent, he eventually set himself up with a bolthole near Baker Street. Warner's millionaire executives at the time joked, "Seymour Stein, see less money," but as events would illustrate, Warner's fortunes in the eighties would owe much to his street-smart ways. As Pretenders singer and Sire signature Chrissie Hynde described their first meeting in London in 1979, "I was given Seymour's address and walked over there, knocked on his door … Seymour answered, asking if I wanted to go out to a nearby antique market. *Okay.* So we walked over to a flea market and just rooted around."

On a typical Saturday in London, Stein would wander around the Portobello Market, then drop into the nearby Rough Trade store, which by 1980 was bursting at the seams, distributing from its back office hundreds of thousands of records for hot groups like the Specials, the Undertones and Joy Division. Through his London connections, Stein signed up the North American rights to the Rezillos, the Undertones, Echo & the Bunnymen, Simple Minds, Madness, the English Beat, Soft Cell, Depeche Mode and the Cure.

One of the fledgling labels being distributed by Rough Trade was also feeling the transatlantic pulse: Factory Records, a Manchester collective dreamed up in 1979 by Joy Division manager Rob Gretton. Five months after the suicide of Ian Curtis in May 1980, the renamed New Order was in New York as supporting act for their funkier sister group A Certain Ratio. Present on the trip were Factory co-directors Rob Gretton, Tony Wilson and Martin Hannett, the label producer.

"The three weeks saw the team spending a lot of time either playing or hanging out at Hurrah's and Danceteria," remembered Wilson. "Cool design. Clubs as venue and disco and style lounge all in one. The kind of clubs that David Byrne could go to the toilet in." That winter, a crazy idea took root as Wilson and Gretton asked themselves, "If New York had them, then why the fuck didn't Manchester?" With profits from Joy Division's posthumous breakthrough pouring in, Gretton and Wilson dreamed up their biggest gamble, a New York-style superclub in Manchester. Including a stage, discotheque and adjoining lounges, the contemporary-designed Hacienda was built in 1981.

Of all the British indies being distributed through Rough Trade's back office, there was one with a particularly modern tang that New York dance floors were going crazy for. Mute was the synth-pop label behind Depeche Mode – Seymour Stein's biggest-ever American import. Mute's founder, Daniel Miller, was also the producer of Soft Cell's seminal 12-inch "Memorabilia," released in 1981 on Some Bizarre.

As the commercial success of British synth-pop acts like Gary Numan, the Human League, OMD and Visage illustrated, the synthesiser was in vogue. Unlike all the competition listening to Kraftwerk, Daniel Miller had a special feel for Germanic futurism. He was the son of Austrian refugees – effectively a love child from the Vienna exodus in 1938. "My parents didn't know each other before they met in London," explained Miller. "My father when he came to London didn't speak a word of English, which is tricky if you're going to be an actor. But during the war, he ran quite a renowned cabaret club for Austrian émigrés called the Lantern, which turned into a meeting point for Austrian and German refugees. My mother joined as an actress, and that's how they met.

"During the war, my parents both worked for the BBC German service," continued Miller. "Because he was a great impersonator, on one April Fool's Day during the war, he spoofed a Hitler speech, which was broadcast in Germany. It was on the edge of being believable. It was hilarious; a lot of people actually thought it was Hitler."

When Daniel Miller was born in 1951, the dark shadow of the war was locked away out of children's reach. In the cosmopolitan neighbourhood of northwest London, Daniel Miller's childhood was immersed in the postwar spirit of rebuilding. "In those days kids were allowed to play on the street, and there were lots of kids my age. But one day when I was about four or five, I must have heard something at school, because I asked them, 'Who is Adolf Hitler?' And I just remember them looking at each other as if to say, 'Okay, we weren't expecting this quite so early … er … what are we going to say?'"

His father, Martin Miller, was regularly in demand for British TV, films and stage plays. He appeared in the first one thousand performances of Agatha Christie's *The Mousetrap* and played roles in *The Pink Panther, The Prisoner, Doctor Who* and *The Avengers.* Daniel remembered going to film sets as a child. "One memory in particular stands out; my father was in the film *Exodus,* which was made in Israel. We made that a big trip, just my mum, my dad and myself. I must have been about nine at the time."

Following their own brand of humanist, liberal Judaism, the Miller family wasn't religious, although they did treasure the cultural side of Jewish history. Daniel also inherited some of his parents' darker memories, which he began to understand as he entered manhood. "My father never went back to Vienna after the war. The bitterness I felt from my parents was very much geared towards Austria rather than Germany because it was so personal, because of the nature of the Anschluss and what happened in Vienna – how people from one day to the next turned against the Jews. You turned up for work and suddenly they'd say, 'We can't employ you any more,' you were thrown out of university, you had trouble getting into the hospitals, you had to wear a star, you had to clean the streets. It was very direct for my parents, the Austrian experience."

At the heart of these old wounds, his parents saw faces of friends and family. "A lot got out just in time," explained Miller, "but not everybody did. Especially the elderly. It was tragic. The leaving behind of people is the most traumatic thing for those who survived. And it forged their characters for the rest of their lives."

Miller says he has come to accept "all that probably did creep into my character. I was very conscious of it." At the same time, "when you grow up in that environment, it is very normal. And I had friends who had similar histories." Also, as a young man, Daniel Miller felt a certain affinity with young Germans, who, like himself, had been born into a type of haunted house. Not only was Daniel Miller's first girlfriend German, his parents didn't object.

Although he had been heavily into music as a boy, Miller's big awakening occurred shortly after his father died in 1969. "There was a combination of things that happened around the same time," explained Miller. "I was looking for something new and then I came across an Amon Düül record in a shop and I heard Can on John Peel. I just thought, 'Wow!' It wasn't Anglo-American, it wasn't based on blues, it wasn't based on traditions of British pop music.

"Don't forget, there wasn't just krautrock," recounts Miller, who at the time was studying film and television at the Guildford School of Art. "There were all the German filmmakers like Rainer Werner Fassbinder, Werner Herzog and Wim Wenders. They were redefining a sort of new German culture that wiped away the hangover from the war, but at the same time, they were conscious of not basing this new culture on American or English influences."

Miller got his first jobs editing commercials, then deejayed in Switzerland. Drawn back to London by the punk explosion, he bought a Korg 700S synthesiser and TEAC four-track recorder and made his own homemade recordings. One fateful day in 1978, aged twenty-seven, he stepped nervously into the Rough Trade shop with a test pressing under his arm. Geoff Travis appeared from the back office and played the record on the store's sound system. Travis nodded his head to the edgy electronica interlaced with abstract spoken word, as customers continued browsing through the racks. When the music came to an end, Travis nonchalantly ordered 2,000 copies. Mute was in business.

When returning from a tour, Miller found a pile of demos on his doorstep. Apparently other musicians who bought his first single had mailed their demos to the address on the sleeve. He started listening to the creations of his admirers, and in 1979 he signed Fad Gadget. The following year, he found Depeche Mode, who in 1981 broke into the British charts with their second single on Mute, "New Life," shortly before scoring their first major hit, "Just Can't Get Enough" – whose American rights Seymour Stein gladly scooped up.

Also listening to Mute's early releases was the Jamaican diva Grace Jones, one of the Studio 54 regulars who in 1977 had struck gold with a stirring disco remake of Edith Piaf's "La Vie en Rose." Since then, Chris Blackwell had taken over her production at his Compass Point studio in the Bahamas. Reoriented and repackaged in stunning sleeve designs, her bizarre poetry was dubbed up by Sly & Robbie, then plasticised by French-Beninese keyboardist Wally Badarou. As well as dance-floor gems like "Pull Up to the Bumper" and a haunting electro-dub remake of Astor Piazzolla's "Libertango," she even covered Daniel Miller's first single, "Warm Leatherette."

Despite plenty of interesting traffic coming through Blackwell's Compass Point, including Talking Heads offshoot Tom Tom Club, Island Records was drifting into the doldrums. In the snakes and ladders of the music business, Chris Blackwell's elusive muse had found a home in Jamaica. Experiencing Bob Marley's global rise as a crowning moment in his own life as a record man, Blackwell understandably hadn't dived into the New Wave with adequate gusto. Inevitably, Island's vulnerability was laid bare in 1981, when Bob Marley died at the shockingly early age of thirty-six.

Compounding the feeling that an era was over, just four months later, Guy Stevens, the estranged A&R man who had been so instrumental in Island's early history, died after a long battle with drug addiction and alcoholism. "Guy got heavily into drugs, and we sort of got him off of it," remembered David Betteridge. "He did a year in jail because of it – ridiculously long – then he took the cure but, what happens quite a lot, he got into drinking. I'd left Island, but I saw him at CBS with the Clash, who he was producing. He was a wreck of a man by then. It was a great, great shame. When he died in 1981, he was only thirty-eight."

Another bereaved friend was Andrew Lauder, one of London's most respected A&R men, whose signatures for United Artists included Can, Motorhead, Dr. Feelgood, the Buzzcocks and the Stranglers. "When we had Radar Records," recalled Lauder of his subsequent job, "Guy used to come around, usually in a horrible state ... stinking of alcohol. I used to dread it but I couldn't not see him. Just the other day when I was opening a box, I found a book he'd given me because I'd lent him some money so he could go see the kids. He went soon after that."

In that dark summer of 1981, Andrew Lauder was cajoled into becoming Island's new A&R man. Flattered but sceptical, Lauder asked his old friend, Island managing director Martin Davis, whether Chris Blackwell really would allow others to sign acts to Island. Davis made a call, whereupon it was suggested that he and Lauder fly out to the Bahamas. Blackwell welcomed him with a smile and "It's great to have you with us!" Too embarrassed to quibble about A&R freedom while enjoying Blackwell's hospitality in the palm-tree setting, Lauder accepted the inevitable, "so by the end of the weekend, various carrots had been dangled; I was head of A&R and a director at Island."

When Lauder arrived at his new job, he found a company in crisis. "A lot of negative things were happening; it was the year Marley died – a very dark cloud hung over St. Peter's Square. Gloom and doom descended ... I had been told, 'Don't worry, Chris is always in America, he hasn't been here for months,' but the day I started, it was a case of 'Good Lord, Chris is here!' ... Almost immediately I got a phone call. 'Can you go and see Vic Godard and the Subway Sect at the Lyceum? Chris would like you to go check it out.' So I did. And I thought it was a pile of old turd – a poor man's Tony Bennett or something. So I passed on the message, 'Yeah, went to see it, didn't like it, these are the reasons.' End of story. Then a couple of days later, you'd get bits of conversations coming back to you: 'Chris isn't very happy.' 'What's he not happy about?' 'That you didn't want to do the Vic Godard.' 'Well, if he wants to do the Vic Godard, it's *his* company!'

Lauder was then called in as firefighter on Marianne Faithfull's follow-up to *Broken English* – a wilted tulip of an album titled *Dangerous Acquaintances.* "The producer had a nervous breakdown and she was in really bad shape," Lauder remembered. "Work was just not getting done. I came home every night at 5:00 A.M. having been sitting on the stairs just talking to Marianne trying to keep the thing from going off the rails ... Then a few weeks later, someone in the corridor asked me, 'Are you going to the Marianne Faithfull release party tonight?' And I'm standing there, 'What,

Phonograph inventor Thomas Edison, 1895. He gave us the technology but didn't have an ear for the music that would drive his world-famous brand. *Library of Congress*

Gramophone inventor Emile Berliner. A musician and idealist, his brief but decisive influence on the fledgling industry would inspire the twentieth century. *Library of Congress*

The first record mogul, Victor Talking Machine founder Eldridge R. Johnson. He inherited Berliner's patents and built the world's biggest label. *Library of Congress*

Italian tenor Enrico Caruso, the first international superstar of the record age. Beside him, the machine that transformed the industry, the Victrola. *Library of Congress*

Ralph Peer journeyed from Okeh field recorder to country mogul, in 1920 he recorded Mamie Smith's "Crazy Blues," then in 1928 the equally seminal Bristol Sessions featuring Jimmie Rodgers and the Carter Family. *Courtesy peermusic*

Harry Pace, founder of Ethel Waters's mythical label, Black Swan. Despite its claims as the first authentic African-American record company, Pace may have been Italian. *Courtesy Peter Pace*

John Lomax, musicologist and field recorder who in 1933 discovered Lead Belly in a state penitentiary in Louisiana. *Library of Congress*

Beatles producer George Martin in the British Fleet Air Arm, 1947. He had just taught himself music theory and in 1950 would join Parlophone, an EMI label on Abbey Road. *Courtesy George Martin*

CBS founder William Paley bought out Columbia in 1938 and remained its corporate chairman until 1983. *Library of Congress*

Motown founder Berry Gordy with Levi Stubbs of The Four Tops. *Michael Ochs Archives/Getty Images*

A&R legend John Hammond (centre) with Count Basie, one of his discoveries. Others included Billie Holiday, Aretha Franklin, Bob Dylan, Leonard Cohen and Bruce Springsteen. *Getty Images*

Sun Records founder Sam Phillips (right) with Elvis Presley and his bassist and guitarist Bill Black and Scotty Moore. *GAB Archive/Redferns/Getty Images*

The music industry's most lovable rogue, Ahmet Ertegun, founder of Atlantic. His star-spangled career spanned five decades. *Warner Music Archive*

Jerry Wexler, *Billboard* writer turned R&B producer who broke Ray Charles and Aretha Franklin. In 1968, he also signed Led Zeppelin to Atlantic. *Warner Music Archive*

A man with a plan, Steve Ross, Warner's corporate boss from 1970 to 1992. *Warner Music Archive*

Highfliers on the Warner jet: (Left to right) Stan Cornyn, Russ Thyret, Joe Smith and Chrysalis founders Terry Ellis and Chris Wright. Mo Ostin is seated on the extreme right. *Courtesy Stan Cornyn*

Columbia boss Clive Davis (left) with Nina and Jac Holzman, New York, 1968. *Jac Holzman Archive*

Jimi Hendrix watched by Dave Robinson, his then roadie, during the recording of Eire Apparent's *Sunrise* album, Los Angeles, 1968. *Courtesy Dave Robinson*

From Greenwich Village to Sunset Strip – Jac Holzman, the Elektra founder who signed the Doors. *Jac Holzman Archive*

Stiff Records co-founder Dave Robinson with guitarist Martin Belmont, 1979. An Irishman in search of London's own folk, Robinson discovered and broke Ian Dury, Graham Parker, Elvis Costello, Lene Lovich, Madness and the Pogues. *Courtesy Dave Robinson*

Arguably Britain's greatest ever record man, Island founder Chris Blackwell. Among many important signatures, he brought Bob Marley to the world. *Courtesy Petersimon.com*

Simon Draper, the ears behind Virgin Records. Signing Mike Oldfield, Tangerine Dream, XTC, the Flying Lizards, OMD, the Human League, Simple Minds, Heaven 17, UB40, Culture Club and Phil Collins, among others, Draper was instrumental in forging the sound of the 1980s. *Courtesy Simon Draper*

Supertramp's *Crime of the Century* launch, 1974. From left, band manager Dave Margereson, A&M London boss Derek Green and a bobby questioning A&M cofounder Jerry Moss about the party serving alcohol after hours. Green and Moss would later break The Police. *Courtesy Derek Green*

Ivo Watts-Russell, cofounder of 4AD, the label behind Bauhaus, Modern English, the Cocteau Twins, Dead Can Dance, Throwing Muses and Pixies. *Courtesy Ivo Watts-Russell*

Punk pioneers: The Ramones with Sire cofounder Seymour Stein (third from right) standing beside band manager Danny Fields (far right). In 1968, Fields brought MC5 and protopunks the Stooges onto Elektra. Seymour Stein would soon sign Talking Heads and, in 1982, Madonna. *Warner Music Archive*

Mute founder and electro pioneer Daniel Miller. Another key taste-maker of the 1980s, he broke Fad Gadget, Depeche Mode, Nick Cave, Yazoo, Erasure and, later, Moby and Goldfrapp. *Courtesy Antoine Giacomoni*

Geoff Travis, the young idealist who started Rough Trade. As an A&R man, he signed Cabaret Voltaire, Stiff Little Fingers, Virgin Prunes, The Fall, and The Smiths. He managed Pulp and, with partner Jeannette Lee, signed The Strokes, Antony and the Johnsons, Warpaint, The Libertines, Alabama Shakes and Palma Violets. *Courtesy Geoff Travis*

Martin Mills, Beggars Group chairman and indie-community chieftain. Forty years in the game, he remains probably the most respected figure in the business. *Courtesy Martin Mills*

The catalyst in Seattle, Sub Pop founder Bruce Pavitt. Inspired by Rough Trade in England, he began America's very own indie charts and eventually discovered Nirvana. *Courtesy Bruce Pavitt*

Hip-hop pioneer and Tommy Boy founder Tom Silverman. Researching break beats as a journalist in 1980, he found Afrika Bambaataa, a path that led him to Queen Latifah, De La Soul and many others. *Courtesy Tom Silverman*

Young mogul Craig Kallman, today's CEO of Atlantic. A former deejay, he has privately built up one of the largest vinyl collections in the world, numbering some 750,000 discs. *Courtesy Grayson Dantzic*

Rick Rubin, Def Jam and American Recordings founder – arguably the most important producer of his generation. As a young man, he mixed rock with hip-hop, producing Run-D.M.C., Beastie Boys and Public Enemy. As well as the milestone *Blood Sugar Sex Magik* by Red Hot Chili Peppers, he produced Johnny Cash's last albums. *Annabel Mehran*

uh, is there a party?' because nobody had told me anything." Just as Lauder had feared, he was playing the role of A&R butler.

The previous year, Island had signed a young postpunk group called U2. So Lauder was sent to Dublin to report on the final stretch of their second album, *October.* "It looked so obvious to me that this group could be huge. They'd just come off the road touring their first album, *Boy,* and of course they were struggling with that difficult follow-up. I thought, why is Island pissing around with some of the things they're doing, instead of giving a big push behind this group that any bozo could see was gonna do something … I remember Chris always having reservations. He was always going 'yes, but…' about U2."

Lauder came up with the idea to include a free copy of the single "Gloria" inside the album sleeve as a release-only special edition. "It was a trick we used to do at United Artists. It got all the fans to run out and buy the new album on release. Chris was against the idea; he thought it would just make a quick stir then the record would fall away. We did it anyway, and sure enough it charted, then fell away. He said, 'Look, I told you so.' And I said, 'It got them their first chart position. What's bad about that?'"

In every department, Lauder noticed "it was very difficult for anyone to make any meaningful decisions without bumping into the ol' 'What does Chris think?' No matter what you suggested or gave them, it always came back as 'Well, what does Chris think?' And after a bit you start to say, 'I don't know. I haven't asked him. But this is what *I* think.'"

Island Records at the time was employing a staff of about 120, a costly operation to keep fed without a major act. Inevitably, under the weight of such an absent, cultlike figure, office politics were rife. Despite the label's origins in the late sixties as a gang of kindred spirits, Island Records in the early eighties had turned into a sort of third-world monarchy – run-down, absolutist, unfair. To get ahead one had to play the game according to local rules, or emigrate.

By 1982, the British market was taking a giant leap into pop. The biggest names of the New Wave, like the Police, Madness, the Jam, the Stranglers, the Clash, Adam Ant and UB40, were still scoring hits, but their sounds were softening. Usurping them at the top of the charts was this new generation of synth-pop groups: the Human League, Duran

Duran, Depeche Mode, Yazoo, Culture Club, Soft Cell, Eurythmics. It took one of Island's affiliate labels, ZE Records, which symbolised New York's so-called *no-wave* movement, to supply Island's only significant hits in 1982 – the album *Tropical Gangsters* by Kid Creole & the Coconuts, whose salsa-infused hit singles included "Stool Pigeon" and "Annie I'm Not Your Daddy."

The very fabric of demand was changing. As Island's head of publishing, Lionel Conway, noted, "We had career bands in the seventies. It all just changed in the eighties. It basically became more like a singles market. There were a lot of one-offs, and we weren't equipped for that."

Others were, however – in particular, clued-in New York deejays whose job was to spot and test individual tracks from all over the world. "It all grew out of the record stores," Craig Kallman believed. "I lived in those stores and I'd bump into Rick Rubin, the Beastie Boys, Larry Levan, Jellybean Benitez, Afrika Bambaataa. There was truly a revolution happening with so much exciting music coming out of New York, L.A. and Miami. The U.K. scene was hot, too, so there was this huge wave of seven- and twelve-inch imports, especially from the big importers like Rough Trade and Important. The club scene was exploding with so many new sounds, dance and hip-hop mixed with U.K. alternative music and U.S. indie rock. And in the record stores, deejays were fighting over new releases as they were coming in – because there were never enough copies to go around."

In May 1982, Tom Silverman's fledgling label, Tommy Boy, released "Planet Rock" by Afrika Bambaataa, a classic hip-hop record notable for its use of a drum machine and sampler. Two months later, Sugar Hill Records released an even bigger genre milestone: "The Message" by Grandmaster Flash & the Furious Five. "I don't think people today can imagine just what a radical departure rap and hip-hop felt like," said Tom Silverman. "There was this confluence of everything coming together at once: the 808 drum machine, the first Fairlight and Synclavier samplers, breakdancing, graffiti, quick-cut deejay techniques, rapping. It was just such a strange synthesis of so many new things."

In fairness to the experienced Chris Blackwell, even at Island's lowest point, he was barking up the right trees. As well as starting a dance sublabel, 4th & B'way, named after the address of Island's New York office, he was considering hiring Danceteria deejay Mark Kamins as a talent magnet. When Seymour Stein heard the news, he was laid up in the hospital undergoing treatment for a heart infection. Going stir-crazy listening to demos while penicillin dripped into his arm, Stein immediately telephoned Kamins, to whom he had given $18,000 to produce some recordings. Unbeknown to Stein, Chris Blackwell had already turned down Kamins's latest discovery – a singing, dancing pop-doll named Madonna Ciccone, whose first effort, "Everybody," Kamins had been spinning at Danceteria. "Can I meet her?" asked Stein – who had, after all, paid for the experiment.

At about three in the afternoon, Kamins called back warning that Madonna would drop by the hospital at eight o'clock. Unbathed, unshaven, with his backside protruding from his hospital gown, Stein worked the telephone all afternoon. His secretary delivered a pair of pyjamas; his barber arrived for an emergency grooming; his doctors allowed him to wash. "I figured that I had to look healthy," Stein remembered, smiling. "It was the beginning of the AIDS epidemic, and I didn't want Madonna to think that she was signing with someone who wasn't going to be around much longer."

Stein knew that to produce and market a pop artist, he would need Warner funding. Because Mo Ostin tried to torpedo the deal, he took Madonna's case to Nesuhi Ertegun, still head of WEA's international division.

"My brother tells me you're in hospital," said Nesuhi Ertegun. "Just listen to the doctors and I'll give you what you need to sign her."

That night, Madonna walked into Stein's ward. "I could have been lying in a coffin," he said. "It didn't matter to her. All she wanted was a deal."

26. CYCLOPS

FOR HOT INDEPENDENTS, THE EIGHTIES BEGAN AROUND 1978. FOR CERTAIN majors, the seventies lingered on to 1983. Moguls like Walter Yetnikoff and David Geffen were, for the most part, blind to the synth-pop, post-punk and hip-hop sounds stirring up the New York club scene. In fairness, so was most of America. As if disco and punk had never happened, the biggest-selling album of 1981 came from seventies rock group REO Speedwagon, on CBS sublabel Epic. The following year, a supergroup of ageing British progressive rockers, Asia, scored America's biggest-selling album – 4 million copies for Geffen Records. Anyone looking at the bottom line was seeing that established names producing high-quality adult-oriented rock remained the most bankable commodities on the market.

Those with ears knew better. In 1981, A&M boss Jerry Moss took his future wife, Anne, on a trip to London via the Concorde. On arrival, the taxi took them to Derek Green's house, where, as coincidence would have it, the Police were on the TV screen, performing on *Top of the Pops*. Discussing which restaurant to eat in, Moss's attention was drawn back to the television a few minutes later. It was "Don't You Want Me" by the Human League. He shared a knowing glance with his girlfriend. "We just couldn't get it out of our heads," said Moss, who the very next day tracked down the infectious tune to familiar faces at Virgin. On Richard Branson's houseboat, Moss negotiated the Human League's North American rights.

Returning to Los Angeles with a copy of the accompanying album, *Dare!*, Moss played "Don't You Want Me" to his head of sales and promotions, Harold Childs. An astute character who only wore white suits and a Panama hat, Childs started making calls in his customary manner – always standing up in his office, no chair, television permanently on. "I recall a promotional trip with Harold to all of A&M's field staff," said Martin Kirkup, the company's artist development VP. Despite the unfamiliar synthesised sound, "the enthusiastic reaction it got everywhere was partially due to the narrative of the lyrics. The promotion guys could relate to 'you were working as a waitress in a cocktail bar.' The story arc of *A Star Is Born* gave it great depth." However, the record's momentum was slow; starting on the progressive Los Angeles stations, it eventually won over Top 40 radio, city by city, reaching the Midwest. The single climbed to No. 1 on *Billboard*'s *Hot 100* as the album peaked at No. 3.

One surprising admirer of the Human League's quirky sound was Neil Young, who had just moved to Geffen Records for another million-per-album advance. In 1982, Young delivered his infamous album *Trans*, a jarring mix of synthesisers, folk-rock and ethereal vocoders. When it flopped with an unrecouped advance, David Geffen interrupted the recording of its country-flavoured follow-up, *Old Ways*, demanding that Young just make some "rock 'n' roll." Picking up on Geffen's choice of words, the pissed-off Canadian renamed his band the Shocking Pinks and banged out a kitsch satire of Elvis-era 12-bar rockabilly. Called *Everybody's Rockin'*, the thirty-minute comedy album ended in an equally farcical $3 million lawsuit – in which Geffen's attorneys failed to convince the court that Neil Young was fraudulently making albums unrepresentative of himself.

Over at CBS, Walter Yetnikoff was also accelerating with his eye on the rearview mirror. Even though Mick Jagger was barely speaking to the tattered Keith Richards, Yetnikoff spent an exhausting year trying to bag the Stones. "It amused Mick to see hungry record execs chasing his skinny ass around the world," admitted Yetnikoff, who was thoroughly teased and outsmarted by the Stones' singer. "His image as the prancing prince of rock belied that side of his character that had seriously studied economics." Following tortuous negotiations, *Rolling Stone* magazine reported that the $25 million deal "shapes up as no apparent moneymaker for CBS." An unnamed source even admitted what staffers were whispering outside Yetnikoff's office – "a prestige move more than anything."

In that difficult year of 1982, CBS's $1 billion turnover yielded a paltry $22 million profit, forcing Walter Yetnikoff on Friday, August 13, to close two factories and lay off three hundred workers. Few in the postwar record business had witnessed anything like it. In urgent need of a win, he picked up his telephone and called Michael Jackson, who hadn't released an album since his 1979 disco blockbuster *Off the Wall*. The message was simple: we need another smash – mixed, packaged and in stores for Christmas trade.

An emergency session was convened in Santa Monica by Jackson's producer, Quincy Jones, who announced the daunting challenge to his production team. "Okay, guys, we're here to save the recording industry!" Working flat-out, they delivered *Thriller* just in time for a rush release on November 30. "You gotta remember the time and place," said keyboardist Brian Banks. "The record business was in the dumps right then. I remember one night, when they were looking at a bunch of proofs, large blow-ups of the centrefold, spread out on the console, and I was just there in the background doing my thing while Quincy was talking. *Off the Wall* sold something like eight million records, and I remember Quincy saying, 'The record business is not what it was a couple of years ago, and if we get six million out of this, I'm gonna declare that a success.'"

To handle *Thriller*'s marketing, Yetnikoff chose the perfect CBS executive, Frank Dileo, an Italian American who was good friends with Joe Isgro, "the Network's" main man in Los Angeles. For $100,000 per song, Isgro and his radio promotion colleagues covering other regions pulled out all the stops, embarking on a strategy of blitzkrieg. While "Billie Jean" was No. 1, CBS released "Beat It" as a single. Such a mass assault hadn't been witnessed since the Beatles invasion of 1964; this time, *Thriller* was a concerted plan. All seven singles from its nine-song track list entered the Top 10, while the album held the No. 1 spot for thirty-seven weeks. Within one year of release, *Thriller* had earned CBS $60 million, immediately wiping away any residual gloom from the previous four years. Conservative estimates begin at 45 million unit sales to date. As monster hits go, *Thriller* was the King Kong of the vinyl jungle.

The industrial renaissance of 1983 had another arm that coincided with *Thriller*. Originally set up in 1981 by Steve Ross and American Express, MTV was a novel channel showing nothing but pop music videos on a twenty-four-hour rotation. When "Billie Jean" was refused by MTV, Jackson's manager, Ron Weisner, called Walter Yetnikoff to flag what was widely rumoured to be MTV's white-only policy. In an uncharacteristically cautious move by a man otherwise known for shouting into telephones, Yetnikoff consulted the powerful Bill Paley, who personally telephoned MTV and threatened that if the video wasn't broadcast that very day, CBS Records wouldn't do any future business with the channel. Fearing the wrath of Paley's long arms, MTV aired "Billie Jean" hours later.

Despite pocketing a record-breaking royalty of 42 percent on the wholesale price of every record sold, Michael Jackson was obsessive about staying on top. Walter Yetnikoff couldn't believe how "I used to get calls from Michael in the middle of the night. 'Walter, the record is not number one ... what are we going to do?' I said, 'We're going to go to sleep and deal with it tomorrow.'" Realising that Yetnikoff didn't share his panic, Michael Jackson came up with a stunt to push *Thriller* back to No. 1. Using the horror film *An American Werewolf in London* as a reference video for the album's title track, Jackson contacted director John Landis.

The only problem was that Landis's idea for a fourteen-minute "theatrical short" would cost half a million dollars. Jackson called Yetnikoff, explained the concept, and passed the phone over to Landis, who later remembered "this blast of flaming – 'You motherfucker! What the fuck's the matter with you?' The one conversation I ever had with Walter Yetnikoff – you know, in movies where they hold the phone away?"

"OK, I'll pay," Jackson told Yetnikoff. However, John Landis and his logistics man, George Folsey, found a better plan – to film forty-five minutes' worth of behind-the-scenes footage to lead up to the actual short film. Thus they were able to pitch a sixty-minute documentary to TV broadcasters. They initiated a bidding war, until MTV and Showtime each pitched in $250,000 for the rights. The landmark "Thriller" video was broadcast in December 1983, a year after the album's official release, sparking a second wave of Jackson hysteria.

Despite the drama, Yetnikoff was, well, thrilled with how the whole episode had played out. Thanks to the excitement aroused by *Thriller* and MTV, the entire record industry in 1983 lifted itself out of recession, registering a 4.7 percent increase. Dick Asher, forced to forget his anti-payola crusade, noted, "When the tide comes in, all the ships go up."

It was probably no coincidence that just as *Thriller* exploded, Warner decided to pump serious resources into its most promising talent, Prince – a singing, dancing multi-instrumentalist, who'd released five critically acclaimed funk-rock records on Warner since 1978. Following his first Top 10 commercial success in early 1983 with "Little Red Corvette," Warner talked its movie division into a risky gamble to relaunch Prince. Filmed throughout the year and released in 1984, the semi-autobiographical musical drama film *Purple Rain* was an instant hit – the turning point in Prince's long and colourful career. The film soundtrack went on to sell over 10 million copies.

As this new generation of televisual pop music exploded across the globe, a technological revolution was sweeping across Japan. Some Japanese and Dutch industrialists believed it had the potential to create a worldwide music boom of historical proportions – the compact disc.

Its most powerful champion was Norio Ohga, a former opera singer and senior executive at Sony. The other industrial giant involved was the Dutch conglomerate Philips, at the time merged with German manufacturer Siemens. Although Sony and Philips had each developed its own variation of the same principle, because Sony had just lost millions with its Betamax videocassette, both companies recognised the wisdom in pooling their patents for one standard format.

The first American company to yield to pressure from CD demonstrators was CBS, who since 1968 were in a joint agreement with Sony to sell their records in Japan. In Europe, it was easy to understand PolyGram's enthusiasm for the CD; the company was owned by Philips. Crawling out of the disco wreckage, PolyGram had hired a new president from the Philips talent pool, Jan Timmer, a former accountant with a flair for spotting opportunities. Like Ohga, Timmer was convinced the CD was the most important invention of the times.

Realising PolyGram lacked the music catalogue to go it alone, Timmer began prospecting for a big American partner. He offered Warner

Communications a merger, finding an ally in David Horowitz and a receptive ear in Steve Ross, who, having bought out Atari, was far better acquainted with new technology than his record moguls. Throughout the early eighties, Ross had even commissioned internal reports investigating whether video games were partly responsible for the waning demands for records. Walter Yetnikoff, however, lobbied Washington and kicked off a public debate in the press. Eventually, the Federal Trade Commission intervened and put an end to the Warner-PolyGram merger on grounds of anti-trust.

Despite a few raised eyebrows in the predominantly Jewish record business because compact discs were a Germanic and Japanese collaboration, the figures coming out of Japan were mouth-watering. After just four months in Japanese shops, Sony was already at maximum capacity, selling 10,000 machines and 300,000 discs per month. Sales projections for 1984 were anticipating 10 million discs for Japan alone. The other key detail was price. Japanese consumers were lining up to pay the equivalent of $17, almost twice the price of vinyl, for records they already owned.

Creeping slowly throughout 1983, the volume of American CD trade rose to $103.3 million. Although record labels couldn't have guessed what lay around the corner, the compact disc was poised to become the biggest boom in the record business's century-long history. Like the radio giants of the twenties and thirties, the world's media and hardware conglomerates of the eighties were gazing down from their towers, salivating over this truly global, multibillion-dollar gold mine.

As the most powerful record executive in the world, Walter Yetnikoff, described the sudden sea change from bust to boom, "In a few years, just as cocaine contributed to the decline of what was left of my moral character, Michael Jackson, who never touched a drug, soared into the stratosphere, creating a buying frenzy that consolidated my power base even further. MTV, compact discs – the decade would see a series of innovations that fattened profits and led to excess on my part. Soon the eighties would make the hedonistic seventies appear altruistic."

27. LEGENDS

IN THE AUTUMN OF 1983, DAVE ROBINSON GOT AN UNEXPECTED PHONE CALL.
It was Chris Blackwell fishing for a new managing director. Although
flattered, Robinson at first politely declined, citing his commitment to
Stiff, then a seven-year-old indie employing twenty-six staff.

Still, Robinson didn't flatly close the door. After Chris Blackwell
helped Stiff Records weather the storm of Jake Riviera's sudden departure
in 1977, "we became pretty close," admitted Robinson. "About three times
a year we'd have dinner. When he'd come to town, I'd be high up on his
list of people to meet and talk about things." Now aged thirty-nine and
awaiting his second child, Robinson was feeling the pressure to provide
security. As for the prestige, "Island was the model."

Eventually, Blackwell came up with an offer too good to refuse. "He
said, 'I'll buy half of Stiff, you run Island, I'll give you a share of Island's
profits.'" The two men met for dinner in a Chinese restaurant in Mayfair,
where Blackwell wrote a two-clause contract on a sheet of facsimile paper
– one clause for 50 percent of Stiff's shares, valued at £2 million, and the
other clause for the 20 percent profit-share system. They signed their
names on the page, shook hands, and ordered their desserts.

Unfortunately, things didn't turn out so simple. "It never occurred to
me that Island would not have money," sighed Robinson. "When I got
into the company and started looking through the accounts, they had no

money; they were broke, and in actual fact, they were probably insolvent." Confronting Blackwell, the legendarily blunt Irishman said, "Look, I should really pull out of this because it's not happening. Number two, how are you gonna pay me for the Stiff shares?"

Producing another carrot on the table, "Blackwell said, 'Look, I'll buy half of Stiff, and three or four years down the road, we'll sell the whole shooting match. I'll do very well and you'll do great.' So I agreed – foolishly – that the money for the Stiff shares was to be paid quarterly, in instalments of £250,000, to help them with cash flow."

Walking in from Stiff, where he made his employees work hard, Robinson "found Island a little baffling to begin with. I listened to all the albums lined up for release, and I thought, 'What's going on here? This is terminal. This can't work. We haven't got the money, we haven't got the release schedule. Who's been doing all this?'" There was also the bizarre office politics. "I'd be having these very enthusiastic meetings with the guys and then I'm getting no reaction. And I'm very people conscious, I see when people don't meet your eye. So I'm thinking, 'What the fuck's going on?' It took me a while to suss it out. Then I got a tipoff from one of the staff. Basically Blackwell would get up late in Jamaica, he'd have a few spliffs, and he'd call people in London and ask, 'What happened today?'

"In those days the fax machine was very new and there was only one in the whole company, so I asked my secretary to copy everything coming in and out. And I read every fax because it was the only way I could find out what was really happening. I was amazed by the faxes. Of course Blackwell was on the end of most of them. Everything was being sent to him – acetates, cuts, artwork. But it wasn't like he ever got back to anything the following day. He'd have a few spliffs, he'd go to Miami, wander around. No decision would be made. So there was an awful lot of apathy inside the company where staff would send something off knowing they wouldn't hear anything back for two or three weeks."

Convinced Blackwell's absentee control was the source of the company's dysfunction, Robinson put him on the spot. "What do you think you're doing? What the fuck? You've got no money. You've sold me a pup." Although Blackwell didn't like getting his nose shoved into the rug stain, in choosing a tough nut like Dave Robinson, he may have been subconsciously asking for a reality check. So, with Blackwell's mixed blessings, Robinson began a series of unpopular but necessary reforms.

Years of rust had eaten into every nook and cranny of Island. Robinson felt it could only be wiped away by a brief but decisive reign of terror. "I put intercoms on all the desks so that I could listen in to their phone conversations. It drove them potty, but they were all talking to fucking girlfriends, or their mother, or their granny, or booking their American holidays. I had several meetings and I said this isn't how it's going to be."

One staffer in the sales division, Ray Cooper, recalled the unforgettable dawn of the Dave Robinson era. "Island was the only company in the U.K. with open-space offices. It was like a charming big war room with gold discs on the walls. There was a massive board on one side where everything was written down – chart positions, live, artist info. But when Dave got in, he threw out all the potted palm trees and plants. He wanted to make it a little more sterile. Then he put a tannoy [intercom] system in, so you'd press a button and he'd tell you what he wanted you to do. When it was installed, his first command was to a guy called Ken Hallett who did things for Chris. The tannoy suddenly spoke in that voice of Dave's. 'Ken Hallett, get me some cheese … *now!*' Everyone just turned and looked at each other."

To Robinson's single-sensitive ears, the one obvious contender in Island's otherwise "crap" release schedule was "Relax" by an unknown group from Liverpool called Frankie Goes to Hollywood. It had been produced by "Video Killed the Radio Star" creator Trevor Horn, whose Island affiliated sublabel, ZTT, had just been set up in the old Basing Street studio. Throughout the autumn of 1983, "Relax" was languishing around No. 70, failing to break through.

Robinson ordered from America 5,000 copies of a seven-minute remix called the "Sex Mix," which he'd heard visiting Island's New York office. Sensing that Christmas was an ideal time to make noise while other record companies were on holiday, Robinson ordered twelve salesmen to tour the strategic retailers, greasing the palms of assistants who played "Relax" on the store's public address system. The 5,000 copies sold out so that after Christmas, the record sneaked inside the Top 40. That week, a big act pulled out of *Top of the Pops* and, grinning in their leathers, Frankie

Goes to Hollywood got their first TV appearance. "Relax" shot up to No. 6 in the second week of January.

Then the media outrage erupted. BBC Radio 1 deejay Mike Read lifted the needle mid-broadcast, branding the song "obscene." Then BBC Radio 1 producer Ted Beston telephoned Robinson personally. "We're banning 'Relax' by Frankie Goes to Hollywood," he announced. "I don't understand, why would you ban it?" Robinson asked.

"It's all about ejaculation."

"Well, how can you say that?" Robinson asked with an air of beguiling innocence. "If you were to ban records that *might* be about something like that, you'd be banning an awful lot of them. The other thing," continued Robinson, "is that I've met Holly Johnson's mother last week, and this is the first job that Holly's ever had. He's been on the dole all his life and suddenly he's in a band that's happening. His mother was very pleased – very Irish she was. I can give you her number. You can tell her you're banning her son's first record."

"I'm not talking to her!" blasted Beston with increasing irritation.

"Well, the least you could do is talk to the press and explain why you're banning it," responded Robinson with equal force.

To Robinson's utter amazement, Beston agreed. "Okay, I will. If you set up a press reception, I'll talk to them."

That afternoon, 175 media operatives were cordially convened to hear a spokesman for BBC Radio 1 explain, as Robinson put it, that " 'Relax' by Frankie Goes to Hollywood is a song about ejaculation."

Bingo! Adding to the song's rebellious cache, *Top of the Pops* was sucked into the affair and banned "Relax" for the five embarrassing weeks it stayed No. 1. In total, the record sold 2 million copies, the third-biggest single of the year in Britain. "I'm happy to accept that 'Relax' wouldn't have *happened* if I hadn't been there." said Robinson. "The records wouldn't have arrived on time. They wouldn't have got out to the sales force. We wouldn't have seized the *Top of the Pops* opportunity, and we wouldn't have had the press conference. They were all Stiff techniques."

With Island still unable to pay its bills, Robinson had no qualms about cancelling titles and cutting off bands who, he felt, "used to smoke dope with Chris but weren't up to anything." With the axe falling in every direction, managers stormed Robinson's office, pleading, "You can't cancel my record, I've got a tour." Robinson would have to explain to them, "This is not a hit. There's no point in us putting this record out. We haven't got the money to support it, and the record is not a hit."

"Well, how do you know that?" the stunned managers would ask.

"That's what I'm here for – *to know.*"

"I'm sure I was quite bolshie and a pain in the ass," acknowledged Robinson, "but we were on a roll and all the Island staff was starting to function properly." Ray Cooper, for example, although initially wary, quickly warmed to Robinson's unorthodox style. On a sales trip together in the north of England, said Cooper, "Dave was pacing around my room, talking in his animated way, then he walks over to the corner and pisses in the sink." Cooper described Robinson's effect on the company as a type of electroshock therapy. "Island in the early eighties was definitely on the slide creatively and financially, and I could see why Chris would have picked Dave ... Dave was hotheaded, he was clever, he was rude, he was careless, and to me, he was a brilliant marketing man. Everything that came out of his mouth was different and challenging – he gave me a real education. He was *alive* when Island was not."

There were plenty of long faces in the war room as Island's pecking order got reshuffled. Island's old guard had what Cooper described as a "cerebral" attitude to music, whereas Dave Robinson was "a man of the street," whose "naked honesty" created some peculiar culture clashes. In one incident, Robinson confessed he knew nothing about R&B and requested a tutorial from the company authority, Ashley Newton. Although, the snobs tutted to each other behind Robinson's back, the irony was, as Ray Cooper also pointed out, "Dave couldn't suffer fools."

A case in point was Paul Morley, media pundit and ZTT's communications director, who described Robinson as "a particularly aggressive version of the record man," expounding that, "if there was previously a certain form of institutional delicacy, almost modesty, at Island that might have interfered with its indeterminate yet somehow incisive plans to achieve a deluxe form of entertainment world domination, and even meant the label's existence might be threatened by the cut-throat commercial fury of the 1980s, Robinson tore that apart."

"Full of shit" was how Factory cofounder Rob Gretton summed up Paul Morley – a description Dave Robinson did not contest. "Paul Morley couldn't stand me. Still can't," said Robinson, "because he had all this artistic highfalutin crap which he thought was going to make a difference. I used to trot out all these Irish proverbs to irritate him, like 'Let the dog see the rabbit' and 'You can't go without the horse.' You needed a good record, you needed some good attitude, and you needed videos you could use. He made some really gay video for 'Relax.' All his friends were patting him on the back telling him what an artistic genius he was, but he couldn't get it on television because it was far too over the top."

In the pseudo-intellectual dialectics of Britain's postpunk scene, ol' Robbo may have come across like a savage chieftain from the bogs of Ireland, but unbeknownst to employees and affiliated producers alike, Stiff had just lent Island £1 million to help pay its bills. There was a reason for Robinson's admirable confidence.

Since their dinner in the Chinese restaurant, Blackwell and Robinson had been discussing a Bob Marley greatest hits disc. What Blackwell hadn't told Robinson was that immediately after Marley's death, he released the Lyceum concerts as a commemorative live album. It had flopped miserably.

Acquainting himself with his new project, "when I found out that sales for [Marley's most popular album] *Exodus* were 189,000 in the U.K., I thought that was a terribly low figure," explains Robinson. "I thought Marley would be closer to a million. I mean, Madness had done seven hundred thousand. Even in America, Marley had been selling around six or seven hundred thousand copies for his best records. So I began wondering – maybe he doesn't sell to white people?"

Robinson called in a market researcher, Gary Truman, with whom he profiled a mainly white, mainstream target audience. Truman conducted eight groups. "He's a funny little geezer who blends into the background," said Robinson. "He gets them on the case but he lets them do their own talking. He's a big fan, as I am, of the spontaneous things people say having listened to four or five tracks [and] looked at some photos or album titles we made up for the sake of conversation. During these sessions, it came out that a lot of people were saying 'legendary' or 'he's a legend.' The public picked the title, *Legend*. They also came up with the rather interesting clue they were worried Bob Marley might be slightly anti-white. People felt that maybe Bob Marley didn't like *them*.

"Island had great photographs of Bob Marley, but the problem was there was nothing smiley about him. There was no friendliness. It was always a bit tough, a bit aggressive. And also quite political." Truman's observations suggested mainstream record buyers wanted to cut through the whole Rastafarian agenda and get to the universal heart – the love songs, the uplifting whistlers. Having pinned down the handsome portrait that pushed all the right buttons, "the running order on *Legend* took me a month at least," Robinson remembered. "I agonised over it."

Released in May 1984 with a campaign of television commercials, *Legend* bolted out of the stable and entered the U.K. album charts at No. 1 – Bob Marley's first ever. Just a week later, on May 14, Dave Robinson turned forty. Island picked up the bill for a birthday party Robinson's pregnant wife organised at their new family home in Hammersmith. In retrospect, that night celebrated the beginning of a dream harvest.

Bob Marley stayed at No. 1 in the U.K. for fourteen weeks, all summer long, while on the singles charts Frankie Goes to Hollywood detonated their second smash hit, "Two Tribes" – No. 1 in Britain for nine weeks, selling 1.5 million copies. With Britain gripped by a second wave of Frankie fever, even "Relax" climbed back to No. 2. As it was happening, the year belonged to Frankie, but in time, the true monster would be *Legend:* 25 million copies to date and God knows how many million more counterfeits in Africa, where Marley has become a giant symbol of freedom and progress – in fact, arguably the continent's biggest-ever music icon.

Fired up by Island's spectacular renaissance in England, Chris Black-well was rethinking his American operations. In need of new blood, he recruited a whole crop of marketing staffers, then appointed a former A&M promotions man, Charly Prevost, as president.

Just before Prevost started the job, he was invited to a small party at Blackwell's New York apartment attended by Malcolm McLaren. Among the group of faces was Blackwell's local sweetheart, a glamorous black lady he affectionately called Chocolate Cake. During the party, she took Prevost to one side and asked, "Are you gonna work for Chris?"

"Think so," replied Prevost, trying to contain his excitement.

"Well, just be careful, because he likes walking on thin ice. But he never wants to go first. He's gonna have you go through – first."

In America, Island was distributed through Atlantic, but due to the astronomical costs of radio promotion there, Ahmet Ertegun had long tried to persuade Chris Blackwell to move to a licence deal. Convinced Atlantic wouldn't work his left-field records, Blackwell battled on as an independent, even putting out his 4th & B'way records through independent distribution networks. "In my conversations with Doug Morris, who was running Atlantic Records at the time," explained Prevost, "he'd look at me and shake his head in despair and say, 'how can you do this with no money?' Because we didn't have a lot of cash to market and play the game. We certainly couldn't play it on Atlantic's level. So Chris was always looking for creative ways to make things happen.

"We did a lot of creative stuff with Frankie Goes to Hollywood," continued Prevost. "We looked at what Robbo did in England and devised our own version of it." Thinking up ways of getting around independent radio promoters, "we brought in a ton of imports and worked them everywhere except radio. And because we worked the retail reports so hard, 'Relax' began selling everywhere, without airplay. The sharper programmers always monitor local sales to check if they're playing the right stuff. We consciously decided not to service the track unless we got a call from a programmer who guaranteed us airplay and a report. In the first two, three weeks we got enough of the trendsetters on board and we coordinated their reports to ensure that the record first appeared on the airplay chart with velocity and a major set of important call letters. We actually got airplay by withholding servicing – the only time it ever happened, to my knowledge."

Prevost adapted the reverse psychology trick when announcing Malcolm McLaren's *Fans,* an innovative operatic hip-hop concept album.

"We took out a full page ad in *Billboard* on the inside front page, saying, 'We don't care if you hate this record. We love it.'

"People used to say Chris was a flake and he smoked pot, but we would walk around the office at night when everybody went home and both get incredibly irritated because somebody spent seven-eighths of a penny writing a note on something with an Island logo on it. So we stopped doing the company stationery." Prevost quickly noticed "he had an eye for detail and he knew about royalties and he knew where the dollars were."

Blackwell replicated in New York his ghostlike presence in London. Prevost described how "he'd come in at night and work all night. Somehow he never slept when he was in New York, he just kept going. But he had installed a very expensive and sophisticated security system so that from his desk he could watch everybody that was walking around the front door, certainly anybody that came into the building. Another set for the elevator and another set for the front door."

After a while, Prevost started to understand Chris Blackwell's idiosyncrasies. "I talked to him on the phone ten times a day and my impression of him was Howard Hughes, a guy you didn't see often. When he goes to Jamaica, he doesn't want to be reached, that's his refuge. But when he's in Nassau, he's totally ready to go. The thing about Chris that everybody always marvelled at was that he had all these different compartments. He had different girlfriends in different countries, he had different businesses run by different people. When he was in the studio he was sort of a different guy than he was elsewhere. Especially if he played music for you; it's a sight to behold, his entire body would start vibrating … It's what's at the heart of it with him. He always told me he'd never sell his label, he'd sell his pants before he'd sell his record company."

In reality, not only was Dave Robinson aware of the long-term plan to sell Island, but Blackwell would soon have to share the secret with U2 manager Paul McGuinness. Considering U2 had scored Island's two biggest hits in 1983 – *War* and *Under a Blood Red Sky,* McGuinness had mixed feelings about Frankie Goes to Hollywood's giant breakthrough. Noticing the tide ebb on raw postpunk, throughout the summer of 1984, U2 was back at the drawing board with producers Brian Eno and Steve Lillywhite. Called *The Unforgettable Fire,* their next album was a deliberate effort to enlarge their sonic canvas with delay pedals and synthesisers. It was released in October 1984 and hit the No. 1 spot in the U.K. for two weeks.

As irony would have it, back in 1979 when McGuinness was shopping U2's demo around London, he had called into Stiff for contacts. "Actually, U2 *were* pretty terrible," asserted Robinson of their early years. "But Blackwell signed them to a deal where they got tour support ... Blackwell introduced [McGuinness] to Frank Barsalona, who was *the* hot agent in America. U2 settled down for two years just touring around America in a station wagon with a U-haul trailer behind it. Frank Barsalona put them on a support of every single gig that he could. So they played with every-body and Bono ripped off everybody. He absorbed everybody's *hot licks.* He would stand at the side of the stage and spot what was *the thing.* That's what he's great at."

"Bono is the manager of U2," ventured Robinson. "If you listen to the early demos of U2, they're not very good, but within two years they had metamorphosed completely because of Bono's media savvy ... McGuin-ness was just the accountant ... He handled the money. The brains is Bono."

In the early years, Island staffers joked that U2 was the only band in the world whose manager partied like a rocker while the saintly boys went to bed early back at the hotel. All that would change with money. A few years before U2 could afford the trimmings of rock stardom, Charly Prevost in particular got a taste of the manager's growing reputation. "McGuinness said to me, 'we just re-signed with Island. If we knew you were here, we never would have re-signed with you. You're a fucker!' And from that moment on, he and his staff would call people in our office by their wrong first names on purpose. We just decided to work the record because it was our job to do it. And we would work it as hard as we could, take no prisoners, spend whatever it took. But we had no relationship with them – at all.

"Because of our lack of funds, it was virtually impossible for us to go after U2 and Frankie at the same time," admitted Prevost. "In those days, it cost about two million bucks to bring a record in – tour support, independent promotion, etc." Prevost remembered "one really uncomfortable evening when we were going to Philadelphia to see them play. This is way before the arenas, they barely sold out a theatre. And we were in the car with his attorney, the two of them facing me, several bottles of wine there. 'Charly, what are you gonna do? You got Frankie Goes to Hollywood or us, which one are you gonna work?' Maybe that's the way U2 did things in the record business, but by the time we got to Philadelphia, I was furious I got put in that position."

In England, U2's brief chart success in October 1984 was quickly eclipsed by the next Frankie Goes to Hollywood tsunami. Their long-awaited double album *Welcome to the Pleasuredome* was the big pay-off after almost one year of singles and remixes. In November 1984, EMI's distribution wing handed Island a £6 million cheque for preorders alone. Charting a third No. 1 single in December, "The Power of Love," Island totted up the year's spoils and celebrated its best-ever financial performance. After a long spell in the doldrums, the rusty Caribbean cruiser had sailed off into the rapidly expanding CD market of the mid-1980s.

Alas, as Robinson bleakly concluded, "all of that was not worthwhile because everything we made, Blackwell squandered on a couple more movies that never came out." After just a year working together, relations between the two record men became strained as Dave Robinson realised large sums of money were being siphoned out the back door into Blackwell's many projects. "In that year of 1984, we made something like £56 million," explained Robinson. "It paid off all of Island's debts, which was pretty amazing, and if you calculate my twenty percent profit share, it would have been £2 million from the £8 million or so profit."

However, in spring 1985, Robinson was not paid his sixth instalment for Stiff and realised "the profit share was bullshit." In fact, the treasure chest was so bare, Island couldn't pay U2 the £5 million they were owed in royalties.

Island's CFO, Art Jaeger, attested, "The royalty cheque [U2] were gonna get was going to be their first big royalty cheque. And they were as excited as could be … And all of a sudden, that cheque wasn't there. That gave those people the opportunity – the absolute opportunity – to do whatever they wanted, including [signing with] CBS Records [who] at the time had offered them a huge North American deal, which made a lot of sense because Island Records in the U.S. wasn't really that great, it hadn't broken them yet. So they could still stay with Chris for the rest of the world and be with CBS [for North America]. A lot of people back then said that Island was bankrupt; that if you had ten percent of Island or ninety-seven percent of Island, you possibly had nothing. Yet Bono decided to stay with Chris. And he took that ten percent and that ten percent became $30 million."

Unlike U2, Dave Robinson was not offered any alternative deal. "Blackwell moved the goalposts constantly," said Robinson, who felt cheated by the whole episode. On the question of how the original deal was undone, Robinson pointed to Blackwell's fiercely loyal money handlers, who "would have taken a bullet for him … They were always trying to second-guess him and lead him onto the path of good, commercial sense, which he seldom was on. And so he allowed them to have the impression that I had up-sold them a company and not given them details of the contracts, the income, the money in the bank, etc. And that's what Blackwell would always do with everybody; he'd sell his operators."

Robinson left in August 1985. His severance was handled by Art Jaeger. "To cut a long story short," Robinson said, "1984 was great, 1985 was shit because all the money had gone. The company was broke and had no more products. There was nothing for me to do. So in that second year, it was starting to get really messy because Blackwell didn't want to address either the company's problems or my problems. His inner circle figured the way to get rid of me was to unhinge Stiff."

In the middle of this mess, Robinson spotted and signed to Stiff a peculiar trad-punk group – the Pogues, his last great discovery before the walls caved in. Although an acquired taste, their 1985 album, *Rum, Sodomy & The Lash* became a classic. Thirty years later, songs like "A Pair of Brown Eyes" and "The Body of an American" are on their way to becoming public domain anthems that future generations, stumbling home from a thousand pubs, will howl at the moon for years to come.

For Chris Blackwell, the battlefront had shifted to the ghettos of Washington, D.C., where millions of dollars were gurgling down a drain. "Oh God," Charly Prevost shuddered at the mere mention of the dreaded film. "*Good to Go* had something to do with our demise – he and I. The deal we had with Atlantic Records was one where we got paid every month, after expenses and reserves. And sometimes the cheque was good and sometimes there was no cheque. And the reason there'd be no cheque was because Chris had taken it to put in the *Good to Go* production ... Island Pictures was the Los Angeles outfit that he was funnelling so much dough into."

Convinced the so-called *go-go* scene of D.C. was the next big thing, Blackwell was signing up a whole pool of go-go acts. "We had this big commitment to go-go," recalled Prevost. "We had to get it to go national. [But] no amount of push, bribes, publicity, or personal appearances could get it going outside the ghetto of D.C." Meanwhile, the whole film production descended into disaster. The director walked out; nobody wanted to finance or even release it.

"It was sucking dollars out of the company, and at the time we were trying to break 'Addicted to Love' by Robert Palmer," continued Prevost. "Chris was on the phone talking about *Good to Go* and 'Why aren't you down here? And how much are you doing to break this?' He thought I did not have enough relationship with the urban community – the African American community – to be able to help him out. And he was right. I didn't have it naturally. I was concerned with the rock side. There was a division in the company between those who helped him on *Good to Go* and those of us who were trying to make profits."

Blackwell was like a gambler hypnotised by a slot machine. His commitment to *Good to Go* went from reckless to suicidal. Pulling out monthly cheques as big as $600,000, he began to bleed the cash cow dry. "Look at the end of 1985," sighed Prevost. "We had just released 'Addicted to Love,' and we knew we had a number-one record." In fact, because Island had a reputation for not paying its bills, Prevost had to pay independent promoters a whopping $400,000 to get the song all over the airwaves. "I had at least sixty people working in the New York office, but we had to get rid of most of them. We came back to work in January with maybe fifteen, because we couldn't afford the payroll." Art Jaeger flew in to handle the mess – laying off staff and earning himself the nickname "*Art the Assassin*." To his credit, Jaeger paid the skeleton staff with his own savings.

In a tense meeting in Blackwell's apartment, Prevost was pushed out just a week before Robert Palmer hit No. 1 in the spring of 1986. For the Canadian, it was tough justice because "when I started at the company they were making one or two million a year. And when I left, we managed to get it up into the twenties. So over a two-year spread it was good. But Chris was, I dunno. You talk about money with him – I don't know if you use a credit card, but if you do, you keep the receipt generally. Chris would always just throw 'em away. He didn't care. So he always had a cavalier attitude about the amount of money we had. And it was tough because you can't compete. And he wanted to compete."

Meanwhile, back in Ireland, U2 was reeling from their royalty shock. Famous but still not rich, they spent over a year building a monster in their backyard – *The Joshua Tree,* a purpose-built American break-through machine. From his Principle Management office in Dublin, Paul McGuinness was investing in U2's very own stage and roof company, Upfront/EGS, a state-of-the-art rig allowing tighter stadium scheduling, which they sometimes rented to other acts. When U2 exploded on tour in 1987, their T-shirt merchandising alone became a multimillion-dollar cash cow.

It was a stark contrast to the fate of that other Irishman, Dave Robinson, who crawled out of the wreckage with a Stiff on his shoulders. Although he got to keep the fifth instalment of £250,000, once the £1 million loan was effectively recouped by four other payments, his lawsuit against Blackwell proved slow and costly. After two days in court, he accepted a settlement of £75,000, which barely covered his legal fees. "It altered my life, it altered my relationships, it altered my kids' relationships," confessed Robinson in a rare flash of emotion. "I think to myself, 'What a fucking idiot you are, Robbo. If you'd been a nasty cunt – which you should have been – you would have put the boot in and you'd be like McGuinness sitting on ten percent or whatever. You were in the driving seat and you should have driven it then.' I was the Irish geezer who was prepared to put up with an awful lot of shit and still fight on to pull his company out of the fucking mire. I was still wanting to stand there and say 'I did it!' It was foolish. It's ego, and maybe Chris Blackwell knew more about me than I knew about myself!"

When trying to explain Chris Blackwell's extraordinary knack of always riding into the sunset, Dave Robinson referred to an old Irish proverb, "The lucky man has only to be born." While still laughing at its cruel simplicity, he pulled out another. "You have to believe in luck, because how else can you explain why people you can't stand are doing well?"

"What [Chris Blackwell] was brilliant at was choosing creative people and giving them their shot. He was not a great boss," said former managing director Tim Clark with a firmly punctuated silence. "He was great at spending money. There were plenty of occasions when there'd be a film in the pipeline and he'd say, 'don't worry, we're just going to put in a little bit of feed money and that's it, I'll raise the rest.' But the money didn't get raised and he carried on spending. And that was just bonkers! But you know, Chris, when approached about this sort of stuff, would just behave like a naughty schoolboy. He grinned and chortled and charmed his way out of it. And at the end of the day, he was actually the one that found the solution to the financial problems."

Another Island lifer, Lionel Conway, offered his own take on the Chris Blackwell enigma. "He's a gambler, always has been a gambler. When we were in Nassau, he'd go in and he liked a bet." It wasn't just movies, said Conway. "There were other things he financed that put a complete dent in what we were doing because he needed cash. He financed this woman with a whole series of exercise videos, plus venues, the equivalent of Jane Fonda. I know we put a lot of cash into it … and it was a huge cash-flow problem. The thing about Blackwell, he's an entrepreneur. You couldn't stop him from doing things if he really wanted to see if there was anything in it."

When it came to replenishing the treasure chest, "his deal-making was just amazing," exclaimed Conway. "The *way* he always had the upper hand. Because everybody wanted to do business with Island. They were a phenomenal label and he was a phenomenal A&R magnet. People wanted to be with him … He was a terrific deal-maker. And it was his charm. 'The baby-faced killer,' yes, absolutely."

As Art Jaeger remembered "In 1985 or 1986, whenever it was, Chris sends me down to South Beach, Miami, to buy this hotel called the Marlin. So I go down there, and the whole place is just a total slum … Basically, he was on the absolute forefront of what now is one of the hottest areas for music and young people and great hotels. After the Marlin, other hotels were bought. A little bit later, he asked me to try and sign this young designer that had just graduated so that he could be the chief designer for what would be the Island Trading Company. And this guy's name was Marc Jacobs."

Ultimately, the secret to Chris Blackwell's long and successful career was probably his capacity to go with the flow yet remain determined. Rather like water, Chris Blackwell easily changed directions yet remained bound by the force of nature to seek one final destination, the ocean-wide vista of his own success. As the man himself admitted, "You adjust, deal with whatever you have to go through at any time. Human beings are very adaptable. I believe you have to play the cards you're dealt as well as you can play them. You can't just throw in the hand."

28. ROMANS

IF ANYONE STOOD ABOVE THE FRAY LOOKING DOWN ON BRITAIN'S LANDSCAPE of tribal chieftains, it had to be Maurice Oberstein. Notorious for his silly hats, *Obie* was a gay, eccentric New Yorker who became the most powerful vinyl warlord in Britain.

Although his father, Eli, had been an A&R man at RCA, young Maurice did not inherit the musical ear. Taking command of CBS's London office, where he clocked up forty British No. 1 singles in ten years, Obie was a red-blooded conquistador who viewed the record business as an animal kingdom. "Think of us as being in the jungle," he told Derek Green in one tense negotiation. "I'm an elephant and you're an ant. I tread on you. And kill you. And I don't even know I've done it."

According to one rumour in the early eighties, every time his A&R man, Muff Winwood, came looking to sign a band, Obie demanded that he beg on his knees like a dog. Another rumour was that if his red setter, Charlie, didn't wag his tail to a visiting band, Obie wouldn't sign the contract. His number two at CBS, former Island managing director David Betteridge, suspects that many of the tales following Obie around began as jokes that lower-level staff, through a process like the telephone game, exaggerated into horror stories. What Betteridge did vividly recall was the eerie manner in which, due to polyps on his vocal chords, Obie's legendary fits of screaming flipped in and out of falsetto.

All who worked closely with Obie agreed that behind his burlesque rudeness was an immensely astute mind. He was a natural-born general who understood how a large record corporation should be led from the front and supported from behind. Parading with his dog, he would inspect the floors, listening intently to employees' organisational problems.

Earning himself the posthumous title of "the Architect," Obie was the first to express highly prescient theories about where the record industry was moving. In the late seventies, Obie warned, "Majors and indies have been competing on 'my music is better than your music' basis. But now it's gonna be my marketing clout is better than yours." From that realisation, Obie began to understand the wider consequences of what chess players call material advantage.

As the record market became progressively global, majors were demanding bigger distribution territories from independents – paricularly in Europe. Instead of regional blocs like Benelux or Scandinavia, majors like CBS, WEA, PolyGram and EMI increasingly wanted sales rights for all of Europe. As Obie rightly predicted, all these independents, being hand-to-mouth operations, would immediately spend the huge advances on new signatures and whatever expenditures happened to be urgent when the money arrived. However, once those licensed records began charting overseas, the artist managers would come looking for money already spent.

In the early eighties, Obie watched the fastest-growing youngster in the British market, Virgin, sail straight past Island. Although not a music man, Richard Branson was another naval commander quick to understand that in the eighties, size did matter. From about 1978 onward, he worked from his houseboat, building a global group, leaving the day-to-day running of the main U.K. label to Simon Draper.

Soon after Chris Blackwell bought Ian Fleming's former Jamaican residence, Goldeneye, Branson bought a Virgin Island – Necker, his very own paradise retreat fit for a Bond villain. Opening recording studios, record stores and record companies around the world, Virgin was becoming an empire. As Simon Draper pointed out, "Consider the artists that we signed in the seventies – all the Soft Machine and Canterbury sort of acts, the German acts, Tangerine Dream, the instrumental music, it was all incredibly sellable throughout Europe. So right from day one we sold records throughout Europe while all of the other record labels were focused too much on the U.K. and America. And of course America was a hard nut to crack. It's much easier, actually, to sell records to Europe."

As well as a significant chunk of the synth-pop and new romantic groups of the era, Virgin signed pop blockbusters like Culture Club, Phil Collins, UB40, the Human League and Peter Gabriel, whose textured sounds were instantly appealing throughout non-English-speaking markets. "I was very idealistic in the seventies, less so in the eighties, more pragmatic," admitted Draper almost apologetically. "In the eighties there was more pressure to have success, to run it as a business, to sell records."

Virgin's success was so sudden that "by 1983, we'd become one of the major labels in the U.K. and had set up companies around the world. I was actually enjoying selling, you know, millions of records, dominating the charts, making lots of money. The negative part of it, for me, was that by having these foreign companies we needed to sign bands in Canada, in Australia, in Germany, in France. And we had a great deal of pressure to do it … We had loads of A&R men in the U.K. and around the world all wanting to find acts. You couldn't have A&R men and not let them have their own room to move. So we signed all these acts. And from there you start to get this thing where the passion starts to go out of it."

Evoking what he terms "the Richard Branson factor," Draper lamented how "we had Richard, entrepreneur par excellence, pushing the thing forward – *pushing,* ambitious beyond belief, always trying to think of new things to do. So in 1984 and 1985, he says, 'I want to be in the airline business!' Problem is, *I* didn't want to be in the airline business. I would have liked to be in book publishing or maybe get involved in the art world, which I did subsequently. And I certainly didn't want to be involved in retail shops. Richard could have been doing anything. And he did. He started countless businesses that failed. So you had this tension between what we were doing with the record company and Richard's driving ambition. I enjoyed the growing process up to a point, but then we get to 1986 and we've gone public and suddenly I own fifteen percent of a company that's worth £250 million and I realise that my stake is now real."

On both sides of the Atlantic, things started going slightly mad somewhere in the mideighties. In America, the already exorbitant cost of independent radio promotion was changing the very game of selling music. By now, musical programming on Top 40 radio was tightly controlled by "the Network" – the allegedly Mafia-connected group of radio promoters including Fred DiSipio in New York, Joe Isgro in Los Angeles, Jerry Brenner in Boston, Jeff McClusky in Chicago, Gary Bird in Cleveland, Jerry Meyers in Buffalo and Jimmy Davenport in Atlanta.

"You couldn't get your records played!" said Harold Childs, A&M's head of sales and promotion at the time. "The radio stations gave independent promoters carte blanche to choose whatever got played. And the majors used independent promotion to basically get rid of the independent labels. A&M couldn't spend that kind of money, nor could Motown. Back in the seventies, it was record company against record company. We all had our own radio promotion staffs and we'd go out there and fight for the radio stations, wine and dine the program directors. We were companies fighting companies. But when the independent promoters came in, which was around the early to mideighties, you were competing with a third entity."

"One of the reasons I sold half my company to Warner Bros. in 1986," admitted Tom Silverman, founder of the hip-hop label Tommy Boy, "was because I didn't have access to the indie promoters that controlled Top 40 radio. This wasn't payola anymore. Actually, I have no problem with payola. It was great for the fifties labels because they could get their R&B records on air by paying a few deejays. There was something democratic about payola. It's when five or six national pop promo guys ended up cutting deals with the radio stations that it turned into an extortion game. They ended up working every record that was on the radio. It wasn't promotion anymore. What they ended up doing was extortion."

As the eighties progressed, all the larger independent record labels were starting to wobble. In chess terms, all the proverbial knights and bishops were exposed as queens and rooks controlled the corridors. A corporate endgame of global dimensions was in motion.

When the increasingly eccentric Maurice Oberstein was fired from CBS in 1985, the British record industry gasped as he moved to PolyGram, the biggest of the continental heavyweights, whose Dutch mother company, Philips, co-owned the compact disc. PolyGram was floated on the stock exchange the very year Oberstein took over its British company; then, in 1987, Philips de-merged from Siemens and reorganised full ownership of PolyGram. Illustrating the tactical importance of the compact disc, Jan Timmer was being groomed to take over the entire Philips group.

As Philips began mobilising for a major assault, in 1986, a 150-year-old German book publisher, Bertelsmann, bought RCA from General Electric for $300 million. Meanwhile, back in Manhattan, cloaks and daggers were dashing around the corridors of CBS Inc. Its corporate president, Laurence Tisch, wanted to sell CBS Records to an American food industry billionaire named Nelson Peltz for $1.25 billion. Determined to block the deal, Walter Yetnikoff telephoned an American senior executive at Sony, Mickey Schulhof, and initiated a rival offer. It was a smart choice. Following the debacle with the Betamax video, Sony understood, like Philips, that the success or failure of the compact disc would depend almost entirely on the availability of good-quality content.

The inevitable haggling and stalling between Sony and CBS Inc. continued for a year until Black Monday, October 19, 1987, brought negotiations to a head. Fearing a massive upheaval in the financial markets, Laurence Tisch panicked and called Schulhof, asking sheepishly if the $2 billion offer was still on the table. Schulhof then telephoned Sony cofounder Akio Morita, who confirmed that despite the turbulence of Black Monday, yes, CBS Records was still worth $2 billion. With that final showing of cards, America's oldest record label, effectively Columbia, went into Japanese ownership.

Although Sony's buyout of CBS had been a tactical success for Walter Yetnikoff, the new owners wouldn't tolerate his drinking and cocaine addiction. Within just months of the buyout, Yetnikoff checked himself into rehab. He came out sober but was ushered into retirement with a generous severance package of $25 million. Yetnikoff's protégé Tommy Mottola took over at the newly named Sony Music. Yetnikoff's track record as a businessman had been as spectacular as his personal story. The jury, however, is still out on the long-term legacy of the court he left behind.

With an arms race officially on, a flurry of indie buyouts followed in close succession. In May 1989, EMI bought out the troubled Chrysalis for $75 million. "A lot of things aren't for life, are they? You change as people," sighed Chris Wright in reference to his fateful split with cofounder Terry Ellis in 1985. "We had our problems throughout our relationship. When we worked well together, we worked really well together. But I think Terry, you know, he had a lot of emotional baggage. Under his own admission, I think he was drinking too much, and because he was drinking too much, he was probably doing other stuff too much. It got a little bit difficult. He became very difficult to work with, and he started wanting to do deals that I felt we shouldn't be doing."

"Partnerships are difficult," Terry Ellis responded. "In my case with Chris, we were and still are very different people. In the early stages of our partnership, that was an advantage. We came at things from a completely different point of view. So often we'd find a compromise. And I think that's a good way to run a business because you never end up in one extreme or another. But I think with success, you get a bit of arrogance. We each became less willing to compromise, and that really was the cause of the split."

"The last straw," said Chris Wright, "was when Terry went down to the Cannes Film Festival and made a £4 million commitment to invest in the film *Santa Claus: The Movie*. I stopped it and he got pissed off, saying, 'If you don't let me do this deal, that's it.' And so that was it." With the benefit of hindsight, Terry Ellis regretted they didn't have a lawyer friend like Allen Grubman to lock them both in a room until peace was reached.

In 1985, Chris Wright bought out Terry Ellis's stake and continued Chrysalis as its sole general. Because Ellis had been running the American company, however, Wright inherited unfamiliar problems. "The cost of business in America had got so big that it was hard for us independent companies to cope. Island, Virgin, Motown, A&M, the same story," reasoned Wright. "Basically, we had too large an operation; we were employing something like eighty-five people in the American company and we had a complete dry-up of product ... and we ran into cash-flow problems."

Looking back with some regret, Wright said, "We could have just closed down the American company, which in hindsight might have been the most sensible thing to do, but we thought we'd do a ten-year joint venture deal with BMG until the negotiations broke down and we ended up doing the same thing with EMI. And the other companies all kind of followed suit quite quickly because they were, in their own way, experiencing similar kinds of problems.

"The reason Island sold," Wright speculated, "was because they had a similar kind of situation to us. Blackwell couldn't pay the U2 royalties, and he had a partner in the company, the film producer John Heyman. When they saw the Chrysalis deal with EMI, I think they thought, 'Shit, if there's that much money around, here's our chance to get out and make a shed load of money.' "

Chris Blackwell's bagmen – his closest confidant, Tom Hayes and CFO Art Jaeger – had spent the previous four years struggling to keep Island financed. "It took a toll on Tom and it took a toll on me," admitted Jaeger. "Tom and I basically kept breathing air into Island for a lot of years. I think we were very successful in insulating the rest of the company to go about and do their jobs. Tom's a goddam genius. Tom Hayes might be the smartest guy I know." Lionel Conway, Island's head of publishing, also recalled the constant scramble to extend subpublishing deals to raise money – mainly to pay U2.

As Tom Hayes described the bigger picture, "There was a realisation towards the end of the eighties, like that old saying, you're too small to be big and you're too big to be small … In America, the cost of promotion is hideous because you've got so many stations and so much coverage and the big companies have much deeper pockets. So as an independent, MTV was useful for us, but at the same time, towards the late eighties, every act wanted a video. Plus, we were an established independent so therefore we didn't have such a niche market anymore. There was us and Chrysalis, we were the big [British] independents, then there were the Beggars Banquet labels who were a younger version of us. So it was clearly the right time to sell."

With the compact disc overtaking vinyl sales in 1988, "probably the late eighties was the most prosperous period in the record industry for the older majors," reasoned Hayes. "They held vast back catalogues that were long since amortised. Certainly on a lot of the classical records, they didn't owe anybody any royalties because they were either public domain or buyouts. And they were selling them at fifteen quid a throw." Thanks to the compact disc, the likes of PolyGram turned their dusty old vaults into cash dispensers.

Island circulated a brochure. "Warner was interested," admitted Hayes, who held a 1 percent stake in the company, "but PolyGram engaged quickly; they were *very* interested." Tactically, PolyGram was the perfect fit – rich, European and with ambitions to break into America. As Hayes explained, "You need a certain critical mass in order to be able to have a proper America-wide distribution. CBS had it, Warner had it, but PolyGram needed sufficient volumes of turnover to justify having regional depots."

In late July, the news was official. Island Records went for $300 million. "We were very happy," recalled Island's chief negotiator, John Heyman. "I think it goes beyond doing a brilliant deal. If the company was going to expand and if it was going to keep pace with all of the changes that were going on, it needed to be part of a larger animal." Earning a tidy $30 million, U2 was celebrating also. Since they were Island's biggest act, Paul McGuinness had been regularly consulted in the negotiations to give PolyGram assurances U2 was not going to throw any tantrums.

PolyGram was simultaneously in negotiations with A&M, whose owners, Jerry Moss and Herb Alpert, were also feeling outgunned by the majors. Now a giant independent that had grown several blocks around the original Charlie Chaplin studio, A&M relied on huge distribution advances from the majors, yet had to compete with the same behemoths to sign and promote hot acts. It clearly didn't add up.

The inherent problem first raised its head when, around 1985, the European distribution arm of CBS failed to get behind A&M's rising star, Bryan Adams – arguing that Adams competed with Bruce Springsteen, a CBS artist whose *Born in the U.S.A.* was America's biggest-selling album of the year. With the distribution deal coming up for renewal, Walter Yetnikoff tightened the terms and effectively gave Jerry Moss no alternative but to find a new European partner.

A&M moved its European distribution to PolyGram, and as a result of this successful partnership, "I got to know [PolyGram chairman] David

Fine very well," said Jerry Moss. "So when it came time to sell the label, Jan Timmer came up with a price." While buying Island, PolyGram splashed out another $500 million to acquire A&M.

Curiously, one of the last straws convincing Moss of the need to have major funding was losing Janet Jackson to Virgin, which was also in a tailspin trying to repair the mistakes of its bionic growth spurt in the mideighties. As Simon Draper explained, "What got Richard into financial problems wasn't the airline. The airline had always been kept out of the public company. The problem was that we'd gone public and suddenly Richard got access to a lot of money; our overdraft went from £4 million with Coutts to £35 million with Lloyd's. Then we had all this public money as well. And he started expanding in a furious way – a property company, you name it. We got into such difficulty, the share price dropped and we had to go private again. And to go private, we had to buy back the public shares. So we had to sell a stake in the record company to Fujisankei while we also tried to sell off other stuff.

"The Virgin retail chain, for example, always lost money, but we kept it going because it was very good for our image. Richard didn't want the shop staff to know; he always played down the bad news. So the public perception was always that Virgin retailing was a profitable business. But it wasn't really. The only shop that actually made money was the Paris megastore … It was a huge thing – groundbreaking – selling records, selling books, selling films, and the scale of it was a monster. But all the other ones were disasters; they lost a huge amount of money … There were always disasters around Richard, but he's always managed to paint them as successes. The airline became very successful much later. But certainly in my time, the only thing making big money was the record company. In the end, because of all the losses, particularly in the property company, we had to sell the record company."

Behind the scenes, Richard Branson's business protégé Ken Berry was shopping around for a buyer as Virgin began making headlines with high-profile signatures. "We put in an extra effort to sign the Rolling Stones just to decorate the nest," admitted Draper. "Also Janet Jackson to some extent, although we probably would have signed her anyway. But signing the Rolling Stones for £8 million as we were negotiating the sale price was definitely just to make the whole thing look more attractive." Thorn-EMI acquired Virgin Records for £560 million.

Once again, observers were stunned at the enormous price tag. As David Betteridge understood, there was one crucial asset Virgin possessed. "I was sort of lucky enough to see both sides of all that," explained Betteridge, in reference to the fact that he ran a Virgin sublabel years after his long spell as managing director for both Island and CBS. Compared to the licence deals Island maintained with its European partner, Ariola, "I then got an insider's view of what Virgin had in Europe, which was an entirely different kettle of fish. You could fly to Italy or France or Germany and talk directly to a guy who would sit down with you, as a fellow member of the Virgin group, and discuss promoting your act. Virgin were hugely successful in Europe," while the likes of Island and Chrysalis were "burning their fingers in America."

For Simon Draper, it was the end of a twenty-year adventure. "I was in favour of going public in 1986, although it was madness to start an American office the following year. But the environment you inhabit as a public company is not comfortable, because you have to deliver profits, you can't take long-term decisions. That's really why I eventually got out. I didn't like the environment of being in a big public company, and I definitely didn't want Richard Branson risking something that I'd built up for twenty years on some venture that was of no interest to me whatsoever. So it was definitely time for a parting of ways."

For Chris Wright, those years also proved to be a painful milestone. Because the Chrysalis deal was structured in two parts, the shock hit him two years after the original signature. "I couldn't sleep for six months … ," admitted Wright with a crackle in his throat. "I was not happy about it. It was the second deal in 1991; that's when it affected me *that* badly." Although he's among the one thousand richest men in Britain today, Chris Wright says, "I don't think you do anything for the money. Certainly not when you're young. Money doesn't come into it. When you're young, you don't *need* money, you just need a hamburger and a plate of fries. As you get older, you get used to a certain lifestyle and the money does become a bit more important. But not when you're young." It was almost as if selling Chrysalis marked the end of his youth.

Jerry Moss was entering a similar place. "I heard stories about corporations taking over," he said, "but I just didn't believe it was going to happen to us ... For the first year, I was relatively happy. David Fine told me 'no changes.'"

Then the PolyGram chairman telephoned one day. "I'm not sure if you're aware of our retirement policy," he began, "but the mandatory age for retirement here is sixty-one, and my birthday is next Saturday."

"David, you mean I'm not going to be working with you anymore?" gasped Moss.

"We're actually choosing who it is now," confirmed Fine.

The successor to the PolyGram throne turned out to be Alain Levy, a notoriously dour record executive who'd risen up through the ranks from the French office of Polydor. "From the outset we didn't get along," admitted Moss. "He had an MBA, which is a dangerous thing to have these days. All those people learned in college was to cut expenditure, so in the short term they show profits, but in the long term the company got shut down. It was just an idiotic way to run anything. He would befriend certain artists who'd get anything they wanted. And the others would starve. His manner of leadership was awful, just frightening. And it didn't work for our company ... Pretty soon they cut our Paris office, they cut our New York office. People left. I made it a smaller, tighter more aggressive company, but Alain just wanted me to leave."

The writing was quite literally on the wall. In a poignant symbol of the culture clash, the new order took a dislike to a mural created by Tubes members Prairie Prince and Mike Cotten. Depicting the A&M logo in different perspectives, it had been proudly exhibited around the soundstages of the lot since the seventies. Visible from the street outside, it was part of the local landscape – until whitewashed in 1993 by the corporate owners. "Now why would anybody do that?" wondered Moss, who knew it was time to pack up his office mementos. He looked at Herb Alpert with a sorry shrug and said, "What can we do about it? This is the deal we made. And this is who they chose to run it. We don't own the company anymore ... So we left. Herb and I had a lot to do with what our company meant, and once we were gone, it just became a PolyGram entity."

One executive, Bob Garcia, attested, "For the average employee who had been involved with A&M for more than fifteen or twenty years, it was almost an assault. It's what I term *the Alain Levy syndrome.* It was a very strange experience to hear the words 'Alain Levy is in the building.' What does that mean? It means 'clean up your shit, even though you have no shit to clean up.' It was like injecting a strange unknown virus into the body. And you never understood it. You never warmed to it. It was never personable. You're dealing with shareholders, you're dealing with a building in New York City that looks like something out of *Ghostbusters*. And it's the heart and soul of the people who own you. A&M had always been the centre of its own universe. Then all of a sudden, we were a satellite circling around someone else's universe."

Even inside the biggest majors, there were casualties. Mo Ostin, in particular, whose corporate owners merged with Time in 1990, was feeling the absence of Steve Ross, who died of prostate cancer in 1992. With bean counters in New York meddling in his decisions, Ostin quickly "found that I couldn't live with it anymore … I was done." Looking back on Warner's spectacular success throughout the seventies and eighties, Ostin believes "a lot of it was attributable that we had this incredible corporate support during the Ross years, with minimum corporate interference. We were allowed to be entrepreneurial and take risks, and because of this, we were able to empower our executives. Philosophically, we stayed close to our basic belief: that music was our highest priority … that whenever there was any conflict between art and commerce, the artist should prevail." By the midnineties, however, that whole ethic had died with Steve Ross.

The ageing record man had become a semi-retired multimillionaire. Some moved on; some stuck around for a while as elder statesmen. For the best minds of a generation, the golden age was over.

29. LAMENTATIONS

"WHOEVER BELIEVES WILL BE SAVED, BUT WHOEVER DOES NOT BELIEVE WILL be condemned." Despite the spread of corporate entertainment, there were still innumerable pockets of resistance – especially one.

Revered by connoisseurs as a sort of temple on the mount, the epicentre for alternative music in Britain was Rough Trade – by all accounts an extraordinary happening in the history of the record business. When the tiny shop opened in 1976, there were only about a dozen indies in Britain, but by the late eighties, there were eight hundred, five hundred of them being handled by Rough Trade's distribution hub – colloquially referred to as *the Cartel*. Never before had a single gateway accepted so many vinyl artisans into such a diverse marketplace of homespun music.

For decades, most record companies operated on the assumption they were delivering the type of music people wanted. However, Rough Trade founder Geoff Travis had always taken the opposite view, pointing out to a BBC journalist in the early eighties, "The record market is artificially created and might not be what people would buy given other alternatives."

"That's as true today as it was back then," Travis believes, thirty years the wiser. "Just look at Fox News. Fox News gives an image of what a country is and what people are meant to be thinking. And it's all very circular; what you make available to the general public – and I don't underestimate the intelligence of the general public, and that's an important premise – but what you put in front of them is completely and utterly determined by available means of distribution: who's in power, what people want you to hear, read, see. Although that's changing hugely with the Internet, it's still a factor in the way people live their lives, how they think. What we get to see on TV, what we hear on the radio, what we read in our newspapers is absolutely key."

Throughout the eighties, Geoff Travis and his colleagues were determined to alter public demand by widening the supply of alternative, independently made music. As Rough Trade's kibbutz model ballooned into a multistorey building, there was a deeper sociological dimension driving demand for moody records that captured the desolation of Britain's postindustrial decline, particularly in the north. By 1982, Britain's unemployment level had snowballed to a massive 3 million, having tripled in the previous eight years. Although the national average was one in eight, as many as one in six were on welfare in most parts of the north. Britain had never been so divided.

As Travis emphasised, however, "It wasn't a conscious thing to sign so many northern acts, it just seems to be that the north was where the best stuff came from. I always wonder why there's not better music from London. It's strange, maybe that old cliché about hard times producing great art has some veracity to it."

While the Cartel incubated a whole generation of indies like Factory, 2 Tone, 4AD, Mute, Creation, One Little Indian, Go! Discs, Some Bizarre, Fiction and Cooking Vinyl, Geoff Travis signed to Rough Trade's in-house label the Manchester band that personified the "indie" moniker – the Smiths. "Not everyone knew how great the Smiths were from day one," said Travis, "but any A&R person knows it's part of his job to help educate and bring the rest of their company along with things. A lot of people liked the Smiths, a lot of people didn't understand it, but for some of us they were absolutely central to what Rough Trade was doing. They were intelligent, educated, groundbreaking, original, innovative, politically aware to a degree, they understood feminism in a way that not many men did at that particular time. They were fascinating people. And they were northerners."

One overlooked phenomenon was Rough Trade's subtle influence on alternative rock in America. While Seymour Stein licensed the North American rights for a wide selection of acts from this indie network, there was a whole other grassroots movement quietly sprouting on the American periphery. One such unsung hero is Bruce Pavitt, founder of Sub Pop, the Seattle label that launched Nirvana.

Pavitt was originally from Chicago; his winding path to Seattle began in 1979 when he was a student in Olympia, Washington, hosting a radio show called *Subterranean Pop*. "I played a lot of West Coast punk, like the Dead Kennedys, X and the Wipers as well as a lot of the Rough Trade catalogue," explained Pavitt. "Rough Trade was my favourite label at the time." In 1980, Pavitt started the first indie magazine in America, also called *Subterranean Pop*. He understood that smaller cities around the country had their own happening bands ignored by the major companies, so in his magazine "all records were reviewed from a regional perspective, with an emphasis on cities outside of New York, Los Angeles and San Francisco."

The originality of Pavitt's perspective aroused the interest of the English magazine *NME,* which first reprinted his *U.S. Indie Chart.* Shortening his magazine title to *Sub Pop* in 1981, Pavitt then began alternating the magazine with mix tapes. Inspired by Rough Trade and then helped by them, he got his first taste of record production when their "distribution picked up two hundred copies and I was off! It eventually sold two thousand – good numbers at the time!"

In 1983, Pavitt made his fateful move to Seattle, where he helped set up a store for alternative music and skateboard gear. Called Fallout Records and Skateboards, it became a meeting point in the bohemian Capitol Hill neighbourhood. "Although I left in 1985 to start the Sub Pop label," explained Pavitt, "I helped establish the vibe, which was mostly SST releases, American hardcore punk, as well as U.K. releases from 4AD, Factory and Rough Trade." Pavitt also began spreading his message to the local street scene; he wrote a "*Sub Pop*" column for alternative magazine *Rocket*; hosted a *Sub Pop* show on Seattle radio; and deejayed at two clubs, the Metropolis and the Vogue. Then in 1986, Pavitt finally set up his own Sub Pop record label, and two years later, he teamed up with a local music promoter, Jon Poneman, who invested $20,000 "and joined me in documenting the Seattle scene, which we both agreed was really taking off." On April Fool's Day in 1988, they opened a tiny office, selling mail-order 45s from bands such as Green River, Soundgarden, Mudhoney and Nirvana.

"Things moved quickly for Kurt [Cobain] and Nirvana," remembered Pavitt. "Despite his intense, guttural singing style, offstage Kurt was shy and quiet. He was also sensitive, creative, and a genuine fan of new music. His ambitions were initially modest. In the fall of 1988, he was stoked to have his first single, 'Love Buzz,' played on the local college station." Within a year of their debut album, *Bleach*, Nirvana made the cover of Britain's *Sounds* magazine, toured Europe, and rocked London at Sub Pop's LameFest showcase.

Meanwhile, in New York, another young man with a giant destiny in the record industry was rising up through his local indie community, producer and Def Jam founder Rick Rubin. As a student in the early eighties, "I hung out at a tiny independent record store called 99 Records on MacDougal Street, run by a guy named Ed Bahlman," explained Rubin. "He was sort of my mentor in the music business because he put out independent records like ESG, Bush Tetras and Liquid Liquid. It was just a really cool indie store where I heard a lot of U.K. twelve-inches and independent punk rock."

Rubin got into break beats and befriended Zulu Nation deejay Jazzy Jay. "I experienced hip-hop as black punk rock," he said. "It was another way of taking music back. It wasn't made by virtuosos, it wasn't about great musicianship, it was made by anyone with an idea or something to say." He was introduced to a black promoter, Russell Simmons, and set up Def Jam in 1984 while still a student. Following initial releases such as LL Cool J.'s "I Need a Beat," Rubin began mixing up all of his diverse influences. "In high school I had listened to stuff like AC/DC and Led Zeppelin. From there I got into independent punk rock – the Dead Kennedys, Black Flag. Then I got seriously into hip-hop, where it all moved full circle because I was missing the old stuff like Led Zeppelin and Black Sabbath." Blurring the lines between what seemed to be alien genres, in 1985 Rubin produced Def Jam's first Top 10 smash hit, "Walk

This Way," on which an old Aerosmith rock song was given a striking slant courtesy of rappers Run-D.M.C.

In the opposite direction, Rubin convinced the hárd-core punk band the Beastie Boys to try rapping. The resulting experiment was a 12-inch, "Rock Hard," which led to a No. 1 album, *Licensed to Ill*, including two Top 10 hits, "(You Gotta) Fight for Your Right (to Party)" and "No Sleep till Brooklyn." From that collision of genres and personalities came a third important Def Jam group, Public Enemy, who in 1988 released the landmark hip-hop album *It Takes a Nation of Millions to Hold Us Back*.

Illustrating the constant reverberation of sounds and ideas across the Atlantic, in around 1988, just as grunge and punk-fuelled hip-hop began to explode on America's coasts, back in England, a new kind of postpunk dance wave – inspired by the New York clubs of the early eighties – was starting to swell up through Rough Trade's distribution networks. Once again, it was coming from northern England, in particular Manchester, where for six loss-making years, Factory Records had poured profits from Joy Division and New Order into their superclub, the Hacienda.

"I'm out of touch with the street," admitted Factory cofounder Tony Wilson in 1987. "Between '76 and '81, I knew everything that was being released and I saw a different band each night. But that part of your life passes, and now I rely on other people to tell me what's happening." As Factory's new A&R man, Mike Pickering, explained, "Rob Gretton and I wanted a dance label; Factory Dance ... you could feel it happening ... God bless Tony, but I don't think he had the vision Rob had. Tony said dance would never happen." As a result of this disagreement, Pickering set up his own dance label, Deconstruction, which competed with other house pioneers such as On-U Sound, FON, Champion and Mute sub-label Rhythm King.

However, Mike Pickering and Rob Gretton still had influence over programming at the Hacienda. Deejay Dave Haslam recalled that "By the middle of 1987, Thursday, Friday and Saturday were packed every week with twelve hundred people a night. My Thursdays were becoming a focus for the city's indie dance fans. Pickering's Fridays were then attracting a slightly harder, blacker crowd." Then, in early 1988, a new drug called ecstasy entered the building, as another deejay, Jon DaSilva, began Ibiza theme nights on Wednesdays. "The music was coming from all angles," said DaSilva, "from the deepest Detroit techno, into hip-hop and into garage, back to house and into acid house. It wasn't just the chemicals, it was the music … The whole thing just hit the Hacienda like a thundering train."

Despite Britain's first ecstasy-related death on the dance floor of the Hacienda in 1989, rave culture surged, sprouting new clubs, new acts and new indies by the handful. That year, Britain's most iconic goth and coldwave label, 4AD, released a one-off experiment, "Pump Up the Volume" by a studio collective of musicians who called themselves M/A/R/R/S – a milestone smash hit. Dance-infused hits followed from the Stone Roses, Primal Scream, and even the original ecstasy dealers from the Hacienda – the Happy Mondays.

Just as dance culture and sampling went mainstream, Rough Trade's distribution arm collapsed in 1991. Although £40 million worth of records were flowing through its nationwide veins, its success had made it too large and unwieldy for its idealistic founders to steer. Cash-flow difficulties on the distribution side capsized the entire enterprise – record company included. "Rough Trade's great flaw was that we never had a financial director who understood the business," sighed Geoff Travis with the benefit of hindsight.

For the hundreds of hand-to-mouth labels involved, it was more than just a distributor going bust. There had been a powerful cultural dimension to the Rough Trade experiment, and its sudden death created a vacuum. For 4AD boss Ivo Watts-Russell, "It was the end of an era. I, perhaps naively, always thought of Rough Trade as being filled with true music lovers. I felt the label was being handled by people, at the lowest levels, who knew its history and, with luck, enjoyed a lot of what we were releasing."

Although another distribution company called Pinnacle provided the same core services, "the dream was over," said Watts-Russell, "and faceless individuals, little different to those working at the major labels, would now be packing boxes with 4AD *product*. I think it was the beginning of the word *independent* or *indie* losing its meaning, its credibility." It was at this crisis point, however, that one indie chieftain began to show his mettle – Martin Mills, the group owner behind Beggars Banquet and 4AD. As events would illustrate, through crises, Mills was in the process of becoming a resourceful guardian of independent values, somewhat like Chris Blackwell in the early seventies – though arguably more disciplined and committed to a collective cause.

As with most record men, the enigma of Martin Mills makes most sense viewed through the boy's eyes. His father, the brightest son from a working-class Yorkshire family, studied at the Sorbonne in Paris, where in 1939 he met his wife, an upper-middle-class girl from the home counties whose family history reached back to the civil service in India.

A product of this socially mixed student romance in Paris, Martin Mills was born in 1949. Unfortunately, "I don't remember my father very well," he confessed, "because he died when I was eleven. I don't really have any clear memories of him apart from a few old photographs." Growing up, Martin Mills was a brilliant student, but the shadow of his father's death followed him to school and back home again. "It made me very insecure in my teenage years. It made me very, very, very insecure," Mills acknowledged as a sixty-two-year-old man.

In the austere gloom of postwar England, the beat boom arrived like a circus coming to town. Listening first to the Shadows, then the Beatles, Mills as a boy got progressively drawn to the edgier sounds of the Stones, the Animals, the Kinks, the Who and the Yardbirds. "I didn't really get into Dylan until around 1966 when I first heard *Bringing It All Back Home* and began working backwards through his stuff," explained Mills. "I wouldn't say that I played Dylan to the exclusion of everything else; he was one amongst many. But I think with the benefit of hindsight, it's pretty clear to see that he is the preeminent artist of that half century."

With his mother working as a primary school head in Oxford, Mills moved into student digs down the road, graduating from Oriel College in 1970 with a degree in philosophy, politics and economics. While England was up to its eyeballs in psychedelia, "those years were not wild at all. I never took drugs, I was very rarely drunk. I had been an *extremely* conscientious schoolboy, and I obviously learned to have a bit more fun as a student. I think I was probably a late developer, to be honest. I was very shy as a teenager, and it wasn't really until university that I began to come out of myself."

After he applied for a job at every record company in London, the Hammersmith labour exchange found him work as a statistician for the Lane Committee, a group of politicians and specialists reporting on the reform of Britain's abortion law. "I ended up being the person that wrote the report," explained Mills. "I actually did all the analysis of all the research and pretty much wrote the statistical side of the report."

Mills teamed up with a friend, Nick Austin, to set up their own specialist record store, Beggars Banquet. They opened a total of five Beggars Banquet shops, and, as with other specialist retailers of the seventies, the punk explosion was cue for a label, Beggars Banquet Records. After three years releasing punk records, their lucky ticket, Gary Numan, arrived right in the middle of the 1979 recession. They were dipping into the cash register to pay for his synthesisers as bills began piling up in the back office. "We were about to go bust. We were bouncing salary cheques. The shop's cash flow just couldn't fund what we were trying to do with the label anymore. We were steering over the cliff at that point."

Luckily the redundant managing director of Arista's London office found them a lucrative deal with Warner. Mills and Austin sighed a shoulder-load of relief cashing their £100,000 cheque – a lifesaver, and in hindsight a smart gamble on Warner's part, comfortably recouped a few months later by Gary Numan's transatlantic smash hit, "Cars." Reinvesting profits into a new sublabel, Mills and Austin set up 4AD, run by one of the store managers, Ivo Watts-Russell. Ironically, the younger imprint, by about 1985, began to eclipse the parent company with a string of dark gems: Bauhaus, Modern English, This Mortal Coil, Dead Can Dance and the Pixies.

By the mideighties, Nick Austin was cartwheeling off on his own artistic tangent. While Martin Mills was focusing his efforts on breaking the Cult, Austin's fascination with New Age music and jazz-funk left him isolated inside his own company. With tensions turning to estrangement, Mills bought him out. Possibly regretting his ill-timed departure, Austin sued a few years later.

334 ★ COWBOYS AND INDIES

"The fallout with Nick Austin was the only big one of my life, and it was a mega fallout," confessed Mills. "We spent three months in court with each other at the end of it. So it was an absolutely enormous event. It put me hugely into debt." Ivo Watts-Russell confirmed that the saga cast a dark cloud over the group. "It was just so strange from my perspective. It just seemed obvious that Nick, having not really succeeded with his new solo venture, decided he deserved more money from Martin. By this time, 4AD was doing really well, was even financially very flush. The Cult, I think, were also doing quite well. Perhaps Nick felt he was entitled to some of that."

To pay for his legal costs, Mills had to tap into 4AD's cash reserves, but in doing so he rewarded Ivo Watts-Russell with 50 percent of the label. "He did not have to do that," said the equally gratified Watts-Russell. "I only went to the courthouse once to see what was going on, but I did go on the day the judge ruled in Martin's favour." Unaware the heavyweight independents from London to Los Angeles were all lurching irreversibly into the jaws of major buyouts, Martin Mills stepped out of the courtroom into a bright future. "In the pub afterwards you could see this *huge* weight lifted from Martin's shoulders," remembered Watts-Russell. "We all had tears in our eyes."

Symbolising their ascension to the top of the indie mountain, it was Martin Mills and Mute financial director Duncan Cameron who ran in as firefighters once Rough Trade collapsed. They set up a new distribution company called RTM. "The objective was to try to preserve the spirit of Rough Trade," explained Mills, "but to put it in a more organised and secure context. And those labels that went from the Cartel to RTM didn't lose any money. We came up with this rather neat idea to subcontract the actual distribution to Pinnacle, so RTM was actually a sales and market-ing organisation, and it subcontracted all the putting of records in boxes to Pinnacle. There was a slice of the distribution fee which went to repay the old debt. It took about eighteen months, but it succeeded in getting everyone's money back."

Not all other chieftains were as determined to salvage the indie spirit from the smoking ruins. "When everything collapsed," recalled Ivo Watts-Russell, "quite apart from the trauma and tedium of having to attend endless meetings in rooms filled with far more people than I tend to feel comfortable being around, there was a feeling of everyone scrabbling around trying to save their own arses. Even before it was inevitable that Rough Trade would not pull through, I had a phone conversation with [Creation founder] Alan McGee trying to persuade him not to jump ship. To no avail."

Sony swooped in and plucked Creation Records from the wreckage – the label behind Primal Scream and, later, Oasis. Then in 1992 another bombshell hit; Factory Records went bust. For the founder of 4AD, these years of upheaval were too much. "Back in 1979, I was given the opportunity, along with Peter Kent, to start a record *label*. By the early nineties, I was running a record *company*. I didn't enjoy it and I was useless at it. More importantly, I felt in danger of losing my love of music." Just two years after Rough Trade's demise, Ivo Watts-Russell relocated to California and retired.

It was the same story for Sub Pop in America. Once grunge began exploding, Nirvana was lured to David Geffen's new label, DGC Records. "Of course Jon Poneman and I were disappointed in the move," admitted Sub Pop founder Bruce Pavitt, who nonetheless received a lucrative override of 2.5 percent for Nirvana's first three albums. "Although in retrospect DGC was able to really get *Nevermind* out to a much larger audience – which it deserved. It's an amazing record. I'm honoured to have worked with Kurt and Nirvana."

Despite the cash injection from Nirvana's success, Sub Pop was forced to sell half the company to Warner. "As the label grew, the culture changed," lamented Bruce Pavitt, "becoming more departmentalised and less spontaneous. Although we were technically *independent,* in reality, we were competing with majors and adopting their characteristics. My partner, Jon Poneman, seemed to be much more comfortable with this approach. I left, moving to Orcas Island in Washington State to raise a family. Jon continued to build the label, and it has done good business under his management. It's just not as innovative, as fun, or as culturally significant as it once was."

With the majors becoming hugely rich and powerful, for Mute founder Daniel Miller, the consensual, bland pop-rock of the nineties was a hostile environment for anyone with an adventurous imagination. In the early eighties, Miller regularly turned down lucrative offers from the likes of Richard Branson, "because why would I sell out? I was young, independent and doing really well." Things turned sour soon after Rough Trade's collapse. "There was a struggle, but not just financially," confessed Miller. "There was a musical struggle, for me to be honest. There was a period in the midnineties – the Brit Pop era – which I hated. It was counterintuitive to me. I didn't really sign very much because anything that wasn't Brit Pop was very difficult to get exposed. Radio 1 and the media was completely taken over and obsessed with Brit Pop. And we were not doing brilliantly financially at that time. So I was a bit depressed about everything."

In the mid-nineties, Daniel Miller convened a supper at Julie's Wine Bar in Kensington. Joining him were twelve or so indie chieftains including Martin Mills; Derek Birkett, owner of One Little Indian; Martin Goldschmidt, owner of Cooking Vinyl; and Derek Green, by now owner of his own indie, China Records. As the evening progressed, the veteran Derek Green surveyed the table: "All these characters sitting there with their eccentricities – it was quite a funny kind of gathering because as a community they're not necessarily close to each other, they're fiercely competitive, very private, not very easy to speak to. Their egos are very big. They need to be just to meet the everyday battle.

"Anyhow, in that wine bar, I'm sitting there and listening to the debate. All the frustrations are coming up. 'We can't get our records on Radio 1; we can't get seen in HMV because all the marketing clout is with the majors.' There was a moment in that dinner when a light flicked on in my head. 'I know what everybody in this room has in common! Everybody around this table is losing money.' And when I clocked that, I laughed to myself. Then I thought, that's probably true, none of us are making money. So why then do we do it? Well, the only reason we do it is because on our balance sheets we have the value of our masters and the value of our contracts marked as zero. Therefore technically every year our accountants tell us we're bankrupt. But what we really know and believe is that the majors will pay millions to buy us."

Half the table did eventually throw in their napkins and ask for a cheque. In 1995, Go Discs!, then enjoying success with Portishead, sold out to PolyGram. In 1997, Green, enjoying success with Morcheeba, sold his label to Warner. The party host, Daniel Miller, held on for the best part of a decade "limping along financially and artistically." The only way to raise enough cash to keep Mute afloat was a big worldwide licence with a major. "But we weren't really getting any interesting offers," said Miller. "Then suddenly, we had this huge hit with Moby's *Play* and of course now everybody wants to do a fucking deal with me!"

Thanks to Moby selling 10 million records, "I was in a really strong position, so I went to [French boss of EMI-Virgin] Emmanuel de Buretel and made up a list of things I wanted, and he said, 'Okay, I think we can do most of that.' So I thought, I'm going to take that opportunity to work with somebody else. Plus, you know, by then I'd been doing it for what, twenty-four years?" In 2002, Miller secured a deal for a tidy £23 million.

Of the dinner guests, one conspicuous holdout was the quiet Derek Birkett, founder of One Little Indian, whose success with Björk helped keep the wolves from the door. Then, of course, there was Martin Mills, who, during his legal wrangles with Nick Austin just a few years previously, almost did consider the unthinkable. "You only ever really think about these things because of money," confessed Mills. "It was a time when things were difficult and I was kind of, hmm, I thought about it once, but it passed. It was a moment of madness. It passed. Ever since then, I've just resolutely always said no."

For his resilience, Martin Mills was amply rewarded in the midnineties when his new sublabel, XL Recordings, directed by the capable Richard Russell, struck gold with the Prodigy. Their dance-rock smash hit *Music for the Jilted Generation* assured the Beggars Banquet Group, and in particular its rapidly expanding XL Recordings imprint, an inside lane into the computer age.

Another determined face walking against the traffic was Laurence Bell, founder of a new indie label, Domino. "I was there when Rough Trade distribution collapsed," said Bell of his formative years holding down odd jobs as a young man. "I was working in that office, saw it all go down. And it was pretty depressing … Everyone was going; Creation, Factory, it was all around; you saw independent labels fail, go bankrupt, or be sold. The majors were taking over everything; they were starting up these bogus independent imprints – the whole culture was being bought up and chewed up. But I was still excited by music and finding things. I just wanted to do something genuinely independent, start again, find some bands, go against everything that was happening. And there was some great music around then – 1991 was a great year for music. That's when I started to realise that I wanted to do this; to work with bands, put out records. So I set up my own label in 1993." Before Domino hit the big time in 2004, courtesy of Franz Ferdinand, it operated out of a basement. Its first release was a simple U.K. licence for an indie-rock group, Sebadoh, originally signed to Sub Pop. The story was moving full circle.

Refugees, exiles, outcasts – the combined effect of corporate concentration and Rough Trade's demise left a generation of England's left-field record men wandering aimlessly along the roadside. Exposed to the elements in the naughty nineties, many a weary warrior was lured inside by a hefty cheque. Only a handful of diehards had enough fire in their bellies to keep *believing*. Dust or pollen? The ruins of the proverbial temple blew away on the four winds – a sad memory for some, but for others, an ideal destined to come again.

30. BUBBLEGUM FOREST

FIRST CAME THE FACTORIES, THEN CAME THE SUPERMARKETS. ENTER THE plastic jungle of artificial fruit whose sugary flavour can only be chewed for a while, then spat out. The new era oozed the musical equivalent of fast food – sold to children at adult prices. Quite literally, suits from food and drinks industries were taking over the conglomerates that owned the majors, and with them, along came their conception of a planned, supermarket industry.

"As the business got bigger, there was an arrogance," said one of the era's few genuine record men, Rick Rubin, who in 1988 left Def Jam for new adventures out west. In 1991, he produced *Blood Sugar Sex Magik* by the Red Hot Chili Peppers, and on his new label, American Recordings, he directed Johnny Cash's last four albums. "From the nineties onwards," said Rubin, "record labels were all being run by accountants and attorneys. It was becoming a less pleasant business."

The compact disc had brought profound changes to the very artifact itself – the record. Since the forties at least, buying the latest pop song had been most people's initiation into the record-buying habit. As Elektra founder Jac Holzman points out, however, "singles did not have a format after the demise of the 45 rpm record. At the beginning of the CD, prices ranged between $15 and $18. They fell over time, but the model ran counter to the business. Singles have historically been important to the record business because they helped point people – they were calling cards for albums."

The cream of the nineties market was certainly capable of making interesting albums. Nirvana, the Fugees, Radiohead, the Red Hot Chili Peppers, Rage Against the Machine, the Chemical Brothers, Massive Attack, Portishead, Beck, Jeff Buckley and many others managed to exploit the full capabilities of the compact disc in a way that justified the price tag. For record buyers, though, the CD age meant that to buy the latest *one-hit wonder* you had to pay at least $15. The price of bubble-gum, a standard commodity in the record business, had soared to an all-time high.

"What went wrong," continued Holzman, "is they all thought they were geniuses. When the CD took hold, it took hold very quickly. The retailers got rid of LPs as quickly as they could. They told the labels, in effect: you take a twelve-inch bin designed for vinyl LPs, cut it in half with a board, and put in twice as many CDs at twice the price. Plus, the labels had clauses in their contracts that royalties would be reduced by twenty percent for any new technology. So suddenly the artist who was supposedly getting a dollar royalty on a CD was getting eighty cents. In some cases, they were getting another twenty-five percent taken off for packaging deductions, which meant the artist was getting only fifty-five cents. The result was that the labels became incredibly profitable. And everybody running a label thought they were a stone genius."

With easy money, even the best companies became complacent. "The enormous growth was based largely on catalogue sales," pointed out Tommy Boy founder Tom Silverman, who, while enjoying commercial success with De La Soul, became a Warner VP attending top-level meetings. "Anybody with a catalogue was getting forty-five percent of their revenue from people rebuying their favourite records on CDs at sixty to eighty percent higher prices. And because it was such a cash cow, the majors didn't have to be ambitious. Whatever they did, it did great."

The joke was that not everybody was even sure the CD sounded better than vinyl. "It was all being heralded as a technological achievement that supposedly improved the way we listen to music," ventured Craig Kallman, at the time an indie specialising in house music who joined

Atlantic in 1991. "When the industry started happily announcing the death of vinyl, I used to have cold sweats and sleepless nights because I started comparing both formats. I'd sync the vinyl and the CD of the same recordings by artists like Led Zeppelin, Miles Davis, Fleetwood Mac, Bob Marley, Van Morrison, Aretha Franklin, Neil Young, Frank Sinatra. Those early CDs were brittle, glassy, edgy and two-dimensional, whereas the vinyl was liquid, open, smooth, inviting and truly euphonic. Yes, the CD offered convenience, but back then, the trade-off in sound quality was too great. Not to mention the whole experience of the vinyl album jacket – the artwork, the liner notes, the tangible nature of it. For me, in the eighties, there was just no comparison between vinyl and CD."

"In the early days, often a cassette master, which was already a substandard master compared to the vinyl master, was downgraded further to be cut to CD masters," confirmed Rick Rubin. "So even though the CD had the potential for higher resolution, the source material tended to be really second-class. We all worked hard mastering our records to sound good on vinyl, but we hadn't worked much on mastering records for CD yet. So they were further down the food chain … There were good and bad things about the CD. They didn't sound good, but they were convenient, they were portable. But originally when they came out in a long box, it was really terrible. I missed the big sleeve artwork. And I missed the sound of analog."

Realising that the true sound of classic records was being downgraded while the originals were being phased out, "I went on a mission to preserve the history of recorded music on vinyl," explained Craig Kallman. "I started making lists every night – notebooks upon notebooks: the complete discography of every artist who was important in virtually every genre. I had to study, do research and then go find perfect copies." Now the proud owner of one of the world's largest, most pristine vinyl collections, measuring some 750,000 LPs, 10-inches and 45s, the Atlantic CEO, while acknowledging he is vinyl obsessed, believes it's no accident the 12-inch LP has endured, even thrived, sixty-five years after it was introduced.

Sure enough, the inherent weaknesses of the compact disc, notably its high price, cold sound and cheap packaging, provoked structural market problems in the second half of the decade as music got corporate. Just as conglomerates bought up record companies, giants like Best Buy, Walmart, Target and Circuit City were muscling in on the lucrative retail market. Aggressively undercutting the established record chains by selling bestsellers at $12, by 1996, Best Buy and Walmart were moving 154 million compact discs per year.

Simultaneously, gargantuan buyouts were further concentrating production. In March 1995, Edgar Bronfman, Jr., heir to Canadian beverage giant Seagram, persuaded his board to spend $5.7 billion on 80 percent of MCA, which Bronfman renamed Universal following his acquisition of the movie group. Meanwhile, in Amsterdam, the new chief executive of Philips, Cor Boonstra – straight out of the food industry – promised worried investors he would cut down the group's "bleeders." Although PolyGram was the biggest record company in Europe, it was put on the market partly because its movie division was littered with money-losing companies.

In 1998, Edgar Bronfman persuaded the Seagram board to buy out PolyGram for $10.6 billion. PolyGram's chief, Alain Levy, was swiftly replaced by former Atlantic co-president Doug Morris, who laid off 980 employees and cut two hundred acts as part of a massive restructuring plan. PolyGram was duly merged with the group formerly known as MCA to create Universal Music Group – the corporate equivalent of Goliath.

Bubbles tend to defy logic just before bursting – and the CD was no different from any property or speculation bubble. In 1999, the Backstreet Boys' album *Millennium* broke all existing records by selling over 1 million CDs in its first week of release. Then Britney Spears's *Oops! ... I Did It Again* broke the record with 1.3 million sales in its first week. 'N Sync smashed it again in 2000 with a historic 2.4 million sales in just one week. Those three acts alone sold 96 million records in America. From that teen-pop wave, in 2001, *Pop Idol* in Britain inspired the first season of *American Idol* on Fox.

In purely financial terms, by 1999, as Napster arrived, the CD business was statistically booming like never before; the annual turnover was $12.8 billion in America alone. In an indication of how the supply of music was getting concentrated, Walmart was enjoying 20 percent of American retail CD sales with an average of just 750 titles per outlet.

"The way music was just pumped out," said Rick Rubin, "it seemed like the people in charge cared very little for quality. Like they had this big switch. They'd have just one song, which they'd push at radio and put it out as a CD with a load of filler – basically trying to trick people into buying albums. And I think that behaviour led to a revolt. If you buy five terrible albums with only one good song, you start to lose faith in the system. I feel like the system was broken, creatively broken. And that's a big part of why the falloff eventually happened. There was very little goodwill built up between fans and the artists on the radio."

Adding to the perfect storm was technological ignorance. Unlike Steve Ross, who moved into video games, MTV and the compact disc, the new emperors reigning over the entertainment industries just kept selling the plastic. As Seymour Stein put it, "The real name of EMI is the Gramophone Company; the real name of RCA is the Victor Talking Machine Company; the real name of Columbia Records is the Columbia Graphophone Company; the real name of Decca is the Decca Phonograph Company. You get it? They made phonographs … In the fifties, Columbia invented the 33 rpm, RCA invented the 45 rpm, rock 'n' roll came along and the record business exploded, so they thought, 'Thank God we don't have to make this furniture anymore.' Luckily, by some miracle, Philips and Sony made the cassette and the CD, so we held on a little bit longer, but we planted the seeds of our own destruction. This could have been avoided. We never should have stopped making hardware."

"Technology has done more to change the record business than any other entertainment medium," reasoned his Warner confrère Jac Holzman. "That's certainly true of film. Television followed a straight evolutionary path – always getting better, but you were using the same frequencies, the same airwaves. Records were fundamentally different, from cylinder to discs to LPs to CDs. And what happened was that this CD model goes along happily for eighteen years until, in 2000, you get Napster and suddenly the majors see they may lose control. This was an issue of control … I once asked one of the guys who is in this book – I can't mention the name – I said, 'Look, there is a big change going to come and we can do all kinds of other things with the new technology.' And he said, 'Oh, Jac, you're always talking about the future. I just want to deal with the present.' I said, 'No, this is going to happen. How are you going to plan to embrace it?' And he said, 'I'm not embracing it, I just want it to go away.' So everybody gets up and they start fighting."

As Napster and other file-sharing systems began eating into retail sales, the record industry was, like Nero, fiddling while Rome burned. In 2000, Edgar Bronfman persuaded his board into a fateful stock-only merger with French water monopoly Vivendi for a theoretical $34 billion, thus creating Vivendi Universal, one of the legendary own goals of that crazy period. Folly was in the air – even among more experienced players who should have known better. In 2001, for example, Ken Berry at Virgin splashed out $80 million in a bidding war to pick up Mariah Carey. Imagine Berry's surprise when he realised the thirty-year-old diva was having a nervous breakdown and past her prime. Bad luck turned the risky investment into a commercial wipeout; Mariah Carey's relaunch on Virgin was scheduled for September 11, 2001.

The most surreal fairy tale from the bubblegum forest was surely the sale of the Zomba Group – the sugariest of the teen-pop factories, whose Jive label brought you Britney Spears, Backstreet Boys, 'N Sync and Justin Timberlake. As a result of a badly thought-out contract signed ten years previously, BMG was contractually obliged to buy out Zomba at a price based on its previous year's turnover. Due to a fortuitous alignment of the stars, Zomba owner Clive Calder sailed off into the Caribbean sunset with an unbelievable $2.74 billion in his hip pocket. For its money, BMG inherited a chocolate factory without its Willy Wonka.

The bubblegum index finally began to crash the following year. First, Vivendi Universal's share price plummeted. Suffering losses of $23 billion, Edgar Bronfman, Jr., had effectively poured his family's beverage empire down a drain. Meanwhile, on the street, with the huge success of the retail juggernauts altering the fragile status quo, the traditional record chains Tower and Musicland were forced to follow all the latest Top 40 junk. After decades of giving the store's prominent positions to artists who actually played instruments, traditional stores all over America and Britain began to lose their feel as places of pop culture. The gaudy covers of manufactured bands paid their way onto the end caps and began scaring away older audiences.

With 65 percent of the market controlled by Best Buy and Walmart, the older record chains Tower and Musicland eventually went bust. "The saddest day was the closing of Tower Records," lamented Craig Kallman. "Tower was obviously such a lover of music, which had a really deep inventory. So for those of us operating on the front line, the business was really changing because you had this consolidation around hit records on your established artists. So for new artists getting going, it became tougher and tougher to find a way in."

Of course, not everyone in those champagne-belching years was buying teen-pop. From the late nineties onward, there was also an adult wave in electronic music. Innovative albums from the likes of Massive Attack, Moby, the Prodigy, Björk, Orbital, the Chemical Brothers, St. Germain, Thievery Corporation, Kruder & Dorfmeister and Daft Punk, brought electronica to mainstream audiences – not just listeners but established artists and small producers also. As this high-tech genre inspired a flood of imitations, the mass of electronic music being produced from home studios became far too vast for labels, shops and consumers to keep track of.

So the adult CD market witnessed a glut of DJ-mixed compilations grouping the best moments of the electronic underground. Specific genre terms began to grow under the increasingly defunct *dance* appellation as *house, ambient, trance, trip-hop, chill-out, lounge* and *electro* became the hallmark sounds inside nightclubs, hotels and restaurants. Gradually a whole new generation of compilation brand names was taking up larger spaces, particularly in European record stores. Ministry of Sound, Defected, Café Del Mar, Global Underground, Hed Kandi, Space Night, Hotel Costes, Buddha Bar, DJ-Kicks and many others sold truckloads of compilations to the urban adult market.

Although nobody noticed what was happening, a deejay-mixed compilation is nothing more than a collection of singles assembled dynamically into a personalised storyboard. All these compilation makers understood that the thirty- to sixty-year-old urban demographic simply wanted the *best of* the electronic underground. People didn't want the sixty-minute albums.

Illegal downloading devices, apart from being free, enabled the public to get the one song they wanted. Because CD stores had ceased to be centres of street culture, all the subversive action was happening on the Internet. Thanks also to MP3 software like Winamp and iTunes, people could become their own deejays. Suddenly, in the first years of the new millennium, pop culture entered the *anyone-can-be-a-deejay* era. The previous century's music became a dusty surplus from which you could assemble the soundtrack to your own life.

To its credit, Apple, the most popular hardware manufacturer among this urban demographic, spotted an opportunity to launch its very successful iPod and from there meander its way into the smartphone market with admirable stealth. A twenty-year trademark saga with the Beatles' production company, Apple Corps, was finally resolved thanks to a rumoured $500 million payout, allowing the Californian giant of the same name to break into the music business. For the third time in 110 years, the jukebox was about to throw the drowning recording business a lifesaver.

In April 2002, Steve Jobs personally telephoned the president of AOL Time Warner, who dispatched Paul Vidich, a Warner Music executive. A technology VP in the Warner delegation, Kevin Gage, described one meeting at Apple's headquarters where he and Vidich argued for "locks" to be encrypted into digital tracks to prevent file-sharing. Just as Gage began his PowerPoint presentation, Steve Jobs pitched a fit, shouting. "You've got your head stuck up your ass!" In an oblique reference to such outbursts, the EMI boss, Robert Faxon, recalled how Jobs "pushed us in ways we needed to be pushed … He sometimes didn't hold the executives in very high esteem, but he always put the creators of music at the pinnacle of the business."

Or so they thought. By personally lobbying the world's most powerful artist managers and pop stars – notably Bono, who became Apple's loudest cheerleader – Jobs was tacitly reminding the majors that if they weren't compliant, they might have a messy mutiny on their hands. In the cut and thrust of business, Steve Jobs ran circles around the shell-shocked executives of the world's rapidly shrinking majors. Amazingly, nobody noticed that, despite Jobs's claims about the iTunes Store being *for artists*, he knew virtually nothing about music. As one senior Apple colleague recently admitted, at the time Jobs hadn't even heard of hip-hop – the genre!

Jobs knew other things, though. What he wasn't telling the record companies in 2002 was that *he* urgently needed content to embark on his hazardous expedition into the terra incognita of handheld devices. "I need you guys to be healthy," he later told Universal CEO Lucian Grainge, "because if you are healthy, then you'll invest in more artists, more talent, and it means I grow my business."

The figures draw the clearest picture. In the first year of the iTunes Store, iPod sales shot up ninefold – becoming Apple's biggest-selling product and pushing up turnover by 37 percent. Between 2003 and 2011, Apple sold a total of 300 million iPods and 10 billion songs via the iTunes Store, overtaking both Walmart and Best Buy as retailers. For Apple, the iTunes Store was the key battle that won them the war. However, over a ten-year spread, music and apps only represented between 5 and 10 percent of Apple's overall revenue – a percentage relatively stable with Apple's growth. Thanks to the increasing volume of iPhone and iPads, the iTunes Store exceeded $1 billion in 2009 and reached $12 billion in 2013.

Meanwhile the major labels were kicked around like deflating footballs. Still determined to leave his mark, Edgar Bronfman bought out Warner Music for an undisclosed sum, then sold it in May 2011 for $3.3 billion to a Russian-born tycoon of Jewish origin, Len Blavatnik. In 2004, Sony and BMG merged to create Sony BMG; in 2008, Bertelsmann sold off BMG to Sony. In 2011, due to £4 billion in debts, EMI was carved up and sold off by its creditor Citibank – the record division to Universal for just £1.2 billion, and its publishing arm to a Sony-led consortium for $2.2 billion. More fire sales will follow.

On balance, viewed from the mountaintop, the recent music industry crash resembles a forest fire that, however cruel, is maybe just a part of Mother Nature's epic cycles. Scientists have learned that, strange as it seems, forests actually need catastrophic fires about once a century to replenish nutrients in the underlying soil.

31. REVELATIONS

LET'S IMAGINE THE FUTURE OF MUSIC. IF YOU BELIEVE THE TECH PRESS, IT is pure and simple: a system of mobile devices through which music flows as a kind of utility, financed by a subscription similar to public television. Tomorrow's listeners will consume music like water. Just as water pours from your tap, old catalogue will be legally available in online libraries. Discerning ears will pay a little extra for premium offerings, in the way that sensitive palates prefer bottled mineral water.

Now open your eyes. When imagining any future in the music industry, the common error is to underestimate the guile, mischief and plain vandalism of lawyers, lobbyists, teenagers and other rogue gremlins in the machine. In the shell-shocked years following Napster, technologists kept predicting that artists would sell themselves directly to the public – because for the first time in history, they physically could. Remember how, in and around 2005, we were all hailing MySpace as a revolution? And then it swiftly degenerated into a jungle of garage bands hustling each other for compliments.

Even the world's biggest technology giants cannot plan a music economy. In 2012, when Apple became the wealthiest corporation in history, its music "ecosystem" looked poised to win the digital music race forever after. Then iTunes sales began falling ominously throughout 2014 and all eyes turned to the new model of subscription-based streaming services, Spotify. Within the year, Apple itself was throwing out the old model and relaunching iTunes as Apple Music, a subscription streaming platform complete with BBC-inspired radio channels.

Apple's shift to streaming, however, wasn't plain sailing. By 2015, the new digital realities were sinking in and the music industry had got a fair bit wiser. Apple faced a far more sceptical and tough-dealing industry than the one Steve Jobs pushed around a decade previously. The first sign of this, for the public, was Taylor Swift derailing their attempt not to pay for content streamed by customers on free trials. But behind the scenes the corporate lawyers were hard at work.

Surprisingly, perhaps, the true survivor of the record industry crash has been our century-old framework of music copyright, and by extension the old hierarchy of record companies and collection societies that control the content. The record label, by consistently pumping fresh hit music into an increasing number of real and virtual channels, has remained the heart of the entire musical organism – artists, publishers, deejays, journalists, advertisers, concert promoters and sellers included.

The marketplace has, however, been fragmenting over the past fifteen years into an extraordinarily multi-dimensional mess of networks and niches. YouTube's head of content, Robert Kyncl, accurately likened today's business to the street chaos of India, obliquely suggesting that the recording industry cannot return to the "Switzerland" of yore. It is a disorder remarkably similar to the arrival of radio in the equally turbulent inter-war years. Then, as now, regional diversity, further compounded by economic inequality between young and old generations, added layers of demographic complexity to the record industry's already confusing technological, commercial and legal transformations.

Today's recording industry, despite having shrunk to less than half the size it was at its $40 billion high point in 1999, measured about $14 billion in 2014, the milestone year when combined digital revenue finally nudged past physical. About $6 billion worth of compact discs were nonetheless sold in 2014, 46 percent of worldwide revenue, and still the single most lucrative format. Japan, the world's second largest market and the birthplace of the CD, has been the notable hold-out. Thanks to its old-fashioned industry which packages beautifully, promotes reissues and blocks digital rights to potential marauders, CD sales accounted for 72 percent of Japanese music revenue in 2014, over $1 billion. Europe's most populous country is another anomaly: 66 percent of the German market in 2014, generating €985 million, came from CDs. Even in America, where the format has steadily fallen to a third of all industry income, some 141 million CDs were sold in 2014.

What many outside observers fail to understand about this supposedly extinct format, is that the majority of music journalists will not review a new release unless there's a physical album to listen to and peruse. Secondly, a vast black market of unaccounted CDs, probably measuring in the tens of millions, operates directly between musicians and their fans, at concerts and on websites. Amongst those struggling to survive in music, physical product is still the hard currency.

The quiet rise of Amazon points to another largely unreported phenomenon in this die-hard market. In Britain, the all-powerful online retailer overtook iTunes in 2014 to become the largest music seller, controlling one quarter of the local CD market. In America, Amazon's share of the CD market has also been growing – the conventional wisdom being that it's taking online what mass merchants such as Walmart and Target are letting go. But inventories suggest that isn't the whole story. Whether it's due to rural isolation, harsh winters, aging, social reclusion or whatever, millions of discerning CD buyers are opting to browse digitally, then have their finds delivered to their doorsteps.

Even more remarkable has been the resurgence of vinyl. In America, vinyl sales have tripled since 2010 to 9.2 million units in 2014, some $181 million of trade. Across Britain, the vinyl market exploded tenfold over the previous six years to over £30 million in 2015. Although vinyl accounted for just 2 percent of global music revenue in 2014, the niche has became a popular symbol of a renaissance in specialist stores and indie labels. Record Store Day, first launched in the U.S. in 2007 to arouse public support for this struggling muso community, has proved so successful that 550 album titles were released exclusively to independent shops for its 2014 campaign. Some 30-40 new independent stores opened each year in America between 2011 and 2015 and the numbers rose steadily in Britain, too. By 2015, there were approximately 1,400 independent record stores across America, and 240 in Britain.

The digital market is even more complex, in particular in the division between downloads and streaming. Global figures for combined downloading platforms in 2014, although falling 8 percent on the previous year, remained the biggest digital format, generating twice the revenues of streaming services. But again, these worldwide averages hide profound disparities. Downloading accounted for 60 percent of American digital revenues in 2014, compared to just 20 percent for streaming, whereas in Scandinavia, the downloading market had almost completely collapsed. In Sweden, the home of Spotify, an incredible 92 percent of the digital market was accounted by streaming in 2014. By contrast, in Germany and Japan, only 8 percent and 3.5 percent respectively of music income came from streaming. Demographically, the trend towards streaming is strongest amongst younger people but preferences for platforms are varied. Google Play and Soundcloud proved the most popular audio-only platforms amongst teenagers, while Spotify scored poorly at 11 percent.

Logically, as Internet connection speeds improve – and every music consumer has a tablet or mobile device – high-quality streaming is likely to gain in appeal amongst all age-groups and social strata. It's far less certain, however, that subscription models such as Spotify's $10-per-month service will ever take off amongst youngsters and low income earners – two demographic groups whose influence on pop music has always been key. At time of writing in 2015, Spotify has 20 million paying subscribers, alongside 50 million people who use its advertisement-based freemium model.

Then behold the true behemoth: YouTube. The Google-owned, advertisement-financed video platform drew one billion viewers per month in 2015, a sizable proportion of them to music content. An estimated 80 percent of American teenagers use YouTube regularly, and if the crowds are anything to go by, YouTube has been number one for music consumers all along. Which is not especially good news for the industry. YouTube announced in February 2014 that it had paid $1 billion (to date) to music rights owners – considerably less than the $3 billion Spotify has paid out – and not overly generous in relation to its *annual* advertising revenues of $4 billion. However, YouTube has long claimed that its ad-financed freemium model has much in common with traditional broadcasting, and it probably deserves recognition for having drawn many millions of its "viewers" away from music piracy. It is also opening up new markets in the developing world and expects gargantuan growth over the next ten years, chasing vast audiences to feed its powerful Google-driven advertising. Alongside it, subscription platforms like Spotify and Apple Music look more like European public broadcasting, geared towards wealthier or more highbrow audiences.

The historical parallels between digital music and the radio boom of inter-war period were highlighted in April 2015, when a new Washington-based lobby called the MIC Coalition was formed between YouTube and the National Association of Broadcasters, America's powerful radio lobby since its formation in 1922. Their purpose was to fight the recording industry's Fair Play Fair Pay act which would have forced both YouTube and American Top 40 radio to come into line with European norms and pay an estimated $400 million in annual royalties to labels and recording artists. Repeating tactics exploited since the 1930s, the MIC Coalition played out the U.S. congressional clock, obfuscating negotiations with the argument that they provide "promotional value" for artists. In other words, that record labels should be happy with the free publicity.

For its perceived abuse of power through lobbyists, YouTube is generally loathed by today's recording industry. Label bosses do accept, however, that the knotty question of exposure lies at the heart of today's marketplace. Freemium music may have turned the business into a game of dimes rather than dollars, but because YouTube can expose artists to many millions of viewers, labels are learning to monetize fame in other ways. "We're now in an attention-getting business," says Craig Kallman, the CEO of Atlantic Records which operates a lucrative division dedicated entirely to merchandising. Other spin-off revenue streams, such as the licensing of music for TV, film and advertisement synchronisation, has also risen steadily since the start of the music industry crisis.

Truth is, the survivors of the crash have long stopped agonising over technology. Take Geoff Travis who, with record woman Jeannette Lee, has successfully rehabilitated Rough Trade inside the Beggars Group. "The carrier question pales in comparison to the content," he believes. "All I've ever cared about is finding music and bringing it to people." Another diehard indie, Daniel Miller, who recently extricated Mute from the EMI wreckage, paints an equally simple picture. "There's a lot of good music out there, and that's what drives us."

Chasing the muse into the great wide open sums up the record man's cosmic bargain. Today, not only is a market recovery quietly in motion, the advantage has moved back to the old-school record man. "God bless the indies!" exclaims Seymour Stein, who never forgot his origins. "They've introduced every new trend since, and even before, rock 'n' roll. You name it, it all started with the indies." Having recently left his co-chairmanship at Columbia following five difficult years, Rick Rubin confirms, "There is definitely a realisation amongst the majors today that they have to get back to a more indie model."

At the top of the indie community, the proverbial Last of the Mohicans is Martin Mills, who now presides over a group that includes XL Recordings, 4AD, Matador and Rough Trade. He is old enough to see history repeating itself. "In 1987, when the house explosion really started to happen," recalls Mills, "it looked very much to us like the punk explosion a decade previously … It was becoming clear that to be a successful label you had to catch successive waves. Although you couldn't catch every one, the way to compete with the majors was not to compete head-on, but to find the niche and take things beyond that niche." That philosophy has landed his group plenty of interesting fish: Gary Numan, Bauhaus, the Cult, Dead Can Dance, the Pixies, the Prodigy, the White Stripes, Bon Iver, Cat Power, the Libertines, and America's biggest-selling artist of 2011 and 2012, Adele.

Sticking to the simple business of finding brilliant music, Mills has resisted the so-called 360-degree deal – securing an artist's rights for recordings, publishing, merchandising, live, everything. Because most signatures lose money, Mills predicted that these "land grab" contracts, being more expensive, would lose more money and, in the exceptional cases of blockbuster success, arouse the artist's resentment. Carefully watching the digital market, he has meticulously adapted his business structure to the changing environment. Thinking big but spending prudently, across Europe he designed a "nesting system" in which his overseas branches handle local promotion from within his chosen independent distributor. The records get plugged by employees who answer to Mills, without the risky costs of running a distribution system. As traditional megastores close, Rough Trade stores are opening in the big cities to cater to a community of specialist music lovers. In many ways, Beggars is a type of multi-tentacled deep-sea creature. Having spent almost forty years feeding off the underground, Mills has learned that survival requires an ability to dart at movements yet maintain a slow metabolism. He has come to expect long waits between feasts.

Former colleague and 4AD founder Ivo Watts-Russell maintains that "If you were shipwrecked with a handful of strangers, Martin Mills is the one you would want in charge of water and rice rations". And indeed, among today's community of struggling indies, that's precisely the role he's assumed. With Alison Wenham, he set up indie trade body AIM, then brought the idea to America with its equivalent, A2IM. He dreamed up Merlin, a digital rights distributor enabling indies and lone producers to sell their music through all the online platforms. Mills has also been a key player in the recording industry's many battles against the tech giants.

Life in the music business has taught Martin Mills that, as a rule, money should be treated with great trepidation. Whether with artists or business partners, "money can be the root of all evil", he laments. "When people are behaving in a way that you find unacceptable, very often money is at the root." The purist values that underpin the Beggars Group are a welcome reminder that some survivors of the record crisis are alive and well.

Perhaps the spectacular collapse of the record industry over these last fifteen years was just a long-overdue purge of all the cynicism and delusional financial logic that clogged up the industry throughout the 1980s and 90s. Those who've been hardest hit arguably had it coming.

This brings us full circle back to the special few who found and fostered most of the important music this last century: the music men, a conspicuously rare species in the corporate era – pushed out and devalued by a generation of smug executives who believed that if they thought commercially, their sleek products would sell better.

So what is it that really makes the record business spin? "A lot of it has to do with why we do what we do to begin with," believes Rick Rubin. "I think people who get into music to make money, it doesn't always work out that way. I've always just done music as best as I can, and wherever that leads, ultimately, it's okay. I see myself as sort of an art collector, not a gambler. The thing I've always found is that it's almost like falling in love. It's not about what you can get out of this. It's not a commercial venture. It maybe becomes one, but that's a by-product. It's almost by not aiming at it, it's able to happen because the intention behind it is pure." Or as the great John Hammond put it, "A hundred times I've seen efforts to make a record more commercial turn the buyers off. Stand or fall on what you are, I tell my people. Be yourself."

The A&R craft operates on many levels, but one quality the greatest producers have in common is a deep-rooted faith in their own judgment – so certain, so capable of recognising genius in its embryonic stages, they often find themselves standing alone admiring things nobody else gets. "With every great musician I have discovered," continues John Hammond, "there was never a moment's doubt. I could hear the singularity of the sound. Always this quality seems obvious. Lights flash. Rockets go off. Where is everybody? Why don't they hear it? This has always amazed me."

Reaching that level of clarity takes years of learning. As John Hammond's blues-singing son of the same name testifies, "[My father] was a complex guy who was on a mission. He was not in it for the money. He saw himself as independently wealthy and yet he died broke. He never took a royalty for any of the artists he produced … he was a straight shooter. He was fastidious about everything he did; dressed well, didn't drink, if you sent him a letter, he replied. He played viola, understood music charts, spoke five languages. He was a rebel in the sense that he wanted to know things for himself. He could read classical

Greek and Latin, and at one point he thought about going into divinity school."

Also a bookworm and engaged humanist, Rough Trade's founder, Geoff Travis, describes the vocation as a form of journalism. "I don't think people have any idea the work you have to do to have the clear sight to make the critical judgments," he explains. "I think all of us who run labels spend our whole lives listening to music. Because to be able to judge something as being special you have to know everything else out there. It's like Ezra Pound's famous quote about the first person to compare their love to a rose is quite possibly a genius, the second an idiot. Then consider the sheer volume of music that comes out these days … The job of being an A&R person is to hear everything. It's not a chore, it's part of the excitement, but it's a real job; hours every single day researching, going out to gigs every night. The only way to run a record company is to have faith in your judgment. But your judgment has to be informed by a lifetime of work."

Curiosity, proximity to the street, an openness to people and their stories – all these qualities also make it relatively easy for artists to find the record men. Bob Dylan cleverly wangled his way onto Hammond's radar, just as Robert Johnson appeared at Henry Speir's counter. Elvis, Johnny Cash, Carl Perkins and Jerry Lee Lewis all turned up on Sam Phillips's doorstep. Bob Marley asked for an introduction to Chris Blackwell. Smiths guitarist Johnny Marr bluffed his way into the Rough Trade warehouse, pretending to be an employee and waited for Travis to appear through a doorway. In the history of music, such incidents are not unique. Great artists, having a strong sense of their own destiny, tend to choose their midwife.

The modern record man has an ancestor in the noble houses of Europe. Centuries of classical music repertoire depended on composers getting recognised and financially supported by wealthy patrons. Having a patron was the gateway into opera halls, theatres and cathedrals. By raising up these artistic mirrors, the patrons sought to enlighten society from the top downward. Rock 'n' roll, a child of jazz and a grandchild of vaudeville, has simply adapted this ancient system to modern times.

The most astute record men in the business are conscious of this heritage. Having spent fifty years flying hit records both ways across the

Atlantic, Seymour Stein points back to the comic-opera composers Gilbert and Sullivan as the missing link. "I believe we owe the start of Tin Pan Alley in America to the whole music hall scene in late nineteenth-century England," he says. However, "because of World War II, we became the world power. Elvis was sort of like Joshua and Jericho. When he broke in 1956, rock 'n' roll was born, and it's lasted to the present day because it's such a melange of music able to reinvent itself." Stein believes England's prolific output of great pop music in the postwar era can be explained by an inherent time lag. "1960 for the English was like about 1952 for America. In rock 'n' roll, we're ten years ahead of England because – well, we started it!" Since the Beatles, England has kept bouncing back theatrical slants on America's old records: skiffle, R&B, Chicago blues, punk, dance, hip-hop – the list is long. "It's just like the stage: Broadway or the West End? Some years the Brits have it. They do definitely have an edge in acting because of the schools and traditions. They have great writers too."

Regularly flying in from California to scout talent around London in the sixties, A&M boss Jerry Moss began to notice something similar. "The Americans were somewhat inhibited, except for a few bands, whereas the dramatic effect of the Stones, the Who, oh my God, it was classic! Almost like Shakespearean actors. And that's how the English believed it was supposed to happen – complete drama. Everything was done with a flourish." Unlike America, England has a deeply ingrained class system. In the early days of EMI, "producers were expected to wear suits and ties, just as they did in the office", explains George Martin. "Engineers wore white coats to distinguish them as being of a lower class. Recording artists, too, were considered to be socially inferior – a bit like actors, not quite decent people, tolerated because they brought in money, but always expected to be of somewhat dubious character." Even among modern, progressive indies, the legacy has lingered on. When the erudite boss of Factory Records, Tony Wilson, asked the cultivated John Cale to produce a dysfunctional group of working-class hooligans called the Happy Mondays, Cale asked, "What are they like?" "The best way I can describe them," Wilson said, grinning, "is scum. They are fucking scum." England's slightly mischievous appetite for social caricature reaches back to at least Shakespeare, and to this day, England still loves its class division pop – even though it's largely unexportable.

Our whole musical world is an ethnic melting pot containing just a few core ingredients. For the Irish-bred Dave Robinson, "England has always been odd because its music has always been theatrical. The indigenous music in England and Ireland is really folk music, but that's not what the British public buys to a large extent. It buys a theatrical kind of pop. It's very different from America, whose music has gone through several ethnic and urban filters." As Robinson points out, country music, centred around East Tennessee, was heavily influenced by Scots-Irish traditional music – as was the folk scene of Greenwich Village. In fact, boiled down to its lowest common denominators, modern music has been built on three main waves: African blues, Irish folk and English vaudeville. "If you mix all that together," reasons Robinson, "that's where the great songs are, that's where the great rhythms and lyrics are. That's where Jimi Hendrix was. And at the end of the day, that's where most of rock 'n' roll came from."

However, Robinson suggests, "If you want to understand the business, you're going to have to get into the whole Jewish side of things. The music business is very Jewish – always has been, still is." Also admitting that he's long wondered why, A&M's former London boss, Derek Green, says with a laugh, "Sometimes you'd be in a negotiation and everyone in the room, on both sides of the table, would be Jewish." The half-Jewish, half-Irish Green came to the conclusion that "Jewish people are good at taking risks. There is a saying in Israel that everyone thinks he should be the prime minister." It's a hunch Jac Holzman shares. "A lot of Jews came into this because it was stuff that serious money businessmen would not do. They would not take the risk."

A&M founder Jerry Moss points out that in the old days, the most predominantly Jewish end of the record business was independent distribution, in contrast to, for example, radio, which had a relatively sparse Jewish contingent. "Stocking merchandise, ordering merchandise – it's what Jews did," reasons Moss, himself also Jewish. This phenomenon began, Seymour Stein believes, because of old WASP restrictions barring Jewish immigrants from certain colleges, professions and influential social clubs. Because wide-open sectors like music publishing, record production, and movies didn't require qualifications, "Jews gravitated to those new businesses," notes Stein, speaking from personal experience.

Behind the stereotypes of Jewish stockists and traders hides a far more interesting psychological area. Jac Holzman, son of a wealthy Manhattan doctor of East European origins, conjures up bitter memories of how "my parents were WASPY Jews. I thought synagogue was a prison. I was there four to five days a week to get prepared for my bar mitzvah. I resented it." He obsessively saw every new picture that came out; "the movies were where I truly lived," he explains. Then, as a student cut off from New York's movie theaters, he threw himself into folk music, which enabled him "to plant my own roots". Branching out from American folklore into what we now call world music, Holzman eventually began seeing his own origins from a more humanist angle.

"I had no interest in the Jewish liturgies," he says, "although some of it was really quite beautiful. I was moved by the constant sadness, which was a strain through Jewish life. Some of it's genetic, having been inherited from people who had to escape Russia or live through pogroms in Poland. But coming out of Israel, there was a rich sense of hope and possibility. So I got interested in the middle of 1955 in recording Israeli songs. Actually, Israel was into singer-songwriters much earlier than we were in America, because of the whole kibbutz thing." Now eighty, Holzman realises that in escaping religion, music became his own, superior brand of prayer. "I'm an agnostic Jew, but a culturally sympathetic one. Not being a believer in God didn't mean I didn't believe in stuff. I believed in the music. And I have always sought to protect it and do it right. I'm a nut on the subject; always the music – it's all that counts. The rest of it is business, and we figure that out so we can keep doing it."

Holzman's story is similar to Geoff Travis's, another teenager who wandered off to find his own artistic promised land. "When I was very young I went through a phase when I took being Jewish quite seriously," confesses Travis, whose family observed a traditional interpretation of Judaism. "I spent half my life in evening school, Hebrew classes and all the rest of it, so they had plenty of chances to get their hooks into me. We used to have our lunches in different places to everyone else, so there was always a bit of separation going on. I just don't really believe in religion, I have to say. Having been inculcated with it hugely since I was a young boy, I just think it's a lot of nonsense really." With age, however, Travis does recognise "you could definitely make an argument for the displacement of religion by music. I'd definitely much rather listen to the Velvet Underground than listen to a rabbi singing tunelessly."

Another Jewish rebel is Rick Rubin. "I'm not religious, but I am very spiritual. I was lucky to have learned Transcendental Meditation at the age of fourteen," he explains. "That and my interest in Dao are probably what have kept me grounded throughout this rollercoaster ride." As someone who has long contemplated the subject of creativity, Rubin instinctively wonders if the puzzle of why so many major players in the record business came from Jewish families should not be widened to that other conspicuously well-represented ethnic group. "In the same way there are a lot of really talented black musicians," muses Rubin. "Both cultures share a strong past of suffering. And maybe both used music as an escape from that genetic suffering. Maybe there's a deeper understanding of music, a deeper insight, because of suffering?"

The cornerstone of Jewish culture is the powerful story of the flight from slavery, as told in the Book of Exodus and celebrated by Passover, one of the holiest of Jewish rituals – possibly why so many humanist record men from Jewish backgrounds identify so strongly with the uplifting music passed down from African slaves. "[Chris Blackwell] always told me the Rastas related to Judaism because of the thirteenth tribe that disappeared," confesses Lionel Conway, a Jewish friend and Island-lifer. "He was very proud of that relationship … He always told me they were Jews."

The founding father of rock 'n' roll, Sam Phillips, a former cotton picker himself, was another who felt a profound identification with black people. What has perhaps intrigued generations ever since Elvis is that beneath all its carefree energy, rock 'n' roll was steeped in black evangelism. "Even the most religious [white] Southern people would have an hour or hour-and-fifteen-minute service," he observed, "but the blacks, their services would go on four hours or even all day. That kind of fascinated me. These people never seemed to be really down in the dumps. And I wondered why. I guess their solace came from their belief in God, and it's gonna be all right somehow."

Nearly every new genre of modern music has evolved from these ancient forms of theatre and religion, and the men at the top know it. "I've always thought what we do is to evangelise, to crusade," says Beggars boss Martin Mills, citing his favourite quote from black punk Don Letts – "If music is a religion, then Rough Trade has always been my church." Chasing the muse, the indie hunter, hearing our Top 40 airwaves as an injustice, plays midwife to ignored, downtrodden genius. Since his retirement to northeastern New Mexico, 4AD founder Ivo Watts-Russell spends one day every week taking impounded dogs from his local animal shelter out for a run in the desert wilderness. "Poor things," he sighs. "While waiting for a Forever Home, they don't really see much of their beautiful surroundings unless volunteers go and walk them. I never had kids, but I went from nurturing musicians to rescuing dogs. There are similarities to all three responsibilities, I would imagine."

As an older man contemplating the historical importance of African-American music, Sam Phillips believed "we've now learned so much from some of these people we thought were ignorant, who never had any responsibility other than chopping cotton, feeding the mules, or making sorghum molasses. When people come back to this music in a hundred years, they'll see these were master painters. They may be illiterate. They can't write a book about it. But they can make a song, and in three verses you'll hear the greatest damn story you'll ever hear in your life."

For centuries, folk and blues was accumulated wisdom passed ever downward. "Think about the complexity, yet simplicity, of music we have gained from hard times," says Phillips, "from the sky, the wind and the earth. If you don't have a foundation, you won't know what the hell I'm talking about." His proudest discovery was not Elvis, or even Johnny Cash, but blues shaman Howlin' Wolf.

Whether it's in dense cities or across open country plains, the search for the divine comedy is a timeless art that just adapts to different environments. In the big city, cut off from the elements, records have become our folklore, our spiritual medicine, our last sacred connection to the tribal godhead. In a game populated by snake-oil salesmen, the real record man is the one selling the magic potions that actually work.

Music is one of several domains – sports, politics, movies, books and fashion included – that will always remain governed by tribal genes inherited from the campfire. Thousands of years of technological progress and where are we? Still huddling up at night around the glow, trying to make sense of it all – dreaming our lives into the stars.

Seek and ye shall find.

BIBLIOGRAPHY

Birch, Will. *Ian Dury: The Definitive Biography*. London: Sidgwick & Jackson, 2010.

Boyd, Joe. *White Bicycles: Making Music in the 1960s*. London: Serpent's Tail, 2006.

Carlin, Peter Ames. *Bruce*. New York: Simon & Schuster, 2012.

Cohodas, Nadine. *Spinning Blues into Gold: The Chess Brothers and the Legendary Chess Records*. New York: St. Martin's Press, 2000.

Cornyn, Stan, with Paul Scanlon. *Exploding: The Highs, Hits, Hype, Heroes, and Hustlers of the Warner Music Group*. New York: HarperCollins, 2002.

Crouch, Kevin and Tanja Crouch. *Sun King: The Life and Times of Sam Phillips, the Man Behind Sun Records*. London: Piatkus Books, 2008.

Dannen, Fredric. *Hit Men: Power Brokers and Fast Money Inside the Music Business*. New York: Times Books, 1990.

Davis, Clive, with Anthony DeCurtis. *The Soundtrack of My Life*. New York: Simon & Schuster, 2013.

Dylan, Bob. *Chronicles: Volume One*. New York: Simon & Schuster, 2004.

Foster, Tony. *The Sound and the Silence: The Private Lives of Mabel and Alexander Graham Bell*. Halifax, NS: Nimbus Publishing, 1996.

Gelatt, Roland. *The Fabulous Phonograph, 1877–1977*. New York: Collier Books, 1977.

George, Nelson. *Where Did Our Love Go? The Rise & Fall of the Motown Sound*. Sydney: Omnibus Press, 1985.

Greenfield, Robert. *The Last Sultan: The Life and Times of Ahmet Ertegun*. New York: Simon & Schuster, 2011.

Hammond, John, with Irving Townsend. *John Hammond on Record.* New York: Ridge Press/Summit Books, 1977.

Harris, Larry, with Curt Gooch and Jeff Suhs. *And Party Every Day: The Inside Story of Casablanca Records.* New York: Backbeat Books, 2009.

Heylin, Clinton. *The Act You've Known All These Years.* Edinburgh: Canongate Books, 2007.

Holzman, Jac, and Gavan Daws. *Follow the Music: The Life and High Times of Elektra Records in the Great Years of American Pop Culture.* Santa Monica, CA: FirstMedia Books, 1998.

Hoskyns, Barney. *Hotel California: Singer-Songwriters and Cocaine Cowboys in the LA Canyons, 1967–1976.* London: HarperPerennial, 2006.

Houghton, Mick. *Becoming Elektra: The True Story of Jac Holzman's Visionary Record Label.* London: Jawbone Press, 2010.

King, Tom. *The Operator: David Geffen Builds, Buys, and Sells the New Hollywood.* New York: Random House, 2000.

Knopper, Steve. *Appetite for Self-Destruction: The Spectacular Crash of the Record Industry in the Digital Age.* New York: Free Press, 2009.

Kusek, David, and Gerd Leonhard. *The Future of Music: Manifesto for the Digital Revolution.* Boston: Berklee Press, 2005.

Lawrence, Tim. *Love Saves the Day: A History of Dance Music Culture, 1970–1979.* Durham, NC: Duke University Press, 2003.

Lippmann, Stephen. "Boys to Men: Age, Identity, and the Legitimation of Amateur Wireless in the United States, 1909–1927." *Journal of Broadcasting & Electronic Media* 54, no. 4 (2010): 657–74.

Marmorstein, Gary. *The Label: The Story of Columbia Records.* New York: Thunder's Mouth Press, 2007.

Martin, George, with Jeremy Hornsby. *All You Need Is Ears.* New York: St. Martin's Press, 1979.

Napier-Bell, Simon. *Black Vinyl, White Powder.* London: Ebury Press, 2002.

Oldham, Andrew Loog. *2Stoned.* London: Vintage, 2003.

Oldham, Andrew Loog. *Stoned.* New York: St. Martin's Press, 2001.

Prial, Dunstan. *The Producer: John Hammond and the Soul of American Music.* New York: Picador, 2007.

Rodgers, Nile. *Le Freak: An Upside Down Story of Family, Disco, and Destiny.* London: Sphere, 2011.

Salewicz, Chris, ed. *Keep on Running: The Story of Island Records.* New York: Universe Publishing, 2009.

Southall, Brian. *The Rise & Fall of EMI Records.* London: Omnibus Press, 2009.

Spitz, Bob. *The Beatles: The Biography.* New York: Back Bay Books, 2006.

Stone, Henry. *The Stone Cold Truth on Payola!* N.p.: Henry Stone Music, 2013.

Sutton, Allan. *Recording the Twenties: The Evolution of the American Recording Industry, 1920–29.* Denver, CO: Mainspring Press, 2008.

Szwed, John. *The Man Who Recorded the World.* London: Arrow Books, 2010.

Wade, Dorothy, and Justine Picardie. *Music Man: Ahmet Ertegun, Atlantic Records, and the Triumph of Rock 'n' Roll.* New York: Norton, 1990.

Wexler, Jerry, and David Ritz. *Rhythm and the Blues: A Life in American Music.* New York: Knopf, 1993.

Wilentz, Sean. *Bob Dylan in America.* London: The Bodley Head, 2010.

Wilson, Brian. *Wouldn't It Be Nice: My Own Story.* New York: HarperCollins, 1991.

Yetnikoff, Walter, with David Ritz. *Howling at the Moon: The True Story of the Mad Genius of the Music World.* New York: Broadway Books, 2004.

Zanes, Warren. *Revolutions in Sound: Warner Bros. Records, the First Fifty Years.* San Francisco, CA: Chronicle Books, 2008.

AUTHOR INTERVIEWS:

Laurence Bell, Derek Birkett, David Betteridge, Harold Childs, Tim Clark, Lionel Conway, Stan Cornyn, Ray Cooper, Simon Draper, Terry Ellis, David Enthoven, Bob Garcia, Derek Green, John P. Hammond, Larry Harris, Tom Hayes, John Heyman, Jac Holzman, Art Jaeger, Craig Kallman, Danny Krivit, Al Kooper, Andrew Lauder, Andrew Loog Oldham, Daniel Miller, Martin Mills, Jerry Moss, Bruce Pavitt, Charly Prevost, Tony Pye, Dave Robinson, Rick Rubin, Tom Silverman, Seymour Stein, Howard Thompson, Geoff Travis, Ivo Watts-Russell, Chris Wright, Trevor Wyatt, Patrick Zelnik.

SPECIAL THANKS TO THE FOLLOWING FOR VARIOUS SOURCES OF INFORMATION

Thomas H. White for his invaluable help on radio history, Patrick Feaster for his research on Thomas Edison, Rick Bleiweiss, Steve Knopper, David Ritz, Stephen Lispon, Nigel House.

INDEX

GARETH MURPHY was raised in Ireland surrounded by the musicians with whom his father worked as a concert promoter. A graduate of University College, Dublin, he has worked at various record companies, produced the Buddha Bar compilations, and composes his own original music. He lives in Paris with his wife and young son.